CARPETS IN NETHERLANDISH PAINTINGS

CARPETS
AND THEIR DATINGS
IN NETHERLANDISH
PAINTINGS

1540-1700

ONNO YDEMA

Antique Collectors' Club Ltd

To the memory of my father Jacob Ydema

Contents

The author and publishers are grateful to the Stichting Charema, Amsterdam, and the M.A.O.C. Gravin van Bylandt Stichting, for the material support to accomplish this book.

Copyright © 1991 Onno Ydema, Leiden/Walburg Pers, Zutphen

Published in The Netherlands by Walburg Pers, Zutphen

Published in the United Kingdom by the Antique Collectors' Club Ltd, Woodbridge, Suffolk IP12 1DS

Book production, design and international publication Uniepers Abcoude, The Netherlands

ISBN 90.6011.710.7 - Dutch edition
ISBN 1.85149.151.1 - U.K. edition

The publishers were unfortunately unable to contact the copyright holders of all the pictures in the book. Those who have not been contacted are asked therefore to get in touch with the publishers.

Printed in the Netherlands by Walburg Pers, Zutphen

British Library Cataloguing-in-Publication Data
Ydema Onno
Carpets and their datings in Netherlandish paintings, 1540-1700
I. Title
746.75095

CIP-Gegevens Koninklijke Bibliotheek
Ydema, Onno

Carpets and their datings in Netherlandish paintings 1540-1700 / Onno Ydema.
- Zutphen : Walburg Pers. - Ill.
Ook verschenen als proefschrift Leiden, 1990. Met lit. opg., reg.
ISBN 90-6011-710-7 geb.
NUGI 912
Trefw.: Oosterse tapijten in de schilderkunst : Nederland ; geschiedenis ; 1540-1700.

Illustration preceding page: G. Terborch, A Lady writing a letter, c. 1655, The Mauritshuis, The Hague.

fig.1 Animal rug, known as the dragon and phoenix rug, Anatolia, first half or middle 15th century (fragment). Staatliche Museen zu Berlin, Islamisches Museum, Berlin.

I
INTRODUCTION

ORIENTAL CARPETS IN WESTERN PAINTING

The present study is focused on the intersection of two civilizations: on the one hand, Islamic textile art, and specifically the art of the Islamic carpet; and on the other, Western European painting. As we will show, the richly designed Oriental weavings with curious ornaments strongly appealed to the taste of Western painters; it has even been suggested that the Oriental use of colour influenced the Great Venetians[1]. Italian paintings frequently display carpets that serve either as the background for the representation of saints, clergy and secular dignitaries, or as embellishment for balustrades, windows and floors to indicate exceptional festivities[2]. Often carpets were portrayed as floor decorations in paintings. In these representations the carpet functions iconographically as a dais in a composition which does not necessarily correspond to the reality of actual use in those times. The rarity and costliness of Eastern carpets usually warranted a careful treatment in actual use, whereby wear was minimalized. Undoubtedly, these carpets were generally used as table-covers or to cover other pieces of furniture such as trunks and chests. As such, they were not subjected to the wear implied in every-day use as floor-covering. It is not until the 18th century that Oriental carpets are commonly used as floor-covering in the Netherlands (i.e. the Southern Netherlands or Flanders and the Northern Netherlands or the Republic of the Seven United Netherlands), and it must have been at that time that many of the remaining earlier Oriental carpets in the Netherlands were worn out and lost. The loss was great; in the Northern Netherlands only three surviving examples of Oriental carpets are known to have been in Dutch possession ever since the 17th century[3]. It is remarkable, given the large number of extant 17th century Dutch paintings representing Eastern carpets (which would suggest that a relatively great number must have been present in these regions in the 17th century) that hardly any of these carpets appear to have been preserved to the present day in the Netherlands. In Southern European countries such as Italy, by contrast, many early Oriental carpets survived; churches in particular have proven to be repositories where some very old and exceptional examples have been preserved.

DATING OF EARLY ORIENTAL CARPETS

As early as the 14th century, carpets were traded from the Near East to Western Europe. The Italian merchants in particular traded actively with the Islamic cultural regions in the 14th and 15th century, and brought home carpets with a knotted pile, which were decorated with brightly coloured floral ornaments or stylized animal figures. It is not surprising, therefore, that the earliest representations of Eastern carpets are found in Italian paintings from 1317 onwards[4]. Although the question of the exact origin of the earliest of the so-called Early Animal Carpets in the Italian paintings remains unclear[5], the Oriental carpets represented in the 15th century paintings are generally attributable to Anatolian Turkish weaving centres.

When in the 19th century the attention of art historians began to be directed toward classical Oriental carpets, it was originally not even clear if genuine early examples could indeed be recognizable: carpets almost never bear inscriptions referring to origin, and dated examples are highly exceptional. Occasionally documents mention place and date of production or purchase, but in the vast majority of cases clear-cut evidence is absent. Comparitive stylistic research only partially produces reliable criteria for dating, since the development of the pattern does not always run parallel with that of Islamic miniature art and other dateable art forms. For these reasons, comparative art-historical research into the stylistic developments of carpet patterns has from its very onset (1870[6])

largely been based upon carpets represented in datable European paintings.

One famous example is an early Anatolian carpet, which was discovered in an Italian church by Wilhelm von Bode in 1886 (fig.1). The coarsely woven fragment is divided into two rectangular compartments with octagonal medallions, each one representing a stylized squirming dragon in combat with a phoenix. The design has been carried out in thick woollen yarns, forming a relatively high pile in a limited number of colours, primarily yellow, red, and blue. The carpet, for which hardly any reference material in Islamic art is available, can be dated with the help of representations of similar Oriental carpets in Western paintings. A more or less identical pattern has been found in a carpet represented between 1440 and 1444 by Domenico di Bartolo in a fresco in the Spedale della Scala in Siena[6a]. Apparently, such carpets were known in the West in the second quarter of the 15th century, and with the evidence of the Domenico painting a *terminus ante quem* for the development of this type of carpet has been found.

Western paintings also constitute equally indispensable references for the dating of later carpets. The tradition of precise realism in representation fashionable among Western painters in the second half of the 15th and in the 16th century provides pictorial source material sometimes detailed enough to justify conclusions concerning technical weaving characteristics of a certain carpet. However a problem is posed by the presence of Anatolian carpets in early Netherlandish painting. Famous representations by Memlinc and his contemporaries are used for reference material by many authors, but the reliability of most of these representations is questionable. Certainly the early Netherlandish painters must have had access to authentic Oriental carpets, as they had obviously been able to study their designs. Still, if all the representations are compared, it appears that many, if not most, show patterns which are composed by the artistic juxtaposition of several separate design elements. Famous representations of floor carpets are those painted by Jan van Eyck in *The Madonna Enthroned with St.Michael and the Donor*, dating from about 1430-31, and the *Lucca Madonna*, dated 1437, showing Our Lady on a rug with a trellis pattern, and also *The Madonna of Canon Georg van der Paele*, dated 1436, showing a small rug on the steps of the throne, decorated with a pattern of interlaced stars[7]. Another appears in his 1434 portrait, *Giovanni Arnolfini and Giovanna Cenami*[8], but the part visible in the scene is too small to allow for detailed conclusions; one cannot even be certain that a pile rug is represented here[9]. The carpet in the Van der Paele Madonna however seems to have a piled surface, which is suggested by the hairy texture, the drawing of the contours of the individual motifs, and also by the representation of the typical way the pile has opened where the rug bends over the steps of the throne.

Some decades later are the paintings by Quinten Massys (active 1465/6-1530) and Hans Memlinc (active 1465-1494). A good example by Quinten Massys is *The Virgin and Child Enthroned with Four Angels*, in the National Gallery in London[10]. The field design is not known from extant examples; it could have been invented by the painter who may have found his inspiration in the repertoire of 15th century Oriental carpet patterns which includes many design

fig.3 Willem Key (attributed to), Portraits of a Man and a Woman, Members of the Smit Family, about 1560. Koninklijk Museum voor Schone Kunsten, Brussels.

elements with similar stars. However, it seems also related to the field design of the rug in Van Eyck's van der Paele Madonna. The carpet also has a very inaccurately drawn kufesque border (so called because it is believed to derive from a rectilinear form of Islamic script known as Kufic), and the solution to the problem of turning the corners is, as John Mills has already stated[11], most unusual. Possibly the painter was generally familiar with the designs of Oriental carpets, but did not have an authentic example before him in his studio while painting the representation.

A characteristic motif found in many of these carpets in early Netherlandish painting is in one of the two borders of the rug in the van der Paele Madonna, showing a non-Oriental undulating clover stem. Similar ornaments can be found in the borders of many representations of carpets painted in the Netherlands in the 15th and the beginning of the 16th century, but are unknown from any surviving carpets of the period. Another remarkable feature is the representation of the fringes, which are often found at the sides of the carpet, and not, as could be expected, at the upper or lower ends[12]. From this it could be concluded either that the carpets in these paintings sometimes have a square shape, which is a feature unknown from surviving examples; or that the painters, using artistic licence, did a lot of improvising with the designs and weaving characteristics of the authentic models; or else that these carpets themselves were Western copies, which would explain the frequent presence of the curvilinear stem with trefoil leaves, which is almost certainly derived from Western Gothic ornament. In summary, the information from the systematic inventory of carpets in these early Netherlandish paintings brings about more questions than answers. For this reason the present study will concentrate on pictorial source material from about 1540 onwards. Around this date, the so-called 'Memlinc' and 'Holbein' design types cease to be represented, and new types appear.

In Italy, Sebastiano del Piombo is the first artist known to have included a rug with a characteristic 'Lotto' arabesque pattern, based on earlier 'Holbein' designs (1516[13]). These rugs, named after the painter Lorenzo 'Lotto', who represented such carpets in two of his works, were introduced in Netherlandish paintings much later, around 1540, and were to constitute the largest group of carpets represented in paintings from the Low Countries (see Chapter III). The other groups of early Turkish carpets apparently first woven in the 15th century, such as the groups named after the city of Ushak (the Medallion Ushak, the Star Ushak and the Ushak 'Double-niche' carpets), occur much less frequently in 16th century Western painting. In fact, only two examples of a Star Ushak in a Netherlandish painting were recorded during the collection of data for this study (Van Somer, *Edmund, 3rd Baron Sheffield, 1st Earl of Mulgrave*, 1614. (fig.2); Stomer, *The Virgin of the Annunciation*, about 1660[14]. Presumably the carpets shown in the two portraits of members of the Smit family attributed to Willem Key belong to the same group (fig.3), although they may also have been examples of another type, the 'lobed Medallion Ushaks'[15]. It must be noted, however, that in the 16th century the Netherlandish pictorial sources are quantitatively far smaller in number, and thus less important for the drawing of conclusions, than the more numerous Italian paintings.

A Comparison of 16th and 17th Century Pictorial Source Material

For the purpose of our analysis of images of carpets in paintings, the end of the 16th century can to some extent be considered a breaking-point. In the first place, as far as pictorial source material is concerned, the interest of Italian painters in representing Oriental carpets had strongly declined by this time. The 17th century style of painting in Italy, which was no longer characterized by a concern for realism in detail, was apparently no longer suited by style or by iconography to the exact representation of carpets. The importance of Netherlandish painting for the study of pictorial source material, particularly the painting of the Northern Netherlands, increases strongly at around the same time. In the Netherlands, carpets are frequently represented in 17th century genre paintings, but equally in still-lives, portraits and in history paintings.

In addition to Turkish carpets, Persian carpets gradually began to be represented in Dutch and Flemish painting at regular intervals: the first examples of Persian carpets forming part of the regular Oriental commerce were traded to Western Europe at the end of the 16th century. The Portuguese were the first to start a flourishing trade with India and Persia, countries which could now be reached directly via the new trade route around the Cape of Good Hope. Whether carpets had initially any significant share in the trade remains to be seen; Donald King states that 'Inventories and other documents indicate that Persian carpets were arriving in Europe in considerable numbers from the second half of the 16th century and possibly earlier'[16], but, in the early 17th century, these carpets were rarely represented in Western painting. The Dutch United East-India Company (*Vereenigde Oostindische Compagnie*) was founded in 1602, and by 1620 the Dutch and the English East-India Companies had succeeded in their attempt to take over the larger part of the trade with the Near and Far East. This explains the strong increase of Persian and Indian carpets represented in Dutch paintings at this time (fig.4). Oriental carpets appear to have been only incidentally depicted in the 17th century in other European countries; even in England, where carpets became an almost indispensable adjunct of the standing portrait[17], the number of English artists that included these objects in their paintings is relatively small. In closely examining Dutch paintings of this period, one is impressed by the extent into which Oriental carpets became an integral part of the furnishing of every self-respecting well-to-do citizen's home in a relatively short period of time. The strong increase in the fashion for portraits and genre paintings (the latter especially in the Northern Netherlands) contributed strongly to the increase in pictorial evidence relating to the importance of carpets as an aspect of interior furnishing in the Netherlands. Up until the end of the 17th century, Anatolian, Persian and Indian carpets are frequently represented in Netherlandish painting; after that date the costly Oriental carpets seem to have grown out of fashion[18]. The present study will therefore focus on representations painted until about 1700.

fig.4   Willem de Keyser, Portrait of a Young Silversmith, 1630. Collection of the Marquess of Bath, Longleat.

Dutch and Flemish 17th century paintings primarily display two types of carpets. First are the carpets adorned with a geometric yellow lattice displayed against a red field, surrounded with a blue-ground border: these, as mentioned, are known as 'Lotto' carpets (Chapter III). The majority of Anatolian carpets represented in 17th century Netherlandish paintings belong to this group. Previously published inventories of 'Lotto' carpets[19] produced some important dating criteria for subgroups of 'Lotto' carpets sharing the common 'Lotto' pattern but displaying slight variations on the general theme, causing them to be subdivided into smaller categories. It can be assumed that a systematic inventory based on a substantially larger sample of representations than those previously published might sharpen the conclusions of the earlier studies. Such a systematic search might also produce an insight into the market share of a specific type of carpet compared to other types of carpets. If the results were converted into graphic form, a possible chronological ordering of the subgroups within the 'Lotto' rubric might emerge. For example, if a certain subgroup were to be found only in paintings dated later than c. 1620, the variant could be assumed to have been developed shortly before, whereas examples which were never or seldom represented after that date might be assumed to have gone out of fashion at that time. When examples of a certain subgroup are represented in paintings over a period of several decades, it might be concluded that the specific type may have been manufactured over a relatively long period of time without a demonstrable change of pattern.

This does not exclude the possibility that early carpets may appear in late paintings; the data provided by the pictorial source material can only be regarded as *termini ante quem*. Still, if several graphs indicate that specific types of carpets appear in paintings in large numbers during a certain period of time, and representations are rare in the following decades, it can be concluded that in general the painters did not use old carpets if newer and possibly more fashionable ones were available. Sometimes relatively early carpets appear in later paintings, but such examples seem to present exceptions, rather than indicating a common practice. An example of such an anachronism is the depiction of what appears to be a late 16th or early 17th century Anatolian so-called Bird Ushak rug in a much later still-life painting in the collection of the Netherlands Art Collections Department in The Hague (fig.5). Although it was signed and dated *J. van Huysum 1714*, it is now attributed to Willem van Royen (c.1645-1723[20]), who may have done this painting early in the 18th century. The rug must have been of some age at the time; one of the colours has faded considerably as the painter carefully demonstrated in his representation: the pile opens at the folding of the rug over the edge of the marble table, showing the bleached tops of the woollen yarns forming the leaves of one of the blossoms.

In this context it should be noted that on occasion a single carpet may have been used as a model over and over again by generations of painters; a good example is a rug of unknown origin, apparently represented in paintings several times, first by Caspar Netscher and later by his son Constantijn (see p.118). Usually a comparison of the minor guard borders and other details will indicate the extent to which a certain particular carpet example is represented in more than one painting; the guard borders are much less stereotyped than the patterns of the field or even of the borders. In the present study, the possible presence of more than one representation of an individual rug in the work of a single painter will be corrected in the graphs.

17TH CENTURY PICTORIAL SOURCE MATERIAL: THE 'FLORAL AND CLOUDBAND' CARPETS

After the Anatolian 'Lotto' type, the second type of carpet most frequently represented in 17th century Netherlandish paintings is the so-called floral and cloudband type (fig.4). The East-Persian province of Khorasan, with Herat as its capital, has been mentioned by many 17th century travellers as the most important centre for the manufacture of such fine-quality carpets with a woollen pile, although scholars are still divided between Central Persia, Khorasan and India as possible places of their manufacture (see Chapter IV). Floral-and-cloudband carpets are characterized by a symmetrical pattern of coiling stems, numerous large and smaller flowers and 'tchi', or cloudband ornaments of Chinese origin. At first sight, the patterns of these carpets are, like the 'Lotto' design, rather stereotyped; even the most carefully painted representations show only minor variations. Perhaps both the stereotyped design and the extensiveness of the group explain why these carpets have never been thoroughly studied; it may have been assumed that a time-consuming study would not produce much significant new material about such an apparently homogenous group of carpets.

In scholarly literature, these floral carpets are sometimes defined as 'Indo-Persian', which denotes the existing uncertainty as to the exact place of origin of certain examples: Persia or India[21]. It is known that the Mughal emperor Akbar (1556-1605) invited Persian weavers to come to India in order to establish new weaving centres (see Chapter V). A 17th century English source describes one of the workshops in Ellora (India) where carpets were made *after the manner of those in Persia*, and woven by descendants of these Persian immigrants. Also the working method is recorded: *The loome is stretched right up an downe, made of Cotton thread, and the Carpett wrought upon them with the woollen yarne of severall collours by young boys of 8 to 12 years old a man with the Patterne of the worke drawne upon paper, standing at the back side of the carpett, and directing the Boyes that worke it how much of each collour of yarne should be wrought in. And every thread being wrought, they share it with a pear of sizers, and then proceed to the next*[22]. A similar procedure can be found recorded in a French source, describing a workshop in Cairo (see p.20). It indicates that these carpets were woven from paper cartoons, which probably explains the uniformity of the designs we see represented in Dutch and Flemish paintings. The products from the Indian centres are sometimes assumed to display identical designs and weaving characteristics to those of Persian manufacture, the potential of dissimilarities not yet being recognized. Some characteristics enable the student to distinguish certain definitely Indian carpets from the larger group of floral 'Indo-Persian' carpets; the frequent use of two shades of one colour side by side without separating outlines presents one such characteristic (see p.89). The

17th century pictorial sources appear to contain a large number of minutely represented carpets which can be attributed to Indian workshops, on the basis of these often minor but significant design characteristics. As the Persian province of Khorasan is often named as the major weaving area of such pile carpets, it will be interesting in the present study to compare the number of 'Indian' examples found to the number of examples which do not have these 'Indian' design elements. If the ratio is such that a substantial share of the representations show Indian products, it becomes less probable that pile carpets with patterns absolutely identical to those used in Persia were made in India as well. In principle, it would seem unlikely that carpets woven in a distinct weaving area in India would be immune to local influences, especially since the Moghul court had a strong impact on the arts in the early 17th century.

In this study we will also look at other types of floral carpets depicted in Netherlandish paintings, such as woollen carpets from North-West Persia and South Persia, and the silk carpets with gold and silver brocadings that are generally attributed to workshops in Isfahan and Kashan.

In summary, we will attempt to isolate subgroups from the bulk of floral carpets represented in paintings, assuming that such a systematic cataloguing might produce an insight into the market share of each specific type compared to other groups of Oriental carpets. Not included in this study are those types of carpet that numerically constitute the smallest groups represented in the paintings. Examples of this situation include: (a) when only a single example is found of a extraordinary type of carpet (e.g. the Isfahan 'Strapwork' carpets[23]), (b) when no new information can be added (e.g. the above-mentioned Star Ushak carpets) and (c) when the pictorial information is difficult to confirm through the evidence of authentic surviving examples (e.g. the so-called Bird Ushak carpets and the Couple-columned Prayer Rugs, of which only a very few representations have been found, adding little in the way of new information to the study of these groups).

HISTORIOGRAPHY

N. Willemin was apparently the first writer to make, in 1839, a reconstruction of an Oriental carpet pattern based on information from pictorial sources[24]; he had discovered a representation of a carpet decorated with so-called Memlinc guls in a 15th century French miniature painting. The history of the art historical research of ancient carpets in Western paintings might have received a major impetus with the publication of this reconstruction, but in 1839 apparently the time was not yet ripe for other scholars to pick up the theme of Willemin's work. It took about forty years before Julius Lessing's pioneering study was published in 1877. Lessing's *Altorientalische Teppichmuster nach Bildern und Originalen des XV-XVI. Jahrhunderts* was the first book exclusively devoted to the study of historical Oriental carpets, and its publication marks the start of the study of carpets in general and carpets in paintings in particular[25]. As the dating of surviving specimens posed serious problems due to lack of inscribed examples and provenance information, Lessing's aim was 'feste Anhaltspunkte in gleich-

zeitigen bildlichen Darstellungen zu finden'[26]. Lessing raised the question of the possible presence of domestic copies of Eastern pile carpets included in the pictorial source material; he also referred to the 16th and 17th century written sources describing the production of pile carpets in France. Still, Lessing regarded the possibility of such copies being depicted in Italian or Netherlandish paintings as quite remote. Therefore he assumed that the pictorial representations which he had used in his book for the reconstruction of the history of old carpet patterns represented genuine Eastern weavings[27].

The second major study of Eastern carpets appeared in 1881 with the publication of Joseph von Karabacek's *Die persische Nadelmalerei Susandschirds*. In this book Karabecek's concern was primarily as an Orientalist working with Eastern reference material, although he did quote Lessing's earlier conclusions[28]. Towards the end of the 19th century, Wilhelm von Bode, the director of the Berlin Kaiser Friedrich Museum and a knowledgeable scholar and connoisseur of Italian and Dutch art, had the opportunity to collect carpets on his frequent travels to Italy, where many ancient pieces could be found and purchased in the churches where they had been kept for centuries. Bode combined his interests in an article on early animal rugs in Western paintings in 1892[29], and published in 1902 his famous standard work *Vorderasiatische Knüpfteppiche aus älterer Zeit*. This publication and its later editions, which had the Islamic art scholar Ernst Kühnel added as a co-author, would become the most frequently quoted studies in the first half of the 20th century as far as pictorial sources for carpet history are concerned. Bode regularly referred to Western painters who had portrayed the carpet types which he discussed in his book, but unfortunately he seldom mentioned a specific painting, apart from those which he had published earlier in his 1892 article. For later students the accessibility to the sources which he had collected and cited was therefore minimal.

In the later publications on carpets which followed Bode-Kühnel, the pictorial sources were scarcely mentioned; authors for the most part confined themselves to references to von Bode's original article on representations of carpets in paintings[30]. The American carpet scholar and specialist in Iranian art Arthur Upham Pope called the datable paintings 'a dependable check'[31], but, as Karabacek before him, he discussed collateral dating in the main by presenting comparisons with other branches of Eastern art and by references to the scarce written sources[32].

The interest in pictorial sources as documentation for the history of carpets revived in the 1950s. The first systematic survey resulted in 1954 in a German doctoral dissertation: Brigitte Scheunemann's *Anatolische Teppiche auf abendländischen Gemälden*[33]. In her thesis over 180 carpet representations, mainly in Italian and Dutch paintings, were listed. This study can *mutatis mutandis* be regarded as an elaboration of the subject as presented by Bode and Kühnel in *Vorderasiatische Knüpfteppiche aus älterer Zeit* (Kühnel was her supervising professor), although surprisingly she was not able to check several references in the earlier study[34]. Unfortunately Scheunemann did not give accurate descriptions of the representations which she had found; in details such as the decoration of the subguards and other secondary design elements there is much information that is of importance for the delimitation of dependable criteria for the dating of surviving carpets. The main reason however that the Scheunemann dissertation fell more or less into oblivion was the fact that it remained unpublished. Perhaps the author had planned a series of articles with the information from her dissertation; a revised version of its most important chapter was published as an article in 1959[35].

In roughly the same period other researchers started to include illustrations of carpets in paintings next to illustrations of Oriental rugs and carpets in their published works[36], and from about 1977 the study of carpets in paintings reached a new level of importance and a vastly broader readership with the publications of John Mills in the British magazine *Hali*, a new journal devoted almost exclusively to carpets. The representations found and published, with extensive photographic documentation, by Dr. Mills partly overlap the data presented by Brigitte Scheunemann in 1954 (Mills did not have access to a copy of the Berlin dissertation at the time of his first articles), but the Mills articles made available a considerable amount of new information as well. This information was presented with short but useful descriptions and as noted with almost all cited examples illustrated, in the pages of *Hali*. The first four Mills articles include in the main information found in paintings from regions other than Flanders or the Dutch Republic, because in those studies Dr. Mills primarily discussed the earlier carpet types, dating from the 13th to the 16th centuries[37], but in an important article published in 1981 (' 'Lotto' Carpets in Western Paintings'[38]), Netherlandish pictorial sources were amply included. In 1983 Dr. Mills was responsible for a booklet entitled *Carpets in Painting* (a revised version of his 1977 *Carpets in Pictures*) that accompanied a small exhibition of carpets represented in paintings in the National Gallery[39], on the occasion of the 4th International Conference on Oriental Carpets. At the same time, Mills also provided a chapter for the catalogue of the important exhibition *The Eastern Carpet in the Western World*[40].

However, the proportions of the study of John Mills were somewhat limited, as the author did not have the time or the opportunity to search for pictorial sources systematically in photographic archives, and because he chose to publish only those sources for which the painter and/or the dating could be established with reasonable certainty. Despite these limitations, the pioneering studies made by Dr. Mills made it possible for researchers after him to compare surviving carpets with logically arranged represented examples. His important work has made him one of the most frequently quoted authors in recent publications on early Oriental carpets. The study of representations of carpets in paintings has thereby become virtually indispensable for the study of actual carpets themselves.

A few years later, Erik Duverger devoted a chapter to early pile carpets in Flanders, in the catalogue of the 1987 exhibition of tapestries from Bruges[41]. In this chapter, in which the author illustrated several carpets in early Flemish paintings, Duverger also paid some attention to the production of pile carpets with Eastern patterns in Flanders in the first half of the 16th century, amplifying on the evidence from the remarks that the Florentine historian Guicciardini made in 1560 on the carpet weavers of Antwerp[42].

At the start of the present study in 1985, it was assumed that it should be possible to find another two to three hundred representations of oriental carpets in Netherlandish paintings, in addition to the approximately two hundred examples which had already been found and published. It was anticipated that a systematic inventory, following the reasoning outlined above, would not only adjust conclusions made in previous incomplete studies, but would also provide valid new criteria for the dating of certain groups of carpets, the pictorial source material of which had not previously been subject to systematic research (e.g. the Indo-Persian carpets). Furthermore, there are certain groups of carpets of which only one or two examples in Western European painting are known (e.g. the Ottoman Cairene rugs); it was hoped that the systematic inventory forming a basis of the present study would bring new examples to light.

A preliminary report of the results of this research project was published in 1988, at the occasion of the exhibition *Carpets in 17th Century Dutch and Flemish Paintings*, held in Maastricht in conjunction with the Maastricht Fine Art Fair[43]. For this exhibition, principal organiser Michael Franses and the present author made a choice from among the new evidence of representations of carpets in paintings found in the course of this study; some of the best examples of Eastern carpets represented in the 17th century were shown next to original 17th century examples from private collections. The exhibition, which was consequently reviewed by John Mills in *Hali*[44], clearly illustrated that pictorial sources remain a crucial and therefore indispensable source of reference material for the study of authentic rugs and carpets preserved in private and public collections. A great deal of useful information can be found in these datable paintings, as mentioned by Charles Grant Ellis, who wrote that 'Photo archives ... need to be sorted through for leads, painter by painter. Doubtless material exists for another thesis, perhaps half a dozen'[45].

The Sources

The larger part of the research material was provided by the impressive photo archives of the Rijksbureau voor Kunsthistorische Documentatie in The Hague (RKD), the Brussels Koninklijk Instituut voor het Kunstpatrimonium (ACL), and the Rijksmuseum in Amsterdam. In addition, publications of 16th and 17th century paintings from the Northern and Southern Netherlands, primarily scholarly monographs, as well as collection and auction catalogues, constituted significant sources of information. In contrast to most previously published studies on carpets in paintings, the present study will provide the reader with a more detailed description of all carpets which have been included in the inventory: we will specify the design of the field, borders, guardborders and subguards, and at times, when possible, even the flat-woven ends of the carpet, the fringes, and the selvedges, as well as any other determinable characteristics of the weaving structure. Unfortunately, a description of the colour scheme of the carpets is

in many cases impossible, as the available photographic material is mainly in black-and-white. On the other hand, the colour scheme within a specific group is usually fairly consistent, so this unavoidable limitation should not be emphasized too much.

Another and larger problem is posed by the quality of the available material; many reproductions, especially in old auction catalogues, did not allow a detailed identification of the carpet patterns. This problem cannot be completely solved at present, although sometimes recent publications and auction catalogues reveal paintings which had previously only been known from bad quality reproductions. On the basis of such new reproduction material, a more detailed identification of the design elements of carpets in paintings will in some instances be possible in the future.

Choices had to be made about the representations to be included; the data consist of interpretations of objects which were themselves in some sense alien to the cultural background of the occidental painter. As a result, many paintings show carpets with ill-represented patterns. A painter such as Van Streeck, for example, obviously studied the 'Lotto' design, which he then depicted several times (cat.152-157). Nevertheless, the original carpet design can only be traced in several of his representations after comparing representations in all his still-life paintings. Eventually, only those representations have been included which are unambiguously identified in the painting as examples belonging to a certain group. Copies of paintings are also excluded from the inventory, even when such copies were made in the 16th or 17th century. An exception is made in cases when a 16th or 17th century copy displays a carpet which differs from the one represented in the original painting. Occasionally in such cases however an unusually designed carpet has been found, the pattern of which cannot be identified. In most cases such representations of carpet patterns may, again, be regarded as inventions of the painter, rather than as dependable representations of an authentic carpet. For reasons of space and focus, such representations have equally been excluded from this study.

The pictorial sources provide *termini ante quem*, as has been stated above. This implies that in a study such as the present one the trustworthinesss of the conclusions depends on the reliability of the dating of the paintings. In the case of an authentically dated painting, we have usually placed a maximal reliance on the work for collateral dating in the catalogue. In most instances however paintings do not bear dates; a stylistic comparison of undated and dated works in the oeuvre of an individual painter must then provide the missing information. Fortunately a firm consensus exists among art historians in dating the works of the best-known artists; the author has gratefully incorporated the data provided in authoritative monographs such as those of Pieter Sutton (Pieter de Hooch), Albert Blankert (Vermeer) and Susan Kuretsky (Ochter-velt). Other sources for a chronological ordering of paintings were the art historical datings given in other publications such as catalogues of museum collections and exhibitions, or in individual scholarly articles. If such previously published datings were not available — where the painting has not previously been published

— the author of the present study has dated the painting by stylistic comparison or by documenting details such as the style of the clothing worn by the persons represented. In the case of several portraits, the known identification of the sitters has been particularly helpful; for example, marital portraits are very unlikely to have been made years before the wedding of the persons in question took place.

The dates have been rounded off in the graphics; should a painting be dated 1637, it is included in the graphics as 1635; should it bear the date 1638, it is included as 1640. If the exact date is unknown, the painting is be dated in the catalogue as 1630-1640; the graphics would then include it as dating to 1635.

The documentary sources available in archives and libraries in the Netherlands provide a great deal of additional information. However, apart from the publications mentioned above that resulted from extensive work in archives, unfortunately major surveys of archival information were only minimally available at the time of writing of this study, from sources such as legal inventories, travel accounts, or the merchant archives of the Dutch United East India Company. For the present study in particular, the large volumes of the *Rijks Geschiedkundige Publicatien* (RGP) on the history of the East India Company were searched through carefully, and subsequently the original documents were studied at the Centraal Rijksarchief in The Hague when the RGP-publications mentioned anything on the carpet trade. Some interesting reports are included in this study (see e.g. p.64).

The analogous publications on the Dutch trade in the Levant include much less information, perhaps mainly due to the fact that the author of the major documentary studies, Dr.Heeringa, focused his attention primarily on the history of the political relations of the Netherlands with the Mediterranean Islamic rulers and thereby on the historical records left by the representatives of the Dutch traders at the courts of Istanbul and the provincial courts of governing Pashas; Heeringa's other major interest was the organization of the trade[47]. It is not surprising that the history of Occidental-Oriental relations at the top of the social and political pyramid does not include much reference to the trade in pile carpets, as the trade in these items of luxury must have played a minor role. It can be expected, though, that a systematic historical study of the archives might bring to light in future a number of interesting facts. However, for the moment, the history of the Netherlands trade in Oriental carpets itself remains rather obscure; we do not know for example which part the South European merchants and traders played in the carpet trade in the Netherlands. Some fragmentary information is available, such as a letter from the Dutch resident Warnerus in Istanbul to the directors of the United East India Company, dated from Febuary 22, 1663, informing his superiors about the Eastern trade routes[46].

Still, many questions remain unanswered. Did the Mamluk carpets come to Flanders via Italy, or were they imported by some individual Netherlandish merchants directly from Egypt? How many Turkish or Persian carpets were sent from Aleppo to South European harbours and hence by land to the markets of Brussels, Antwerp or

Amsterdam? What percentage of the Indian carpets brought to Amsterdam were transported to Europe from the East by English or Portuguese ships, and what percentage of the carpets sold in the international trade centre of Amsterdam in the 17th century remained subsequently in the possession of individuals and groups in the Netherlands? These questions will have to await further scrutiny, as the limitations of the present study did not permit such a time-consuming systematic research through the enormous amount of written sources in various archives.

Storage of the Information in the Catalogue

From the beginning of the project it was quite clear that the storage or retrieval of the information could not be done conveniently by hand. Therefore, a standard data dictionary was designed by the author as a code book for the processing of the information through an automatic data base system. The project required a data dictionary, with descriptions of all carpet design systems visible in painting.

The dictionary is divided into three chapters: a classification of 1. the field pattern, 2. the border pattern, and 3. the guard border patterns. The field pattern can be listed according to the assumed provenance as either Anatolian (a), (Indo-) Persian (b), Indian (c), other Oriental: Egyptian or Caucasian (d), or as possibly Occidental (e). A subdivision can be made by adding a digit in Roman figures to the aforesaid characters: pre-Ottoman Anatolian patterns, like the 'Lotto' pattern for example aiv; the 'Medallion Ushak' design av. and the 'Star Ushak' design avi.; aiv2 would mean the 'Anatolian' style subgroup of 'Lotto' carpets, and aiv3 indicates the 'Kilim' style 'Lotto' carpets. Capitals have not been used. The Persian subgroups are listed in the same way as the Anatolian subgroups: bi. for example, stands for the usual floral and cloudband pattern of the main group of Indo-Persian carpets represented in the paintings; and bv. for carpets from North-West Persia. A dot is added to some codes to avoid communication failures in the data base; otherwise if the user would recall a list of all ai carpets in the inventory, he would get the aii. and aiii carpets as well, not to mention all records with words like 'available', or names like 'Bailly'.

The border patterns are classified similarly: a2 indicates the usual cartouche-border of the Anatolian group of 'Lotto' carpets; a6 stands for the cloudband border of the 'Lotto' carpets and the so-called double-niche rugs. Persian border patterns are characterized by the letter b, such as b6 for the cartouche design.

No geographical distinction is made in the patterns of the guard borders. A zigzag ornament on either an Anatolian, Persian or other carpet is g6, and the 'barber-pole' ornament is g9. An i as in ig9 is added when the inner guard border is described, and an o when it is an outer guard border. For the classification of a carpet such as that represented in *The Annunciation* of Hendrik ter Brugghen (fig.6), all the necessary codes to describe it as aiv3/a6/og6 are now available (the inner guard pattern can not be identified and is hence not given a code). The rug in this painting is a 'Kilim style 'Lotto' rug, with a cloudband border, and unidentified inner guard border. The outer guard border seems to be decorated with a zigzag ornament. The pattern of this rug is classified as follows:

fig.6 Hendrik ter Brugghen: Annunciation, 1629. Municipal Museum, Diest.

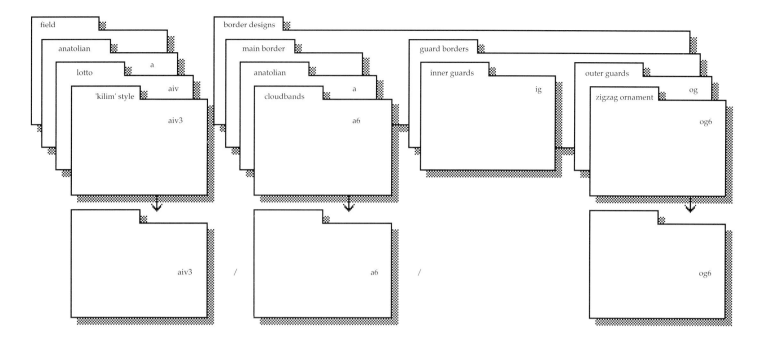

Still, not all the relevant information turns up when, for example, the aiv3 code is entered in the computer for retrieval of the required data. In many representations, if not most, the exact subgroup type of aiv carpet can not be positively identified. When the aiv3 subgroup pattern in a representation of a 'Lotto' carpet is assumed or suspected, but not positively identified, the carpet should be catalogued generally as aiv. In order to make these general records available when the specific aiv3 carpets are retrieved, the specifying code is added in brackets to the standard description: (aiv3); an example would be aiv/a6/og6 (aiv3). This form of entry is also applied to incomplete representations of carpets; in cases where only the a6 border and the g6 outer guard stripe of a presumed 'Lotto' carpet are visible on a painting, the carpet is entered as a6/og6 (aiv).

THE INFORMATION IN THE REPRESENTATIONS

Statistical analysis is the logical result of such a systematic inventory as described above. Nevertheless, the information in this study does not consist of hard facts which are not open to interpretation themselves. Rather, this study is an art historical project that deals with interpretations only; interpretations of carpet patterns by painters who would not have expected to find their names in these files. The results of the research depend entirely upon the degree of care with which each painter 'portrayed' his models. It will be clear from the results of this study, that in general Dutch and Flemish painters took great effort to represent the costly Oriental weavings in great detail with particular regard for accuracy of representation.

II
EGYPTIAN CARPETS IN NETHERLANDISH PAINTINGS

MAMLUK CARPETS

A very exceptional group of carpets was produced in Egypt, presumably from the middle of the 15th century onwards. They are characterized by a dominant central medallion; the larger ones have from three to as many as five medallions in the field, set out along the vertical axis. Numerous smaller ornaments have been placed meticulously around them. These smaller ornaments, such as eight-pointed stars, or small octagons of stylized floral ornaments, are usually arranged within small, square fields, marked by small triangles in the corners (fig.7).

The Egyptian carpets were quite popular in Western Europe, as evidenced from various early 16th century sources. A famous incident in this context was the donation of some sixty of these carpets to the English Cardinal Wolsey in 1520, in exchange for a license for Venetian merchants to import wine into England. These carpets were valued at almost a thousand ducats, an amount which placed stress on the budget of the Venetian Signoria to the extent that it was forced to sell some precious diplomatic gifts which had been given to Venice by foreign monarchs[1]. The enormous appeal of this characteristic group of carpets lay primarily in the kaleidoscopic effect of the innumerable small geometric and floral ornaments added to the relatively simple basic pattern. The kaleidoscopic effect is reinforced by the restrained use of colour (omitting white, and sometimes restricted to crimson red, deep green and blue) and by the soft, shining wool.

The earliest known Western painting representing an Egyptian carpet of the Mamluk group is Giovanni Bellini's *Portrait of the Doge of Venice Loredan and his Four Advisers*, painted in 1507[1a]. On the table, we see a carpet displaying the characteristic kaleidoscopic elements of the Mamluk design[2]. The carpet has a double border, the outer one showing an unmistakably kufesque interlace ornament, as can also be found on a Mamluk carpet fragment in the Victoria and Albert Museum[3].

One of the principal difficulties in tracing the stylistic development of the Mamluk pattern is the small number of representations of these carpets in paintings. In an article published in 1981 John Mills mentioned only seven examples; since then the presence of a Mamluk carpet has been demonstrated in a painting from about 1555 by an unknown French master, entitled *The Three De Coligny Brothers*, in the collection of the Mauritshuis in The Hague (cat.1a)[4]. A monumental representation can be found on Ambrosius Francken's *The Last Supper* at the Royal Museum of Fine Arts in Antwerp (fig.8), painted about fifteen years after the French example. In Franken's depiction, the large star-shaped medallion functions as a nimbus round the head of Christ. In the field, the characteristic umbrella-shaped ornaments are clearly visible. The border however is represented in sketchy fashion. Relatively late is the representation in a painting attributed to Rubens: *Portrait of a Lady, Member of the Imperial Family with her Grandchild* (cat.14). Only a small part of the border is visible. A characteristic Mamluk oblong lobed cartouche is clearly recognizable in spite of the fact that the representation is only roughly painted.

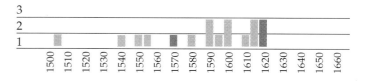

Mamluk carpets in Western Paintings 1500-1700. The Netherlandish paintings are indicated by a ▓ , the paintings from other European schools by a ▓.

fig.7 Mamluk carpet, 16th century, Gemeentemuseum The Hague.

fig.8 Ambrosius Francken, The Last Supper, about 1570. Koninklijk Paleis voor Schone Kunsten, Antwerp.
fig.9 Ludovicus Finsonius, The Annunciation, about 1600. Present location unknown.

In the data-base compiled for the present study, 16 dateable representations of Mamluk carpets could be recorded, of which only 3 are found in Netherlandish paintings, and these exclusively in paintings of Flemish origin. In all probability these carpets were available in such small numbers in the Northern Netherlands of the 17th century, that the statistical chance of representation was minute, if indeed these carpets were available there at all. The assumption that the production of these carpets was suspended in or shortly after the third quarter of the 16th century[5] is therefore supported by the absence of these carpets in Dutch paintings, indicating that Mamluk carpets were not traded to the Northern Netherlands in significant numbers in the 17th century.

CAIRENE OTTOMAN CARPETS

In 1517 the Ottomans conquered Cairo, bringing the dominion of the Mamluks to an end. For quite a long time after the conquest of Cairo, the Ottomans apparently left the Mamluk carpet workshops undisturbed, and production in traditional designs appears to have continued. In the meantime, in the second part of the 16th century, a new refined curvilinear style had been developed at the court of the Ottoman Sultan in Istanbul. This style, known today as the 'saz' style, is characterized by sickle-shaped feather-like leaves, sometimes complemented by naturalistically represented flowers. Famous examples of the 16th century decorations in the new style are the dated tile panels in Istanbul mosques and palaces which were manufactured at Iznik, the classical Nicaea. Similar patterns were also designed for carpets which were to be manufactured at the Cairo workshops that had originally produced Mamluk carpets. Several 'transitional' examples survive that show typically Mamluk motifs and Ottoman ornaments combined in their patterns (e.g. the so-called Ostler rug[6], also a rug in the Rijksmuseum, hereafter fig.10), indicating that there had been a gradual shift in style. In 1580, Sultan Murad III ordered the governor of Cairo to send eleven Egyptian carpet-weavers and some Egypt spun and dyed wool to Istanbul. It may well be that the weavers that came to Istanbul worked on a special commission; the surviving Ottoman carpets cannot be divided in two distinct groups, one of which would be attributable to court workshops close to the Ottoman capital, and the other to the large production centre of Cairo, where somewhat coarser commercial examples might have been woven[7]. It would seem, on the contrary, that the Sultan summoned the Egyptian weavers because they had special skills: the Egyptian weavers were using the asymmetrical knot, a technique possibly better suited to the representation of curvilinear designs than the technique using symmetrical knots that had traditionally been used in Anatolia for the production of pile carpets. Furthermore, the soft wool used in the Egyptian carpets and/or the characteristic colours of the traditional Mamluk Egyptian carpets may have been preferable for the intricate court designs.

In 1663 Thevenot visited a workshop in Cairo where these Cairene carpets using Ottoman court designs were produced...*il se fait au Caire de fort beaux tapis, et en quantité, qu'on envoye a Constantinople et en Chrestiente, et on les appelle tapis de Turquie.* To this he added an account of the procedures used in the workshops where these carpets were woven: *il y a quantité de gens qui y travaillent parmy lesquels sont plusieurs petits garçons, mais qui font tous leur ouvrage avec tant d'adresse et de vistesse, qu'il ne se peut pas croire; ils ont devant eux leur mestier, et tiennent de la main gauche plusieurs bouts de pelotons de laines de diverses couleurs, qu'ils appliquent chacune en leur lieu; de leur main droite ils tiennent un cousteau, avec quoy il coupent la laine a chaque point qu'ils y touchent avec le cousteau. Le maître a eux de temps avec un patron, sur lequel regardant, il leur dicte comme s'il lisoit dans un livre, et plus viste encor qu'il ne se peut lire, disant, il faut tant de points d'une telle couleur, et tant d'une telle autre, et autres choses semblables, et eux ne sont pas moins prompts a travailler que luy a dicter*[8].

If there are today relatively few representations of Mamluk carpets known to us from Western paintings, the situation is vastly improved from 1983, when D. King knew of the existence of only one painting representing an Ottoman carpet[9]. In contrast to the Mamluk carpets, which were less suited for representation in paintings because of their kaleidoscopic patterns and minimal contrasts of colour, the representation of the floral pattern of Ottoman carpets would not have constituted any more serious problem to 16th and 17th century European painters than the representation of Persian floral carpets, of which a great many representations in Western paintings are known. Apparently Ottoman carpets were simply not available as models for painters to use at that time. Yet a relatively large number of these carpets has been preserved. This paradox may be explained by the possibility that Ottoman carpets were primarily exported to those European countries where at the time interest in the depiction of Eastern carpets in paintings had diminished. This would certainly apply, for example, to Italy where only few carpets were reproduced in 17th century paintings. In the present study, only one instance of an Italian painting representing an Ottoman carpet has been found, whereas some seven representations of such carpets were found in Dutch paintings from that same period. Although the Ottoman style had been fully developed by the last quarter of the 16th century, it was apparently not until the turn of the century that these carpets began to be traded to the West in significant quantities.

Early in the 17th century Ludovicus Finsonius represented an Ottoman carpet in his work *The Annunciation* (fig.9). His representation of the carpet is not very detailed; its texture is not clearly discernable, and the pattern is not always exact. The painter may have seen the carpet somewhere, and may have made a rough sketch he later used as a basis for the representation of the carpet in his painting. The carpet in the painting has the same border design and decoration of the guard borders as a carpet in the Rijksmuseum (fig.10). In the corner medallions, however, it shows the so-called 'tiger stripes' that are well known from Ottoman silk velvets in the

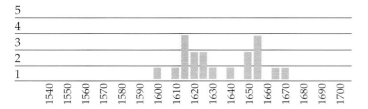

Cairene Ottoman carpets in Western paintings 1540-1700.

so-called 'chintamani' pattern, and which were sometimes used for the embellishment of Ottoman carpets[10]. A similar carpet, also on a table, was painted by Adriaen van der Venne about 1630, in *Geckie met de Kous* (cat.16). The colouring of this carpet representation is more or less identical to that of the above-mentioned example in the Rijksmuseum. Although the decoration of the central medallion is not clearly visible (the corner medallions are not depicted), the field clearly shows Ottoman ornaments, and the Ottoman border of pomegranates and tulips, as well as the typical Ottoman guardstripes, are distinctly recognizable. A third example can be found in *Christ in the House of Mary* (1610-20) by Rubens and Brueghel (cat.15), although this carpet displays a divergent border (cf. fig.11). An example in French painting can be found in a group portrait by Philippe de Champaigne. The carpet is depicted on the altar steps in his *The Mayor and the Municipal Council of the City of Paris* (cat.3a). It has the same floral ornaments as those in the field of the Rijksmuseum rug (fig.10), represented in hues of ochre and green.

The border design of the rug in the Rubens and Brueghel *Christ in the House of Mary*, characterized by S-stems ending in double sickle-shaped lancet leaves, can also be found in various carpets in 17th century paintings. An Italian example is a small carpet painted around 1670 by an artist from the circle of Evaristo Baschenis (fig.12). The second example, though less distinct than the previous one, is visible in a painting by Jan Gerritsz van Bronckhorst's *Merry Company with a Girl Playing the Lute*, painted around 1625 (cat.3). A third and very fine example was painted around 1640 by Elias Vonck, in his *An Elderly Couple in an Interior* (fig.13). This unpretentious painting shows us the couple sitting at a table covered with a small Cairene rug. Although this rug is somewhat sketchily represented, it is easily recognizable. The field pattern may be slightly different, but the all-over impression must have been quite similar to that of another small Ottoman rug in the Rijksmuseum (fig.11).

In 1656 Gerrit Lundens portrayed the couple Joris van Oorschot-Coymans in a pair of portraits, with husband and wife each shown seated at a table covered by an Ottoman carpet (cat.9,10). Although the representation of the carpet in both paintings is definitely sketchy, the border pattern is nevertheless distinctly Ottoman (compare fig.11).

The field design is hardly visible; its corners display small blue rosettes. The fringe of the carpet in the portrait of the wife, which is plaited in braids in the same way as the fringe of the comparable Rijksmuseum carpet, is more distinctly represented here than in the portrait of her husband, where a fringe on all four sides is shown. This divergence, as well as the disproportion between the borders and field of the husband's portrait, and the quick strokes of the brush with which the painter rendered the pattern — as if to disguise the 'black holes' in his memory — seem to suggest that Gerrit Lundens did not paint his carpet working directly from an original.

The border pattern of the cautiously draped carpet represented in Cornelis Gijsbrechts' *Still Life with a Servant* is unknown (cat.7). Clearly visible, however, is the large centre medallion, which is identical to that of the above-mentioned Rijksmuseum carpet (fig.10). In view of the pictorial information included, the painting by

fig.10 Ottoman Cairene Rug, late 16th or early 17th century. Rijksmuseum, Amsterdam, inv. R.B.K. 1959-1.

fig. 12   Evaristo Baschenis, Still-life with Musical Instruments, about 1670.
Present location unknown.
fig. 13   Elias Vonck, Portrait of an Elderly Couple Seated in an Interior, about
1640. Private collection, Germany.

Hendrik van Balen and Jan Brueghel in the Munich Alte Pinakothek (cat.2) can be said to be quite useful. The subject of the painting is a Bacchanal, showing a float decorated by a carpet on which the merry Bacchus is seated. Both the patterning of the medallion in the field and the decoration of the edging bear great similarity to the carpet of figure 10. A second carpet is draped on a table in the left corner of the painting. The field is evidently covered by a piece of cloth, but the border pattern is visible. The pattern corresponds to that of the second Ottoman Cairene rug in the Rijksmuseum (fig. 11). Both types of Cairene Ottoman carpets are thus represented in one painting.

Finally, a third, and relatively fine group of Ottoman Cairene carpets was represented in painting by Daniel Mijtens. A 1623 painting, *Portrait of Charles, Prince of Wales, later Charles I*, shows us the prince standing on a carpet with a rich design of scrolling stems and curling feathery leaves (fig.14). Under his feet is a small medallion, decorated with a quatrefoil motif with small pendants at both ends. This field design is known from several famous fragments of an Ottoman court carpet, divided among collections in Paris, London, Stockholm and Washington[11]. The border design cannot be identified with certainty, but seems to have floral ornaments similar to those in the border of the Rijksmuseum rug in figure 11. Less clearly shown is the design of the carpet under the feet of Nicolo Molino, painted by Daniel Mijtens one year earlier, in 1622 (cat.11). It has similar curvilinear floral ornaments to those in the carpet in the 1623 painting, and a medallion with presumably identical outlines and the same small pendants at both ends. Both representations may have been painted after one single Cairene Ottoman carpet.

It can be concluded that in the 17th century Ottoman Cairene carpets were available in the Netherlands, but in relatively small numbers. Presumably these carpets were traded to the Occident in the last quarter of the 16th and the first half of the 17th century, as may be inferred from the documentary data concerning the above-mentioned paintings. The evidence found in the paintings themselves is supported by current scholarship both from stylistic research and from written source material[12], whereby dates of the authentic examples within this period can be determined. These data equally explain why Ottoman carpets rarely occur in paintings of other than Dutch origin. As stated before, especially in Italy the interest in the depiction of Eastern carpets had strongly declined by the 17th century, whereas in the preceding century Cairene carpets of Ottoman design would not have been available. But this fact does not fully explain the relatively small number of representations of these carpets in Netherlandish paintings. Both the working methods of the workshops as described by Thevenot, and the considerable number of carpets which have been preserved, indicate that a substantial production existed. Perhaps the trade in these Cairene carpets was dominated primarily by Mediterranean merchants, while the bulk of Oriental carpets available on the Dutch market may have derived mainly from other trading ports, more frequently visited by the North European traders.

fig.14 Daniel Mijtens, Portrait of Charles, Prince of Wales, 1623. Coll. Mrs. P.A. Tritton, Parham Park, Pulborough, West Sussex.

III
ANATOLIAN CARPETS AND CHESSBOARD CARPETS IN NETHERLANDISH PAINTINGS

'LOTTO' CARPETS

In 1516 Sebastiano del Piombo painted a carpet which had a field pattern of stylized yellow arabesques on a red ground. As far as we know he was the first to represent such a carpet in a painting[1]. Despite this fact, the characteristic pattern of stylized arabesques has in carpet literature been named after Lorenzo Lotto, who more than thirty years later included similar carpets in a number of his paintings[2]. The Lotto pattern may be characterised as a variation on the so-called 'small-pattern Holbein' design. The latter, a repeating pattern of alternating quatrefoils and octagonal medallions, probably originating in the 14th century, appears frequently in European paintings over the 15th century (fig.16). The new, partly geometrical and partly floral ornaments of the 'Lotto' pattern have been cast in yellow on a red ground, with small dark blue and white accentuations. This colour scheme, both in the surviving carpets and in painted representations, is highly stereotyped; only a very small minority of examples depart from this model through a different use of colour.

fig.16a The 'Holbein' design.　　　　*fig.16b The 'Lotto' design.*

Representations of 'Lotto' carpets are found in Dutch paintings from 1543 onwards; although they were initially only rarely represented, from about 1610 onwards these Anatolian carpets appear to have been well liked as models by 17th century painters. Although they are sometimes represented in Biblical or mythological paintings, where they often function to create an exotic atmosphere, these carpets most frequently occur in portraits, and, from 1630 onwards, in genre and occasionally in still-life paintings. It can be assumed that the colourful 'Lotto' carpets in the portraits and genre paintings not only served as simple embellishment in order to add a touch of colour; their emphatic presence in portraits suggests that they equally served the representative function of precious showpieces indicating the wealth and status of the sitter.

It was Wilhelm von Bode who, in 1902, was the first to produce an enumeration of Western painters who had represented 'Lotto' carpets; Bode rightly regarded evidence found in paintings as the primary source of information for dating these rugs. He regarded the Italian representations as most important because of their earlier dates. He found that most representations in Dutch paintings were made shortly after the middle of the 17th century, and established that interest in 'Lotto' carpets as models for painting had decreased by the end of the century[3].

Brigitte Scheunemann continued von Bode's study by updating his material and by systematically enumerating sources (the paintings) with their dates and references in scholarly literature including location and attested illustrations. Von Bode had only published the names of various painters who had depicted such carpets, without giving systematic references[4]. Although she did recognize and define two subgroups within the rubric of the 'Lotto' pattern, Scheunemann's major basis for classification of 'Lotto' carpets was by border pattern. While such a classification is useful, methodologically speaking the relation between the different border de-

signs and the different sub-groups of field designs should have been addressed first. The two different types of 'Lotto' field design Dr. Scheunemann recognized are now known from their description by Charles Grant Ellis as the 'Anatolian' style (fig.17), and the 'Kilim' style (fig.15): 'Die Gabelblätter an den Eckabschrägungen der einzelnen Musterschätze sind treppenformig stilisiert'[5]. Scheunemann regarded the 'Anatolian' style to be the earlier; of the 'Kilim' style, she remarked that she had not been able to find depictions of such carpets dating earlier than the 1650s[6]. This assertion cannot be confirmed in her dissertation, as the illustrations are not organized on the basis of field patterns. It is not appropriate here to attempt a thorough critique of Dr. Scheunemann's classification system and her conclusions; one can however pose some serious objections concerning the methods and results of her study. In an authoritative publication entitled ' 'Lotto' Carpets in Western Paintings,' John Mills entirely recast the problem as it had been set up by Brigitte Scheunemann nearly thirty years earlier. Dr. Mills' publication in turn relied upon the work of Charles Grant Ellis, who, in his article 'The 'Lotto' Pattern as a fashion in Carpets'[7] distinguished three sub-groups in the 'Lotto' pattern, which Ellis dubbed the 'Anatolian' style, the 'Kilim' style, and the 'Ornamented' style (see below). Mills listed 44 representations in Netherlandish paintings; apart from these some 37 were found in non-Netherlandish paintings, of which 17 were in Italian paintings. Mills' publication will be subjected to closer examination below.

Three years later, Thomas Reimer added some annotations to Dr. Mills' observations[8]. Reimer was particularly interested in the knotted-pile end panels (elems) or flat-woven kilim ends at the upper and lower ends of actual and depicted 'Lotto' carpets. Based on representations in paintings, Reimer came to estimations of the length of the fringes and the width of the elems or flat-woven end finishes. Although the length of the fringes of 'Lotto' carpets, which sometimes appear to be rather long in representations, may be of some marginal importance in the identification of groups, Reimer's conclusions, giving exact estimations in centimetres (with a possible deviation of 2%, according to the author!) are hardly realistic or useful. The distinction made by the author between elems and kilim ends is also questionable, since quite often in paintings the weaving technique of the unpatterned areas cannot be clearly distinguished. Reimer's attempt to convert the findings of John Mills into graphics and to compare these with figures from a study of surviving 'Lotto' carpets, may be of some interest, however. Still, the data from Dr. Mills' study are not complete enough to allow precise statistical conclusions, which Mills himself did not attempt to make either; moreover, a systematic survey of surviving 'Lotto' carpets has not yet been undertaken. For these reasons Thomas Reimer's article does not add much information to the already existent material.

For the study presented below, the research studies of Dr. Scheunemann and Dr. Mills have been re-executed, with the limitation that only paintings originating from the Southern and Northern Netherlandish schools have been studied. In the processing of the data, no distinction has been made between representations which could be identified with certainty (e.g. a clear representation of an 'Anatolian' style 'Lotto' carpet), and those which because of limitations in the painted evidence can only be hypothesized to belong to a specific subgroup. The results of our new study will then be compared with the conclusions of Scheunemann and Mills.

In all, some 190 'Lotto' carpets have been found depicted in paintings from the Netherlands. After the approximately 290 representations of floral carpets discussed in Chapter IV the 'Lotto' carpets take second place in numbers of depictions in Netherlandish painting. In diagram 1 the dates of the paintings showing 'Lotto' carpets have been arranged chronologically in periods of five years; this diagram also includes painted examples that are reasonably assumed to be 'Lotto' carpets even though only parts of borders and not fields are shown.

The diagram shows that representations of 'Lotto' carpets are highly exceptional in Netherlandish paintings before 1610 (nine examples found in a period of almost sixty years), whereas from 1610 onwards the type occurs in a considerable number of paintings.

Field Patterns

The classification of the 'Lotto' field pattern into three subgroups is based upon the classification propounded by Charles Grant Ellis. In the subsequent diagrams the depictions of carpets have been arranged in periods of five years and by subgroups according to field pattern.

The 'Anatolian' group, which is commonly regarded to be the oldest variety of the 'Lotto' design (fig.17), can be found in paintings made by an unknown Flemish painter (cat.20), in paintings by van Balen and Brueghel (cat.29), presumably in a painting attributed to de Baen (cat.23) in, paintings from Coques (cat.66), Duck (who, like van Balen, Coques and Honthorst also depicted at least one 'Lotto' carpet belonging to the 'Kilim' style, cat.68,69), van Dyck (cat.72), Floris (cat.78), Francken (cat.80), Gheeraedts (e.g. cat.84), and in paintings from Honthorst, whose representations derive from at least two different authentic models (a usual red-ground 'Lotto' carpet with a cartouche-border (cat.91) and another example with a blue-ground field, framed by the characteristic a93 border (cat.96). Examples were also depicted by Jordaens, Key, Kick, Lievens, and in a self-portrait which has been attributed to van Mieris (cat.134). A presumed example is seen in the 1555 painting by Massys (cat.118) and further examples are found in paintings by Mijtens, van Oost, van Rossum (fig.18), Schalcken, Steenwijck, Teniers, Valckert, Victors and in works by both Cornelis and Simon de Vos.

In spite of the fact that it is difficult to prove exactly to what extent a painter may have used a single carpet as a model in more than one of his paintings, it is highly probable, as a matter of practicality, that repeated use of one carpet as a model for several paintings was a regular practice. Diagram 2a represents the earliest depiction of 'Anatolian' style 'Lotto' carpets represented by each of the painters listed above, unless some details convincingly suggested that the painter in question almost certainly depicted more than one authentic example as a model. In such cases, the earliest representa-

diagram 1

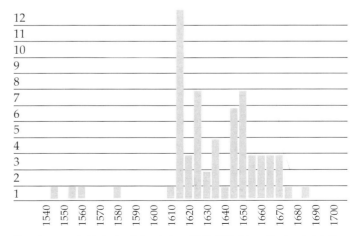

'Lotto' carpets in Netherlandish paintings 1540-1700 (aiv).

diagram 2

'Lotto' carpets in Netherlandish paintings 1540-1700, 'Anatolian' style (aiv2).

fig.19 A 'Lotto' carpet showing the 'Ornamented' style field design (aiv4) and a cartouche border (a2). Wher Collection, Switzerland.
fig.20 Jan van Ravesteyn, Portrait of an Unknown Officer, 1621. Royal Picture Gallery The Mauritshuis, The Hague.

tions of each separately identifiable example are tabulated in the graph. No distinction has been made for field colour; pattern type alone has been tabulated.

Both diagrams 2 and 2a show a continued interest on the part of Netherlandish painters between 1610 and 1670 for 'Anatolian' style 'Lotto' carpets. Although the diagrams display certain peaks, the numbers are too small to allow for detailed conclusions. Still, the peak around 1660, as is shown in diagram 1, can not be found in diagram 2, which suggests that the 'Anatolian' style gradually lost a part of its share of the numbers of 'Lotto' carpets represented in paintings to the other subgroups.

The term 'Kilim' style was launched by Dr. May Beattie and subsequently adopted by Charles Grant Ellis. The style forms a

diagram 2a

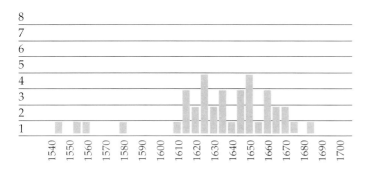

'Lotto' carpets in Netherlandish paintings 1540-1700, 'Anatolian' style (aiv2), arranged according to the earliest depiction of a particular example by each painter.

diagram 3

'Lotto' carpets in Netherlandish paintings 1540-1700, 'Kilim' style (aiv3).

variant of the 'Anatolian' style, whereby portions of the field arabesques are broadened and serrated in such a manner as to be highly reminiscent of slit-tapestry kilims (fig.15). 'Kilim' style 'Lotto' carpets have been found in Netherlandish paintings from 1584 onwards. The earliest representation can be found in the portrait of an unknown man by an anonymous artist, dated 1544 (cat.19); further representations have been found in paintings by van Linschoten, van Balen, possibly Brueghel, Ter Brugghen, van der Burgh, Codde, Coques and Duck (who also represented 'Lotto' carpets from other subgroups, as did Brueghel and Honthorst), Duyster, Fabritius, Gallis, Gheeraedts, Helst, Honthorst, and de Keyser. Depictions also occur in a painting attributed to van Mander or Isaacs, and in the work of van der Meer, Mesdach, van der Neer, Ochtervelt, Steen, Seghers, van Streeck, Terborch, Tielius, Vermeer and finally Weenix. When converting these data (earliest example by each painter) into graphics, the ensuing picture (see below) arises. The combined data of diagrams 2a and 3a now seem to point out the existence of a point around 1645-1655, in which many Netherlandish painters started to use 'Lotto' carpets as models. Together with diagram 1, these data agree with the findings of Wilhelm von Bode[3].

A third subgroup is the so-called 'Ornamented' style. This group bears a somewhat greater similarity to the 'Anatolian' style than the 'Kilim' style. The design has '...additional hooks and curls, most prominently along the slanting sides of the arabesque octagons (fig.19). In a rug large enough to show a good repeat, the pattern appears from a distance to dissolve into rows of large tangent circles of red within the yellow framework of the arabesques'[9]. Ellis called this type the 'Ornamented' style 'for lack of a more suitable name'[10]. The 'Ornamented' style has been found in the work of a small group of painters: Brueghel, and Rubens in cooperation with Brueghel (the earliest representation found, dating from 1614 or 1615 (cat.156)), Ravesteyn (1620s; fig.20), Bronchorst (some representations dating from ca.1640 onwards) and finally Metsu. Gabriel Metsu represented a 'Lotto' carpet in at least 13 paintings. Most of these representations are very vaguely painted or show only a small part of the carpet. Despite this ambiguity, all Metsu representations seem to have been painted after one authentic model, which is almost certainly of the 'Ornamented' style, judging from paint-

ings in the National Gallery (cat.124) and the Musée Fabre (cat.126). The characteristic additional curls are vaguely visible.

The number of 'Lotto' carpets in paintings dating from before 1614 is relatively small (diagram 1). As to the dating of actual carpets suggested by this data, it could be argued that although the subgroup does not appear in paintings earlier than 1614, the first examples of the subgroup may still have come on the Netherlandish market at an earlier date. The small number in the sample above suggests that they may have been traded to the Netherlands in relatively small numbers, and this fact, if true, has reduced the chance of an example being used as a model by a painter until the representation of such carpets became far more common. Surviving 'Ornamented' style 'Lotto' carpets are commonly dated to the 17th century. However, a (late) 16th century date for the earliest examples seems entirely possible.

When the data of diagrams 2, 3 and 4 are compared with those of diagram 1, it can be concluded that diagram 1 registers a considerable larger number of total representations than the accumulated number of first-time representations registered in the former diagrams. The explanation is obvious; large numbers of depictions cannot be precisely identified due to the sketchiness of the representation, or because the field pattern is only partially visible or not visible at all, or a combination of the two. The data of diagrams 2, 3 and 4 are combined to form diagram 5, and are represented by a ■.
The results are projected on the data of diagram 1, whereby the results, if not coinciding with those of diagrams 2, 3 and 4, are represented by means of ▨.

The data in this diagram are of general interest for the final conclusions of this study, because they indicate a generally high degree of accuracy and realism in representations of Oriental carpets by painters. This diagram shows that of the 190 representations thought to be of 'Lotto' carpets, 132 have been painted meticulously enough to allow determination of the subgroups to which the models belonged. In other words, about 70% of the

diagram 3a

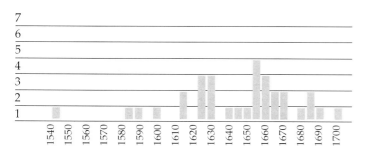

'Lotto' carpets in Netherlandish paintings 1540-1700, 'Kilim' style (aiv3), arrangeed according to the earliest example depicted by each painter.

diagram 4

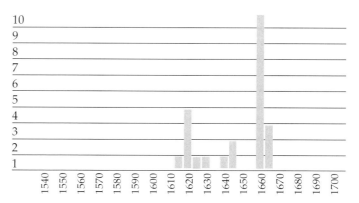

'Lotto' carpets in Netherlandish paintings 1540-1700, 'Ornamented' style (aiv4).

representations display enough detail to allow us to determine not only the general type, but even the subgroup.

Some may think this is a relatively disappointing percentage as about 30% of the representations cannot be identified in some detail; others will possibly regard it as an unexpectedly high percentage. The percentage mentioned however hardly constitutes a significant contribution to the formulation of general conclusions concerning the reliability of representations of carpets in paintings for two reasons. On the one hand, the group of as (aiv) classified carpets in paintings comprises a number of carpets which have a minutely represented border pattern, whereas their field has not been represented and can therefore not be classified more specifically. On the other hand, there are representations classified among the (aiv2), (aiv3) and (aiv4) carpets where the classification depends on a supposed relation between these and other representations of 'Lotto' carpets by the same painter. A significant example is found in the 13 representations by Metsu, of which only 2 were positively identified as 'Ornamented' style 'Lotto' carpets, whereas all 13 have been by inference listed as 'Ornamented' style 'Lotto' carpets in diagram 4, because it can be reasonably hypothesized that Metsu used the same model for all 13 representations. Moreover, a sharp distinction is kept in this chapter between the 'Anatolian', the 'Kilim' and the 'Ornamented' style, while it is clear from study of

actual rugs that this distinction is a rather arbitrary one at times, some examples falling into a 'crack' between the classifications. Future studies of both actual and represented rugs will undoubtedly bring about nuances and modifications of the present tripartite classification.

As appears from diagrams 2, 3 and 4, 59 representations of 'Anatolian' style 'Lotto' carpets have been found (the earliest dating from 1543), against 50 representations of 'Kilim' style 'Lotto' carpets (the earliest dating from 1544) and 23 representations of 'Ornamented' style 'Lotto' carpets. Since the earliest known representation of an 'Anatolian' style 'Lotto' carpet in Western painting has been found in an Italian painting dating from 1516 (Mills 1981, nr.1), and the earliest known representation belonging to the 'Kilim' style has also been found in an Italian painting, dating from 1538[11], this study of 'Lotto' carpets in Netherlandish painting does not provide new data which would make it necessary to adjust the general chronological conclusions of John Mills' publication as to date of manufacture of the carpets. Diagram 4 however indicates that 'Lotto' carpets belonging to the 'Ornamented' style are not only depicted in Western paintings from 1640 onwards, (as concluded from the 1981 study by Dr.Mills), but appear to have been represented as early as about 1614[11a].

fig.21   *Carel van Mander or Pieter Isaacs, St.John the Baptist Preaching, about 1580-1600. Present location unknown.*

Border Designs

Most border designs of the represented carpets can be divided in two main groups: on the one hand the borders which have a pattern of repetitive cartouches (a2; fig.17), and on the other the cloudband borders (a6; fig.15). Representations of kufic or kufesque interlace border patterns are relatively rare. By contrast, the a93 border, which occurs only on 'Lotto' carpets with a blue field, was found represented a number of times. Other designs, such as a91 or a92, appeared in our survey only occasionally.

diagram 5

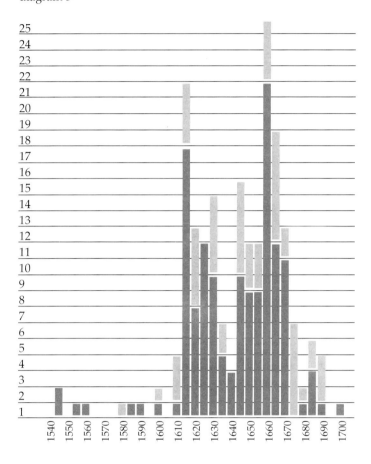

'Lotto' carpets in Netherlandish paintings 1540-1700,
classified and unclassified.

diagram 6

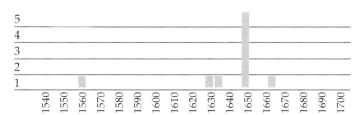

Border design a11 (kufic ornaments).

The fact that kufic border patterns were only rarely represented in Netherlandish paintings was undoubtedly due to the late dating of these paintings. These were obviously produced in a period in which the kufic interlace border was no longer commonly used in new carpets. This conclusion evidently tallies with current conclusions from stylistic research on surviving 'Lotto' carpets: kufic borders grew out of fashion over the course of the 16th century. In 16th century Italian paintings however, they appear to have been represented relatively frequently[12]; a fine Netherlandish example of a painting representing a 'Lotto' carpet with a kufic border was executed by Frans Floris in 1561 (cat.78). Individual early examples of 'Lotto' carpets with kufic borders must have been known to painters like Simon de Vos and Gerard van Honthorst, causing a certain outflowering of depictions of the pattern in paintings about 1640 (diagram 6), although the numbers do not testify to a large scale circulation of 'Lotto' carpets with this border design in the Netherlands in the 17th century.

The border design most frequently found on 'Lotto' carpets in Netherlandish paintings is the cartouche design (a2), which seems also to be the most frequently occurring border design on extant pieces (fig.17). It was found in 48 representations. Diagram 7 shows two peaks in the period 1610-20 and 1655-65; these peaks owe their existence primarily to the relatively large number of 'Lotto' carpets with this border represented by painters like van Balen and Metsu. Diagram 7a displays the number of cartouche borders arranged according to painter, whereby, as in diagrams 2a and 3a, only the earliest example per painter is indicated. From this diagram it appears that 'Lotto' carpets with cartouche borders were constantly within easy reach of the 17th century painters.

This cartouche design has not been found on 'Lotto' carpets in Italian paintings of the 16th century; the earliest representation mentioned by Dr. Mills was painted in 1611, by the Flemish painter Marcus Gheeraedts[13]. A painting attributed to either Carel van Mander or Pieter Isaacs, *St.John the Baptist Preaching*, (fig.21) shows

diagram 7

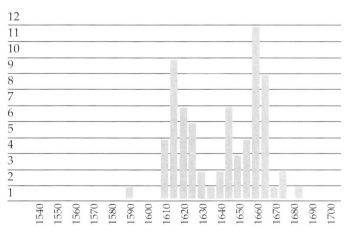

Border design a2 (cartouches).

a considerably earlier representation, dating from about 1580-1600. Apparently the a2 border pattern was developed before the last quarter of the 16th century, but not much earlier, replacing the older kufic interlace borders.

fig.23 Three versions of the floral ornament in the a2 cartouche border.

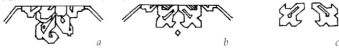
a   b   c

John Mills observed two variants of the cartouche design: 'in one form, typified by the large carpet in the Bargello Museum, Florence[14] and in the Baschenis pictures, the drawing is crisp and clear and the outlines interlace between adjacent cartouches to form little diamonds. In another form, the outlines have become more curved and blurred and have sprouted large hooks or tendrils (...) the first form is, however, definitely earlier'[15]. It may be easier to look at the secondary ornaments of the cartouche design, the stylistic development of which runs parallel to that of the outlines of the cartouches, as described by Dr. Mills. The purest form of the secondary ornaments[16] shows clearly recognizable half-represented flowers (fig.23a). These have consequently been represented in a simplified form[17]. In its most stylized variety only clock-shaped ornaments remain (fig.23c[18]). The issue now focuses on the date of the first representations of the individual versions of the cartouche design. The earliest representation of a 'Lotto' carpet with a cartouche

border found in a Western painting (fig.21) already displays flowers of the most stylized variant; the archetypal variant of figure 23a could not be found in paintings from the Netherlands. As actual carpets with the archetypal cartouche design, as well as representations of the same type of design in paintings, are relatively rare, we may surmise that these date from the 16th century. Such a dating would explain the fact that 'Lotto' carpets with the archetypal cartouche border seem not to occur in Dutch paintings. At any rate, our research on carpets in Netherlandish paintings can not provide data that support the assumed chronological stylistic development of the cartouche design.

The cartouches are usually red and white, and placed on a blue ground. Less frequent is the depiction of a red ground, examples of which have been found in works of Brueghel (e.g. cat.50). A surviving 'Lotto' carpet with such a red-ground border was illustrated by Végh and Layer (as nr.4).

diagram 7a

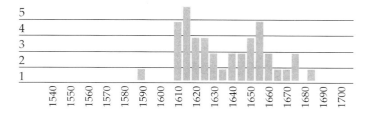

Border pattern a2 set out per painter (earliest example).

fig.24 'Lotto' carpet with a blue field, and the characteristic a93 border, 17th century. Metropolitan Museum of Art, New York.

Cloudband borders (fig.15) have been found by John Mills in 16 paintings from 1611 onward. Earlier examples could not be found in in the present study (diagram 8). As stated by Dr.Mills, the poorer variety of the cloudband pattern, known from the white-ground 'bird' Ushaks, does not occur in the borders of 'Lotto' carpets.

Border pattern a93 (fig.25) is exclusively known from an exceptional group of 'Lotto' carpets. The representatives of this group do not display the usual yellow arabesques against a red ground, but against a dark blue field. These carpets have a change of ground colour within some design elements like the octagons and the quatrefoils, varying from red to green. This unusual group was mentioned only briefly by Brigitte Scheunemann[19] as well as by John Mills[20]. The data of the paintings showing carpets with a93 borders are included in diagram 9. Perhaps the so-called 'eli-belinde' border design of a 'Lotto' carpet in Jan Massys' *Merry Company* — possibly a fore-runner of the a93 pattern — should have been included in the diagram as well (cat. 118); If however we accept Mills' reconstruction of the a93 pattern[21] then exclusion of the example from our diagram is justified. As the a93 border and the blue-ground field are always found together (this appears from the study of representations in paintings as well as from the rare surviving examples), diagram 9 gives a survey of the 'Lotto' carpets belonging to the exceptional group of 'Lotto' carpets with a blue ground, regardless of whether the painter depicted the field of the carpet or not. Thus in the case of incomplete representations, like Honthorst's self-portrait and the pendant portrait of his wife, showing only a93 borders (cat.99-2,3), it can be assumed with reasonable certainty that the field pattern, which is not visible on either of the paintings, will have been identical to that of the other carpets with the a93 border found in paintings by Honthorst and other painters: Duck (dating from about 1645-50; cat.69), van Dyck (1630s), Francken (1620s; cat.80), Pickenoy (1630; cat.76), Pourbus II (1620 c; cat.148) and Cornelis de Vos (several paintings from 1620s onwards). With respect to the work by Frans Francken it should be mentioned that this representation shows a a93 border with a presumably non-blue ground, but this is most likely due to the carelessness of the representation.

diagram 8

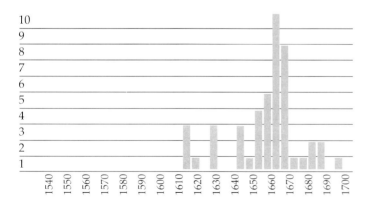

Border pattern a6.

fig.25 Unknown Dutch painter, Portrait of a Man at a Table, ca. 1640. Louvre, Paris.

fig.26 Johannes Verkolje (attributed to), A Young Boy with a Viola da Gamba, 1675-80. Wawel, Krakow.

It is due to the deviating colour scheme and to the careless drawing of the 'Lotto' ornaments, that the three surviving blue-ground 'Lotto' carpets, preserved in the Museum for Turkish and Islamic Art in Istanbul, the Metropolitan Museum of Art in New York and in the Rijksmuseum in Amsterdam, are usually regarded to be of a late date (late 17th or even 18th century[22]). However, the dates of paintings in which such variants have been represented, or in which the a93 pattern is found, point out a dating which is significantly earlier (diagram 9). Presumably these carpets were manufactured from at least about 1600 onward; since representations are not found after the middle of the 17th century, these carpets may not have been imported in large quantities after that date. The three extant examples may therefore most likely be regarded as dating from the first half of the 17th century. For sheer speculation, if Jan Massys' representation had been included in the study of blue-ground 'Lotto' carpets in paintings, a remarkably earlier date would emerge for the start of production in Anatolia. However, the 'Lotto' ornaments in the field are not correctly represented, which, in combination with the unusual colour scheme (the carpet has a green field) probably indicates that Massys was relying on his imagination to a high degree. The 16th century original carpet, which may have been studied by the painter at some place or other, could have belonged however to the same group as the three extant 17th century examples. The existence of a blue ground 'Lotto' carpet in the Buccleuch collection, which was copied in Europe after Anatolian model about 1585[23], could equally be indicative of the possibility that blue-ground 'Lotto' carpets were produced as early as the 16th century. The place of production of these rugs is still unknown. Since both the surviving examples and the represented ones are all of small size, the colour scheme is unusual and the drawing of the extant pieces is carelessly executed, they may have been produced in smaller village workshops.

Other border patterns are seldom found on the represented 'Lotto' carpets. The a92 border for example has only been attested 8 times (e.g. fig.22,26); equally in authentic examples this proves to be an unusual border pattern. a7 was found only once, in a 1598 painting by an unknown Flemish artist working in Italy (cat.18). This type of border pattern is also unusual for authentic examples (the above-mentioned copy in the Buccleuch collection shows this a7 border). The occurrence of exceptional border patterns is probably not an

diagram 9

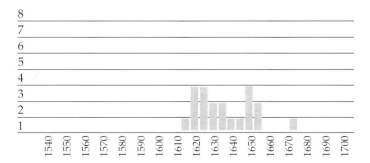

Border pattern a93.

indication that weavers started to experiment with combinations of patterns, 'bridging the gap between the kufic-bordered and the seventeenth-century types'[24]; non-kufic borders have already been attested in paintings from 1529 onward[25]. It might be argued that village weavers at times took over designs from the larger commercial workshops, changing these to their own liking (such as the colour scheme of the red-ground 'Lotto' design, which became blue in the variants described above) and inserting local design elements, like border patterns.

Combinations of Field and Border Patterns

We have stated repeatedly that the a93 pattern has only been catalogued as occurring on blue-ground 'Lotto' carpets. In his article John Mills demonstrated that kufic as well as cartouche borders usually combine with 'Anatolian' style fields. Cloudband borders generally occur in combination with the 'Kilim' style. The results of the research into the Netherlandish source material are condensed in the following table:

	aiv2	aiv3	aiv4	aiv
a11	7	-	-	2
a2	13 (9)	16 (5)	20 (11)	17 (7)
a6	5 (2)	21 (7)	-	19 (1)
a91	-	1	-	-
a92	2	-	-	4
a93	19	-	-	-

The numbers in brackets present the number of represented carpets which either lack an inner guard border or have a simple 'barber's pole' stripe instead.

It appears that Brigitte Scheunemann's classification after border pattern does not hold, since strict relations between border and field patterns seem to occur only in the case of the a93 pattern. A remarkable discrepancy between the data represented in the table above and those presented by Dr. Mills lies in the ratio between the number of 'Anatolian' style 'Lotto' carpets with the cartouche border on the one hand, and the number of 'Kilim' style 'Lotto' carpets with the same border on the other hand (1:1 instead of 5:1). Although the ratio between the number of 'Kilim' style 'Lotto' carpets with the cloudband border and the number of 'Anatolian' style 'Lotto' carpets with this border differs from the one presented by Mills, the outcome is identical, namely, that cloudband borders primarily occur in combination with 'Kilim' style fields.

An important issue in Mills' publication concerns the suggestion by Charles Grant Ellis that a large number of the extant 'Lotto' carpets may have been manufactured in Transylvania. John Mills' conclusions are supported by the present study; the table gives the numbers of 'Lotto' carpets which have no inner guard border or merely a small 'barber's pole' stripe between brackets. Both possibilities are catalogued as g14, as the sketchiness of many representations makes it often difficult to tell them apart. In the catalogue section of this study the g14 code is specified, if possible.

In summary, 'Lotto' carpets were represented by Netherlandish painters in a period in which the development of border and field patterns had already come to an end. The break-point between the older 'Lotto' carpets with kufic borders and the later 'Lotto' carpets with cartouche borders appears to reside in the last quarter of the 16th century, when the number of carpets represented in Italian painting decreased. The numbers of represented carpets in the 'Anatolian' style seem to decrease in favour of those in the 'Kilim' style shortly after the middle of the 17th century, although examples of both subgroups appear in Netherlandish painting in about the same period. Examples of the 'Ornamented' style, which occur relatively rarely in surviving 'Lotto' carpets, are exclusively found in Dutch paintings (cf. also[10a]).

The cartouche border design evidently occurs most frequently; 66 representations against 45 cloudband borders; apart from these, some 33 representations of other border designs have been attested, 19 of which are the a93 border providing frames for the blue-ground carpets. If we compare the 'Lotto' carpets which were traded in this period to the Netherlands (primarily in the 17th century), with those traded to Europe earlier on, the former group constitutes a rather homogenous group. Exceptions hardly occur.

From 1665 onward 'Lotto' carpets are less frequently represented in painting. John Mills remarked that they 'seem to have gone out of fashion in Western Europe since they are displaced in the paintings by other types'[26]. However, a diagram showing the number of Indo-Persian carpets in paintings, for example, shows that these too were less frequently represented in the last quarter of the 17th century (p.60). It is true that the Indo-Persian carpets were introduced later than the 'Lotto' carpets (mainly due to the late date that trade relations between the West and Persia started), but since diagram 1 and the diagram on p.60 largely overlap, it cannot be concluded that one group of carpets in paintings succeeded the other.

DOUBLE-NICHE USHAK CARPETS

Apart from the two groups of large carpets with either lozenge or star-shaped medallions (the so-called Medallion Ushaks, see Chapter III, and the so-called Star Ushaks), another group is named after the Turkish production center of Ushak: the so-called Double-niche Ushaks. These relatively small rugs are characterized by the corner elements, which seem to form niches at both ends of the field. A variable ornament is usually placed like a hanging element in one of the two niches, and gives the rug a directional design. For this reason, these rugs are generally believed to have been intended as prayer rugs[27].

A hexagonal medallion is placed in the centre of the field, decorated with a quatrefoil motif; the rest of the field is left without decoration. There are two variant types of corner medallions. The first type (fig.27), possibly the earlier variant, has almost the exact same shape and arabesque infill as the medallions of a variant Star Ushak, formely in the Ballard collection[28]. The second type has a simpler shape (fig.28). The outlines are less expressive and it seems as if the corner pieces have become spandrels, instead of preserving their character as quarter medallions cut by the border. The arabesques are replaced by small Chinese cloudbands; in each corner element one is represented in full, the other in half. The borders usually show a rich pattern of arabesques and stylized floral forms (a7).

fig.28 The two different types of spandrels of the Double-niche Ushak rug.

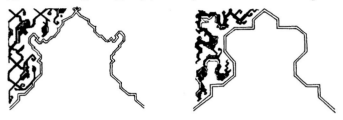

This type may have been developed in the course of the 16th century; the earlier datable representations show borders characterized by the large cloudbands (a6), which can also be found on 'Lotto' carpets.

The colour palette of these double-niche rugs together with their weaving structure are clearly related to the characteristics of the other types of carpets attributed to the Ushak area; the colours may be somewhat deeper and the knotting more refined, but these differences may well be explained by the hypothesis that the Double-niche Ushaks must have been relatively more expensive than the larger and coarser products of the area.

The earliest representation of a Double-niche Ushak was found on a 1519 painting by Girolamo da Santacroce[29].
Only a few years later Jacob Claesz van Utrecht represented another representative of the group in his *Annunciation*. This painting, kept in the Leipzig art museum (fig.29), shows on the floor a small carpet which can easily be recognized as a Double-niche Ushak. It has a plain red field, with somewhat distorted corner medallions with arabesque ornaments. The painter had some difficulties rendering the cloudband pattern of the dark blue border in perspective, but the individual ornaments are in fact rather minutely represented. The inner guard border has no floral or geometrical ornaments; the outer guard shows an archaic-looking stylized vine. Apparently these carpets were available in the Netherlands in the first half of the 16th century, but presumably not in large quantities, as it took three or four decades until the second recorded example in Netherlandish painting was depicted, in 1564. It is found in *A Family Portrait*, by Cornelis de Zeeuw, which is in the Westfälisches Landesmuseum für Kunst und Kulturgeschichte in Munster (cat.251). As in the example painted by Jacob Claesz van Utrecht, the border pattern is more or less carefully represented: cloudbands, endless knots and somewhat deformed rosettes. The corner solu-

tion is unusual, and may well be invented by the painter. The field pattern is less carefully represented. The authentic model presumably had corner medallions with arabesques, like the above mentioned carpet in the painting by Jacob Claesz van Utrecht. Apart from these medallions, the field shows some floral ornaments that are alien to the Oriental style of drawing and were undoubtedly added to the pattern by de Zeeuw. It may be deduced from the irregularities in the representation that he did not have an authentic double-niche carpet in his studio, and that he had to depend upon studies of the design which he may have made earlier.

In contrast to the two represented carpets discussed above, most other double-niche carpets in Netherlandish painting have a rich border design of arabesques and stylized plants (fig.30). The fields of most examples found still have corner medallions with arabesque ornaments.

Sometimes a variant field pattern is encountered, with spandrels filled with cloudbands. The ornaments in the corners of a Double-niche Ushak in a painting attributed to van der Pluym, *A Philosopher* (cat.240), are very vaguely drawn. Still, from the shape of the corner medallions, it is clear that the painter must have based these sketchily represented motifs upon the usual cloudband ornaments known from so many surviving pieces. Cloudbands decorate the spandrels of the Double-niche Ushak in Michiel van Mierevelt's *Portrait of Prince Rupert* (1625, cat.237), and in Cornelis de Vos' *Portrait of a Family* (about the same date, cat.250).

Jan Steen represented in several of his paintings a double-niche rug, which differs from the examples discussed above as it has a gold-ochre border and medallions. The field however is red, as is usual for the larger group of Double-niche Ushaks. The border has the cloudband design; cloudbands also fill the spandrels. Authentic examples with this variant colour palette are very rare. The Victoria and Albert Museum in London preserves one very similar to the one represented by Jan Steen[30]. The rug is dated to the first half of the 16th century, a dating based upon pictorial sources from Italy and England showing representations of Double-niche Ushaks with cloudband borders[31]. There are some differences between the surviving rug and the one represented by Steen: apart from the shape and decoration of the corner medallions, the cloudbands show small variations. Whereas the originally Chinese motifs are placed on a plain gold-ochre ground in the authentic double-niche rug, the ground colour of the border changes within the areas enclosed by the cloudbands in the rug represented in Steen's *The Human Life* (fig.31). However, these differences can not be found on the rug represented by Jan Steen in his *A Lady at her Toilet* (cat.243) or *Soo Voer Gesongen, Soo Na Gepepen* (cat.244), suggesting that the changing ground colour apparent in the rug in *The Human Life* was an invention of the painter.

The represented variant Double-niche Ushak should be dated as older than 1663, the first recorded date of a representation by Jan Steen. It is possible that the carpet was quite old at that time: in for example Steen's *The Human Life* it is obvious that the carpet shows signs of considerable wear; the outer guard border is missing at the end. In any event, the Dutch pictorial sources presenting *termini ante quem* do not bring new information about which might contradict the 16th century dating of the double-niche rug in the Victoria and Albert Museum.

fig.30   Gerrit Dou, Woman Looking Out of a Window, c. 1660. National Museum, Prague.
fig.31   Jan Steen, The Human Life (detail), 1665-67. Royal Picture Gallery The Mauritshuis, The Hague.

The earliest recorded example in a Western painting is, as we have seen, dated 1519. Ushak double-niche rugs were presumably invented at least some decades earlier, that is, prior to the beginning of the 16th century; this would agree with the dating of the related Medallion and Star Ushak types which were introduced in the West in the same period[32]. Presumably the double-niche Ushaks were still being produced well into the 17th century, as examples were depicted several times as late as the 1660s (fig.30).

The data in the diagram indicate that not many examples have been recorded in Netherlandish paintings. An increasing number of examples were found in paintings dating from the 1660s, but this is due to the fact that Ochtervelt and Steen represented a single example more than once in their paintings.

Presumably a systematic study of double-niche Ushaks in paintings from the Mediterranean countries, especially Italy, would bring forward more data.

MEDALLION USHAK CARPETS

The pattern of these predominantly large carpets, characterized by a medallion with pointed ends and pendants, either singly or in repeat in the centre of the field (fig.33), may have been developed as early as the reign of Sultan Mehmed II (1451-1481[33]). Ushak, traditionally mentioned as the place of production of these carpets, is a town already named in late 15th century sources as a weaving centre for carpets[34].

According to a register of 1640 from Edirne (Adrianople), red ground carpets with medallions in the middle were produced in Ushak in various sizes[35]. Evliya Celebi, the famous traveller, gave the following account of the city in 1671: *Bales of wool are untied and tied in this great city (or, for the transit trade of wool, Ushak is a great center). It is a kind of entrepot where camel caravans and wagons from all over the province of Anatolia come and go. Though quite a small town, it is extremely prosperous and well built. Since the neighboring areas are very prosperous and developed, the bazaars of this great centre of commerce are extremely crowded. Of the various crafts in the town, carpet manufacturing is the most famous. Its carpets can be compared to those made of Isfahan of Iran and Cairo. But Ushak carpets are exported to all countries in the world[36].*

The earliest specimens were undoubtedly made for the court, while the commercial production for the foreign market is assumed not to have evolved until much later ('If you had been Mehmed II, the

diagram 10

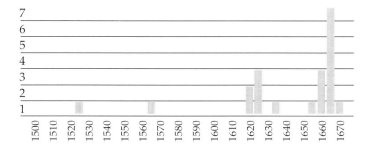

Double-niche Ushak rugs (avii) in Netherlandish paintings 1500-1700.

fig.32 *Gerrit van Honthorst, Amalia van Solms and her Daughters as Spectators of Frederik Hendrik's Triumph, 1649-1652. Oranjezaal, Royal Palace Huis ten Bosch, The Hague.*

fig.33 *Medallion Ushak carpet, Anatolia, 17th century. Photo courtesy Franz Bauback, Mannheim.*

fig.34 *Johannes Vermeer, The Procuress, 1656, Gemäldegalerie, Dresden.*

Conqueror of Constantinople, would you have been content to rest your felicitous derrière on the type of rugs exported to the donne nobili of Venice?'[37]). This would explain the late date at which these medallion carpets appear in Western painting. The production continued through the 19th century[38], apparently without the pattern being subject to a strong stylistic development. The dating of surviving Medallion Ushaks to a certain time is therefore often problematic, especially since the stylistic characteristics ascribable to the time of Mehmed II were also revived in Istanbul in the mid 1530s[39]. Generally speaking, the number of surviving examples may be expected to bear an inverse ratio to their age. Although the diagrams drawn in the course of this study indicate that the carpet trade on the whole declined at the end of the 17th century, suggesting that the inverse ratio does not hold here, several Dutch sources (e.g. advertisements of carpet traders) indicate that a lively trade in Anatolian carpets continued through the 18th century. Due to the thus assumed post-17th century date of the larger part of the extant Medallion Ushaks, the inventory of these carpets in 16th and 17th century Netherlandish painting is not as helpful to the study of the surviving examples as the inventory of other types of carpets.

Altogether 28 representations have been found. This relatively small number is remarkable because of the large number of examples, usually dated quite early, which are preserved in public and private collections, and which seems to point at the existence of a flourishing export to the West from the 16th century onwards. Presumably a large part of the early dated examples may have arrived in Western Europe at a much later date than the style of their rather stereotyped patterns might indicate.

Anatolian carpets were traded to the Netherlands in the 16th century. A 1560 source even mentions craftsmen in Antwerp who made Turkish carpets or imitated them[40], but does not include information about the patterns they copied. Anatolian carpets with the Medallion Ushak design were certainly copied in the Occident, as becomes obvious from a fine 17th century Polish copy in the museum for Islamic Art in Berlin[41].

The carpets in the paintings can roughly be divided into two groups: first, the carpets with an apparently fine weaving structure and rich patterns, and second, the coarser examples with patterns where the curvilinear designs of the earlier models have degenerated. The representations in paintings of the earlier group are the most interesting for the study of surviving Medallion Ushaks. As a whole, the pictorial source material at this point hardly provides spectacular new information, apart from the fact that the small number of representations should presumably be regarded as an indication that these carpets were at the time not found in the Netherlands in large quantities. The dates of the paintings are all within the boundaries of the period to which most authors attribute surviving specimens.

A famous example of a Medallion Ushak in a Netherlandish painting was painted in 1656 by Vermeer, in *The Procuress* (fig.34). The large carpet fills almost one third of the picture. It is placed horizontally; the upper or lower end of the carpet can be seen on the right. The finish consists of a yellow kilim strip, whereas the fringes are red, presumably made of wool. The dominant ornament of the represented carpet is the star-shaped corner medallion. As is usual

for the type, not just one quarter of the medallion, but rather almost one third is visible. (compare fig.33). Unusual is the fact that the edge of the inner guard border at the right side does not coincide with the vertical axis of this medallion. Usually the side medallions are shown in halves[42], or even less than halves[43], whereas the carpet which Vermeer used as a model had side medallions which, apparently due to the width of the carpet, were rendered in such a manner as to show more than half. Under the woman's hand which holds the glass, a part of the whimsical outlines of a characteristic Ushak medallion can be seen, which was apparently visible for a small part on the upper and the lower end side of the carpet along the vertical axis of the field[44].

The suggestion is made that the field shows only part of a continuous pattern; Dr. Spuhler's remark that the comparable extension of the field of another Medallion Ushak in Berlin is presumably due to the wishes of a specific principal[45] cannot be held as applicable to the major part of the surviving examples; and apparently examples in paintings show the same phenomenon.

Usually the field of Medallion Ushaks has a red ground. The carpet painted by Vermeer is an exception to this rule, as it has a dark blue field colour like the Medallion Ushak in the Thyssen-Bornemisza collection and the fragment in Berlin[46]. This, in combination with an equally unusual archaic border design, suggests a considerably earlier date for the rug in the painting than the date Vermeer's painting (1656) actually suggests.

A carefully represented carpet on Daniel Mijtens' *Portrait of Lady Martha Cranfield* (about 1620-25) has a somewhat simpler pattern (cat. 215). The field has an angular, presumably blue medallion against a presumably red ground with rigid, strongly stylized floral ornaments. It was possibly because of the similar, stiffly drawn ornaments and the angular shape of the central medallion that Mildred Lanier regarded an authentic Medallion Ushak with similar characteristics in Colonial Williamsburg as a 19th century example[47]. Although that example may be datable to the 19th century for other reasons, the sample shown in Mytens' painting proves that stylistic comparisons sometimes provide poor criteria: the most commonly used criterion, a coarser structure or a cruder pattern, need not always indicate a later stage in a chronological stylistic development. Earlier carpets can be of inferior quality, while later ones may have been carefully woven in the better workshops using rich, traditional designs.

A second representation of a Medallion Ushak by Daniel Mijtens can be found in his *Portrait of Prince Frederik Hendrik of Orange* (fig.35). Again, Mijtens presents us with a unusual example. The medallion under the feet of the the prince is relatively small, and slightly angular. The pendant motif is small, and has a simple ornament which may not be exactly identical to that of the authentic Oriental model the painter used. Remarkable is the continuous outline of the partly visible medallion on the bottom left part of the painting. The floral ornaments surrounding the medallions are quite stiff, the tendrils and leaves being drawn feebly and with arbitrary lines. A similar authentic carpet was published by Kurt Erdmann[48] and another similar carpet is in the Metropolitan Museum of Art[49].

The largest part of the representations of Ushak carpets found in Netherlandish paintings belongs to the second group. This group is characterized by an apparently coarse weaving structure and consequently by cruder, more geometric patterns . A well-known representation, and a good example of this group, is the large carpet in Vermeer's *Music Lesson* (cat. 230). Without a doubt, the design was meticulously copied by Vermeer; even the individual knots of the pile can be distinguished on the painting.

This representation is often referred to as a classic example of a Medallion Ushak on a Western painting[50]. However, there are several differences to be noted between the surviving authentic examples and the carpet painted by Vermeer. The central medallion, for example, has an unusually large pendant motif, whereas the corner medallions are smaller than usual. The latter have a strongly simplified pattern, compared to that of the carpet represented by Vermeer in *The Procuress* and the surviving Medallion Ushaks. The ornaments filling the space between the medallions too are simplified: these floral ornaments have degenerated into more or less abstract whimsical ornaments. The border has a design which is equally unknown from authentic examples. It has stylized ornaments resembling rosettes, composed of four ovals around a cross-form motif. These rosette-shaped ornaments are connected by a straight line coinciding with the parallel axis of the border. Small diagonally placed leaves are connected to alternate ornaments. As far as can be deduced from the three paintings by Vermeer (see also *Girl Reading a Letter at an Open Window* (cat.229) and *The Concert* (cat.231)), the carpet shows a restrained colour palette. The most prominent colours are brick-red and dark cobalt blue, while black or dark purple are used for the contours. Yellow wool is also applied, for some details. Other colours are not used, as far as can be concluded from the paintings. The fact that the three representations hardly show any differences in the details of the design or the weaving structure is an indication that all three can be traced back to a single authentic model Vermeer might have had in his studio.

The type must have been available in the Netherlands in the 17th century; the assumption that this unusual type of Medallion Ushak was not invented by Vermeer is proved by the fact that similar carpets can be found in the works of other painters as well. A fine example is the carpet painted several times by Jan Steen, for example in *Soo Gewonne, soo Verteert*, dating from 1661 (cat. 222). Like the carpet in Vermeer's paintings, it has a coarse weaving structure and the same border design. The field designs are even more deformed. The corner medallions are further shrunk, while the pendant motif has obtained an even more dominating role, and the ornaments surrounding the medallions are hardly reducible to the elegant tendrils and leaves of the authentic earlier Ushak carpets. The colour scheme corresponds with that of the examples painted by Vermeer: sombre tones with some details in yellow.

A similar coarse carpet was represented in a painting by Nicolaes Verkolje in 1694 (fig.36). It clearly belongs to the same group painted by Vermeer and Steen, but is distinguished from those by the slightly lighter colours. The explanation for these carpet representations is presumably to be found in the style changes during the three preceding decades; the painter may simply have used tones lighter than the ones of the colours in the authentic model. It is perhaps worth mentioning that in the Verkolje representation, in

fig.35   Daniel Mijtens, Portrait of Prince Frederik Hendrik, Present location unknown.
fig.36   Nicolaes Verkolje, Young Couple with a Dog, 1694. Present location unknown.

addition to the previously mentioned colours, there is an occasional use of orange wool.

There are no authentic Medallion Ushaks corresponding to the representations of this group of paintings that are known to have survived. Representations of the type have not been found in other than Netherlandish paintings. If these atypical represented carpets are not found in any works by painters from non-Netherlandish schools, it could reasonably be assumed that such carpets were not available outside the Netherlands. The arguments concerning the possible Dutch origin of the group of coarse pile carpets first discovered by Brigitte Scheunemann[51] could also be applicable here, although in the case of the variant Medallion Ushaks, examples are also found in the works of painters from Flanders[52].

'TRANSYLVANIAN' CARPETS

The name 'Transylvanian' is used to denote two separate groups of Anatolian carpets which have been found in considerable quantities in Transylvanian Protestant churches. From 1526 until 1699 Transylvania was dominated by the Ottoman Empire, and, according to contemporary documents, there was an extensive trade with Anatolia; various documents mention the import of Anatolian carpets[53].

The first of the two groups has at both ends of the field a niche or arch-like form, formed by parts of corner medallions. In a relatively small number of these rugs, the corner medallions are decorated with a complicated pattern of interlacing arabesques (axi1, fig.37). They can in this respect be considered as the successors of the other and earlier type of small so-called Double-niche carpets, woven in the Ushak area. The latter often have an identical arabesque pattern in the quarter medallions[54]. Sometimes these Double-niche Ushaks have cloudbands in the corner medallions, in which case the medallions have slightly stiffened outlines[55]. It is interesting to note that the later 'Transylvanians' have corner medallions filled with arabesques similar to those of the first-mentioned group of Double-niche Ushaks, whereas the shape of the corner medallions is more stylized, as with those of the second-mentioned group.

The larger number of examples of the 'Transylvanian' carpets however are characterized by even more heavily stylized corner pieces; these can best be regarded as spandrels to the niches, rather than as quarter medallions (axi2; fig.39). From the niche a double vine extends left and right into the spandrel ending in a curved leaf. In the centre of the spandrels stands a rather large, plain rosette,

diagram 11

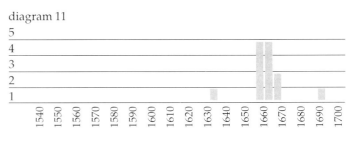

Medallion carpets of the crude 'Medallion Ushak'-type in Netherlandish paintings 1540-1700.

while the remaining space is filled with crude floral ornaments.

*fig.40   The arabesque motif in the field of Cairene Ottoman rugs (a) and in
'Transylvanian' rugs (b).*

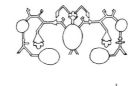

a   *b*

The centre of the field of Transylvanian carpets is usually decorated with a pattern of stylized vines and flowers, sometimes with a vase or lamp shape in the top of both 'niches.' The design is thought by some to be based upon Persian prototypes which have not yet been identified[56]. In fact, the floral composition recalls the intricate patterns of Cairene Ottoman rugs (fig.40). The Cairene prototypes show an elegant double curvilinear arabesque, bound together by a floral ornament in the middle, which is crowned by a flower bud with two leaflets. The arabesque in the Anatolian derivatives has angular outlines, and one can see that the designers had difficulties in adapting the intricate and finely woven prototype to a coarser weave. The flower bud with the two leaflets is still there, but it does not overlap the scrolling stems anymore; the coiling stems sprout from a different angle from the floral ornament in the middle.

The non-floral ornament in the top of the niches does not form a part of the floral pattern itself; it is clearly superimposed on the floral design. It may therefore be compared with the lamp that is traditionally represented in many prayer rugs, albeit heavily stylized at times[57], rather than with a vase from which spring floral stems that bear the flowers of the field[58].

A variant field design, presumably also based on Cairene patterns, shows a more simplified floral ornamentation, with large palmettes along the vertical axis of the rug, and some stiff vines[59]. A third variant has in the centre of the field a diamond shape outlined by rosettes on short stems[60].

The dating of these 'Transylvanian' carpets is primarily based on the 17th century pictorial source material[61]. An impressive representation of such a rug in Thomas de Keyser's *Portrait of Constantijn Huyghens and his Clerk* (1627, cat.261) has been referred to frequently, not only because it is a very good example, but also because it is a very early one[62]. Wilhelm von Bode gave at the beginning of the century a list of painters who had more or less frequently displayed these colourful rugs in their works; hereafter the 17th century representations which are now recorded will be listed and briefly discussed.

Representations were found in 46 paintings from the Netherlands. When the data were classified according to five year periods and transferred onto a diagram the following figure (see diagram 12) resulted.

The peak occurs in the period 1663-1667, mainly because of the large number represented by Caspar Netscher. As a correction, in diagram 12a only the earliest recorded representation of a specific carpet in the work of the individual artists has been included;

whenever a painter seems to have taken several authentic samples of this type as models, the earliest recorded carpet of each variation has been listed.

The earliest pattern of the corner medallions is undoubtedly the one with interlacing arabesques. A rug with such corner medallions was meticulously reproduced by Thomas de Keyser on several occasions. The famous portrait of Huyghens has already been mentioned; another, perhaps even more interesting representation as it indicates that the rug had in fact two niches at one end of the field, is his *Portrait of an Unknown Man*, dating from 1632 (fig.38). The earliest Netherlandish representation of a 'Transylvanian' carpet with floral ornamentation in the spandrels is from a later period, dating from 1644 (cat. 252). This variation may therefore have been developed some decades after the production of 'Transylvanian' rugs with arabesques in the corner medallions

diagram 12

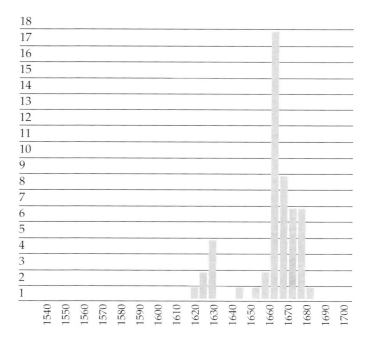

'Transylvanian' carpets in Netherlandish paintings 1540-1700.

diagram 12a

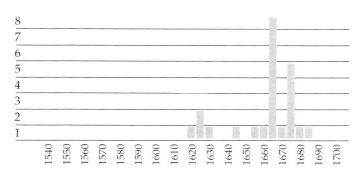

*'Transylvanian' carpets in Netherlandish paintings 1540-1700, grouped
according to the earliest recorded representation per painter.*

started. The field of the rugs in these relatively early representations invariably has the elaborate vine pattern with the lamp or vase form at the top of the niches. The simpler variant described above, which is characterized by some large palmettes along the vertical axis of the rug, flanked by two pairs of angular vines, appears about 1665 in paintings (e.g. Caspar Netscher, *Lady at her Toilet*, cat.274). In general, 'Transylvanian' carpets have a cartouche border. The centre of the cartouches is decorated by a lotus flower, surrounded by a stylized arabesque shape (fig.37; fig.41a). A simpler version of this arabesque shape, diamond-shaped, can occasionally be found, as in works by Cornelis de Man (fig.42) and Caspar Netscher (*Woman Teaching a Child to Read*, cat.272). Authentic examples with this simple variation of the border design are generally dated to the 18th century [63]; apparently however 'Transylvanian' carpets with similar borders were present in the Low Countries in the middle of the 17th century. For the rest, it may well be that the older variation was still being woven in the 18th century: representations of 'Transylvanian' carpets with the richer border design are found in many 18th century Dutch paintings[64], and advertisements of rug dealers in Dutch early 18th century newspapers suggest a continuous trade in Anatolian carpets at the time. Unless the carpets in these late pictures are presumed to be very old when they were depicted, a plainer decoration of the cartouches clearly does not always indicate a later date.

Another simplified variation is also made up of cartouches with arabesques; these form mirror images along the horizontal axis of the cartouches (fig.41b). This variation was not found in 17th century representations in Netherlandish paintings; an early 18th century representation was found in a painting by J. van Schuppen, *Woman with Guitar*[65].

fig.41 *The arabesque motif in the cartouche border*

A floral pattern of S-vines which bear lotus flowers that turn towards the middle and the edge of the carpet at the points of contact (a17) appears less often as decoration for the main border. Three examples, dated between 1660 and 1670, have been recorded (Netscher, *The Music Lesson*, cat.271; id. *Couple Making Music in an Arched Window-bay* (fig.43); Toorenvliet, *Piskijker* (cat. 294)). Authentic examples with such a border have been found in Transylvania[66]. The example in the painting by Toorenvliet is an exception as 'Transylvanian' rugs with a diamond-shaped cartouche in the field are not recorded in other Netherlandish paintings.

The accepted dating of examples with arabesques in the corner medallions to the early 17th century is supported by the information from the paintings. As the pattern was based on those decorating the Cairene Ottoman carpets, dating to a period before 1600 seems less secure if we accept the theory of Denny, suggesting that the latter carpets were woven from a point not long before the fourth quarter of the 16th century[67]. The *hausse* in the pictorial sources can be found in the third quarter of the 17th century, when

fig.42 *Cornelis de Man, The Faint, 1666. Present location unknown.*
fig.43 *Caspar Netscher, Couple Making Music in an Arched Window-bay, 1665. Gemäldegalerie, Dresden.*

examples with floral ornaments in the spandrels were frequently included in paintings. These variants may have been invented around the middle of the 17th century.

Examples of the second group of 'Transylvanian' carpets (axi3) appear seldom in Netherlandish paintings. Only three are listed in the present study. These belong to a group of prayer rugs characterized by a red and empty niche, white spandrels with a waving floral stem bearing various kinds of flowers and flowerbuds, and gold-ochre borders with floral patterns plainly showing the relation with the designs of Ottoman Cairene rugs; the borders have a stylized variant of the d222 pattern (fig.44). Undoubtedly the finest representation of a carpet from the second group is found in *A Family Portrait Group Making Music*, made in 1663 by Pieter de Hooch (fig.45). The rug has been draped over the table in such a way that the upper end with the top of the niche is visible; above the niche it had an extra panel which is uncommon in surviving pieces. The rug had a green elem and green fringes. It is interesting to note that the painter may have used a model which was kept folded until shortly before he started portraying it.

An extraordinary variant was painted in 1683 by Adriaen Backer, in his portrait of *Four Governesses of the Burgher Orphanage* (cat. 253). It shows an unknown type of 'Transylvanian' rug with two niches side by side. Dr. John Mills called it a prayer rug in his review of the 1988 Maastricht exhibition *Carpets in 17th Century Dutch Paintings*[68], and perhaps it is, but if we look closely at the carpet, it appears that the red medallions are not pentagonal, but have an oval shape. This could mean that the rug had a quadruple niche; two niches at both ends of the field. A similar decoration of the field has been noted in the carpet painted several times by de Keyser (fig.38). The question whether such a variant had ever existed or had been invented by the painter can thus be answered in favour of the first possibility; still, even without the evidence of the rug in the paintings by de Keyser, it would seem unlikely that Adriaen Backer could have doubled the floral infill of the spandrels in the elegant way shown in his group-portrait.

The examples of the second group of 'Transylvanian' carpets found in 17th century paintings are too small to allow for detailed conclusions; in fact, the three pictorial sources are all of such a late date that it would seem that the carpets illustrated were examples of a type which had been invented several decades before 1663, the year when Pieter de Hooch painted the earliest representation recorded.

Unfortunately, despite the substantial number of 'Transylvanian' rugs found in Dutch paintings, not one single example is known to have survived after the 18th and 19th century in a Dutch collection. In this respect it is quite a pity that Dutch Protestant ministers did not care to decorate their churches with carpets like their Calvinist colleagues in Transylvania.

SMYRNA CARPETS

'Smyrna' carpets take their name from the Western Anatolian port of Smyrna (Izmir) on the Aegean Sea. In the first half of the 17th century, Smyrna seems to have played only a minor role in the history of the Dutch-Turkish trade relations. In his account of the Dutch trade in the Levant, the earliest record dr.Heeringa published is a 'memoriael' from Cornelis Haga, the Dutch ambassador at the Porte at the time, dates from 1600[69]; a record from 1633 mentions that no ships from Holland had called at the port for several years[70].

However, the situation had changed considerably around the middle of the century; in 1656 Smyrna had by far become the most important trading centre of Asia Minor[71], while the importance of Istanbul as a trading centre diminished. In a letter dating from 1663, the Dutch resident Warnerus described the situation in Istanbul as follows: *dient te weten, dat -beginnende van Constantinopolen- de trafique alhier langen tijt heell slecht is geweest. France schepen comen weynich, Engelsch nogh minder (...) en Nederlantsche bijkans geen (...). De principale oorsaecken, dat de negotien alhier soo vervallen, is d'eerste, dat alle coopluyden, sowel uyt Romelia als Anatolia, die alhier pleegden te trafiqueren, naer Smirna haer vervougen; d'ander, het universael brandt van Constantinopolen heeft een gemeene armoede gecauseert (...); daer oock bijgevought can worden, dat den vorigen visier duysenden van de grootse ende voornaemste van 't landt gemassacreert, dewelcke met haer grooten aenhangh verbruyckten menighte waeren, van de Francken alhier getransporteert*[72]: there has been little trade in Constantinople for a long time, and few Western ships come here. The main reasons are that the merchants have moved to Smyrna, and that the consuming market has fallen down as a result of the conflagration of Constantinople, which has caused a lot of poverty, and the massacre among the original consumers by the former *vezir*.

Apparently Smyrna provided a somewhat safer harbour for the foreign trade. Another interesting source, dating from 1671, consists of letters from a Dutch sea captain named Eland du Bois, who was privately requested by a certain Willem van Wassenaer, a director of the Dutch admiralty, to buy two or three Turkish carpets for him in Smyrna. The carpets had to be of beautiful and lively colours, *schoon en levendigh*, and should cost no more than six hundred and fifty guilders. Eventually du Bois could report that he had bought the rugs for a third of the maximum price indicated by van Wassenaer[73].

Undoubtedly a large part of the Anatolian carpets represented in Netherlandish paintings must have been shipped from Smyrna, such as the rugs ordered by van Wassenaer, but only a relatively small group has been named, and rather arbitrarily so, after this port city.

Smyrna carpets have a pattern of large palmette blossoms on each side of which are branches with flower buds and rosettes producing different floral decorations interspersed with lanceolate leaves (fig.46,47). Like the so-called 'Transylvanian' carpet patterns, this pattern presents a simplified version of Ottoman Cairene patterns. A related example of the latter group is preserved in the Victoria and Albert Museum in London[74]. Like the so-called 'coupled-column prayer rugs', the border of the 'Smyrna' carpets is often decorated with cartouches, which alternate with a row of two or three small rosettes which are either produced in full[75] or cut by the guard borders[76]. Less usual is a floral pattern of an undulating floral stem with flower calices and rosettes which incline steeply towards the viewer, as in the border of the Rijksmuseum rug (fig.46)[77].

fig.44 Transylvanian carpet, 17th century. Photo courtesy David Halerim Gallery, Milan.
fig.45 Pieter de Hooch, Family Portrait Group Making Music, 1663. The Cleveland Museum of Art, Cleveland.

Few early Smyrna carpets seem to have been preserved. Although carpets of this type appear regularly in the trade, the majority are presumed to have been made in the 19th and 20th centuries[78]. The pattern was recorded in thirty 17th century Dutch paintings. As far as could be established from the study of the actual paintings and colour reproductions, the colour of the field is usually dark blue. The field colour also appears to be dark in many paintings of which only black and white reproductions are available. However, no 18th century paintings have been found showing examples with a dark blue field. At this time all examples found have a green or yellow field colour. This could be a criterion for dating original examples with a dark blue field.

The earliest representations found are those by Willem Duyster (cat. 305, 306). In these paintings the field pattern has been meticulously reproduced while the border pattern seems to have been painted less carefully; the rosettes differ from those in original examples. They are simpler and the alternating ornaments seem to point to a certain arbitrariness on the part of the painter. The inner guard stripe is shown without decoration and in front there are three parallel stripes in varying colours. It is possible that Smyrna carpets with similar inner subguards have not been preserved. It may be an early variation which fell into disuse during the 17th century. Slightly more richly drawn and comparable rosettes can be seen in Bronchorst's *Vanitas* (cat.303). The rosettes have small, white V-shaped ornaments, which can also be found in the rosette border of a Smyrna carpet in the Islamisches Museum in East Berlin (fig.47). Presumably the representations of the rosette border by Duyster and Bronchorst derive from a similar model.

No fewer than 14 representations by Michiel van Musscher have been recorded. He must have known at least two original examples, as he depicts Smyrna carpets with a rosette border and also with a meandering floral stem (cat. 318). This second border pattern corresponds with that on the Rijksmuseum rug already referred to. The carpet on the floor that Musscher painted in his *Portrait of Thomas Hees* is remarkable (see fig. p.75). The border has a relatively rich design of stylized rosettes and palmettes which face out, and — very unusual for carpets of this type — exhibits an attempt at a corner solution, rather than arbitrarily ending the border motifs at the corners. Corner solutions are rarely found in Anatolian carpets. No clear explanation is available, either for the unusual border

diagram 13

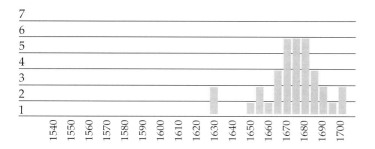

Smyrna carpets in Netherlandish paintings 1540-1700.

fig.46 So-called 'Smyrna' carpet, Anatolia, 17th century. Rijksmuseum, Amsterdam.
fig.47 'Smyrna' carpet, Anatolia, 17th/18th century. Islamisches Museum, East Berlin.

53

pattern or the existence of a corner solution. The explanation may be found in the historical context of the painting. Thomas Hees was the President and Commissioner of the States General to the Governments of Algiers, Tunis and Tripoli. In the painting he is shown with his two nephews in the midst of mementos of his 'Turkish period': eastern weapons, a copy of the Koran, etc. It is not impossible that the carpet on which he is resting his feet is a relatively valuable one from one of the better workshops, which Thomas Hees may have bought himself in the East as a souvenir of the Mediterranean world. This might perhaps explain the rich border design, but not the presence of a corner solution. It is also possible that the corner solution has been invented by the painter. Apart from this example, Musscher painted several differently sized carpets with the Smyrna pattern. While the carpet in the portrait of Thomas Hees and his nephews is rather large, that shown in the painting of An Alchemist in his Studio (cat.318) for example is small. The differences in size could be taken as an indication that he used several examples as models, which possibility is supported by the presence of different inner guard borders, although naturally he could have adjusted the dimensions to fit the composition of the painting.

Apparently Pieter de Hooch also used several original examples of Smyrna rugs for the depictions of carpets in his pictures. In A Woman at her Toilet with an Officer only a small part of the field is visible, just enough to enable the pattern to be identified (fig.48). The border pattern of the carpet is very remarkable, as it has never been found on the border of a 17th century carpet; it is however well known as a border pattern on later Ladik prayer rugs, dating from the 18th and 19th centuries. It is derived from late 16th century Ottoman patterns, like those decorating the fine carpets made in Cairo[79]. In de Hooch's Portrait of the Jacob Hoppesack Family (cat.309) a Smyrna carpet with the usual cartouche pattern in the border is visible.

It can be concluded from the diagram that Smyrna carpets were available in the Netherlands in the second quarter of the 17th century. It is plausible that the production of this type of carpet started at the beginning of the 17th century. An associated piece of evidence is that the luxurious Cairene Ottoman prototypes were probably only designed as late as the second half of the 16th century[80]. Probably most samples available in the 17th century had a dark blue background. With this information an early date could be given to the small Smyrna carpet in the collection of the Rijksmuseum (fig.46).

'CHESSBOARD' CARPETS

The field of the so-called 'Chessboard' or 'Checkerboard' rugs is divided into rectangular compartments, each containing an eight-pointed star composed of an endless knot of interlaced bands (fig.49). This star is encircled by small abstract radiating ornaments, among them what appear to be stylized representations of cypresses and rosettes. Triangular cornerpieces mark the corners of the compartments. All of these ornaments can be found in the repertoire of secondary motifs of the Mamluk carpets from Cairo,

where they are used fill the space around the medallions[81]. The ground colour of the field of 'chessboard' rugs is vermillion with the motifs constituting the design woven predominantly in light-blue or blue-green. The ground colour of the border is blue-green. These carpets tend to be thick and heavy in their construction.

The place of origin of these compartment rugs is still uncertain. They employ the asymmetrical knot, like the related Mamluk carpets, but the construction and materials (Z-spun wool, and madder dye instead of lac for the red colour), and the treatment of the motifs strongly recall those of Anatolian carpets.

Dr.John Mills found thirteen 'chessboard' examples in European paintings of the 16th and 17th centuries[82], two of which were depicted by Netherlandish painters: one by Marcus Gheeraedts (cat.334) and one by Simon Kick (cat.336). Mills mentioned the latter attribution as uncertain, but compared with other paintings known to be by Kick there seems little reason for doubting the attribution. The earliest representation seems to have been made before 1581 by the Italian artist Marco dall'Angolo[83]; the above-mentioned work by the Flemish artist Marcus Gheeraedts, painted by him in England, was presumably done shortly after that date in the 1580s.

There is a lapse of four decades before another example appears in a painting by a Netherlandish artist (cat.341). Simon Kick is responsible for four representations, one of which is dated 1648 (cat.338). The other three paintings seem to have been made in roughly the same period (fig.50). The carpet depictions are not given in much detail, but still appear as fairly correct representations of the authentic model; the borders may be drawn a bit too wide compared with surviving examples, and there may also be some divergences in the rendering of the original colour scheme, but these differences are of minor importance. The rug in Kick's *Five Young Men at a Table* has a border with a very light ground colour (cat.335), whereas in the other representations by Kick, the ground colour of the borders seems to agree more with the bluish-green ground colour of the surviving examples. Apparently the painter allowed himself some freedom in rendering this rug, most likely using the same model in all his representations.

The sketchy representation by Kruys (cat.339) may have been made a few years earlier, but dates from the same decade. Gabriel Metsu painted his version in 1659 (cat.340). C.G.Ellis described the colour

fig.50 Simon Kick, Portrait of the Artist Painting. National Gallery of Ireland, Dublin.

diagram 14

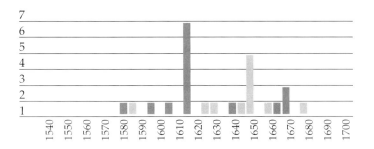

Chessboard rugs in European paintings. The Netherlandish paintings are indicated by a ▢ *, the paintings from other countries by a* ▪ *.*

scheme of this rug as 'abnormal'[84], but when the represented rug is compared with surviving examples, there seems no reason to support that observation.

A remarkable carpet was depicted in 1680 by Eglon van der Neer in a genre painting called *The Faint* (cat.342). This carpet, which is draped over the table in the foreground, has a border decorated with the cartouche design which is a characteristic of the 'Chessboard' rugs. The field however is adorned with a curvilinear pattern of lotusflowers and stems reminiscent of Persian designs. It is possible that van der Neer has combined the patterns of two different carpets that he may have studied somewhere in the carpet represented here, but in fact some carpets have survived which technically belong to the 'Chessboard' group, although they are decorated in a very different —Persian— style[85]. Possibly Eglon van der Neer in this painting represents another example of these rare 'Persian' variant 'Chessboard' carpets.

In summary, only a small number of 'Chessboard' compartment rugs appear in Western paintings. The often repeated explanation for the few representations of Mamluk carpets in paintings does not apply here — the pattern is not sufficiently complicated to make the design less fit for reproduction in a painting. An obvious explanation is that these carpets were not produced in very large quantities for export to the West; this is also suggested by the fact that only a small number of these rugs have survived: F.Spuhler mentions only 29 extant pieces with a consistent 'chessboard' design[86]. On the other hand, Dr.Spuhler pointed out that these carpets were woven in a diverse range of sizes, from large-format examples to smaller pieces with only six compartments, and — as we have seen above — that technically closely-related carpets exist with entirely different designs. 'We must presuppose that the weavers were experienced, and that they possessed a workshop tradition, which allows us to exclude third-rate and little known production centres'[87]. Perhaps patterns of trade relations might explain the apparent contradiction between a theoretically large production and a small number of surviving examples, and a consequent paucity of representations in Western paintings.

Based upon the dates of the paintings, the production of the compartment rugs was at its height in the last quarter of the 16th and the first quarter of the 17th century. At that time, the overall number of representations of Oriental carpets in Italian paintings decreased, partially explaining the relative small number of examples found in these sources. Possibly such carpets were still sold at that time, primarily through Italian and Middle Eastern dealers, in trade centres less frequently visited by the Dutch. In marketing centres such as Smyrna or Aleppo, where Dutch traders were located, these 'Chessboard' carpets may not have been part of the regular stock. This in turn might imply that the weaving center of the compartment rugs may not have been located in Anatolia after all, since for other Anatolian groups the Dutch merchants seem to have had their substantial share of the carpet trade. This might also —to some extent— support F.Spuhler's suggestion that these carpets were produced in or near the same weaving centre that had produced Mamluk carpets from the 15th up to the second half of the 16th century, since similarly only a few examples of the then flourishing production of Cairene Ottoman carpets are found in Netherlandish paintings.

The technical characteristics of the carpets in question, on the other hand, seem to argue against this attribution. Moreover, if only a relatively small number of these carpets were traded to the West, as is suggested by the small number of these carpets that is known to have survived, it is not surprising to find only a small number of representations in Western paintings. The question of the location of the mysterious production centre is, not surprisingly, not illuminated further by the study of the appearance of these carpets in Western paintings.

The dates of the paintings however provide us with a *terminus ante quem*: the export of 'Chessboard' rugs for the Western market presumably started in the third quarter of the 16th century and stopped during the second quarter of the following century.

IV
PERSIAN CARPETS IN NETHERLANDISH PAINTINGS

Judging from the number of both surviving and represented carpets, the floral and cloudband type must have been the most popular in 17th century Persia[1]. The carpets with this pattern are characterized by a decoration of floral scrolls in warm colours (fig.51)[2]. The coiling stems are arranged symmetrically with respect to the vertical and horizontal axes of the carpet, which made it possible to view the pattern from all four sides right side up. According to travel accounts, carpets constituted more or less the only form of interior decoration in Persia; they were spread out on the floor and those present sat down *als kleermakers in 't Vaderland, met een goudlakens kussen tegen hunnen rug*: 'like tailors in the homeland, with a gold-brocaded cushion in their backs'[3]. In the West, however, these carpets were so extremely valuable that they were only exceptionally used as floor coverings. Usually they were draped over tables as decoration and were either carefully pushed away or covered by a damask tablecloth when the table was used for eating or writing. Although several paintings display carpets as floor coverings (fig.52), this usually applies in the case of stately full-length formal portraits. Such representations do not necessarily point to an everyday usage of carpets on floors in Netherlandish 16th and 17th century interiors.

The field of the early examples is usually depicted with a red ground with a double system of coiling stems in contrasting colours. The stems bear palmettes, lotus flowers and numerous smaller flowers, buds and leaves. These, as well as the undulating cloudbands which seem scattered through the field or find themselves partly hidden behind palmettes or lotusflowers, are motifs borrowed from examples in Chinese art. Sometimes even birds and

fig.51 Carpet with the floral and cloudband design (bi.), in combination with the b1 border design (detail).

animals in combat are included in the pattern, a usage that may equally bear testimony of an East-Asiatic influence on the vocabulary, if not the syntax and grammar, of design.

Several 17th century sources indicate that woollen carpets were bought by European traders in Isfahan, at that time a pre-eminent centre for trade. In caravans these goods were taken to the port of Gamron (Gombroon) on the Persian Gulf where the *Vereenigde Oostindische Compagnie* (V.O.C), the Dutch East India Company, had its warehouses. Other routes were through Mediterranean ports (Aleppo and Smyrna) or ports in Arabia (Mocha[4]). Considerable numbers of these carpets were also shipped from the Indian ports of Surat and Goa, or were even transported over land through Turkistan, Russia and Poland. Representations in paintings suggest that the carpets exported by Persia in this period predominantly belonged to the group of floral and cloudband carpets described above (fig.51). Animal figures, such as those found in many 16th century woollen carpets, together with a pattern of spiralling scrolls, lotus flowers and cloudbands[5], seem not to be any longer included in the standard 17th century design vocabulary; representations of floral carpets with animals in Dutch painting are highly exceptional.

FLORAL AND CLOUDBAND CARPETS

Up to the present little research has been done into the floral and cloudband carpets represented in 16th and 17th century Western paintings. A considerable number of these carpets have been preserved. In comparison with the research on 'Lotto' carpets in paintings, the study of floral and cloudband carpets is confronted with the difficulty of stereotype patterning. An example of the former group could be assigned to a particular subgroup on the

diagram 1

49
48
47
46
45
44
43
42
41
40
39
38
37
36
35
34
33
32
31
30
29
28
27
26
25
24
23
22
21
20
19
18
17
16
15
14
13
12
11
10
9
8
7
6
5
4
3
2
1

1540 1550 1560 1570 1580 1590 1600 1610 1620 1630 1640 1650 1660 1670 1680 1690 1700

Floral and cloudband carpets (bi.) in Netherlandish paintings 1540-1700.

basis of additional curls in the pattern or the zig-zag contour of a small stylized leaf. However, on the basis of the inventory in the present study, floral patterns of the latter group can hardly be classified according to subgroups. Although the pattern of a particular example may have been relatively richer than that of another example, such differences do not result in a subdivision of the group. The outcome of the inventory is presented in diagram 1, with the understanding that incomplete representations, such as those displaying only a border design which usually frames a floral and cloudband field, are included as well.

From about 1620 the floral and cloudband carpets occur in large numbers in Netherlandish paintings, particularly in those from the Northern Netherlands. This date largely coincides with the arrival of the *Vereenigde Oostindische Compagnie* in Persia; before that time only exceptionally did carpets of this type find their way to the Netherlands, as indicated by diagram 1.

Until about 1630 their number in painting increases, among other reasons because of the relatively large number of representations by painters from Flanders, such as Rubens and van Dyck, and by Dutch painters like de Keyser. The largest number of depictions of these carpets however is found between 1660 and 1680; after this period painters lost interest in the representation of this type of carpet. A letter written by the governors of the English East India Company in 1686 presents the possible cause for this decline in interest: *You must never send us any more Persian Carpets, for those we*

diagram 1a

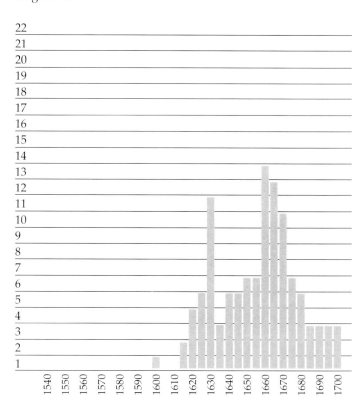

22
21
20
19
18
17
16
15
14
13
12
11
10
9
8
7
6
5
4
3
2
1

1540 1550 1560 1570 1580 1590 1600 1610 1620 1630 1640 1650 1660 1670 1680 1690 1700

Floral and cloudband carpets (bi.) in Netherlandish paintings 1540-1700, arranged according to earliest example per painter.

had last by way of Surat will not yield us here above a third of what they cost in Persia, which gives us just that cause to fear that we were abused in the price of them, the greater cause of our loss being that such rich carpets are now grown much out of use in Europe [6].

After this date some painters, like Willem van Mieris in particular, continued to represent floral and cloudband carpets in Dutch paintings, although with less frequency.

In diagram 1a only the earliest representations per painter are included; if it is clear that one painter must have used two or more different examples as models, the earliest example of each type has been indicated. Several painters represented at least two distinctly different carpets in their work: van Anraadt, Bol, Coques, de Crayer, van Dyck, Eliasz, van Everdingen, Kemper, Luttichuys, Metsu, Frans and Willem van Mieris and Netscher. Pieter de Hooch and Pieter van Slingelant represented at least three different variants. As appears from diagram 1, the number of floral and cloudband carpets represented in paintings quickly increased in the 1620s. Diagram 1a confirms the conjecture that in this period these luxury goods excited the interest of numerous painters. The representations undoubtedly reflect the arrival of the first stream of Indo-Persian carpets traded by the V.O.C. to reach the Netherlands.

diagram 2

23	
22	
21	
20	
19	
18	
17	
16	
15	
14	
13	
12	
11	
10	
9	
8	
7	
6	
5	
4	
3	
2	
1	

1540 1550 1560 1570 1580 1590 1600 1610 1620 1630 1640 1650 1660 1670 1680 1690 1700

b1 borders on carpets in Netherlandish paintings 1540-1700.

Borders

As has been mentioned above, the floral and cloudband carpets in paintings can not be classified to subgroups according to field patterns. However, a classification according to border patterns is in many representations possible. Occurring most frequently is the b1 pattern of repeating S-stems with large palmettes, which alternately point inwards and outwards (fig.51). A lotus flower is visible in the middle of each S-stem, generally pointing outwards; diagonally around this flower smaller lotus flowers and palmettes have been placed on the stem. A secondary spiralling stem with still smaller floral ornaments fills the remaining space. This border pattern, with small variations seldom recognizable in the generally sketchy representions, occurs most frequently on surviving examples.

The results of diagram 2 are at first largely parallel with those in diagram 1; a relative decrease however can be noticed in the second half of the century, after 1660. This decrease can be explained by the results of diagram 5 (see page 62). The b1 border is bound by smaller guard borders on both sides, displaying either floral or geometrical ornaments. The g46 design, a small meandering stem with leaflets on short tendrils, appears to have been most frequently used to adorn the guard borders. The richer g45 design, a double meandering stem with flowers and leaves, regularly occurs in the inner guard border, usually in combination with the g44 ornament in the outer guard border: a double meandering stem with lotusflowers and blossoms.

Less commonly used are reciprocal ornaments for the inner guard, which now and again occur in the shape of reciprocal lilies (g11a). Usually however they occur in a simplified form, as small triangles with diamond-shaped figures on top (g11b). Although, as diagram 3 indicates, this geometrical design has not been found very frequently, it did occur at regular intervals over a relatively long period of time (approximately 50 years).

The geometric g62 ornament, a repetition of triangles with usually a small dot in the centre, most likely constitutes a derivation of the g11b ornament, in a simplified form. This ornament occurs fairly frequently on represented carpets, as becomes clear from diagram

diagram 3

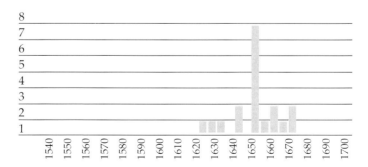

8	
7	
6	
5	
4	
3	
2	
1	

1540 1550 1560 1570 1580 1590 1600 1610 1620 1630 1640 1650 1660 1670 1680 1690 1700

Floral and cloudband carpets with reciprocal ornaments in the inner guard border (g11), represented in Netherlandish paintings 1540-1700.

4. It seems to occur exclusively in combination with the b1 pattern (fig.53).

The numbers used above must be interpreted with some caution; when we assume that a painter like Willem Kalf used one single example of a floral carpet over and over again as a model for most of his paintings included in this study (fig.54), then an even larger number should have been included in the diagram; only those g62 ornaments actually visible on the paintings have been registered above. At any rate, this ornament may be regarded as one of the most frequently occurring ornaments used in inner guard borders on carpets depicted in Netherlandish paintings. It is surprising therefore that the g62 pattern rarely occurs in floral carpets that have been preserved.

The b2 border is characterized by repeated curved stems, ending in a flower calyx. Large lotus flowers are placed diagonally on the points of contact of the stems. This border pattern particularly occurs on floral and cloudband carpets represented in paintings of the second half of the 17th century (fig.55,56). This could imply that the major part of the authentic carpets with this type of border may equally have been woven about the middle or third quarter of the 17th century.

The b2 border is in representations usually accompanied by a 'chevron' ornament on the field side. From the 20 representations of b2 borders distinct enough to allow an identification of the inner guard border design, 16 appear to have 'chevron' ornaments and 5 to be decorated with a small running stem (g46). The outer guard borders all display the same running stem, irrespective of the pattern of the inner guard border. One example of a bi./b2/ig46,og46 combination is a fragment from the Thyssen-Bornemisza collection[7]; a complete example is in the collection of the Museo Poldi-Pezzoli in Milan[8].

diagram 4

16
15
14
13
12
11
10
9
8
7
6
5
4
3
2
1

1540 1550 1560 1570 1580 1590 1600 1610 1620 1630 1640 1650 1660 1670 1680 1690 1700

Floral and cloudband carpets with g62 ornaments in the inner guard border 1540-1700.

Borders with interlacing arabesques and half-geometrical and half-floral bands ending in split stylized leaves (b5) regularly occur in authentic carpets[9], but rarely occur in represented specimens. The earliest representation of a carpet with a border composed of interlacing arabesques dates from 1628 (fig.57). Paulus Bor carefully represented a border pattern against a dark blue background which, at first sight, seems closely related to the border pattern of preserved carpets. However, Bor's border pattern does not exclusively consist of two clutching pairs of red and gold coloured arabesques, but incorporates green S-stems in addition. These are formed by broad stylized leaves ending in split leaves on one side and in flower buds on small thin stems at the other. Two of these buds, placed over the gold-coloured arabesques, are clearly visible in the representation. The points of contact of these S-stems have been adorned with smaller floral ornaments than those in the previously mentioned authentic carpets. The border pattern painted by Bor appears to be more closely comparable to that of a group of 'Polonaise' carpets[10].

In at least eight of his paintings, executed between 1645 and 1657, Ferdinand Bol represented a carpet with a border comparable to the one painted by Paulus Bor (fig.61). In contrast to the Bor example, the carpet used as a model by Ferdinand Bol has large composite palmettes with an arabesque band on both sides ending in a split leaf. Spuhler's reconstructions 18b and 20a[11] to some extent agree with Bol's border pattern; the latter seems to have arabesques which sprout from the palmettes ending in a split leaf, whereas the 'Polonaise' carpets show curved stems with split leaves on one end, and curved leaves on the other end.

A border design closely related to the one painting by Bol was represented in a Moghul miniature of about 1633, *Royal Lovers in a Garden*[12]. The pattern is not exactly identical to that in Ferdinand Bol's paintings, although this could be explained from the artistic licence common among Oriental miniaturists when they represented carpets. The carpet under the baldachin of the royal lovers displays alternating inward and outward pointing cartouches, with arabesques which are less compact than those in Bol's representations but they display the same design principle. This does not yet necessarily imply that the carpet in the paintings by Ferdinand Bol will have been of Indian manufacture.

Several sources report an export of carpets from Persia to India; the

diagram 5

9
8
7
6
5
4
3
2
1

1540 1550 1560 1570 1580 1590 1600 1610 1620 1630 1640 1650 1660 1670 1680 1690 1700

b2 borders on floral and cloudband carpets in Netherlandish paintings.

fig.52   Caesar van Everdingen: Count William III Grants a Charter to the Polderboard of Rijnland, 1654. Hoogheemraadschap van Rijnland, Leyden.

carpet in the miniature may have been such an example. Even the decoration of rosettes interchanged by small colonettes in the outer guard border, which is definitely Indian in character, does not necessarily indicate an Indian provenance; the miniaturist may here have departed from the original and even if he did accurately depict his model the weavers of the authentic carpet may have borrowed the Indian motif from Indian artefacts. Bol's variant has a richly adorned inner guard with a double meandering stem with leaves and flowers (g45); the double meandering stem with blossoms and flowers (g44) which decorates the outer guards is also richer than the decoration of most guard borders on floral and cloudband carpets. Finally, Jacob van Loo represented a similar carpet about 1650; although the representation is somewhat sketchy, the use of colour and the drawing agree with those in Bol's version. Authentic woollen carpets with this particular border pattern of interlacing arabesques are unknown. The border of a fragment from a clearly different weaving centre than that of the carpets in the paintings, exhibited in Milan in 1982, could be regarded as a variant [13]. Quite familiar however is the decoration of a border of a late 16th or early 17th century tapestry-woven silk rug with metal thread, which is kept in the Louvre[14].

A border pattern which is often found on early Persian carpets[15] displays shield-shaped and lobed cartouches (b6). In early examples these are formed by meandering interlacing bands. This type of border pattern does not occur often in paintings from the Netherlands (see for example cat.387 and 682). In fact, it only occurs — as far as the evidence indicates — in combination with a double inner guard border; if the guard border which connects with the field has a dark ground with X-motifs interchanged with dots (g131), shield-form ornaments with small volutes (g132) or even S-forms, then an Indian rather than a Persian origin should be considered (see p.91). The carpets in Netherlandish paintings that display the cartouche border in this study are therefore discussed in Chapter V.

Carpets with borders composed of S-stems ending in curved lanceolate leaves (b73), were represented by Dou, de Hooch, Musscher and van Slingelant round 1670. The curved lanceolate leaves surround a small rosette which has been placed in the middle of the S-stem (fig.59,60[16]). However, four examples (the floral carpets with this border painted by de Hooch can all be deduced to one original model) are, despite their approximate agreement in date, insufficient proof for a relatively late date of all extant carpets with this type of border pattern. Still, their dates can be regarded as an indication in that direction.

A variant of the b73 pattern (b74) was found in paintings by Verschuring (cat. 627, about 1660), Gijsbrechts (fig.62, 1672) Christian (cat.372, 1677) and van der Plaes (cat.594, about 1690). The S-stems in this border pattern equally end in curved lanceolate leaves, but the latter do not encircle a rosette placed in the midst of the S-stem. These dates more or less agree with those of the paintings discussed above showing b73 borders. Authentic examples of floral carpet with similar border designs are illustrated by Kühnel[17] and Ellis[18].

The relatively rare border pattern b8 consists of a series of large connected, lobed or star-shaped cartouches, alternating with smaller star-shaped cartouches. The cartouches of the latter kind are accompanied by small graceful W-shaped cloudbands on the upper and lower sides. Characteristic of this type of border pattern is the way in which the ornaments have been drawn: sharp edges seem to have been avoided as much as possible. The inner and outer guard borders seem to have been adorned with a meandering stem with flowers and leaves (g46); the field is in all examples decorated with some kind of floral pattern of stems, lotus flowers, palmettes and small, elegant cloudbands similar to those in the borders.

Representations of carpets with the b8 border have been found in works of Rubens (cat.606, 1623-25), Metsu (cat.515, 1660-67), van der Sluys (1684, fig.64), Musscher (cat.554, 1685) and Willem van Mieris (cat.535, 1690-1700). A closely related carpet is kept in the Musée des Arts Décoratifs in Paris (fig.65). The border pattern of this authentic carpet is identical to that of the carpets represented by the above-mentioned painters; also the field pattern largely agrees with the floral ornaments in the represented carpets. The central medallion of the carpet in Paris, however, has not been represented in any of the paintings. The Paris example may be considered as a richer variant of the type that served as a model for the 17th century Netherlandish painters.

North-West Persian Carpets

In 1675 Gerard Terborch minutely painted a North-West Persian carpet with a cartouche border (fig.66). The place of origin is apparent from, among other things, the angular spiralling stems in the field and the characteristic drawing of the cloudbands and lotus flowers. An authentic example with such a field pattern is in the collection of the Islamic Museum in East Berlin (fig.129). Although such a carpet — like the one represented by Terborch — has a cartouche border, it does not agree with the border in Terborch's painting: the latter has, instead of interconnected cartouches (b6), a design of partially overlapping cartouches, a type of design known from some early surviving northwest Persian carpets[19].

A carpet represented by Bartholomeus van der Helst (fig.67) has a field pattern comparable to the one painted by Terborch. The drawing of the scrolling stems, the chi-motifs and other ornaments seem to indicate a North-West Persian origin. The border has a simple and stiff pattern of interlacing bands; it is found on an authentic carpet in the Keir collection, and, in a somewhat richer variation, in a carpet which can likewise be ascribed to the north-west part of the Safavid Persian kingdom[20].

Carpets from this part of Persia occur only rarely in paintings from the Netherlands. An obvious explanation is not at hand. The area of their production was not inaccessible to merchants and foreign travellers. Still, the commercial situation may for some reason not have allowed the export of these carpets to the Netherlands in large quantities at the time; if this indeed were not the case, and import of such carpets had flourished, then logically more examples would have been recorded in Netherlandish paintings. Another, somewhat remote possibility that may have affected the import of such carpets might be that the somewhat starchy drawing of the North-West

Persian patterns simply did not attract the V.O.C. (Dutch East India Company) merchants or their customers in the Netherlands.

fig.60   Carpet with a floral design in combination with the b73 border pattern, 17th century. Musée des Arts Décoratifs, Paris.

SILK CARPETS WITH SILVER AND GOLD BROCADINGS

Several European travellers who visited Persia in the 17th century made extensive mention of the rich silk carpets, adorned with gold and silver threads, which they had seen in palaces and bazaars. The fact that in their records they pay much more attention to these exceptionally precious pieces than to the 'ordinary' woollen ones they must have seen much more often, indicates the extent to which the travellers were impressed by the rich and flashy materials used in these carpets.

Artistically, the 17th century silk carpets brocaded with gold and silver threads may not have been equal to the famous 16th century silk carpets (e.g. the large Swedish Royal Hunting Carpet[21]), but the richness of colourful and shiny materials still had a strong impact upon the 17th century Europeans; for example *...the ground* (of the Shah's palace was) *spread with rich and curious carpets of silk and gold, without other furniture*, according to the traveller Thomas Herbert[22]. Tavernier, who travelled in the Middle East as a merchant in precious stones, and visited the court of Shah Abbas II in 1644, described the entry of the Shah into one of the halls of the palace as follows: *Tous mes joyaux furent aussi exposez, & le Nazar de sa propre main rangea le tout sur le plancher couvert d'un tapis d'or & de soye (...). Un quart-d'heure apres le Roy entra par une porte qui donne de son appartement dans la salle, suivi seulement de treize Eunuques pour sa garde, & de deux venerables vieillards, d'ont l'office est de tirer les souliers du Roy quand il entre dans les chambres, couvertes de tapis d'or & de soye, & de les luy remettre quand il en sort*[23].

These rich silk carpets equally contributed to the prestige of other Islamic courts: Joan Ketelaar, envoy of the V.O.C. in India, in 1712 described a tent at the court of the Moghul Emperor: *seer oude groote thent van zij met goud en silver doorwerte tapyten en agter deselve de keyserlyke throon, staande op een van aarde, omtrent vijff voeten hoog gemaakt vierkant, met cierlyke met goud doorwerkte tapyten belegd...*[24]: 'a very large old tent constructed of silk tapestries interwoven with gold and silver, and at the back, the imperial throne standing on an approximately five foot high square earthen dais, covered with graceful carpets embellished with gold.' Even in the Occident these carpets were renowned: in 1601, for example, King Sigismund Sava III of Poland sent an Armenian merchant out to Persia in order to have some silk carpets with gold brocadings woven in Kashan[25]. At the end of the 19th century, these silk carpets were generally — and erroneously — considered to be of Polish make, due to the European coat of arms interwoven in the carpet of Prince Czartoryski, displayed in the 'salle Polonaise du palais de Trocadero' at the Paris 1878 World Exhibition[26]. Ever since, the name 'Polish' or 'Polonaise' has been used as a term of convenience to denote these carpets.

The 'Polonaise' carpets were pre-eminently suited for state gifts; some examples found in the treasure of San Marco in Venice were presumably brought to Venice as gifts by envoys in the diplomatic missions of 1603 and 1621[27]. Likewise the Persian envoy Mousa Beg, who visited The Netherlands in 1625, brought some carpets as diplomatic gifts. Unfortunately it is not mentioned if these carpets were made of silk, although this may be assumed to be the case[28].

It was Shah Abbas the Great (1587-1629) who realized that these costly silk carpets had a commercial value in addition to their value as royal gifts and presentation pieces. During his reign, workshops in which all forms of precious textiles or ceramics were manufactured were set up under state patronage in major cities throughout Iran. Western travellers were offered these costly goods for sale in the bazaars of several Iranian cities.

Carpets equally proved pre-eminently suitable for Dutch diplomatic gifts to the Far East. In 1633 the Dutch commercial establishment in Persia was assigned to purchase *25 goude alcativen, om tot monsters naer 't Vaderlandt te seynden ende eenige tot geschenken in Indien te gebruyken*[29]: 'carpets brocaded with gold threads, so as to be sent to The Netherlands as samples, as well as to be used as gifts in the Far East.' The *alcatijff met silver ende gout doorwrocht*, which was presented by Dutch merchants to the emperor of Japan at the occasion of an audience in 1635[30], may well have been one of the 'Polonaise' carpets ordered in 1633. In 1642 a Portuguese diplomatic mission presented the Japanese emperor with gifts which had a collective value of more than one million pounds, among which were included *un grand nombre de tapis d'or, d'argent et de soye qui se font aux Indes et en Perse*[31].

The V.O.C. sent in 1650, among other things, *een groot Persiaens alcatyf*, a large Persian carpet, as a *geschenck aan de May.t* (gift to His Majesty) to Japan[32]. The archives make further mention of the tragic end of this carpet: *Het groot alcatyff voor den Keyzer van Japan was (...) op de reyse van Batavia naer Naugasacqui 't enenmael verrot ende vergaen, waertegen op Amadabath een ander in 't werck gestelt was*[33]: 'the large carpet to be given to the emperor has been utterly wasted and putrefied on its way from Batavia to Nagasaqui; a replacement was ordered to be manufactured in Ahmadabad.' Some years later, returned from his mission to Edo (Tokyo) the V.O.C. envoy Gabriel Happart reports on January 26th, 1655, that *'t Aengenaemste onder deselve (geschencken) is geweest aen den Keyser het alamber, bloetcorael, groote alcatijff...*: 'the emperor was most pleased with the gifts of amber, corals, the large carpet...' It is not known, unfortunately, whether the carpet under description was made of silk or wool; woollen carpets were equally in demand in Japan: '(the Japanese want)...*een moy wol alcatijff...*'[34].

The Chinese likewise appear to have been greatly impressed by the precious 'Polonaise' carpets: (in Tonkin, 1653)...*den Coningh, prins en andere grooten des rijcx ter eerster aencomen ende dat voor 't nieuwe jaer over het behouden varen der schepen sich in een goet humeur vertoonden, doch corts daeraen de Coningh, siende, dat sijnen eysch van barnstene coralen, goude chits, sijde alcatijven etc. niet voldaen wiert, was 't enenmael daerover gemiscontenteert...*[35]: 'the King, the prince, and other dignitaries were at first pleased with the prosperous voyages of the ships; however, shortly after the King had realized that his demand for amber, coral, gold chintz, silk carpets etc. had not been complied with, he was greatly discontented.' Consequently, on January 19, 1654, the Dutch merchants in China wrote to the governors of the V.O.C. that *Belangende Comp.s welstandt ten hove, waerop de gunstige ende vredige negotie eenigszins gefondeert sij, deselve staet omtrent de oude May.t redelijk wel; can oock doorgaens gepreserveert werden, soo wanneer 't geeyste van barnsteen, corale kettingen, goude alcativen, d.o chitsen, mortieren etc. daer van tijt tot tijt het roepen om is,*

jaerlicx volcht[36]: 'The relations of the V.O.C. merchants with the court of the old Majesty, the basis for a prosperous trade in the country, are quite good. This situation can be continued, when the regular demands of amber, coral strings, carpets interwoven with gold and gold chintz, guns etc. are met every year.'

On November 7 of the same year, after his audience at Tonkin, the chief merchant Baffaert declared that he had entered into a very favourable contact with the emperor. He *had de ordinarie vereeringhe gedaen, die hem* (den Coninck) *aengenaem was, bijsonder de barnsteene coralen, goude chits ende alcativen, zoodat daerom desen jare geen silver op leverantie van sijde en heeft genoomen*[37]: he had exchanged the usual courtesies and had presented gifts which clearly pleased the emperor: especially amber, coral, golden chintz and carpets. Consequently, he did not have to pay extra in silver for the silk that year. And in Siam, 1677: *'t Barnsteen (...) en zijde-alcatyffen heeft daar soo hooge estime dan wel een groote oogh vullingh van laken niet gevonden en waerom het wedergeschenck oock van 1500 tayl swaarte sijde vermindet is...*[38]: 'the amber (...) and silk carpets are highly valued, which is not to say for the woollen cloth, so the gift of silk they presented to us was reduced by 1500 taels in weight.'

Kashan may have been the principal weaving centre of silk carpets in the second half of the 16th century; otherwise the carpets for the King of Poland would certainly have been ordered elsewere. The famous silk carpets from this period and earlier, such as the aforementioned Swedish Royal Hunting Carpet, are consequently attributed to the Kashan workshops[39]. However, there were undoubtedly other 16th century weaving centres where carpets of the same style were woven for domestic needs. After Shah Abbas the Great had transferred Persia's capital from Qazvin to the more centrally situated town of Isfahan in 1597/98, a new important weaving centre came into existence in the proximity of the court, while Kashan presumably lost some of its importance.

Friedrich Spuhler believes that 'Polonaise' carpets were woven exclusively in Isfahan and Kashan, as there exists 'no documentary evidence for any other place in the Safavid empire producing comparable work in the 17th century'[40]. However, notwithstanding the special stimulus which must have issued from the court towards the workshops in Isfahan, Yazd too appears to have been an important weaving centre at the time. As early as 1604, Yazd was described as the site where many rich carpets were made; these were, according to the traveller Pedro Texeira, the best in the whole world[41].

Dutch merchants in 1633 apparently shared his opinion about the quality of carpets from Yazd: *Wy verstaen dat deselve* (goude alcativen) *meest in Spahan gemaeckt werden alsmede in Jeest, die ordinaris beter vallen als die van Spahan*[42]: 'we understand that the same carpets with gold brocadings are primarily manufactured in Isfahan, as well as in Yazd; the carpets from Yazd are better liked by our executive than those from Isfahan.'

Generally, the attribution of preserved carpets to certain weaving centres is a precarious matter. Clear-cut criteria such as differences

fig.66 Gerard Terborch, Portrait of an Unknown Man, about 1675. Present location unknown.
fig.67 Bartholomeus van der Helst, Portrait of a Gentleman, about 1650. Present location unknown.

in style or weaving characteristics indicating local traditions are absent or as yet not recognized.

Besides Kashan, Isfahan and Yazd, 17th century sources make mention of other weaving centres. Silk carpets with silver and gold brocadings were woven even outside Persia. Tavernier, for example, described the carpets from Ahmadabad which he regarded as of equal beauty to that of the Persian examples: *C'est dans Amadabat ou se fait comme j'ay dit, quantite de ces etofes d'or & de soye, d'argent & de soye toute pure, & de tapis d'or, & d'argent & de soye: mais les couleurs de ces tapis ne durent pas si longtemps que celles des tapis qui se font en Perse. Pour ce qui est du traivail il est aussi beau*[43].

J.A. van Mandelslo reported in 1658 that the Indian silk carpets were comparatively cheaper: *Sie machen auch gute Seidene Tapeten/ gleichen aber nicht den Persianischen/ seynd derwegen auch viel besseres Kauffs. Ein Pahr schoene grosse Tapeten umb 100. Rupi dergleichen in Persien kaum umb 200. sollen gekaufft werden*[44]. Dutch sources also mention the Indian 'Polonaise' carpets. The V.O.C. merchant Francisco Pelsaert, for example, wrote in 1626 of *goude ende silvere geweven alcatijven van Lahoor en Agra*[45]: 'carpets with gold and silver made in Lahore and Agra.' And elsewhere we read of *weven daar* (in Amadabad) *oock alcatijven met sijde en goudtdraet doorwerct*[46]: 'in Amadabad silk carpets are woven brocaded with gold threads.'

None of the preserved 'Polonaise' carpets can be attributed to India with certainty, but as the Indian ones were apparently relatively cheaper than the Persian examples, they were undoubtedly exported to the West also. It is likely therefore that some of these have been preserved among the carpets now classified either as made in Kashan or Isfahan.

The determination of the exact place of origin of the Indo-Persian woollen carpets appears to be at issue for the 'Polonaise' carpets as well. The production of the precious silk carpets with gold and silver brocadings continued in Persia until about 1725. Thadaeo Krusinski, who visited Persia round 1720, reported that after the fall of Isfahan in 1722, when the city was plundered by the Afghans, *ars ipsa, speciali modo serico panno argentei fili intertexendi (…) totaliter interiit*[47].

Representations of these costly carpets are extremely rare in Western paintings of the 17th century; not one single representation could be found by the authors of previous studies. A possible representation is the carpet in a painting of *Vertumnus and Pomona* by Caspar Netscher (cat. 565). The pattern of the field cannot be identified with certainty, due to the way the carpet has been draped. It seems to have had a field divided in diamond-shaped compartments which had changing ground colours; a white, a red and a dark blue compartment are visible. These compartments are divided by leaflet stems, in the same way in which the field of the socalled two-plane lattice design 'Vase' carpets are divided those also have compartments with changing ground colours[48]. The compartments are decorated with a floral pattern of large lotus flowers or palmettes and stems. The latter seem to form no continuous secondary lattice pattern, as in the 'Vase' carpets, but merely enter the surrounding compartments where they end in curved lanceolate leaves.

fig.68a Reconstruction of the pattern of the carpet on the table in Metsu's A Visit to the Nursery.

fig.69 So-called 'Polonaise' carpet, 17th century, Rijksmuseum, Amsterdam.

Similar variations on traditional patterns are quite usual for actual 'Polonaise' carpets. An example of an early 'Polonaise' carpet in the Rijksmuseum, for example, displays a design of scrolling stems based on the pattern of the East-Persian floral and cloudband carpets. The single stems in the woollen prototypes are replaced by curved stem-segments, ending at both sides in curved leaves, that show the same scrolling figure[49].

If the carpet represented by Caspar Netscher indeed belonged to the group of 'Polonaise' carpets, then the pattern will most likely have been adopted from the woollen two-plane 'Vase' carpets from Kirman. Several examples of authentic 'Polonaise' carpets with a design borrowed from Kirman 'Vase' carpets are known; the Metropolitan Museum of Art in New York owns a pair of very good examples[50].

In his search for 17th century pictorial sources in the collection of the Metropolitan Museum of Art relating to the study of classical Oriental carpets, Maurice Dimand found a carpet painted by Gerard Terborch, in the genre painting *A Lady Playing the Theorbo*. Dimand erroneously identified the carpet in this painting as a 'Polonaise' carpet[51]. Another painting however, also in the Metropolitan, escaped his attention; he did illustrate it in the museum's catalogue, but regarded the carpets in the scene as floral rugs of the Herat type[52]. The painting in question, *A Visit to the Nursery* by Gabriel Metsu, displays on the table a distinct representation of a 'Polonaise' carpet (fig.68). The field has been divided in compartments which are partially vermillion red and partially purple red. These compartments are shield-shaped, as the compartments in a major group of 'Polonaise' carpets (fig.69). The shield-shape is clearly visible in the purple-red compartment just on the edge of the table. The straight lines at the upper side of the shields are embellished with polyp-shaped ornaments which are usual in this carpet design, and which can also be found on the Rijksmuseum rug. Even the ornament crowning the shield shapes in the authentic carpet can be found along the border of the represented example. The weaver of the latter carpet however seems to have made less abundant use of metal threads, just like the weaver of a closely related 'Polonaise' carpet in the Museo degli Argenti in Florence[53].

The dark blue colour of the borders of the carpet in the painting by Gabriel Metsu are relatively unusual; most 'Polonaise' carpets have a dark green colour. The border pattern could not be identified with certainty, it seems to present a variant of the b73 border design.

A third carpet which could belong to the group of Safawid silk carpets with gold and silver brocadings was represented by the Flemish painter C. Gijsbrechts in 1670, *A Vanitas Still-life* (fig.63). The pattern of the field is hardly visible in the painting, but the border design is characteristic for several 'Polonaise' carpets[54]. The represented carpet displays lotus flowers at the point of contact of the curved stems, and half-represented stylized palmettes cut by the guard borders. The latter show an unusual feature however, as the inner guard borders are doubled. Multiple guard borders are unusual for 'Polonaise' carpets. The corner solution is rather clumsily drawn. This indicates an irregularity in the carpet for which the weaver is presumably to blame; apparently he made a miscalculation which was hard to correct on the loom.

From the painting it appears that the carpet has been only sparingly embellished with gold and silver. The leaves of the lotus flowers in the dark green border, as well as the background of the inner guard borders, are decorated with gold threads. Silver threads are less clearly present, although it seems that the rosettes in the outer guard border are alternatingly adorned with silver and gold brocadings.

Representations of 'Polonaise' carpets in 17th century Western paintings are clearly extremely exceptional. Perhaps these carpets were not within reach of the painters because of their rarity and costliness.

'VASE' CARPETS FROM KIRMAN

The 'Vase' carpets take their name from the vases which are included in the floral lattice design of many examples (fig. 70); however, today the term 'Vase' carpet refers to all carpets from Kirman woven in the distinctive technique of the group, whether or not their designs actually incorporate vases. The pattern of the most frequently occurring type shows a triple system of staggered ogivals, formed by a lattice of wavy stems. Each ogival encloses six large flowers, sometimes interspersed with the aforementioned vase forms. Often the pattern is represented against a red ground, but other ground colours, especially blue, are frequently encountered. Technically these carpets have characteristic features, including complete depression of alternate warps, and the use of a single sinuous weft and two tightly-pulled straight wefts between each row of asymmetrical knots. Carpets woven in this technique are attributed to Kirman[55].

Several 17th century sources mention Kirman as a production centre for carpets; Pedro Texeira, who travelled from Goa in India through Persia to Europe in 1604, wrote *...the second best* (carpets) *are those from the kingdom of Kermon...*[56]. When Engelbert Kämpffer visited the court in Isfahan in 1684 he reported: *Als hervorragenster Schmuck der Festhalle nenne ich die Teppiche, mit denen alle drei Bühnen auf das verschwenderischte ausgelegt waren, meist Kermaner Wollteppiche mit Tiermustern, aus edelster Wolle geknüpft*[57]. The carpets with vases in the design do not incorporate motifs of animals, but a subgroup of carpets technically belonging to the same group often displays birds and animals in combat[58]. Abu'l Fazl described the carpets from Kirman as constituting an important part of the Indian trade with Persia. Clearly, 17th century Kirman was an important weaving centre for pile carpets.

Unfortunately the study of Oriental carpets in 17th century Western paintings provides little information concerning the 'Vase' carpets. One reason may be that in the 16th and 17th century carpets were almost exclusively used on furniture such as tables and chests. 'Vase' carpets were not very appropriate for such usage because of their weaving construction, which made them stiff and unpliable. In our survey, only one posssible example of a 'Vase' carpet in Netherlandish painting was found (fig.71). The carpet is draped over the table in Michiel van Musscher's *Portrait of Thomas Hees*, the painting being dated (on the carpet) to 1687. The pattern shows stems and flowers here and there intersected by lanceolate leaves in the same way as in the so-called three-plane 'Vase' carpets[60]. The carpet painted by Musscher seems to have a triple system of staggered ogivals as well. The border design is characteristic for 'Vase' carpets, showing S-stems with lotus flowers, ending in floral sprays. The decoration of the inner guard border is replaced by the signature of the painter, but reciprocal ornaments such as those used in the outer guard border are not infrequently found on authentic 'Vase' carpets. Usually however, these reciprocal ornaments occur in the inner guard border.

The singular presence of this particular type of carpet in this particular painting — this type of carpet not having been commonly found in 17th century Netherlandish interiors — may be due to the status and profession of the persons portrayed. As we have seen above, Thomas Hees, the main subject of the painting, was resident and commisioner of the States General of The Netherlands to the governments of Algiers, Tunis and Tripoli. If the represented were actually a personal possession of Thomas Hees, he could just as well have acquired it not in Holland, but during some of his travels to the Middle East. Its inclusion among possessions portrayed in his portrait, where he is sitting amidst what appear to be various souvenirs of his travels, or perhaps attributes referring to his formal status, may be entirely deliberate.

Systematic research in Netherlandish pictorial sources produced no new unpublished examples of portrayals of 'Vase' carpets. The 'Vase' carpets apparently were not of sufficient interest to the Netherlandish merchants to have resulted in their importation in significant numbers into the Low Countries.

fig.70 So-called 'Vase' carpet, Kirman, 17th century. Private collection, The Netherlands.

fig.71 Michiel van Musscher, Portrait of Thomas Hees, Resident and Commissioner of the States General to the Governments of Algiers, Tunis and Tripoli, with his Nephews Jan and Andries Hees, and a Servant, 1687. Rijksmuseum, Amsterdam.

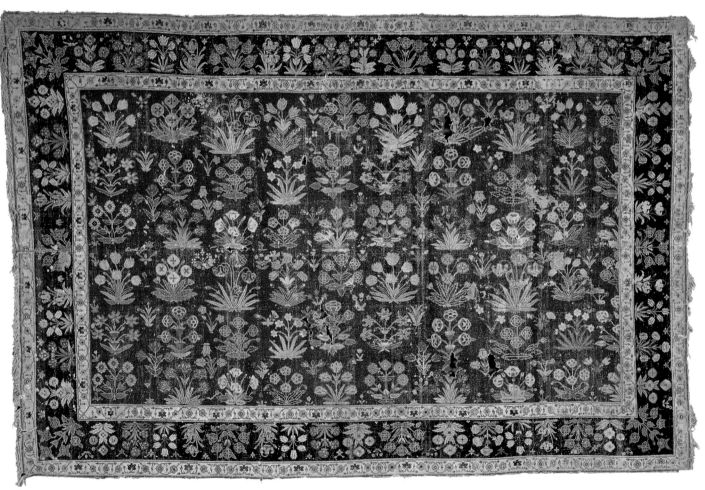

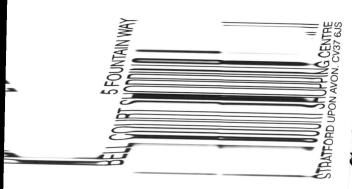

V

INDIAN CARPETS IN NETHERLANDISH PAINTINGS

De Tapijten worden by de Persianen Kaluchey genaemt: by de Portugesen Alcatifas; en gemeenelijk by andere volken van Europe na den voorgang der Portugesen, met een bedorven naem Alkatijfs. (…) De kostelijkste, fijnste en dierste worden gemaekt in Yazd, een stadt van Hyerak, zoo dat eenigen over de duizend dukaten gelden: hettweede slag zijn die uit het Kerman, en het derde uit Karason: 'In Persia, carpets are called Kaluchey; the Portuguese call them Alcatifas. In other European countries the latter term was corrupted to Alkatijfs. (…) The richest, finest and most expensive examples are woven in Yezd, some of which value over a thousand ducats. Second to these are the carpets from Kirman, and third the carpets from Khorasan'[1].

This description of the three regions which were apparently regarded to be the major production centres for pile carpets was taken over by the Dutch scholar Olfert Dapper from Pedro Texeira's account of Persia, made during his tour through Persia and India in 1604. Texeira's original account continues as follows: 'they are also made in Agra, Bengala, and Cambaya, but not fine ones'[2].

Several written sources including information about the production of carpets in India exist; some which compare the quality of the Persian and the Indian carpets tally, with Texeira's report. Persian carpets were in general apparently of a better quality than the comparable Indian examples.

In the 17th century, India had not yet gone through a long tradition of carpet weaving. According to Abu'l Fazl, prime minister and biographer of the Moghul emperor Akbar (1556-1605), it was the latter who had introduced this particular art to India. Akbar is said to have appointed 'experienced workmen' to staff court carpet workshops, and subsequently carpet weavers seem to have established themselves individually in various cities in the country[3]. Abu'l Fazl refers in his '*Ain-i-Akbari* to Agra, Fathepur Sikri and Lahore as the pre-eminent weaving centres. The word 'experienced' used by Abu'l Fazl in his report has led scholars to believe that Persian weavers were brought to India by Akbar[4]. In fact, many artists left Safavid Iran after the era of the art-loving Shah Tahmasp came to an end, and they found a new maecenas in the person of Akbar. An interesting record in this respect can be found in the diary of Streynsham Master, who was in 1679 chief agent of the English East India Company on the Coromandel coast: *We set forward early in the night, and by 9 or 10 in the morning came to Elloor…This Elloor is reckoned one of the greatest Townes in the Country, that the King in his*

last progress came to see it, where are made the best Carpetts after the manner of those in Persia, by a race of Persians which they told us came over above 100 years ago[5].

These Persian weavers may have continued to use their traditional Persian floral and cloudband patterns. The matter of the attribution of a large part of the floral and cloudband carpets is therefore highly controversial. If they were indeed manufactured in India as well as in Persia, it will often be impossible to distinguish between the Persian and the Indian products as they share a common pattern and equally have identical weaving characteristics[6]. Therefore, these carpets are often named 'Indo-Persian' or 'Indo-Isfahan'. Other scholars however assume that the floral and cloudband carpets should be divided into three groups: two Persian groups made respectively in Eastern Persia and in Central Persia, which can be distinguished on the basis of weaving characteristics and materials (quality of the wool; colours etc) and an Indian group characterised by Indian design elements included in the pattern or with a distinctly Indian style of drawing[7].

From the sales figures of a cargo of 'Lahore' carpets shipped from Suratte to England in 1615, it appears that the larger examples were most valued[8]. However, these were not always available. This is suggested by a letter written by an agent of the English factor in Agra to the governors of the East India Company on December 15, 1619: *Carpets of such length and breadth as your worships desire them we shall hardly ever be able to procure; for of such sizes we find that very few were ready made, and we perceave, by experience of a few bespoken here, that the tardiness, slowness and poverty of the workmen to be such that it is endless labour to bespeak them, and those bespoken to cost dearer than others ready made. Of the ordinary sizes here made we have sent you all sorts this year, and a good quantity, as hereafter you will perceave; and of other sizes than these you may never expect them, unless we can persuade the workmen of themselves to make them broader; which we will endeavour[9].* A second letter bearing the same date deals with the same matter: *and they neither make them so well nor good colours as they make them without bespeaking[10].* In other words, when carpets were made on order the weavers saved on material because the products would be sold irrespective of the quality.

Around 1625 the Dutch started to import carpets from India. In a letter dated December, 1624, from the governors of the *Vereenigde Oostindische Compagnie* (V.O.C., the Dutch East India Company) to the factory in Suratte they ordered 540 high-quality Persian carpets to be used as table covers, 500 of which should be 4 to 5 yards long, and some 40 of which should have an average length of 7 to 8 yards; the width of all of these should vary between the 2 1/2 to 3 1/2 yards. To this they added that, in case the Indian goods might be of a better quality and less expensive than the Persian ones, then in addition to 300 Persian carpets, some 500 Indian carpets should also be sent, or in any case 100 should be sent as samples[11]. On March 23, 1626 the arrival was reported in Suratte of a *caffila van Agra, starck 45 cammelen salpeter en alcatifen:* a caravan coming from Agra, with 45 camels carrying saltpetre and carpets[11a], possibly a part of the group of carpets ordered some sixteen months earlier by the governors of the V.O.C. in Amsterdam.

Francisco Pelsaert, a V.O.C. merchant, wrote in 1626: *In dese stadt Agraa, als mede Phettapour 12 coss van hier worden tamelijcke partijen alcatijven geweven, die men aenbesteden kan, soo fijn en groff als men*

begeert…: there is a rather large production of carpets in this city of Agra, and also in Fathepur Sikri. These are made to order, as fine or as coarse as you want[12]. Another Dutch source mentions Masulipatam as a weaving centre: In 1666 a number of carpets were sent to the Netherlands as samples:…*geschoren ofte cortharige alcatijven, curieus van werk ende alle van hair, van levendige beesten geschoren in de quaretieren van Masulpatam, gemaekt sijnde op de Cust..*: carpets with a short pile, having curious patterns. They are made from hair which is cut from living animals in the area of Masulipatam, near the coast[13].

Initially, the results of the trade in Indian carpets must have been disappointing to the English. Persian carpets sold in London obtained far better prices than Indian carpets of identical dimensions, and the merchants in the factory in India soon noticed that Persian carpets could be sold profitably even in India[14]. The logical conclusion was that the East India Company should primarily buy Persian carpets, which could either be shipped from the port of Hormuz (Bandar Abbas) or bought in India and shipped from there. Dutch V.O.C. sources indicate that in the year 1683 the English ordered no fewer than 1500 carpets in India, which is twice the number of carpets ordered by the Dutch in that particular year[15]. Whether these carpets were to be of Indian or Persian manufacture is not clear. Any way, this order did not turn out to be a commercial success, for in 1686 the London Governors notified their factory in India that no more Persian carpets should be sent from Surat, as these rich carpets were growing out of fashion in Europe (see p.61). In Dutch paintings we find representations of Indian carpets until far into the 18th century. The *Portrait of the Brak Family*, painted in 1752[16] by Tibout Regters, constitutes a fine example. It must be said, however, that the carpets in these representations correspond rather closely to some representations in 17th century paintings, and may therefore well have been of respectable age at the time of their portrayal in the 18th century. It is unknown when the regular trade in Indian carpets stagnated. The above-mentioned observation of the governors of the English East India Company, that such carpets were getting out of fashion in Europe in 1686, might equally have been made by the other European East India Companies at that time.

The 1624 letter of the governors of the V.O.C., ordering carpets from India as samples, apparently had a sequel. This appears from several sources, one of which is mentioned above. However, the exact extent to which Indian carpets took a share in the Dutch market in the 17th century is unknown. Our research on the representation of carpets in Dutch and Flemish 17th century paintings will provide supplementary information relevant to an examination of east-west trade at the time.

Carpets of the 'Lahore'-group

The carpets woven in the court workshops of the Moghul Emperors were not all simply copies of Persian examples. During the reign of the Emperor Jahangir (1605-1627) a new and distinctly Moghul style developed, based on the studies the Emperor ordered made of the flowers and fruits of Kashmir by his court painter Ustad Mansur, who took his inspiration from prints in European herbals[17].

This style appears from the 1620s onwards on carpets, many of which were so finely woven that the floral ornament could be rendered in detail and the flowers are easy to identify by botanical type. These carpets were woven in wool of an exceptionally fine quality with a silky sheen, producing a texture like velvet. It can be assumed that these expensive carpets were not made for export; nearly all the examples known in Western collections seem to have been brought to the West from India in the 19th century. A number of them came from the collection of the Maharajas of Jaipur. Many of them were probably made for the palace built by Raja Jai Singh (1622-1668) at Amber, which was completed in 1630. The Textile Museum in Washington owns fragments of a carpet from that palace (fig.72), of which there is a much larger piece in Jaipur and some small fragments in the Rijksmuseum[18]. The field was adorned with rows of flowering plants, and while the density of the knots is not unusually high for this type, the fragments have a beautiful velvety texture and sharp contrast between the plants and the wine-red ground.

Some of the carpets from the important find at Jaipur bear labels showing them to have been made at dates between 1650 and 1680 in Lahore[19], which is mentioned as a centre of carpet weaving by Abu'l Fazl, and is also known from Western trade archives.

Although many 17th century Dutch paintings show carpets which can be presumed to have had an Indian provenance, none has previously been found with this distinctly Indian flowering plant design. However, a painting of 1673 by Ludolf de Jongh of a family in an interior shows two renderings of what seems to be the same carpet, which the artist may have had in his studio (fig.74). The narrow borders separating the wide border with shield-shaped cartouches (g132; see below) from the central field are found on, among others, a 17th century Indian carpet in the Musée des Arts Décoratifs (fig.76), while the field is decorated with flowering plants. The carpet has been so carefully painted that the flowers can be seen to be stiffer in line than those on the Washington fragments, as is more usual for Moghul carpets of this type (e.g.fig.73). Thus it seems that carpets from the same group as the fragments in the Textile Museum were occasionally brought to Europe.

Another carpet which clearly comes from one of the best workshops of Moghul India, appears in Michiel van Musscher's portrait of 1686 of Johannes Hudde, burgomaster of Amsterdam; the burgomaster is shown wearing a costly silk *Japonsche rock* and sitting at a table with objects relating to his public office (fig.75). The carpet has a distinctively Indian colour scheme, the wine-red field showing naturalistically designed ivory flowers and green, elegantly drawn stems like some of the best surviving Moghul carpets. Unfortunately however only a fragment of the rug is visible in the painting, which does not allow for a more precise identification of the pattern. If these carpets were not part of a regular trade from India to Western Europe, in view of Hudde's status the fine carpet on that same table may have been a gift from a Moghul official, and may have been brought to Amsterdam at some unknown date. On the other hand, as a 'Lahore' carpet appears also in the above-mentioned portrait of a middle-class family by de Jongh, it seems more plausible to assume that specimens of this group were available in

fig.77   So-called 'Portuguese' carpet (detail), 17th century. Rijksmuseum, Amsterdam.

fig.78   Anonymous Dutch artist, A Scholar in his Studio, 17th century. Present location unknown.

the Western art market. However, as these two representations are the only examples of Moghul court carpets of this 'Lahore' type so far known in Dutch 17th century painting, these carpets were apparently relatively quite exceptional at the time.

THE SO-CALLED 'PORTUGUESE' CARPETS

A small group of carpets, characterized by a peculiar design of superimposed 'layers' of what appear to be flaming medallions, have become known as 'Portuguese' carpets by reason of the presence of European figures wearing European, possibly Portuguese, costumes and shown in sailing vessels, in the corners of the field (fig.77).

The innermost of these concentric medallions in such carpets is elliptically shaped and has complex outlines. Its centre has a rosette between four compound palmettes, interchanged with diagonally placed lotus flowers. The remaining space in this medallion is filled with vines bearing flowers and leaves; pairs of bird have sometimes been represented above each compound palmette. The larger concentric medallions are decorated with similar vines, and often have a strongly accentuated palmette along the vertical axis of the carpet.

The 'flaming' impression of the layered medallion design is intensified by the vivid use of colours in a variety of bright hues. This palette is clearly related to that of typically 17th century Indian carpets[20]. The borders of all preserved 'Portuguese' carpets have wide blue bands on a red ground forming pointed oval-shaped cartouches, and symmetrical vines ending in split leaves.

For the scene depicted in the four spandrels of the Portuguese carpets various interpretations have been suggested. It has been explained as the biblical story of Jonah and the whale[21] or as a depiction of the arrival of the members of the Portuguese diplomatic mission in the Persian Gulf[22]. Charles Grant Ellis compared the representation with a Moghul miniature painting depicting the death of Bahadur Shah, Sultan of Gujarat while visiting the Portuguese fleet in 1537[23]. On that occasion the Sultan is said to have been either treacherously killed and cast overboard or to have drowned after he had been cast overboard in a more or less seriously injured state. Ellis assumes that the representation in the 'Portuguese' carpets memorizes the latter historical event and presumes that the carpets will have been manufactured in Gujarat, where the people will have been most closely involved in the death of Bahadur Shah. Murray Eiland however points out the existence of other miniatures displaying scenes which equally correspond with the representations on the 'Portuguese' carpets[24]. Finally, Daniel Walker regards the scene in the same line as a representation of a stock Indian scene adapted to the Western taste, with the figures being dressed in Western dress. Although he does not concur with Ellis' identification of the scene, in his opinion the representation does support the Indian attribution of the carpets[25]. In each case, the fact that the figure in the water is absent in the Rijksmuseum 'Portuguese' carpet (fig.77) suggests that the weavers of this carpet were not particularly involved in the events of 1537. Although written sources do make mention of Gujarat with regard to the carpets manufactured in that region in the 17th century, the acceptance of

fig.79   Indian carpet (detail), 17th century. Metropolitan Museum of Art, New York. Gift of J.Pierpont Morgan.

fig.80   The characteristic sickle-shaped wistaria ornament that can be found on many carpets of Indian origin. Detail from fig.79.

other models as prototypes for the maritime scene in these carpets
to some extent undermines the attribution of the group to the
province of Gujarat.

Only one representation of a 'Portuguese' carpet has been found in
Western painting. It was painted by an anonymous Dutch artist in
the 17th century (fig.78). The carpet, displayed on the desk of a
scholar, can be identified as an example belonging to the group
under discussion on the basis of the flaming contours of the
medallion field design, the drawing of the vines and various other
details of the pattern. The carpet is shown from one of the short
sides. A large lotus flower placed in an almond-shaped cartouche,
which can be seen on the left, locates the vertical axis of the rug. A
smaller lotus flower, represented somewhat higher in the painting
and more towards the right, indicates the prolongation of the axis.
It will be evident that the pattern has not been represented completely. The concentric medallions are cut by the border as if the
carpet has been reduced in size. The scene of the European vessels
has therefore not been represented. The pattern of the border is
exceptional. Instead of wide bands, less elegant S-shaped vines
with buds, small flowers and cloudbands are shown. This pattern,
except for the cloudbands, seems similar to that of the inner guard
border in the Rijksmuseum carpet, which has a subguard on the
field side which is identical to the inner guard border of the
'Portuguese' carpet in the painting. The stylized ornament of the
outer guard border on the latter example is unknown from surviving 'Portuguese' carpets. It is symmetrically represented; the vertical axis of the carpet serves as a line of division between two
mutually reflective halves. This detail might be an indication that
the painter followed his model quite minutely in the representation
of the borders; a similar feature, symmetrically drawn borders, can
also be seen on the floral borders of the extant 'Portuguese' carpets.
If the representation of the borders is therefore to be accepted as
reliable for stylistic comparisons, the carpet in the 17th century
Dutch painting must belong to a subgroup of which no other
examples have come down to us. However, all 'Portuguese' carpets
which are now known to us belong to a more or less homogenous
group. It is hard to establish the former existence of an exceptional
variant on the basis of a single representation in a painting. In
conclusion, the most important information for the study of these
carpets is the dating of the painting and therefore of the carpet
included in this painting. However, the 17th century dating of the
'Portuguese' carpets had already been established on stylistic
grounds. Apparently the study of carpets in paintings in this case
leaves us with more questions than answers.

FLORAL CARPETS WITH FLOWERS AND SCROLLING STEMS FROM INDIAN WORKSHOPS

Indian floral carpets in paintings are sometimes difficult to distinguish from Persian products. This is most of all evident from
representations where only a small part of such a carpet is depicted.
The floral carpets described below are restricted to those showing
certain characteristic Indian design elements.

Fields

These carpets generally have a decorative system which derives from Persian models, including floral scrolls in the field and S-stems in the borders. However, many variations were added to the basic pattern, and the individual floral ornaments often show a typical style of drawing. Well-known surviving examples are the Moghul carpet from the J.Pierpont Morgan collection in the Metropolitan Museum of Art (fig.79), the Girdlers' Carpet in London which was manufactured in Lahore between 1630 and 1632[26] and a carpet in the J.Paul Getty Museum in Malibu, that displays floral scrolls and hunting animals[27]. One of the typically Indian characteristics is the use of two shades of the same colour side by side without a separating outline. This peculiar use of colour is visible in several of the represented carpets. In many cases this feature coincides with another Indian characteristic: the sickle-shaped ornament, which is compared by Murray Eiland to a cluster of wisteria blossoms[28] but which could also be compared with flowers such as larkspur (fig.80).

The three different guard borders of carpets represented by Jan de Baen all seem to frame one specific type of field pattern (fig.81). The rather coarse structure as depicted by de Baen does not necessarily reflect the fineness of the structure of his model, as Jan de Baen may have worked from a previously-made study of an Indian carpet without having the authentic carpet in his workshop. This is suggested by the above-mentioned fact that he used different and mostly anomalous guard borders in combination with a single field pattern, and by the fact that most of the floral ornaments approximate the authentic Oriental motifs reasonably well but not exactly. It is therefore quite possible that he deliberately blurred the details by suggesting a coarse weaving structure in order to conceal the places where his memory or his study failed him. This could equally explain the irreducible border patterns visible in his paintings: the double main border of the carpet in *The Governors of the East-India Company of the Chamber of Hoorn* (cat.653) is a good example, as well as the border of the carpet in his *Portrait of Steven Wolters* (cat.644). If this presumption is correct, all the similar carpets in his paintings might be reduced to a single authentic example which may have been available to Jan de Baen as a model. The most reliable representation of this carpet is evidently the one in *The Syndics of the Cloth Hall in Leyden* (fig.99). The field pattern resembles more or less that of an Indian carpet in the Burrell collection in Glasgow (fig.82); the border pattern appears to be identical to that of a 17th century Indian carpet with flowering plants in the Metropolitan Museum of Art[29].

A remarkable field pattern here given the denotation ci.2 shows a repetitive design of angular, meandering vines. The pattern is most clearly represented in an early 18th century portrait, *The Daughters of Sir Matthew Decker*, by Johannes de Meyer (fig.83). The vines form a double overlapping system of ogivals reminiscent of those in the Kirman 'Vase' carpets. A floral ornament has been placed on the intersection or points of contact of the vines; this may be a bud or a rosette, but usually the ornament consists of a lotus flower. In places where two stems touch, they consequently run parallel for

fig.83 Johannes de Meyer, The Daughters of Sir Matthew Decker, 1718.
Fitzwilliam Museum, Cambridge.
fig.84 Michiel van Musscher, A Scholar and his Son. Present location
unknown.

two or three centimetres. Tendrils sprout symmetrically from the stems, ending in the typical sickle-shaped ornament (fig.80) or a stylized leaf. These have been placed alternately pointing to the top of the carpet or to the bottom side.

The ci.2 pattern is seldom found in paintings. Abraham van den Hecken presents us with what initially appears to be a rather disorderly representation of the pattern; however, both the details and the layout of the vines, as well as some secondary floral details have been represented fairly minutely (cat.681). The field of the carpet painted by de Meyer in 1718 is framed by a dark blue border with white and primarily red cartouches, within which the typically Indian use of two shades of the same colour side by side without separating outline becomes visible. The latter aspect, together with the presence of the sickle-shaped ornament in the field is indicative of an Indian origin for the carpet. Equally indicative of this origin are the adornment of the inner guard border, the geometrically designed subguard on the field side, and the reciprocal ornament in the outer guard border (see page 95).

Another field pattern found in representations of carpets in paintings, sometimes liable to be confused with the ci.2 pattern is here given the denotation ci.3. It consists of curvilinear S-shaped vines forming a repetitive design. At the tangent places of the vines, lotus flowers or palmettes have been placed; the vines end in buds or in composite lanceolate leaves. A fine authentic example is in West Berlin[30]. Another example is a carpet exhibited by art dealer Adil Besim at the Art and Antiques Fair in the Hofburg in Vienna in autumn 1982; this carpet has a more stiffly executed version of the pattern (fig.91).The pattern was represented in paintings by Barent Graat (cat.672), Michiel van Musscher (fig.84), in a painting attributed to Jacob Ochtervelt (fig.94) and presumably also in two much earlier paintings by Jan Miense Molenaer, dating from about 1630 (cat.695, cat.696). The representations show rather large-scale floral ornaments in the field, and stiff vines, which may indicate that the carpets used as models by these painters had a pattern closer to that of the carpet in the Vienna fair than the example in Berlin. The carpet painted by van Musscher seems to have a slightly more elegant design than the other examples.

Carpets with representations of animal figures in the field are of infrequent occurrence in 17th century Netherlandish paintings. Examples can be found in paintings by Bol (fig.61), Backhuyzen (cat.348,643), and in two portraits attributed to Pot (fig.87). The carpets painted by Backhuyzen and Pot seem to have originated in India; this is indicated by the sickle-shaped ornaments and the use of two shades of red without separating outlines in the field of the carpet in the painting by the former, and the geometrical ornamentation of the double inner guard border as well as the white ground of the main border in the portraits by the latter (see below). 17th Century Indian carpets showing representations of animals have been preserved in several collections; one of these, in the J.Paul Getty Museum, has already been mentioned; another was was formerly in the von Pannwitz collection, Heemstede, and turned up again in the art market in 1979 (fig.85[31]). Persian carpets with animal figures in the field are generally dated as 16th century (see p.59); the representation of animal combats and other figural scenes in car-

fig.85 Indian carpet, 17th century, formerly the von Pannwitz collection, Heemstede. Collection Vojtech Blau Inc. New York.
fig.86 Michiel van Musscher, Portrait of an Unknown Gentleman, 1698, present whereabouts unknown.

pets apparently went out of fashion in Persia by the turn of the century. On the basis of the pictorial source material it can therefore be stated that these 16th century datings of authentic carpets with animals included in their patterns, need no direct adjustment. An exception may be the afore-mentioned carpet represented several times by Ferdinand Bol; this richly decorated, apparently finely woven carpet shows representations of birds in the field. There are

no design elements in the pattern of this carpet indicating an Indian provenance, so it seems most secure to adhere to the traditional Persian attribution for this piece. It was either already an old carpet at the time Bol used it as a model for his paintings, or an exceptionally fine 17th century piece from one of the better workshops. The bulk of floral and cloudband carpets in 17th century Western paintings undoubtedly belonged to those groups of carpets which were produced for export, and therefore must have been the best commercial compromise between cheap production and decorative appearance. The more expensive products with much richer designs and a very fine weaving structure may also have been exported occasionally, but most likely in far lesser quantities. The carpet portrayed in Ferdinand Bol's paintings may have been an example of this group.

Borders

It is to be assumed that the Persian carpets and the majority of the carpets manufactured in India not only share a common basic thesaurus of ornaments to adorn the fields, but equally share a common design repertoire for the embellishment of the framing. Some border patterns that are presumably Indian variants on originally Persian themes are discussed below. First the adornment of the main borders will be subjected to a closer examination. Rather common is the design of S-stems (b1) which adorns the major part of most floral and cloudband carpets from Persia and also forms a part of the floral carpets which can be assigned to India on the basis of certain design elements. Still, there also exist typical and distinctive Indian border designs; one has already been mentioned in the case of the carpet depicted by Jan de Baen (fig.99).

An Indian variation on the Persian b1 theme is visible in the border of a carpet preserved in the Glasgow Museums and Art Galleries (fig.88). The border is decorated with a row of thin S-stems bearing large lotus flowers at the points of contact, and large palmettes placed diagonally on the middle of each stem. Contrary to the Persian b1 border, the last-mentioned diagonally-placed ornaments are not surrounded by four less conspicuous palmettes or lotus flowers, but rather by a number of small flowers and rosettes. This variation, catalogued under the code c23, can be found on several Indian carpets in paintings dating from about 1625 onwards.

Some surviving carpets from India have a rich border design of palmettes and broad arabesque bands with flaming outlines (c27). Usually the arabesque bands are alternately red and white, placed on a dark blue ground. A very good example of a surviving carpet with this border design is the above mentioned carpet exhibited in Vienna at the 1982 Hofburg Art and Antiques Fair (fig.91). Another example is a fragment in the Keir collection, with a meticulously drawn pattern[32]. The earliest representation of a carpet with such a border was made in 1650 by Johann Spilberg. It is draped over the

fig.87   Attributed to Heindrik Gerritsz Pot, Portrait of Willem de Vrij Frederiks, 1634, and of his Wife Aeltje Cornelisdr Dankerts. Private collection, Laren.

table in his group portrait *Feast of the Civic Guard in Honor of the Appointment of Burgomaster Jan van de Poll as Colonel* (cat.738). Only a small part of the carpet is visible, namely the border, as the major part of the carpet is covered by a linen cloth. Three years later Abraham van den Hecken painted the second recorded example (cat.675); the other representations, by van Musscher (fig.90, 1671), Caspar Netscher (cat.724, c. 1680) and Constantijn Netscher (cat.727, about the same period) were painted at a considerably later date. Only 7 examples have been found in paintings; it is not known how many surviving carpets show this rich arabesque design in the borders. Judging from the pictorial source material, the pattern must have been invented in the second quarter of the 17th century or earlier.

Michiel van Musscher is responsible for a number of representations of a rug with a remarkable pattern of irregular cartouches (fig.86). One of these has been mentioned above (cat.706). The main border of the carpet in this painting has a remarkable pattern of irregular cartouches. This border pattern can be found on a 17th century Indian carpet which I referred to earlier (fig.85). This border pattern is composed of dark blue or dark green circular and oblong cartouches on a light ochre ground. The ground is decorated with small, elegantly drawn arabesques in dark ochre; the cartouches are decorated with stylized floral motifs in red and light blue or light green. This unusual border pattern is rather rarely found, both in surviving carpets and represented examples.

Around 1630, Jacob Jordaens at least twice represented a floral carpet with a relatively simple border pattern composed of a row of S-stems bearing large rosettes at the points of contact (b78; fig.93).

The stems end in a split leaf and bear a lotus flower in the middle of each S-shape. Apart from these a few small rosettes are visible in the background, along with a large rosette which is cut by the guard borders. This border design was also represented in a painting from about 1640, attributed to Jacob Backer (cat.642); all three carpets have a similar geometrical pattern of the inner guard border. A fourth example of such a main border design can be found in a painting which was presumably made by Nicolaes Eliasz in 1628 (cat. 670). The inner guard of this carpet is adorned with a variant of the g89 pattern: the small S-vines, like the stems in the main border, all end in small split leaf forms, relatively simply drawn. At the points of contact of the S-vines we find lily-shaped ornaments reminiscent of the individual ornaments of the reciprocal g11 design.

In the paintings by Backer and Eliasz, the pattern of the field is only partially visible. At first glance it seems to consist of small-scale floral ornaments such as lotus flowers and whimsically drawn palmettes and flower buds scattered over the background. On closer examination however the floral ornaments are seen to be interconnected by thin vines and are accompanied by small rosettes that are shown in orange against the red ground, without separating outlines. This aspect may also indicate an Indian origin of the group.

The dates of these paintings approximately coincide. Apparently such carpets were available in the Netherlands in the first half of the 17th century, although not in large quantities. From the fact that only one authentic example with this type of border was found and that the pattern was recognized on only four representations in Netherlandish paintings, it can be deduced that the pattern was not widely used.

In his *Discussion in a Laboratory*, Cornelis de Man painted a carpet with the floral and cloudband pattern in the field (cat.692). The border pattern (c24) is very unusual; it displays a meandering vine with chrysanthemum-like flowers and half-opened flower buds partly turned towards the spectator. The same type of border pattern occurs in Ochtervelt's *The Dancing Dog* in the National Museum in Stockholm (cat.729) and in some paintings by Naiveu (cat.711, 712, fig.92). The drawing is characterized by the strong contrast of the motifs with the background. The Museu Nacional de Machado de Castro in Coimbra, Portugal, preserves a rug with the same border design (fig.89). The field of this extant piece as well as the field of the examples recorded in Netherlandish paintings, has a pattern of floral scrolls, palmettes, lotus flowers and cloudbands. It differs from the common floral and cloudband carpets both in detail and in the presence of a diamond-shaped medallion in the centre of the field, having flaming contours. Charles Grant Ellis considers this rug to be an Indian made free copy of the floral and cloudband carpets, exported in large numbers to Portugal, Spain and the Low Countries in the 17th century[33]. The pictorial source material confirms Ellis's remark that such carpets were readily available in the Netherlands at that time. His attribution of the carpet in Coimbra seems to be confirmed by the representation in the 1715 painting by Naiveu, *Woman with a Parrot in a Window*; a typical Indian sickle-shaped ornament is clearly visible in the field (fig.92). Presumably the entire group of carpets which have this border pattern was made in India.

fig.88 Indian carpet, 17th century. The Glasgow Museums and Art Galleries, Glasgow.

fig.89 Indian carpet, 17th century. Museu Nacional Machado de Castro, Coimbra, Portugal.

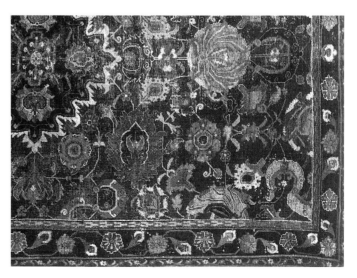

A clear representation of another border pattern (c26) that is equally seldom found in paintings, was recorded in a painting attributed to Jacob Ochtervelt (fig.94). This painting has already been referred to above, in connection with the ci.3 field pattern. The framing shows S-stems, filling half the width of the main border stripe. It is mirrored in the other half of the border; the axis which runs parallel to the border constitutes the line of reflection. The vines in the border as well as in the field are of a slightly angular shape. This border pattern was equally represented by Jan Miense Molenaer (cat.695,696, c. 1630), and Gerrit Horst (cat.684, c. 1640). Authentic examples of carpets showing this particular border pattern are unknown to me.

Other criteria used for the attribution of carpets represented in paintings derive from the patterns of the guard borders. A relatively frequently recorded pattern, that is used exclusively as adornment of the inner guard border, consists of small shield-shaped or eliptical geometrical motifs, having a small volute-shape on either side (g132). This ornament, while often seen in paintings, occurs relatively infrequently in extant examples of carpets. It is for example visible in the above-mentioned fragment in the Keir collection[34] and in the carpet in the Musée des Arts Décoratifs (fig.76). Charles Grant Ellis described the ornament as 'typically Moghul Indian'[35]. The Indian classification seems plausible, in the first place because it is found almost exclusively on authentic carpets which can be attributed to Indian workshops, and secondly because the ornament has been recorded in many carpets in paintings which, as far as visible in the representations, also seem to have several other design elements indicating that the carpets in question were most likely of Indian origin (e.g. fig.74). Only one clear exception was found in the pictorial sources, an apparently North-West Persian carpet in a painting by Bartholomeus van der Helst, *Portrait of an Unknown Gentleman* (fig.67), which shows a carpet with the g132 ornament in the inner guard stripe. The exception could possibly be explained as an eclectic composition of field- and border patterns by the painter; representations are not always as reliable as photographs, and the possibility of deviations from the authentic models must always be kept in mind. With regard to the carpet in the painting by van der Helst, this explanation is, however, not entirely satisfactory as the carpet seems minutely represented. Another possible exception in the paintings is presented by the beautiful representation of a 'strapwork' carpet in a late 17th century Dutch painting by an anonymous artist, *Portrait of Don Francisco Suasso* (fig.95): the pattern of the white inner guard border is composed of circular ornaments flanked by simple spiralling lines. This pattern seems to be an abstraction of the g132 ornament; in this form it is not known to me from surviving carpets and other elements of the carpet pattern, such as the design of the outer guard border, show equally deviations from the authentic Oriental design. The pattern as it occurs here looks like the 'classical' g132 design cut in half: if it had been reflected along the upper contour of the white inner guard border, the part represented here together with its mirror-image would show the g132 design virtually complete. Extant examples of such exceptions, showing the g132 ornament in combination with a field pattern other than Indian are also known; these include a perished 17th century fragment of a so-

fig.90 left: Michiel van Musscher, Portrait of an Astronomer or Cartographer, 1671. Amsterdams Historisch Museum, Amsterdam.
fig.91 Moghul carpet, 17th century. Photo courtesy Adil Besim, Vienna.

fig.92   Matthijs Naiveu, *Woman Feeding a Parrot at a Window*, 1715. State-
owned Art Collections Department, The Hague.

fig.93   J. Jordaens, *St. Martin Curing a Possessed Man*, 1630. Koninklijk
Museum voor Schone Kunsten, Brussels.

fig.94   Attributed to Jacob Ochtervelt, *Letter-writer and a Maid*. Present
location unknown.

fig.95   Unknown Dutch artist after a lost painting by Nicolaes Maes, *Portrait
of Don Francisco Lopez Suasso*, ca.1688. Amsterdams Historisch Museum,
Amsterdam.

called Tree carpet (so named because of the flowering plants in the field, resembling trees) which is attributed to North-West Persia[36], adorned with an inner guard border showing the g132 ornament, and an interesting Anatolian carpet, datable as second quarter of the 16th century or later, with a rather eclectic pattern; the field has a design clearly borrowed from North-West Persian examples while the main border stripe has been decorated with Anatolian cloudbands (in this study called a6). The outer guard border at the lower end side of the carpet shows the g132 design[36a]. Still, it must be kept in mind that these examples are exceptions. In general, the presence of the g132 ornament in a represented carpet may to some extent be considered indicative of an Indian origin of the pile weaving.

The g131 pattern, mainly used for the decoration of the narrow subguard which borders the field, also occurs fairly frequently and may equally be indicative of an Indian place of origin. The pattern consists of alternating circles or dots and X-shapes. Although in surviving Indian carpets this ornament is also used for the decoration of other subguards (fig.79), this pattern is in representations exclusively found in the subguard separating the field and the inner guard border. This subguard often has a certain accentuation in comparison to the subguard on the other side of the guard border, as in the above mentioned carpet in New York (fig.79); it is either depicted as much darker or simply as the only subguard accompanying the inner guard border.

In Persian carpets such an accentuation of the subguard under consideration is unusual. This aspect therefore deserves closer examination. When depicted, the subguard is usually of a dark value (dark blue or black). The red or yellow circles or dots are easily visible; the X-shapes, which often only have a lighter value of the same hue as the background, are not always discernible in a painter's representation. A comparable use of different values of the very same hue occurs in the S-motifs (g8) which can also decorate the accentuated subguard, as in, for example Jan de Bray, *The Governors of the Poor Children's Home* (fig.96). In that representation of a carpet, as well as in the carpet painted by de Meyer, on the side of the main border the subguard is absent; in other representations the subguard separating the inner guard border

and the main border stripe may be present but may have a lighter colour scheme. In these instances, the motifs are often shown in the same hue but with only a very slightly lighter value than that used in the background.

As we have seen, the carpet from the J. Pierpont Morgan collection (fig.79) is a good example of a surviving carpet with this feature. In a depiction in a painting, such a subguard separating the inner guard stripe and the main border would appear as in Jan de Baen's *The Syndics of the Cloth Hall in Leyden* (fig.99). Another variation on the same theme can be seen on a carpet in the Cincinnati Art Museum[37], which has a subguard separating the inner guard border from the field with a zig-zag pattern (g6), and a narrower subguard at the side of the main border with a simple decoration of alternating light and dark cubes.

The above-mentioned authentic carpets are clearly of Indian origin (with the exception of the Cincinnati rug[38]); the carpets in paintings showing the g131 subguards, as far as the representations permit detailed conclusions, appear to belong to the same groups of Indian carpets, or at least of the Indian variants of the Persian floral and cloudband carpets, this being indicated by the presence of Indian design elements.

g131 subguards with circles or dots alternated by X-shapes are not found frequently in authentic oriental carpets. The form does however sometimes occur in Indian chintzes. The pattern remained in use in Indian workshops until well into the 19th century[39].

The previously mentioned small zig-zag lines and S-motifs were relatively frequently recorded as the patterning of the accentuated subguard; the accentuation of the subguard can be recognized from the codes identifying the carpets, when the code iig (and sometimes iiig) is used. The g131, g6 and g8 ornaments can to a certain extent be regarded as mutually interchangeable. The specific use of one of these patterns in a carpet may possibly convey a clue for the attribution to a certain weaving centre or workshop, but the little documentary information presently available about weaving centres or workshops does not allow for detailed conclusions.

List of paintings displaying carpets with an accentuated subguard separating the field and the inner guard border, c.q. carpets with the g131 border design.

cat.650 ci./c23/iiig46?,iig46,ig8
cat.651 ci./ig131
cat.652 ci./iig131?
cat.653 ci./ig131
cat.657 ci./ig131
cat.658 ci./ig131
cat.662 bi./b6/iig8,ig46,og11b (ci.)
cat.663 b6/iig8?,ig46?,og11? (ci.)
cat.664 ci./c1/iig8,ig421
cat.665 ci./c2/iig71,ig132
cat.666 b6/ig132,og11? (ci)
cat.670 ci./c2/iig131?
cat.675 c27/iiig6,iig46,ig8 (ci.)
cat.676 ci./b1/iig6,ig42,og11c
cat.677 ci./c23/iig6,ig46?,og11c
cat.678 ci./b1/iig6,ig42,og11c

cat.679 ci./c23/iig6,ig46,og11c
cat.681 ci./c2/iig8,ig46,og11c
cat.682 ci.3/b6/iiig131,iig46,ig8,og6,oog46
cat.686 ci./b6/iig131,ig132,og46
cat.689 ci./c27/iig131?,ig132
cat.691 ci./b6/iig8,ig132,og86
cat.693 ci.2/b6/iig6,ig132,og12
cat.695 ci.3?/c26/iig8,ig132,og122
cat.696 ci.3?/c26/iig8,ig132,og122
cat.697 ci.?/iig8
cat.699 b6/iig8?,ig132?,og44? (ci.)
cat.701 ci.?/c27?/iiig131,ig46,og46?
cat.707 ci.2?/iig8,ig46,og11c
cat.708 ci./c2/iig46,ig62,og62
cat.714 ci./c11/iig8,ig42
cat.718 bi./ig131 (ci.)

cat.720 ci.?/c26?/iig8?,ig46,og46
cat.721 ci.?/b1?/iig131?,ig46?,og46?
cat.723 b6/iig131,ig46 (ci.)
cat.726 c11/iig131,ig132,og11c
cat.727 ci./c27/iig8?,ig122,og86
cat.728 ci./c11/iig131?,ig132,og11c
cat.730 ci.3/c26/iig8,ig46?,og46?
cat.731 bii./b6/iig6,ig63 (ci.)
cat.732 bii./b6/iig6,ig63 (ci.)
cat.733 ci./iig8,ig46
cat.736 ci./b6/iig6,ig46?
cat.737 ci./b6/iig6,ig46?
cat.741 ci./b1/ig46,og11b
cat.742 ci.?/c2/iig131,ig12,og11b
cat.743 ci./c23/iig6?,ig132,og46

When listing together all represented carpets which have an accent on the relevant subguard, it becomes apparent that most of these carpets are already attributable to India on the basis of other design elements. Several representations e.g. display reciprocal ornaments in the outer guard border (og11), may be regarded as an indication of an Indian place of origin (see below). The two examples possibly painted by Pot (fig.87) deviate from the common Persian floral and cloudband carpets, apart from the animal figures in that they display an unusual geometrical design of the double inner guard stripes (cf. Backer cat.642, Jordaens cat.687,688; fig.93). Sorgh painted two examples with an exceptionally large-scale whimsical floral pattern (cat.736,737); the original model apparently had an unusual white ground colour, as in the cartouche border in the works by Pot and Coques (cat.666).

The carpet in Netscher's *A Man in a Silk Gown* (cat.721), possibly identical to the one in his *Portrait of a Member of the Citters Family* (cat.723), is remarkable because the framing is disproportionately wide. A comparably wide framing can be found on the carpet in van den Hecken's *Portrait of Cornelis Jansz Meyer* (cat.680); in the latter portrait the Indian origin of the carpet is suggested by the presence of the characteristic sickle-shaped ornament in the field (fig.80).

In conclusion, if we consider the pattern as a ground for attributing the carpets in the paintings to certain weaving areas, the represented carpets that have a certain accent in the subguard separating the field from the inner guard border, belong — as far as the representations permit a detailed identification of the rugs in question — to the group of floral carpets for which an Indian attribution is more likely than a Persian attribution. Following this premise, it can be logically assumed that less completely represented carpets showing a similar accentuation on this particular subguard may also belong to the same group.

The g122 pattern, consisting of rosettes interchanged with colonnettes, has seldom been recorded. The pattern occurs as decoration of the inner guard border of the previously mentioned Indian carpet in Glasgow (fig.82). The same pattern has been attested in carpets represented by Lambert Doomer (cat.669), Jan Miense Molenaer (cat.695,696) and Constantijn Netscher (cat.727);

fig.96   Jan de Bray, Governors of the Poor Children's Home, 1663. Frans Hals Museum, Haarlem.

all carpets which are attributed to India on the basis of other design elements. The identification of this guard border pattern therefore contributes only supplementary information to this research.

Reciprocal ornaments (g11) are not uncommon in the borders of both Persian and Indian carpets. The pattern is frequently found in authentic examples as an embellishment of the inner guard border[40], but is less common for the decoration of the outer guard border. We can generally distinguish between two variants. First, there is an elegant lily-shape with flowing lines (g11a). An example is the border pattern of the previously mentioned Girdlers' Carpet[41]. A stylized variant (g11b) is found in several carpets in paintings (fig.96), but the presence of this stylized version may, in *some* cases, be due to the sketchiness of the representations, as this variant is quite rare in authentic examples. In the third variant the lily-like trefoil ornaments are interconnected by S-shaped lines (g11c). This variant occurs regularly in both represented carpets (cat.694) as in surviving pieces, which are of Indian origin (fig.82). A list of carpets in paintings displaying g11 ornaments in the border is set out below.

fig.97   Cornelis de Man, Still-life with a Servant and a Parrot, 1667 or later. Historisches Museum, Frankfurt.

cat.648 ci./og11c
cat.659 c2/ig46,og11b (ci.)
cat.662 bi./b6/iig8,ig46,og11b (ci.)
cat.663 b6/iig8?,ig46?og11? (ci.)
cat.666 b6/ig132,og11? (ci.)
cat.676 ci./c23?/iig131?,ig46?,og11c
cat.677 ci./c23/iig6,ig46?,og11
cat.678 ci./b1/iig6,ig42,og11c
cat.679 ci.c23/iig6,ig46,og11c
cat.681 ci.2/c2/iig8,ig46,og11c
cat.684 cii./c26?/ig132,og11c
cat.688 ci.?/c2/og11
cat.690 bi.?/c23?/ig46,og11b
cat.694 ci./c25/ig46,og11c
cat.717 ci./c25/ig46,og11c
cat.722 ci./c11/iig?,ig132?,og11c
cat.726 c11/iig131,ig132,og11c (ci.)
cat.728 ci./c11/iig131?,ig132,og11c
cat.735 ci./c23/og11c
cat.739 ci./c25/og11c
cat.741 ci./b1/ig46,og11b
cat.742 ci.?/c2/iig131,ig12,og11b
cat.744 ci./c25/og11

List of paintings displaying carpets with g11 ornaments in the border.

It is again remarkable that a significant proportion of the above-mentioned representations is considered to be of Indian origin on the basis of certain other design elements in the field or borders. For this reason, an Indian origin may well be considered likely for floral carpets in paintings with a reciprocal design in the outer guard border, even when the representation does not allow a detailed identification of other design elements.

Cartouche borders (b6) occur fairly infrequently in floral carpets in Flemish and Dutch paintings. One of the clearest examples is the carpet in Cornelis de Man's *Still-life with a Servant and a Parrot*, painted in or shortly after 1667. This representation constitutes a classic example of an Indian carpet in a Dutch painting (fig.97). The afore-mentioned characteristically Indian elements of pattern, such as the g132 ornament and the accentuated subguard alongside the field with S-motifs, are clearly visible, as is the use of two shades of the same hue side by side without separating outline in the cartouches. A list of carpets in paintings showing cartouche borders is presented below. The probable origin of these carpets can in most cases be deduced from a comparison of the decoration of the guard borders.

cat.366 bi./b6
cat.382 biv/b6
cat.387 bi./b6
cat.637 b6 (ci.)
cat.662 bi./b6/iig8,ig46,og11b (ci.)
cat.663 b6/iig8?,ig46?,og11? (ci.)
cat.666 b6/ig132,og11? (ci.)
cat.691 ci./b6/iig8,ig132,og86
cat.699 b6/iig8?,ig132?,og44? (ci.)
cat.723 b6/iig131,ig46 (ci.)
cat.731 bii./b6/iig62,ig63 (ci.)
cat.732 bii./b6/iig62,ig63 (ci.)
cat.736 ci./b6/iig6,ig46?
cat.737 ci./b6/iig6,ig46?

The model which Jan de Bray used twice, namely in his *Governors of the Poor Children's Home* (fig.96) and in *The Haarlem Painter Abraham Casteleyn and his Wife Margarieta van Bancken* (cat.663), may well have been of Indian origin; the presence of the accentuated subguard separating field and inner guard border as well as the presence of the reciprocal outer guard border is significant. The g131 and g132 guard border designs in the carpet in Caspar Netscher's portrait *A Member of the Citters Family* (cat.723) are likewise indicative of an Indian origin. The rugs in the portraits attributed to Pot (fig.87) and the ones by Sorgh (cat.736,737) were discussed above. The large carpet painted by Cuyp (cat.382) can not be attributed either to Persia or to India, as the representation of the individual design elements is unfortunately rather sketchy. In the case of the painting by van Dyck (cat.387), the representation displays too small a part of the carpet to allow for detailed conclusions.
The rugs in the remaining representations can be plausibly attributed to Indian weaving centres. This seems to mean that the commonest type of floral Persian carpet with cartouche borders was never — or at least hardly ever — represented by painters from the Low Countries in the 17th century. It may well be that the large-scale production of floral carpets with such borders came to an end in Persia at the close of the 16th century.

A variant cartouche border design was represented in a group portrait by an unknown Dutch painter: *Portrait of a Family, with the Amsterdam City Hall in the Background* (fig.98). The exact pattern of the field is not clear, as it was not very carefully painted, but the border pattern can comfortably be identified. A classic example of a carpet with such a border is kept in the collection of the Museum für Angewandte Kunst in Vienna (fig.108). It has the same pattern as the borders of the carpets in the paintings discussed above, but in this case these cartouches are all cut in half by the guard borders. It is remarkable that this unusual border pattern, which was re-corded on a floral carpet in only one painting from the Netherlands, was also used for the decoration of the borders in another group of carpets with a medallion design, of which the oriental provenance is rather questionable: namely the carpets of the 'namenlose Gattung' (see chapter V). Although the portrait of the Amsterdam family must be given a rather late date (about 1700), the dating of the medallion rugs in Dutch paintings proves that carpets with this unusual border pattern must have been already present in the Low Countries before the 1660s.

An extraordinary border pattern is visible in a genre painting mentioned above in connection with the g11c border pattern: Willem van Mieris' *Young Woman with a Boy Blowing Bubbles at an Arched Window* (cat.694) in the Rijksmuseum. The carpet in question has a border with large S-stems ending in curved and serrated leaves. Lotus flowers are placed at the place of contact of two adjacent stems, pointing outwards, and in the middle of each stem we find a diagonally placed palmette. The lotus flowers and the palmette are enclosed within small twigs bearing red flowers. Remarkable is the fact that there is no corner solution; as in Anatolian carpets the border ornament does not turn neatly round the corner with the help of diagonally placed floral ornaments. The pattern consists of friezes which seem to have been cut arbitrarily at places where the borders of the long sides and those of the end sides meet. The same border pattern is visible in a portrait by Aleyda Wolfsen. The Indian origin of these carpets seems evident from the sickle-shaped cluster of blossoms in the field of the carpet in the painting by van Mieris, and equally from the presence of the characteristic reciprocal ornaments (g11c) in the outer guard border; the rather elaborate version of the g46 (see fig.88) guard border pattern might be another indication of the Indian origin of the carpet. Authentic examples with this type of main border pattern are unknown to me.

Conclusion

From the material presented above, it appears that certain design elements are most probably of Indian origin, as they generally occur in combination with other, also presumably Indian, design elements. A handicap affecting the study of carpets in paintings is above all that most painted representations display only a mere fraction of the carpet, so that certain characteristic motifs which may have been present in the actual carpet are not visible in the representation. It is possible, therefore, that some representations of rugs decorated with curvilinear designs, of which only a small part is depicted, are in this study erroneously listed in the chapter discussing carpets with Persian field patterns.

Nevertheless, it has become clear that certain combinations of individual design elements, such as reciprocal ornaments in the outer guard border instead of as decoration of the inner guard, or the introduction of an accentuated narrow subguard between the field and the inner guard border, are highly unusual for floral carpets which can be attributed with reasonable certainty to Persia, and relatively common in carpets more easily attributable to India. However, this does not necessary imply that all depicted carpets showing Indian design elements are all of Indian manufacture: the above-mentioned carpet in the Cincinnati Art Museum that includes some Indian ornaments in its pattern, for example, was probably woven somewhere other than India[42]. Clearly the successful Indian patterns were sometimes copied in other weaving areas[43].

diagram a

Carpets with Indian design elements (ci.) in Netherlandish paintings 1540-1700.

fig. 99 Jan de Baen, The Syndics of the Cloth Hall in Leyden, 1675. Municipal Museum de Lakenhal, Leyden.

The datings of the paintings displaying Oriental carpets with Indian design ornaments largely coincide with those of the larger group of Persian floral and cloudband carpets.

The diagram shows that the carpets with Indian patterns were first represented in Flemish and Dutch paintings round about 1620. From 1655 onwards an increasing number of representations have been recorded, while the interest of painters in these carpets decreased after 1680 — also the period when the numbers of Persian carpets in depicted in Netherlandish paintings decrease. In all, 105 17th century representations have been listed in the catalogue part of this chapter, against 293 representations in the chapter on floral carpets that we have tentatively attributed to Persian workshops. This means that up to about 27% of all carpets with flowing floral patterns (with the exception of Ottoman carpets) represented in Netherlandish paintings may have been woven in India. Moreover, this percentage presents only a tentative estimate; there is still the strong possibility that some Indian carpets portrayed by Dutch and Flemish painters have been classified among the Persian examples, in those cases where the pictorial sources give only a glimpse of the represented carpet. Undoubtedly a few of the models for these depictions may have had characteristically Indian design elements that remained undetected due to the limitations of the pictorial sources. Furthermore, the number of carpets attributed to India on the basis of their designs could also increase were one to reject the possibility of an Occidental origin of, e.g., the rugs classified as ei.3 (Chapter VII).

If the data recorded in diagram b are compared with those in the similar diagram 1a in the chapter on Persian carpets (p.60) supplemented with the other groups attributed to Persia in that chapter, yet another relative percentage is found. In these diagrams only the earliest recorded example of a carpet with Indian patterns or a Persian carpet in the work of the various painters is listed, unless it appears that individual painters have used more than one example of such a carpet as models; then the earliest recorded representation of each model is listed. Diagram b includes 75 representations, which means that 30 representations of certain Indian carpets were omitted; diagram a includes 105 representations. If we compare the diagrams on carpets with Indian ornaments to the supplemented diagrams 1 and 1a in the chapter on Persian carpets, it appears that the latter would include respectively 293 and 106 representations; 187 of the representations of these carpets in paintings presumably were painted by an individual painter for a second time, or sometimes more often.

Thus a comparison of the numbers of individual carpets, rather than of total representations, encompassed in diagram 1a and diagram b results, in figures respectively 106 and 75, or ca. 60% Persian carpets against ca. 40% carpets with Indian patterns in Netherlandish paintings.

The different percentages of 27% and 40% illustrate that numbers derived from our study have to be interpreted statistically with some caution; however it seems plausible that over a third of the floral-design carpets used as models by Dutch and Flemish painters originated from Indian workshops or from workshops using characteristically Indian patterns or combinations of designs.

The relative proportion of carpets with Indian ornaments among all carpets in paintings with floral designs — more than a third of all carpets, and over a quarter of all depictions — is remarkable. 17th century travellers in the Orient name as the major weaving centre for woollen carpets the North-East Persian province of Khorasan, which in the 17th century bordered Moghul India. If the major part of the two-thirds of depicted carpets displaying Persian patterns is thus to be attributed to Khorasan, then the theory that carpets with patterns absolutely identical to those of Persian carpets were also being produced in large quantities in India becomes less likely.

The Indian weavers, some of whom were immigrants from Persia, as the Streynsham Master told us, may have adapted their traditional Persian patterns to their own taste or to the local style of drawing. An important question is whether the pictorial sources from the Netherlands present reliable information about the relative quantities of the carpets that were being traded not only to Flanders and the Dutch Republic, but also to the rest of Western Europe in the 17th century. If so, this information, combined with the fact that the most important weaving centre of the time was located in Khorasan, and the large proportion of examples with Indian patterns in paintings among those represented with floral patterns, leaves little room for the existence of a shadowy group of 'Indo-Persian' carpets indeed. In other words, it would seem logical to infer that the extant carpets that show no characteristic Indian design elements may be more confidently attributed to Persia.

In any case, it is clear, from the number of carpets with Indian design characteristics in pictorial sources, that the arrival of the samples ordered by governors of the *Vereenigde Oostindische Compagnie* in 1624 must have marked the beginning of a very profitable import of such carpets in the Netherlands.

diagram b

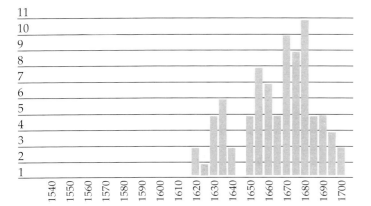

Carpets with Indian design elements (ci.) in Netherlandish paintings 1540-1700, arranged according to the earliest example depicted by each painter.

VI
THE 'NAMENLOSE GATTUNG'

In her dissertation 'Anatolische Teppiche auf abendländischen Gemälden' Brigitte Scheunemann devoted a chapter to 'Eine namenlose Gattung'[1]. In this chapter she describes a group of small, simple carpets that are only known from their appearance in Dutch paintings of the 17th and early 18th centuries; as far as it is known, no original examples have survived.

Field

The middle of the field contains a star-shaped medallion which touches the border on the horizontal axis; above and below the medallion are stiff floral motifs, not unlike fleurs-de-lis. Inside the star there are eight lotus flowers radiating from a smaller concentric eight-pointed star. The latter is decorated with a single large rosette.

Sections of the central star pattern are repeated in the corners of the field; quarter medallions are placed at each corner and meet across the shorter sides of the field at the location where the vertical axis of the carpet intersects the border. The remainder of the field contains crudely drawn floral motifs which are not altogether well understood in Scheunemann's reconstruction (fig.101).

A floral ornament grows out from the fleurs-de-lis, and extends towards the niches on the short sides of the carpet. This ornament divides in two a few centimetres from the top and touches the side arms of the corner medallions at right angles. The fleurs-de-lis on the corner medallions are cut in half by the border. A similar floral ornament extends from these in the direction of the horizontal axis of the carpet. Although the latter floral ornaments are hidden by the inner guard stripe, they are clearly suggested by the half-visible

fig.100 Pieter de Hooch, The Music Lesson, 1667-70. The Taft Museum, Cincinnati, Ohio.

flower and leaf motifs. Finally, a plant-like ornament protrudes from the diagonal arms of the corner medallions and turns towards the horizontal axis of the carpet to decorate the rest of the field.

This field pattern (coded ei.) is clearly a standard form because of the uniform way different painters reproduce it. The patterns they use as models for the full field show little variation. Only Pieter de Hooch used as a model a variant of the field pattern (coded ei.2; fig.100). The carpet he used as a model apparently had a lobed partition round the corner medallion with geometric heart-form ornaments on it. Inside this area the ground colour is orange while the rest of the field is red. Further, the central medallion is surrounded by a zig-zag band that is absent in the 'Scheunemann' carpets portrayed by his contemporaries.

Borders

The border pattern is less stereotyped; a number of variations occur. The most frequently occurring pattern (d11) is composed of two irregularly meandering stems. They have unusually drawn palmettes; Dr.Scheunemann in her reconstruction mistakenly drew this motif as a lotus flower, occurring at the point where the stems are at a 45-degree angle to the border. The stems also carry small rosettes, flower buds and oblong, sickle-shaped leaves. The manner in which the tendril is carried into the corners can be seen in several paintings. The corner solution shows a palmette placed on the diagonal. On this palmette there is a thin little tendril with a flower bud which fills the remaining space.

The reconstruction by Brigitte Scheunemann (fig.101) shows the vertical and horizontal axes of the border as symmetrical. This seems to fit as far as the vertical axis is concerned. The possibility of one side of the vertical axis being a mirror image of the other can also be seen in other border patterns (d12: cf. Voorhout, The

fig.101 Reconstruction of the ei. field design, after B.Scheunemann. On the reconstruction, the carpet has the d11 border; the inner guard border is decorated with the g84 motif, whereas the outer guard border shows the g102 ornament.

fig.102 Reconstruction of the d12 border design.

Footwashing, cat.867; d13: cf. Terborch, *Lute Player and an Officer*, cat.861; d14: Brakenburg, *A Picture Gallery*, cat.749). The horizontal axis of the carpet was not always used to mirror the side borders, as suggested by the reconstruction of fig.101, at least not for the d11 border pattern (e.g. Frans van Mieris, *The Music Lesson* , cat.794). In Niwael's *The Annunciation* (cat.800) it can be seen that the horizontal axis of the carpet was actually used in this mirror reverse manner, but in this case a different border pattern has been used (d14). Finally, on the carpet in the paintings by Jan Steen, the palmettes of the d11 pattern that are closest to the axis turn towards each other and not away, as in the reconstruction.

Brigitte Scheunemann could not find the d11 pattern on original Eastern carpets, so 'wegen der…höchst mangelhaften Abbildungen der Borte auf Gemälden muss für das ergänzte Bortenmuster ein Beträchtlicher Unsicherheitsfaktor einberechnet werden'[2]. However, this is not entirely fair, for the d11 border pattern is reproduced so minutely by various painters that a detailed reconstruction is certainly possible.

d12 can be considered to be a variation of b1, which is the usual border of floral-and-cloudband carpets (see chapter IV). There is no meandering stem as Dr.Scheunemann supposed[3], but there are S-shaped stems that run into leaf ornaments and have a palmette at the point of contact (fig.102). These palmettes conform in shape to those of the d11 pattern. A large flower bud is placed diagonally in the middle of the S-shape. In Terborch's *Lady Washing her Hands* (cat.856) it is striking how the vertical axis of the carpet mirrors the border pattern. It is not, as in Voorhout's painting, in the most logical spot (namely, the middle of the palmettes), but is apparently on a fortuitous spot so that two thirds of the S-shaped stems are reproduced on both sides of this axis, resulting in a remarkably broken pattern that dwindles out.

The corner arrangement however is quite elegant; the stem forms a large C-shape and there is a four-leafed flower in the remaining space. It is obvious that the designer began to draw the border pattern from the corners and was prepared to accept the occasions when this produced a less satisfactory result on the vertical axis of the carpet.

The arrangement at the corner of the cartouche pattern d13 is made from a fusion of two cartouches. In Terborch's *Two Girls Making Music* (fig.103) this can easily be seen. The rosette in the centre of each cartouche appears twice in the fused cartouches in the corner. Presumably the manner in which the cartouches fuse is intentional. Comparable corner solutions are common on both Persian and Indian carpets[4]. In the middle of the d13 border on the short side of the carpet there is a comparatively small cartouche; this one is formed by a fusion of the small branches of the full drawn cartouches (fig.104). As with the d12 border, it appears that the designer began to draw from the corner. Clear parallels of cartouches with a similar stylized floral decoration cannot be found in surviving Eastern carpets. A stylistic connection with the cartouches of the 'coupled-column prayer rugs' is not evident (fig.105).

d14 is difficult to reconstruct in detail (fig.106a). All the representations of this pattern that have been traced have been unclear to a

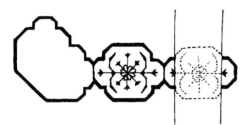

greater or lesser extent. Consequently the reconstruction has some 'grey' areas. Scheunemann called the ornaments 'einzelne recht einfach gezeichnete Blumen' (simple floral ornaments), which is partially correct. In fact they present a succession of S-shapes, which are partly formed by the characteristic composed leaf ornaments that resemble flower buds on the point of breaking into bloom, and partly by the thin little tendrils that continue the curves and end in flower buds. A rosette is usually placed on the points of contact of the S-shapes. Sometimes these are missing, and then the leaf shapes hook together in a chain-like manner. When this occurs, the little tendrils with flower buds are missing. The corner solution interrupts the continuation of the S-shaped ornaments; this perhaps has the effect of making the corners a bit awkward. The prototype of this pattern is unknown. It is possible that the border pattern is related to a particular border pattern known from 'Transylvanian' carpets (see Chapter III) with stylized leaves (a10). The d14 pattern seldom appears. The majority of examples were found in Richard Brakenburg's pictures, one in Niwael's oeuvre, one in a late work by de Vois and one in a group portrait by Weenix. In these last two paintings it is remarkable that the d14 border does not frame a 'Scheunemann' field (see Chapter VII). The example in the painting by Jan Weenix is especially interesting because the artist has depicted the pattern in much more detail than Brakenburgh, Niwael and de Vois.

d16 also seldom appears. It can only be found on 'Scheunemann' carpets depicted by Jan van der Heyden (fig.107) and on a sketchy representation of a carpet in a portrait by Pieter van Slingelant (cat.822). It consists of a half-visible shield shape cut by the guard stripes and lobed cartouches. The space in between shows changing ground colours and is decorated with a thin, curved tendril. A closely related form appears in the cartouche pattern of a 17th century Indian carpet preserved in the Museum für Angewandte Kunst in Vienna (fig.108). However, the floral ornaments in the cartouche of this carpet are somewhat more elaborate than those in the 'Scheunemann' carpets depicted in paintings. The g86 pattern of the inner guard border in the painting by van der Heyden is also found in the inner guard border of the Indian carpet.

d17 is a succession of S-stems and, like d12, is a variation of the b1 design (fig.106b). It is found almost exclusively in paintings by Pieter de Hooch. An almost identical pattern can be found on a late Kirman 'Vase' carpet in East Berlin[5]. In a variation of this pattern the stems always vanish into the adjacent guard stripes. At these points there is a stylized leaf ornament on the side of the guard stripe which is touched by the cut-out lily-shaped silhouette. These shapes are comparable to the fleurs-de-lis that can be seen below and above the medallions in the 'Scheunemann' field design and, in addition, one can point to a similarity with the plant motifs which were described together with this field pattern and which also merge with the guard border. This phenomenon is unusual in the design of Oriental carpets, and remains unexplained.

The inner guard stripe was often decorated with either a continuous row of flowing S-shaped motifs (g84) or angular S-motifs which end in heart-shaped ornaments (g86). The outer guard stripe has either a stylized angular S-motif (g102) or a heavy but flowing S-motif ending in spirals (g85). Dr.Scheunemann has not noticed that the pattern of the guardstripes, like that of the main border, is symmetrical along the vertical axis of the carpet. In both the g84 and g102 patterns a red geometric ornament is generally placed on the axis (see Jan Steen's *The Captured Samson Mocked by the Philistines*, cat.833, for the g84 pattern and *The Seduction*, cat.845, for the g102 pattern). In the g85 pattern there is no interpolated ornament allowing motifs to turn elegantly at the corners. Whenever the S-shaped motif cuts through the axis the effect is of the motif being reflected on the other side of the line (see Johannes Voorhout's *The Footwashing*, cat.867). The reflection line of the g86 pattern falls along the midline of the heart-shaped motif (ibid.); the effect of the reflection is therefore absent.

Colours

The use of colour in the field pattern is rather stereotyped. The background is invariably red with a darker coloured medallion. This medallion is generally dark blue but some moss green can be found, for example in the work of Frans van Mieris (*Death of Lucretia*, cat.795,[6]). The corner medallions are mostly orange though white is also used (as for example in Bartholomeus van der Helst's *Portrait of Daniel Bernard*, cat.763). The centre of the corner medallions is black. According to Brigitte Scheunemann the border is dark blue[7]. However, in the paintings which were studied in situ and those available in colour reproductions the border seems to be predominantly black or dark green. The guard borders are generally white. The other colours used in the carpets shown in the paintings are yellow, beige, light blue and purple.

Structure

As far as the weave is concerned Scheunemann confined herself to the observation that the carpets had a 'grobe und vermutlich lockere Knüpfung'[8]. Although it is certainly true that the 'Möglichkeit einer technischen Untersuchung fehlt'[9] in the absence of surviving examples from the 17th century, a careful analysis of the carpets in the paintings can still produce more clues. So far as recorded, the fringes are always white. They were probably formed by the ends of the warps, rather than added as decoration after the completion of the carpet, as in some Persian carpets; in those paintings where the carpets seem worn (fig.109; Pieter de Hooch's *Woman and a Child Feeding a Parrot*, cat.781) the warps are the same colour as the fringes. Usually they hang loose, but sometimes the fringes are shown as small cables of two warps twisted together and ending in a loop (see for example Adriaen van der Werff's *Portrait of Three Children*, cat.879). A similar effect is produced when, after completion, the carpet is removed from the loom by loosening the beam to which the warps are attached and pushing it out through the loops without cutting the ends of the warp threads. The cable-like effect is the result of the release of the tension that exists in the twisted threads being stretched on the loom. This effect can be seen on different types of Eastern carpets from various weaving areas. The warp was probably made of wool, as the cable-like effect is most noticeable when wool is used, and much less so in the case of

a

b

cotton; and the lustre of some of the fringes shown in the paintings can hardly be expected from a cotton warp. A third possibility, that flax has been used, is unlikely because flax is a fine material whereas this materiaal seems from the evidence of the paintings to be relatively coarse.

The carpets seem to have a double selvedge (either 2x1 or 2x2 warp threads) that was overcast with orange wool. The white wefts are clearly visible in the painting by Frans van Mieris referred to earlier. In this painting part of the back of the carpet can be seen, revealing a low density of knots. The white weft threads on the pile side can hardly be seen as they are hidden by the long pile of the carpet, but wefts can clearly be seen in the places where the draping of the carpet has opened up the pile. This need not indicate a large number of weft shoots after each row of knots, but rather a looser weave structure, as Scheunemann has already described. This can be deduced from the suppleness of the draping in the represented carpets. The low density of knots can also be deduced from the coarse drawing of the pattern in the field and borders. The d11 border pattern contains finer detailing, but this is probably because designers or weavers did not introdue contrasting contour lines to separate the motifs from the dark background.

As far as can be seen, it appears that the short sides of these carpets have usually been finished off with a small strip of red plain weave which sometimes contains a white stripe. In several pictures this strip seems to have a ridged or ribbed effect; in his *Portrait of an Unknown Gentleman* (fig.110) Adriaen van der Werff painted a Scheunemann carpet minutely enough to establish that alternate warps were depressed so that a ribbed effect appears in the kilim strip.

Origin

In 1953 Brigitte Scheunemann put forward her thesis that 'die namenlose Gattung nicht in Persien geknüpft worden sein (kann)'[10]. Although comparable medallion patterns have some forms thought to originate in the area of North West Persia in and around Tabriz, the rough drawing of the separate elements of the pattern do not, according to her, conform to the fine stems which decorate the Persian carpets. The presence of relatively large undecorated spots between the ornaments suggested to her an Anatolian origin. She also pointed out connections with patterns on carpets generally attributed to Ushak. For example, the medallions could be viewed as simple imitations of the corner medallions of Medallion Ushaks: 'ein grosser Teil der Bortenmuster kann an Kolonnenladiks, Medaillon Ushaks oder Gebeds-Ushaks nachgewiesen werden'[11]. The colours also suggested to her an origin in Anatolia: 'Die verwendung von Rot und Dunkelblau als Grundfarben von Feld und Borte, sowie die in den details hinzutretenden Farben bestärken die Vermutung, dass hier eine Teppichgruppe zusammengestellt worden ist, die im engsten formalen und farblichen Zusammenhang mit den Ushakteppichen steht und diesen als spätere Variante zugeordnet werden kann'[12].

At first sight there seems indeed to be some conformity in the use of colours between the carpets of the 'namenlose Gattung' and Anatolian carpets, but this cannot be securely established. Firstly, there is the question of the colours of the borders: these are probably black or dark green (see above) which are unusual for Anatolian carpets. Also the combination of red for the field and orange for the corner medallions is uncharacteristic of the products of Anatolian workshops. As far as the relationship with Anatolian border patterns is concerned, it is evident from the reconstruction of cartouche pattern d13 that the connection with the cartouches of the so-called coupled-column prayer rugs is rather slim. The drawing of the d11 border pattern contrasts with Scheunemann's observation that there is a suggestion of a 'typisch anatolische Stilisierung'[13], and it is certainly not comparable with Anatolian border designs. A closely related comparison for the irregular course of the tendrils of this pattern can not be found on any 17th century Oriental carpet, nor can we find parallels for the use of leaves and small flowers in this form. This also applies to the shapes of the palmettes. The g84, g85 and g88 decorations of the guard stripes are equally unknown on Anatolian carpets. The g86 and g102 variants however are sometimes found on Anatolian carpets, although it must be said that g86 is not only found on Anatolian carpets, but also on carpets from other areas, as far away as Moghul India.

In 1959 Brigitte Scheunemann retracted her earlier attribution. She made a short list of characteristics of the carpets under discussion, which are indeed unusual for Anatolian carpets[14]. The application of a corner solution of the d11 border pattern is certainly the most striking feature. Whether this can be used to demonstrate a Persian origin, as she wanted, is still questionable; as stated earlier, there is no comparative material for the drawing of the d11 pattern in any group of Eastern carpets. The corner solutions in the main border of the other groups of the represented carpets (d12, d13, d14, d15 and d17) were not discussed by Dr.Scheunemann.

The resemblance between the star-shaped medallion in the field and the medallion patterns in carpets from North-West Persia was also emphasized[15]. However, she did distinguish the corner medallions that have a niche form on the short sides of the carpet[16]; this is a design characteristic well known from Anatolian carpets (see chapter III) but not from Persian examples. Scheunemann compared the flowering plants in the field with those on a specific group of North-West Persian 'Garden' carpets[17]. The 'Vase' carpets were mentioned in relation to the large rosettes in the centre of the medallions[18]. She connected the d12 pattern to another South Persian example[19]. Here, however, her suggestion that it is related to the guard border design of a North West Persian example[20] is less convincing.

With regard to the highly decorated frame of the corner medallions on the carpet depicted by de Hooch (fig.100) Scheunemann showed closely related decorations on the corners of North-West Persian carpets. Still, similar motifs can be found on other Persian carpets[21]. Dr.Scheunemann came to the conclusion that the 'namenlose Gattung' must have come from North-West Persia, although she admitted that the use of colour did not entirely support this conclusion. She also recognized that certain elements of the pattern are not found in North-West Persian carpets, but 'wir können annehmen, dass die vorliegende Gruppe eine Spätform nordwestpersischer Teppiche dastellt, die artfremde Motive in sich aufnahm, wie das bei Stücken jüngeren Datums häufig der Fall ist'[22].

fig.107   Jan van der Heyden, Still-life with a Red Curtain. Tiroler Landesmuseum Ferdinandeum, Innsbruck.

C.G. Ellis included some observations on the 'namenlose Gattung' in his review of the exhibition held by the Philadelphia Museum of Art in 1984, 'Masters of 17th Century Dutch Genre Paintings'[23]. He suggested that the field pattern may have been based on an Indo-Persian variety represented by a carpet in the Vienna Decorative Arts Museum, shown in the upper half of plate 20 of Sarre and Trenkwald's volume on carpets. The field of that carpet (which was 'regrettably a war casualty') had eight-pointed stars with lobed outlines, in the centre of which were placed similarly lobed medallions. Inside is a diamond-shaped motif out of which leaves and flower buds grow. The lobed medallion in its turn also carries lilies alternating with smaller flower buds that extend to the points of the star motif. This recurring eight-pointed star does indeed bear a resemblance to the star motif in the Scheunemann pattern. However, the overall differences are more noticeable than the similarities. Above all, the rest of the field of the presumably Indian carpet from Vienna, bore a decoration which had no parallel with the pattern of the represented carpets: it had a pattern of scrolling stems with curled lanceolate leaves and lotus flowers. There are also no links between the decoration of the main border and the guard stripes of the Vienna carpet and the Scheunemann group.

The argument in support of an Anatolian origin appears rather forced in Brigitte Scheunemann's dissertation, and the same criticism applies to her article from 1959. The connections between the depicted carpets and authentic examples of all known oriental carpet groups, from Anatolia to India, cast some doubts on the attribution which Dr.Scheunemann herself had already established. In fact, design elements characteristic of various widely separated weaving areas can be perceived in the 'namenlose Gattung'. Scheunemann's explanation for this (see above) seems to be a very tenuous hypothesis, as is her hypothesis that we are dealing with carpets from later periods with eclectic patterns, produced in a period when other cultural and economic factors were operating. We have established that certain elements of the Scheunemann pattern are found neither on authentic Eastern carpets of the relevant period nor on those of later periods. Perhaps Mr.Ellis' suggestion that carpets depicted in Dutch paintings should sometimes be considered as domestic products of the Netherlands should be taken seriously in relation to the 'namenlose Gattung'. Perhaps if an actual contemporaneous example surfaces some day, a technical analysis of the weave structure might establish a European attribution for the group.

Unfortunately this is to date impossible, perhaps because 'Ihre grobe und vermutlich lockere Knüpfung bewirkte, dass sie relativ schnell verfielen'[24]. The numerous paintings showing examples of carpets of this group, that are represented in a greater or a lesser state of decay (fig.109) might support Brigitte Scheunemann's explanation for the lack of authentic 17th century examples. Another argument for the absence of authentic examples might be that over the centuries only two classical carpets are known to have survived in the Netherlands, and if the carpets under discussion were made exclusively for the Dutch market then perhaps they all perished with the other early examples. Finally, the coarse weave structure shows that these carpets were relatively cheap products of moderate value, another possible explanation for the fact that no

fig.109 *Cornelis Dusart (attributed to), A Man and a Woman Making Music,*
1685-90. Art Gallery, Glasgow.

diagram 1

49
48
47
46
45
44
43
42
41
40
39
38
37
36
35
34
33
32
31
30
29
28
27
26
25
24
23
22
21
20
19
18
17
16
15
14
13
12
11
10
9
8
7
6
5
4
3
2
1

1560 1570 1580 1590 1600 1610 1620 1630 1640 1650 1660 1670 1680 1690 1700

'Scheunemann' carpets (ei.) in Dutch paintings 1540-1720.

example from the 17th century is known to have survived. One could even consider the possibility that these carpets never actually existed, that the pattern was copied by one painter from the works of another. For example, the results of recent studies suggest that the stereotype, abundantly rich garments of the women in the genre paintings were to a greater or lesser extent invented by the artists instead of based on their observation of authentic clothing[24a]. The 'Scheunemann' carpets could likewise have been invented by the genre painters. However, apart from the fact that the weaving characteristics of the pile weavings are represented extremely carefully, which suggests that the artists painted from existing models, some authentic carpets in the exact pattern and colours of the 'unbekannte' group are known to be preserved in a Kyoto collection. This group has been studied on location by Charles Grant Ellis, who came to the conclusion that the carpets are dateable to the 18th century. Mr. Ellis does not believe these examples to be of Dutch manufacture, much less Persian or Indian. In fact, he considers these carpets as exact copies of lost originals, possibly 'made in Japan'[24b]. Any way, following for the moment the conclusion of Mr. Ellis, the existence of these 18th century copies in Japan (a country which, in the 17th century, gave a monopoly on foreign trade to the Dutch East-India Company for many decades) demonstrates that the 'Scheunemann' groups must have been available in the 17th century.

Dating

The dating of this group can be deduced from the dates of the paintings (diagram 1). The margin that must be taken for the earliest picture could, on the grounds of the attribution given above, be smaller than the margin Scheunemann held: 'Ihre Herstellung muss bereits in der 1. Hälfte des 17. Jh. angelaufen sein, da für die Ausfuhr einer Teppichgattung immer ein Höhepunkt ihrer Produktion Voraussetzung ist'[25]. The production of these carpets probably began about the middle of the 17th century.

The large numbers (137 examples found) seem to indicate that a large production of these carpets existed at the time. However, the results of diagram 1 cannot fully be transposed into conclusions about the extent of the production. Indeed, although the number of paintings in which these carpets appear is high, only a small number of actual carpets appear to have been used as models. Some individual rugs were portrayed many times by a few artists (compare diagram 1 and 1a).

It is unclear as yet how long the production continued. From the diagrams it could be concluded that the interest in portraying these carpets slacked off in the last quarter of the 17th century. This interest seems to have run concurrently with the demand in the carpet trade for other types of carpets.

fig.110 *Adriaen van der Werff, Portrait of a Gentleman, half length, Wearing a Grey Cloak, in a Landscape, 1680-90. Present location unknown.*

diagram 1a

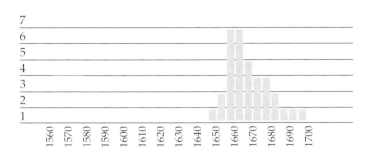

'Scheunemann' carpets in Dutch paintings 1540-1720, classified in five year periods from the earliest known example per painter.

VII
Carpets Related to the 'namenlose Gattung'

Undoubtedly the most important contribution of Brigitte Scheunemann's thesis was her discovery of the exceptional group of carpets discussed in the previous chapter, of which no examples seem to have survived. However, several other groups of carpets that appear to be related to the 'Scheunemann' rugs, and which are also known exclusively from representations in Dutch paintings, apparently escaped her attention.

The highest common factors consist of the coarseness of the weaving structure, the colour scheme (with frequent use of red and orange shades side by side), and of the fact that the weavers of both groups to a greater or lesser extent drew on the same thesaurus of design elements. In general the relatively smaller dimensions also constitute a common factor. Naturally, the discovery of a representation of an individual rug displaying a pattern unknown from any authentic example does not necessarily imply that it is a depiction of an authentic carpet seen by the painter; the pattern may just as well be invented by the artist who, according to his own fancy, may have combined Oriental-like ornaments to form a new whole. Only when several carpets with an identical pattern are found, in paintings by more than one individual artist, does it become possible to hypothesize that a new group has been found. Due to the extensiveness of the present systematic inventarory, there came to light certain unknown groups of such carpets that are found depicted in the work of more than one painter.

Richard Brakenburg, for example, represented a number of carpets characterized by a strongly stylized floral pattern (ei1). In all representations this pattern appears to have been represented rather schematically. Although some individual design elements

fig.111   Richard Brakenburg, Merry Company, 1692. Present location unknown.

are recognizable, it has proved impossible to draw a reconstruction. The floral elements are coarsely drawn and seem to have been placed in the field in a rather arbitrary way; although the represented and recognizable design elements display a clear relationship with Oriental ornaments, in detail they deviate significantly from comparable design elements in preserved contemporary Oriental carpets. The border pattern likewise deviates from those framing familiar 16th/17th century Oriental carpets, in spite of the fact that the individual design elements once again seem to derive from those in authentic Oriental examples.

At first, I assumed that the pattern of the carpets in these representations was invented by Brakenburg himself, possibly due to lack of authentic carpets which could have served him as models. This would explain the coarseness of the drawing and the sketchiness of the representations; in this way the painter could suggest the presence of a pile carpet in the scene without having to recollect actual carpet patterns in their totality from his memory.

However, a representation of a similar carpet in an early work by Michiel van Musscher, *A Scholar in his Studio* (cat.917), suggests the possibility that here we may be concerned with representations of actual carpets. Evidently the lack of detail in the representations is not to be explained solely from the free hand of the painter: Musscher's version does not display detailed ornamentation either. Remarkable in this context is the representation in Brakenburg's *Merry Company* (fig.111). The centre of the field has a large medallion. Around this medallion a band of white volute-shaped ornaments has been placed; these ornaments transect the inner guard border. A similar medallion becomes visible in the field of a carpet in *A Couple Making Music* (cat.888), and in *Lovers in an Interior* (cat.892).

The representations do however allow for a reconstruction of the border pattern, which appears to have a very simple design. It is decorated with repeating S-stems, coarse lotus flowers and diagonally placed stylized palmettes. In the corners we find a simple straight ornament with buds (d18, fig.111,112). The inner guard border has either angular S-shapes (g82c) or an angular meandering vine with tendrils bearing a stylized leaf ornament (g65). When represented in painting, these two roughly similar ornaments can not always be distinguished from each other with certainty. As far as we can establish the outer guard consists of g65 ornaments only. This specific type of pile carpet only occurs in works by Brakenburg, Musscher and Brekelendam. That might be an indication of the fact that examples of this type were not available in large quantities in the Netherlands in the 17th century.

The sketchiness of the representations can presumably be partly explained from the free hand of the painters (Brakenburg also produced sketchy representations of 'Scheunemann' carpets), although in all probability the sketchiness will equally be due to the coarse weaving structure of the carpets under discussion, especially if it were accompanied by a high pile. Evidently the group under discussion is comprised of coarsely woven high-pile carpets with a strongly simplified pattern related to floral carpets from Persia or India.

The earliest representation of the ei2 pattern is found in a work by Willem Duyster (fig.113). In several scenes Duyster painted a carpet with a curious field design, composed of stiff and straight orange floral stems constituting a square or rectangular lattice pattern on a light-red field. These floral stems are usually placed in a horizontal or vertical position; in Eglon van der Neer's *A Lady Playing the Lute in an Interior* however these were placed diagonally, thus forming diamond-shaped compartments (fig.125). On the points of intersection of the stems, and also arbitrarily along the stems, we find simple rosettes formed by a dark blue dot surrounded by orange specks. Equally simple dark blue stylized three-lobed and white-contoured leaves are also placed along these floral stems, usually in mirror-image pairs; such ornaments are placed in radiating fashion around the above-mentioned rosettes. Connecting tendrils have not been represented here by the painters, either because these were absent from the rugs themselves or because they were hardly visible against the background; a separating contour line seems generally not to be used, or in some instances it is formed by white lines. In the middle of each compartment formed by the lattice we find rosettes that are very large in proportion to the compartments they adorn, or large palmettes that are comparatively coarse when compared to related ornaments on

diagram 1

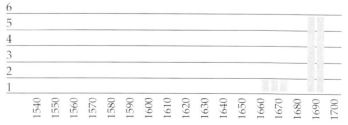

Carpets with the ei1 pattern in Netherlandish paintings 1540-1700.

authentic Oriental carpets. It appears that the painters are not to be blamed here for the crudeness of the ornaments, as identical crude motifs appear in the example in Barent Fabritius' *Portrait of Willem van der Helm with his Wife and Son* (fig.118); clearly visible are the white contour lines of the three-fingered leaves and the large palmette half cut by the border. The field design of the carpet in this family portrait seems at first glance to be rather carelessly represented, but on closer examination appears to be identical to the pattern of the carpet in the painting by Duyster. Clearly these representations must all be fairly reliable.

In 1669 Jan de Bray produced a very impressive group portrait, *The Banquet of Antony and Cleopatra* (presumably a portrait of his family), showing a detailed representation of a carpet with the same field pattern, on top of which large medallions are placed (fig.115). These medallions consist of a star shape, surrounded by a band of volute or spiral motifs. Comparable motifs decorate the edges of the medallions of the above-mentioned rugs depicted by Brakenburg and Brekelendam (ei1; fig.111). The carpet in the painting by de Bray agrees further with those depictions in that the medallions tend to transverse the inner guard border that constitutes the delimitation of the field. The ei2 pattern thus appears to be at least related to the ei1 pattern. If we agree that (a) the ei1 pattern cannot be reconstructed, with the exception of the occasionally-depicted central medallion and certain design elements, and that (b) the ei2 field pattern has many individual design elements in common with the ei1 pattern, then it follows that we cannot rule out the possibility of the ei1 and the ei2 patterns being identical.

The carpet in the family portrait by Barent Fabritius (fig.118), and the previously-mentioned carpet in the genre painting by Eglon van der Neer (fig.125) have an identical border pattern. It consists of a repetitive ornament constructed of eight circles constituting an octagon, between which geometrical rosette shapes have been placed (b75). The rug represented by Willem Duyster has instead a border pattern of large stylized leaves, the veins of which are formed by a stiff tendril (d19). Both this tendril, and the floral stems embellishing the field, display uniform simple rosettes as well as identical small stylized leaves. A fairly coarse pattern of X and O motifs embellishes the inner guard stripe; the outer guard stripe consists of two parallel stripes without decoration. Yet another border pattern is found on the carpet painted by de Bray in 1669, that has what appears to be a variation of the X and O pattern, consisting of large rosettes interposed with geometrical X-shapes. A number of unidentified floral carpets that show decoration systems possibly related to the ei2 pattern appear in paintings dating mainly from the 1660s and 1670s. Jan Verkolje represented in some of his works a rug which corresponds with the other types described in this chapter, in that it is characterized by a stiff pattern, an evidently coarse texture and by the use primarily of relatively light colours such as light red and orange (fig.114). The field exhibits a symmetrical pattern of floral stems bearing lotus flowers and palmettes. The drawing of the pattern vaguely reminds one of some Indian carpets[1], but in detail it diverges from authentic Oriental pieces. The type, which was also represented by Thomas van der Wilt in *A Couple Playing Backgammon* (cat.960), has a large saw-toothed contoured palmette in the centre of the field; the same form

takes a predominant position in the rug in Verkolje's *A Lady at her Toilet* (cat.942). This palmette sends forth a stiff floral stem running parallel to the axis of the carpet to a lotus flower. In his *Portrait of a Naval Officer* (fig.114), the lotus flower is visible in the place where the carpet bends over the edge of the table, close to the hand of the subject; in the painting by van der Wilt, this lotus flower is only partially visible under the black discs of the tric-trac game. Stiffly drawn white-contoured twigs with stylized three-fingered leaves, buds and other ornaments also sprout from the above-mentioned stiff floral stem. In the remainder of the field we find other stiff stems that bear simple ornaments comparable to those on the floral stem running along the vertical axis of the carpet. The former have fairly heavily cast leaves which diverge in form from the elegant lanceolate leaves familiar to us from surviving Persian and Indian carpets. As we have seen in the case of the ei2 carpets, the weavers of these carpets also had a predilection for white contourlines.

The border has a cartouche pattern reminiscent of the cartouches in the border of the 'Scheunemann' carpets in several of Terborch's paintings (d13,[2]). In the centre they display a rosette, from which sprout tendrils bearing a calyx in sideward directions, whereas the tendrils issuing in a vertical direction bear a smaller rosette. The space between the cartouches is filled with lotus flowers pointing in a direction parallel to that of the border, half-traversed by the guard borders. The inner guard ornament has a fairly extensive g46 ornament, which has been represented in a somewhat large scale, possibly as a result of the coarse weaving structure of the original model; it takes more space to draw a specific ornament correctly if a low knot-count is used, than if the weaving is very fine.

The carpet in figure 6 displays reciprocal lily shapes in the outer guard border, each lily displaying two small dots. These were meant to indicate that the sidewards-pointing leaf ornaments slightly curve into the reciprocal ornament; apparently it is due to the coarse weaving that this effect has not been realized in all instances.

Matthijs Naiveu is responsible for two representations of another rather coarse carpet, in *A Family Portrait with a Landscape Beyond* (cat.919), and in *A Scholar in his Studio*, dated 1677 (cat.920). The field seems to have a double system of scrolling floral stems, one in dark blue and the second in orange or yellow. These stems bear large and somewhat clumsily drawn palmettes and lotus flowers, coarse rosettes and smaller lotus flowers that are drawn in a manner reminiscent of North-West Persian ornaments. The latter ornament

diagram 2

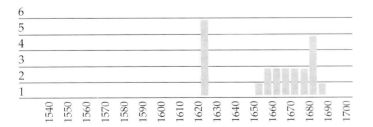

Carpets with the ei2 pattern in Netherlandish paintings 1540-1700.

— composed of four dark leaflets around a white core forming the shape of a butterfly and a three-lobed leaf — is clearly visible in the family portrait, near the woman's elbow. In the other painting such an ornament is seen in the foreground, partly in the shadow of the large fold in the rug and of the book. The other floral motifs however have a drawing which is not found in identical form in surviving carpets. A related carpet in a Dutch painting can be found in a 1699 group portrait by Arnold Boonen, in *The Governors of the Burgerweeshuis* (orphanage) *in Amsterdam* (fig.116). It has a very similar pattern of scrolling floral stems, and the same colour scheme. The palmette in the middle of the field, near the edge of the table, seems identical to the one intersected by the border in Naiveu's family portrait, and also to the palmette in yet another rug, in Backer's *Portrait of Boudewijn Anthony and Antonie de Bordes*, dated 1674 or 1679 (cat.883). The smaller lotus flowers, sketchily represented by Boonen, can be seen at various places in the carpet that Naiveu used as a model, as well as in the group portrait by Backer, where they are very carefully reproduced. Remarkable are the two curved, feather-like ornaments in the latter example, placed symmetrically along the vertical axis of the carpet. They may be related to the characteristic curved 'cluster of wisteria blossoms' which is almost a trademark of some Indian carpets (see p.83).

The large rosette near the shin of the governor sitting at the left in the 1699 portrait by Arnold Boonen looks un-Oriental; it reminds one of the large rosette which plays such an important role in several designs of the carpets described in this chapter, as well as in the 'Scheunemann' design, where it can be found in the heart of the medallions. If we return to the group portrait by Boonen, we see a somewhat distorted, white-contoured floral motif partly hidden from the eyes of the beholder by the folding of the rug, near the legs of the governor sitting at the right hand side on the painting. A similarly distorted white-contoured motif can be seen in what appears to be a meticulously represented carpet in a double portrait by Jan van Rossum, *Jan Willemsz Verbrugge and his Wife* (fig.119). The ornament under discussion can be seen near the large rosette, and is reflected on the other side of the straight stem which may coincide with the axis of the field.

Although straight floral stems are not visible in the carpet in the paintings by Naiveu and Boonen, it seems that we have in the portrait by van Rossum a closely related carpet that is represented with great care. Only in representing the ornaments near the gloves of Jan Verbrugge does the artist seem to have lost some of his concentration. The colour scheme, the frequent use of white or at least light coloured contour lines (see also the above-mentioned group portrait by de Bray) and the presence of the unorthodox large rosette motif are characteristic of the carpets related to the 'Scheunemann' group.

The drawing of decoration of the borders of the rug in Naiveu's portraits described above is highly unusual. The multiple framing has a dark blue or black main border stripe with cruciform green and red medallions (best visible in the scholar's portrait, cat.920) alternating with crude orange star-form rosettes. The medallions

fig.115 Jan de Bray, The de Bray Family as Antony and Cleopatra, 1669. Currier Gallery of Art, Manchester, New Hampshire.

and rosettes are connected by a straight line, partly orange and partly green. From the rosettes sprout four short twigs that run in a diagonal direction, ending in white lily-shaped ornaments, half traversed by the sub-guard stripes. Similar lily-shaped ornaments are found in 'Scheunemann' carpets along the axis of the field attached to the medallion, and equally at the tops of the corner medallion, intersected by the border[3]. The colour palette of the main border of the carpet in the painting by Naiveu is basically identical to that of the d11 borders of the 'Scheunemann' group. Perhaps the relationship can be extended to the pattern of the outer guard stripe, showing an undulating stem with rosettes, leaflets and flowerbuds; it may be an elaborate version of the not entirely satisfactorily reconstructed pattern of the outer guard border of some 'Scheunemann' carpets in paintings by Pieter de Hooch (g88, see fig. p.98). The stiff, geometrically designed inner guard border (g83) seems not entirely appropriate; it is usually found in Anatolian carpets[4]. The rug shown by Naiveu has a double inner guard border, the second one being empty, without any decoration. This emptiness is unusual for Persian and Indian carpets, in which patterns are often characterized by a strict *horror vacui*. A similar feature can be seen in Jan Weenix's *Portrait of Lodewina Schey* (cat.952); it seems to have parallels with the undecorated stripes forming inner guard stripes of the carpets with the ei3 pattern, for example those in paintings by Caspar and Constantijn Netscher (see below).

The particular multiple framing of this type of field pattern has only been found in rugs depicted by Matthijs Naiveu. This could on the one hand mean that the concept does not derive from an authentic example, but that the painter himself may be partially responsible for the combination and realization of the different design elements. On the other hand, Naiveu painted exactly the same ornaments in the borders of the rugs in both *A Family Portrait with a Landscape beyond* and *A Scholar in his Studio*, and also seems to have been fairly consistent in the representation of the field design. Presumably a carpet with such a border design really existed, although it may not have been part of a large production, as specimens of similar rugs are not found in authentic examples or in the works of other artists. The border of the rug in the *Portrait of Boudewijn Anthony and Antonie de Bordes* has S-stems and appears to be identical to the border design of the one in Verkolje's *The Message* (fig.120); the colour scheme of the floral stems and leaves, green against a dark blue or black ground, concurs with that of the d11 border design of the 'Scheunemann' group.

The carpet represented by Arnold Boonen has a border with the stylized floral ornaments characteristic of the 'Scheunemann' rugs represented by, among others, Richard Brakenburg (the d14 or-

fig.116 *Arnold Boonen, The Governors of the Burgerweeshuis (orphanage) in Amsterdam, 1699. Amsterdams Historisch Museum, Amsterdam.*

nament), the prototype for which was found on an unidentified rug with Indian sickle-shaped 'wisteria blossom' ornaments in the field, painted by Arie de Vois in 1680 (cat.950). This raises the question of whether these carpets should for that reason not be attributed to India; the S-border with the heart-shaped leaves (g86) decorating the inner guard border in the paintings by Boonen and de Vois could to some extent support such an attribution. However, aside from the fact that the d14 pattern is a characteristic of 'Scheunemann' carpets, the carpet in the painting by van Rossum has a border pattern also indicating that the origin is to be found in the region where the 'Scheunemann' carpets were designed, as this example shows perhaps the best recorded representation of the d11 border.

That border design, unknown from any surviving Oriental carpet, and found almost exclusively in combination with the 'Scheunemann' pattern, has guard borders with the same g86 design as the carpet in the painting by Boonen; this guard border design is used quite frequently in 'Scheunemann' carpets as well (e.g. J. Voorhout, *Portrait of a Gentleman Seated Full Length by a Table Draped with a 'Turkish' Carpet*, cat.871). The carpet in the van Rossum painting is not unique, as apparently a similar rug was used more than once as a model by Adriaen van der Werff (fig.117) Furthermore, Vermeer included such a carpet in his *Woman with a Water Jug* (cat.948); it apparently has a closely related, if not identical floral pattern. Where the rug bends over the edge of the table we can see the characteristic large rosette, and somewhat to the right the butterfly rosette, far to the right half of the typical palmette. The framing of the field shows a dark blue or black main border stripe with the d11 small leaves in green (somewhat discoloured over time since the painting was made), an inner guard border with z-shaped geometrical motifs (g102) like those in many 'Scheunemann' carpets, and an outer guard border with large S-motifs (g85), which are a characteristic of the borders of the 'Scheunemann' group.

One might in this context refer to a small but remarkable group of carpets with floral field patterns strongly reminiscent of the Persian floral and cloudband type. A clear example can be found in a painting attributed to Cornelis de Man, *A Man Weighing Gold* (fig.121). In contrast to the Persian pattern, the cloudband accompanying the large lotus flower has been only partially drawn; although the coiling ends are clearly visible, the apex of the cloudband is absent. The ends just overlap two large curved ornaments deriving from the double lanceolate leave ornaments adorning some floral-and-cloudband carpets[5]. A carpet in a few paintings by Jan Verkolje shares this remarkable characteristic (fig.120, cat.945 and 946); however, in these paintings the particular ornament does not point outward, but points in the direction of the horizontal axis of the carpet.

Yet another difference between the Persian floral-and-cloudband group and the type under discussion becomes visible in *The Message* (fig.120), and lies in the unusual course of the floral stems and the drawing of the smaller floral ornaments. In the authentic examples the comparable large lotus flowers or palmettes are placed in the tangent planes of two mutually reflective spiraling stems, each of two or three coils. The spiraling movement in these represented examples is much shorter; there are in fact no spirals, but short curved stems filling the vacant space as if forming a second twist of

a spiraling stem. The remarkably narrow main border stripe has a floral pattern seemingly identical to that of some 'Scheunemann' carpets (d17). It has proven impossible to reconstruct the pattern of the outer guard border. However, the narrow subguard near the edge of the carpet has Z-shapes identical to those which regularly occur in the 'Scheunemann' group (g102). Also noteworthy is the embellishment of the inner guard border; it has heart-shaped motifs visible in the g86 ornament, interchanged with Z-forms composed of pairs of triangles. This ornament is known from Indian examples (see fig. p.100). The subguards have a simple zig-zag ornament. Authentic carpets with this type of field pattern (or likewise those with this border pattern) have not come down to us, nor have they been inventarized in paintings from other countries. Presumably we see here a carpet type that is based upon Indian or Persian examples, the field pattern of which has either been misunderstood or misrepresented. Because the inventarized representations occur in a number of paintings made by at least two painters, and because both representations show distinctive characteristics that cannot be explained by the arbitrary whim of the artists (the direction of the palmette), it seems plausible that these representations can be traced back to two authentic and almost identical carpets which these painters must have used as models. The relatively coarse texture, the colour scheme and some of the above-

fig.117 *Adriaen van der Werff, Two Men Playing Chess, 1679. Staatliches Museum, Schwerin.*

fig.118   (left) Carel Fabritius, Willem van der Helm, Municipal Architect of Leyden, 1656. Rijksmuseum , Amsterdam.

fig.119   (below) Jan van Rossum, Portrait of Jan Willemsz Verbrugge and his Wife, 1670. Rotterdams Historisch Museum, Rotterdam.
fig.120   (right) Jan Verkolje, The Message, 1674. Royal Picture Gallery The Mauritshuis, The Hague.

mentioned design elements agree with those found in other types of carpets described in this chapter.

It is possible that Vermeer's somewhat hazily represented carpet depicted in his *Woman with a Water Jug* (should it not directly be related to the ei2 pattern) and the carpet in Ochtervelt's *The Tric-trac Players* (cat.576), showing a carpet with a floral and cloudband design in combination with a d11 border, belong to the same family of variant Eastern carpets. At first, because of the fact that Jacob Ochtervelt painted several 'Scheunemann' carpets with such a border between about 1664 to 1676, and because the carpet in *The Tric-trac Players* has a field design apparently identical to that of the Persian floral and cloudband carpets, it seemed justified to assume that in the latter painting this design was composed by the artist simply using motifs or designs borrowed from various different authentic models. However, since the pictorial sources indicate that in the 17th century Holland was full of carpets with some kind of floral and cloudband patterns, the assumption that Ochtervelt in fact might have had such a remarkable carpet in his studio becomes more credible.

In summary, in this chapter we have so far discussed a group of carpets of which the exact drawing of the pattern cannot be determined: the ei1 group. We have also discussed a group of carpets of which the field pattern alone could not be entirely reconstructed, although the drawing of a great part of the design can be determined in some detail: the ei2 group. The distinction between the two groups may be forced by the limitations of the information included in the pictorial sources, because both groups may present mere variations on the same theme. Finally, we have seen some other unidentified carpets such as the ones in paintings by Backer, Naiveu, van Rossum, van der Werff and Verkolje.

From the organization of this chapter, the reader may already have drawn the conclusion that the author sees a relation between all represented carpets discussed here so far. Indeed, the fact that all examples found present crude variations on the main types of Eastern carpets with floral patterns, and are mutually related in various ways, justifies their presentation in one chapter. This holds true even for the coarse rug that Verkolje and van der Wilt included in their paintings; the predeliction for light colours for the contours of some floral ornaments here constitutes the primary argument. If it is true that all these types are subgroups of a large heterogeneous group of carpets with its origin in the same region, then the fact that most examples found share some characteristics with the 'Scheunemann' group (especially but not exclusively the border patterns) justifies their presentation in this particular chapter.

The field pattern ei3 displays large palmettes, rosettes and other floral design elements, comparable to those occurring in surviving 17th century Oriental carpets. The pattern in general however seems to differ from closely related preserved examples. As far as the representations permit a reconstruction (fig.123), the following picture arises. The pattern consists of broad stems forming octagons; these octagons are used repetitively.

On the points of contact of the octagons, we find a large palmette or a lotus blossom placed in such a way that whenever the ornament points upward on the one vertical side of the octagons, it points

fig.122   Cornelis de Man, A Man Weighing Gold, 1665-75. Present location unknown.

downward on the other vertical side. The same kind of variation becomes visible on the horizontal sides of the octagons. In the heart of each octagon we find a rosette consisting of eight radiating petals within which a star form may be found. From this rosette twigs depart in the four diagonal directions. These twigs end in buds that intersect the oblique sides of the octagon. A late group portrait by Constantijn Netscher, *Three Children in a Window-bay* (cat.934), presents a relatively clear view of this carpet pattern. The painter may well have represented the same carpet as the one used by his father Caspar, some thirty years earlier, in, among others, *Portrait of a Man* (fig.124).

An examination of representations that allow for a study of colour make clear that the colour schemes are rather uniform. The field is red, and the floral ornaments, mainly orange with red parts and small light-blue and white accentuations, do not particularly contrast with their background. The weaving structure is quite coarse.

A representation by Michiel van Musscher (cat.702) displays a variant of the ei3 pattern. The small twigs, which in the ei3 pattern as described above all sprout from the rosettes, are in this version clearly connected to a design element outside the octagon. It seems that we have found the prototype of the ei3 pattern in this painting; a similar pattern decorates the field of a 17th century Indian carpet in the Islamisches Museum in Berlin-Dahlem[6]. The prototypal pattern consists of graceful repetitive S-stems bearing in their tangent planes either a palmette or a lotus flower. The stems split in three smaller twigs at either end, the middle one bearing a rosette or a small lotus flower. The border pattern of the carpet in the painting by Musscher has small sickle-shaped floral ornaments, the

fig.123   *The ei3 field design.*
fig.124   *Caspar Netscher, Portrait of a Man, Wawel, Krakow.*

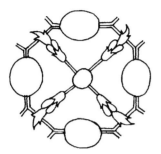

'wisteria blossom', indicating an Indian origin. It could be argued therefore that the discovery of the prototype, apparently an Indian carpet, implies that the origin of the carpets with the ei3 design is therefore to be located in India. The differences between the ei3 and the authentic Indian pattern could be interpreted as resulting from the possibility that the surviving Indian carpets with this pattern and the one painted by Musscher, belong to another subgroup, such as the small group of coarser examples with the ei3 pattern. The existence of patterns closely resembling the ei3 design in later Oriental carpets, represented by a possibly 18th century Khorasan carpet in the Victoria and Albert Museum[7], and a 19th century Central Asian Ersari *chuval* (large wall bag) in The Textile Museum showing the so-called *Mina Khani* design[8], support the possibility of an Oriental origin of the ei3 carpets. Still, the ei3 pattern has so far not been found in contemporary paintings from other European schools. Again, this could be an indication that these coarse carpets were not available outside the Dutch republic.

Border pattern d03 occurs exclusively in combination with the ei3 field pattern. It consists of a meandering floral stem bearing palmettes that are closely related to the palmettes of the d11 pattern (see p.99), as is the case in the carpet represented by Constantijn Netscher (cat.934). A variant is presented by the border pattern of the carpet in Verkolje's *A Portrait of Three Children in a Garden*, showing rotating rosettes instead of palmettes (page 117, fig.121). In Netscher's example, a small tendril sprouts from each palmette top as is the case in the g46 pattern; the tendrils end in open calyxes turned three-quarter to the spectator. Three leaves form the contours while the fourth appears to be in perspective so as to allow a look into the core of the flower. In the case of the carpet depicted by Verkolje we see comparable calyxes, although these have a rather more closed contour. The colour scheme of all examples roughly agrees: dark blue or black for the background, and red, orange, white and light blue for the floral ornaments. The fringes of the carpets can be red, green or white. The guard borders accompanying this type of main border design can be decorated with various patterns. In the carpet in the painting by Verkolje these have S-shapes; the corner solution closely agrees with that in Brigitte Scheunemann's reconstruction of the g84 design of the 'Unbekannte Gattung' (see p.100). These S-shapes have been presented alternately in blue and red against the white background of the inner guard stripe, and presumably orange and dark blue against the light red background of the outer guard stripe. In the guard borders of the carpets represented by Caspar and Constantijn Netscher, floral as well as geometrical ornaments are absent. In these examples the guard borders consist of three parallel lines, respectively orange, white and blue as seen from the main border. Both the absence of any decoration of the guard borders, (uncommon Indian or Persian contemporaneous carpets) and the fact that the d03 border pattern is absolutely unknown from any surviving Oriental carpet, are possibly to be regarded as indications that the place of manufacture of these carpets is not to be found in Persia or India, and perhaps not even in any country in the Orient. The coarseness of the weaving structure might also be an indication in that direction, as such coarseness is a characteristic of the 'Scheunemann' group and the ei1 and ei2 group. However, it must be noted that some of the depicted carpets attributed to India also seem to have a very coarse weaving structure (e.g. Naiveu, *Woman with a Parrot in a Window*, cat.713).

In conclusion, the carpets discussed in this chapter seem not to have had a very fine weaving structure, which can be deduced from the relatively coarse patterning. Some even appear to be of a rather poor quality, presumably with a low knot count and a high pile. The juxtaposition of red and orange in the field, as well as green on a dark blue or black ground in the borders, are of frequent occurrence. These characteristics agree with those of the group described by Brigitte Scheunemann in her dissertation and 1959 article. With the latter group they share two other characteristics: first, no extant examples have been found; and second, all representations of such carpets have been attested in paintings from the Northern Netherlands. Moreover, the carpets described in this chapter and the 'Scheunemann' carpets have various design elements in common, and also exhibit a coarse style of drawing, for which the assumed low knot count cannot be blamed in all cases. Finally, with the exception of the rug in the paintings of Willem Duyster, the datings of both groups approximately agree; the data in diagram 4 roughly concur with those in the diagram visualizing the datings of the paintings showing 'Scheunemann' rugs (see p.106).

It could be argued that both groups have one and the same origin. The question however is, whether the place of production should be located in the Islamic world, or, as I have suggested in respect of the 'Scheunemann' group, in the Dutch Republic. If we were to consider an Oriental origin of these carpets, many arguments for an Indian attribution can be found in the patterns which were used for the decoration. The ei3 pattern can be linked to both Indian and Persian carpets, as we have seen. Other groups discussed above seem to show various variants of Indian design elements such as the curved leaf-ornaments resembling the 'wisteria blossoms,' the geometrical Z-ornaments (g102) or stems with heart-shaped leaves (g86). These ornaments may not be exclusively Indian but they are frequently found in Indian carpets. In the case of the 'Scheunemann' carpets, an Indian origin of the field pattern has been suggested by Charles Grant Ellis (see p.104).

If we adhere to the theory that the latter rugs are domestic products of the Netherlands, it would appear that both the 'Scheunemann' and the related rugs must have been woven in various different workshops producing pile carpets in the Northern Netherlands. This can be concluded from the fact that several subgroups have been recorded in this chapter, some accounting for a larger share of the market, and some of a relatively smaller share, deduced from the fact that some of the subgroups are found more and others less frequently in painting. The 'Scheunemann' group is by far the largest. The workshops where these carpets were produced must have existed side by side in approximately the same period: the second and third quarter of the 17th century. By the last quarter of this century the interest in the depiction of such carpets had clearly decreased, indicating a decline in the interest in these objects and presumably also a decline in production.

diagram 3

Carpets with the ei3 pattern in Netherlandish paintings 1540-1700.

diagram 4

Carpets related to the 'unbekannte Gattung' in Netherlandish paintings 1540-1700.

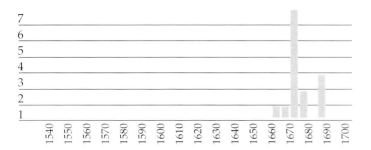

VIII
CONCLUSION

The systematic survey of the pictorial source material from the Netherlands 1540-1700 relating to the study of Oriental carpets has resulted in the cataloguing of about 960 representations. The conclusions available from a survey of this large amount of data have on occasion confirmed or sharpened those of other scholars published in earlier publications. At other times, the conclusions reached here allow us to cast new light on a number of questions of importance to oriental carpet scholarship.

For example: a new dating emerges for the group of 'Lotto' carpets, and the conclusions of earlier studies concerning the subgroups were sharpened (p.31). New information was also found relating to the study of Smyrna carpets (p.53) and Transylvanian rugs (p.49). Representations were found of groups of carpets for which no pictorial sources were previously known, such as the Moghul carpets from the Lahore group (p.80) and the 'Portuguese' carpets; (p.81) and furthermore the amount of source material relating to other groups has been enlarged.

Finally, we have suggested that certain groups of carpets documented in paintings have not survived in any authentic examples. Further, perhaps significantly, clear depictions of Caucasian carpets were not found in any of the thousands of paintings surveyed.

FLEMISH AND DUTCH PAINTINGS

Although Flemish painters such as Brueghel, van Balen, Rubens, van Dyck and Jordaens represented many pile carpets in their paintings, the major part of the depictions of paintings listed in this study were made in the Northern Netherlands during the Golden

fig.126 left: Jan Steen, The Seduction. Museum Bredius, The Hague.
fig.127 right: Gerrit Horst, Isaac's Blessing of Jacob. Dulwich Picture Gallery, London.

Age. Dutch genre paintings in particular provided a large number of examples. Gabriel Metsu, for example, included several fine examples of minutely depicted floral and cloudband carpets in his works and even a silk 'Polonaise' rug, as well as 'Lotto' rugs which he for some reason, in contrast to his meticulous rendering of the floral carpets, depicted only in a very sketchy fashion. The main contribution of Gerard Terborch to the study of pile carpets is the large number of 'Scheunemann' carpets in his paintings, and the related carpet in his portrait of Pieter de Graeff (cat.941). His representation of a large Medallion Ushak is, like the more colourful version by Jacob van Oost (cat.220), one of the finest to be found in Netherlandish paintings (cat.226).

The number of careful depictions of 'Scheunemann' carpets in the works of Jan Steen makes him one of the most important contribu-

tors to the conclusions drawn in this study, notwithstanding the fact that Jan Steen's favourite subject was interiors of less than surpassing tidiness. It must be admitted that in Steen's allegories of slovenly housekeeping the carpets look quite worn, but this observation only confirms the assumption that he depicted his models with great care. Also interesting is the red-with-ochre variant Ushak Double-niche rug, which likewise shows signs of wear, that Steen showed several times in his work.

Pieter de Hooch can be named as well in this respect, as he represented a 'Scheunemann' carpet quite frequently, and also depicted two different Smyrna rugs (cat.308,309), a Medallion Ushak (cat.212), a fine Transylvanian prayer rug (cat.259), a 'Lotto' rug with a cloudband border (cat.100) and at least two different types of floral carpets from Persia or India (cat.427,428).

Floral carpets are found repeatedly in paintings by Bol and de Hooch, but no painter seems to have been as loyal to his model as Willem Kalf, who included the same type of floral carpet in most of his paintings recorded in this study.

With all of this focus on Dutch painting, we should not fail to note that some very important information on carpets was found in Flemish paintings, like the Persian carpet in works of Jacob van Oost (cat.591,592) and the Indian carpet in paintings by Jordaens (cat.687,688). Of special importance are the early Flemish paintings from the 14th and 15th centuries, which are not included in the present study for reasons explained in the Introduction (Chapter I). The carpets in those paintings, showing early Anatolian patterns, could perhaps be the subject of another study in combination with the study of early pile carpets in 14th-16th century Italian paintings.

From the pictorial sources, it seems clear that 16th and 17th century Netherlandish painters often used some rugs as studio props, which accounts for the repetition of similar types in their works. An unexpected side-effect of this fact is that in some instances paintings may be attributed to a certain painter on the basis of the carpet included in the painting (e.g. cat.684). This is not to say that the artists, or even the people who commissioned a painting, actually must have possessed the carpets which are represented. An interesting note was found recently by Prof. Willemijn Fock of the University of Leyden, in the municipal archives of Leyden, saying *Aen Abram Pietersen betaelt voor 5 weecken drie dagen huer voor een cleed voor Frer Nicolaes groote schilderij ƒ 3.6.-.* In this note a Johannes Spilleurs apparently registered that on April 8th, 1645 a payment was made for the rent of a carpet which was to be represented in the portrait of his brother Nicolaes Spilleurs the Younger, an Amsterdam merchant[1].

CARPETS IN INTERIORS

As already remarked briefly in the Introduction, represented rugs are usually found on tables. It is unusual to find carpets in Netherlandish paintings used in other locations in domestic interiors. If so, they are usually found in portraits showing the portrayed individual in full length, where the carpets are used on the floor to denote the social status of the subject (e.g. cat.216); these representations hardly show the carpets as they were commonly used. It is true that some representations show carpets on the floor in genre

paintings as well, for example under a canopied bed which usually is richly draped with costly curtains. One such an example appears in Emmanuel de Witte's *Interior with a Woman at a Clavichord* (about 1665) in the collection of the State-owned Art Collections Department in The Hague[1a], cf. cat.668; see also a design from Daniel Marot's *Nouveaux livre de paramens inventee et gravee par D.Marot, architecte de sa Majesté Britannique*, about 1690, showing the ideal of a stately formal bed placed on a richly decorated carpet[2]. In these paintings the bed in the picture seems not only to be represented as a comfortable place to spend cold nights, but probably bears a deeper significance as well. Such a significance is clear enough in scenes depicting lovers or a doctor's visit; in other scenes the bed has yet another social function, as a representative piece of furniture; the carpet on the floor in these interior scenes has the same function as the carpets which can be seen laying on the floor in several full-length portraits. *Een Turcx aerttapyt*, mentioned in a 17th century Antwerp inventory, may possibly have been used in this manner[3]; *Een Turckx ofte Persiaens tapijt onder 't ledicant leggende* was certainly used under a bed[4].

The source material found in 17th century inventories confirms the supposition that Oriental carpets were mainly used on tables and other pieces of furniture. Carpets are usually described as *Een Turcx tafelcleet* (a Turkish table carpet,[5]) or somewhat more elaborate *Eene herthouten uttreckende tafele met een Turcx tafelcleet dairoppe* (a hardwood draw-out table covered by a Turkish tablecloth,[6]). Sources mentioning any other mode of use of an Oriental carpet are exceptional. An Antwerp inventory dating from 1617 mentions some carpets which were kept in a trunk, the first in the list being *Een slecht Turcx tapyt dienende tot buffet* (an ordinary Turkish carpet which is used on the buffet,[7]). The pictorial sources provide some rare representations of carpets used in this way, such as van Balen's *The Feast of the Gods* (cat.32), and van de Velde's *Musical Party* (cat.187). The second carpet in the same list was *Een ander Turcx tapyt lanc twee ellen dryquart dienende totte dagelyckschen tafel* (another Turkish carpet ... for daily use on the table), and the third *Noch een Turcx tapyt daerop de vrouwen gewoonlyc syn te sitten lanc vier ellen* (another Turkish carpet ... which is used by the women to sit on (representations of carpets used in this way could not be found).

In a few instances a carpet was found depicted draped over a bed. Charles Grant Ellis assumed in these paintings a use as a counterpane for expected seduction[8], a view that could very well be supported by the depiction in Jan Steen's *The Seduction* (fig.126) — however as an exception rather than as a rule. In *The Blessing of Isaac* by Gerrit Horst (fig.127) as well as in the version by Jan Victors (cat.192), a carpet was used on the bed presumably merely to add an Oriental touch to the scene. There are no 16th or 17th century sources, either written or pictorial that convincingly indicate that pile carpets were used regularly as adornments of beds.

PLACE OF PRODUCTION

Most entries in written sources mentioning carpets describe these as Turkish carpets. The adjective 'Turkish' is not in all instances to be accepted literally; the 16th and 17th century officials and clerks who drew up the inventory lists can hardly be expected to have been specialists in the field of attributing pile carpets to the various weaving centres in the Orient. Presumably the term *Turcx* was the common adjective used to describe a pile carpet with an Oriental pattern (see e.g. p.21); the first Oriental rugs traded in bulk to the West were produced in Turkey and the later pieces, i.e. the Persian and Indian carpets, were often transported over land to Turkish cities and traded to the West from there. Resident Warnerus' report from 1663, quoted twice before (p.15), describes the land route of goods from India to Istanbul: *...carrowanen (...) dewelcke (...) uyt Parsia comen, niet alleen met Parsiaensche, maar oock veel met Indiaensche goederen, welcke Indiaensche goederen ten deele ter zee over de schala van Bender Abaes gebracht warden, ende vandaer in vier en twintigh daeghen in Spahan, ende van Spahan binnen vier maenden in Constantinopolen. Ten deele warden gememoreerde goederen uyt Cadich oock over landt door de passagie van de gerenommeerde stadt Candehaer gebracht, vanwaer se vorder in Spahan binnen veertigh daegen worden vervoert; genoemde wegh wort van de coopluyden -om minder oncosten- veel gefrequenteert in tijt van stilstant van wapenen tusschen de Parsiaensche ende Indiaensche coningen (...). Vorder warden de Indiaensche goederen oock over Basra gebracht, alwaer voorleden jaer de Engelsche met ses gehuyrde Turcxe schepen met commertie sijn gearriveert; welcke goederen vandaer in veertigh dagen door de rivier Euphrath in Babylonia, en van Babylonia in sooveel tijt in Aleppo, en van Aleppo in Constantinopolen in gelijcke veertigh daegen overgevoert warden. Noch compt hier oock Indiaensch goet over Mucha, haven van 't landt Jemen...*[9]: Indian as well as Persian commodities were transported to Constantinople. Indian goods over sea to Bandar Abbas, and then via Isfahan, or over land via

fig.128 Gabriel Metsu, A Young Woman Composing Music, c. 1667. Royal Picture Gallery The Mauritshuis, The Hague.

Candahar to Isfahan and thence to Constantinople. Another route is via Basra and over river Euphrat to Aleppo and from there to Constantinople, or even via Mocha.

Apparently not only Turkish, but also Persian and Indian merchandise was available in Istanbul, albeit in 1663 not as much as in previous times; the record begins with the remark *De Turcxe carrowanen sijn oock niet soo frequent als voor desen, van dewelcke nu omtrent twintigh in 't jaer uyt Parsia comen...*[10]: Of these caravans, nowadays only twenty reach Constantinople each year....

At any rate, in the 20th century the denotation 'Persian carpet' is in the Netherlands most commonly used for any pile carpet from the Orient, just as in the everyday nomenclature of the seventeenth century in the Low Countries, 'Turkish carpet' seems to have been synonymous with 'Eastern pile carpet'. Supporting this is a 17th century description of *Een zyden Turcx tafelcleet* (a silk Turkish tablecloth,[11]); 17th century Turkish carpets with a silk pile are not known, although it must be admitted that the inventory could refer to an original silk cloth from Anatolia; Godfried Schalcken represented a beautiful and precious Ottoman silk with metal brocadings in his *Portrait of a Family Making Music* [11a]. Another such enigmatic rug appears in an entry in a 1632 inventory of the Stadholder's quarters in The Hague: *Een houten tafel met een Turcx tapijt met gout ende silver gemengt*[12]; it may have been a 'Polonaise' rug from Persia or India. Naturally, it is also possible that the observations of the notaries who made up the inventory lists were otherwise incorrect. Sometimes descriptions are found like this one: *Twee Persiaense tapyt tafelcleen: d'een tot tafel, d'ander tot dressoor*[13]. This geographical adjective may well be dependable, as the author of this inventory made a distinction between these two carpets and the *Turcx aerttapyt* mentioned before[14].

Even India is sometimes mentioned as the place of production of a carpet, as in a 1617 inventory: *Een Indiaensch tapyt oft tafelcleet lanc dry ellen* which is followed in the list by *Een ander tafelcleet Turcx lanc vier ende een half ellen*[15]; in these instances the geographical description may have been correct. A complicating fact is that the adverb *Indiaensch* was at times also used to denote everything imported from 'pagan' countries. But even if it was not, the entry seems to prove that India was known in the Netherlands as a regular producer of carpets next to Anatolia and Persia as early as 1617. This is quite early indeed, given the fact that the date of the earliest representation of an Indian carpet found in Netherlandish painting is about 1620 (see p.96, diagram a). At this early date the trade in Indian goods by sea was mainly in the hands of the Portuguese; the English and the Dutch East India companies only started to expand their actions to India in the 1620s. At that time the proportion of carpets from Persia and India traded to the Netherlands must have grown considerably. As for the conclusions of the study of Indian carpets in Netherlandish paintings (p.96; see also the diagram below), we see that India was an important producer of floral carpets in the 17th century as well, and that substantial numbers of these carpets made their way to the Netherlands.

THE DEVELOPMENT OF PATTERNS AROUND 1600

The 16th and 17th century pictorial sources show little of a chronological development of carpet patterns. Only a relatively small number of chronologically significant subgroups of carpets have been found, that show those small stylistic characteristics that may allow for some sort of chronologic conclusions. Apparently in the period under study the largest part of the production was concentrated in professional workshops weaving for the export markets, using successful stereotyped patterns. The earlier centuries of carpet production were apparently artistically more creative periods, as is suggested by the few studies presently available dealing with Oriental carpets in 14th/15th century Italian paintings. During the 15th century several new types of carpets were invented that appear in many Western paintings. The paintings themselves, as opposed to the carpets, appear however to be of significantly later date in many instances; the Medallion Ushak and 'Lotto' carpets, the Star Ushaks and Double-niche Ushak carpets appear in painting at a considerably later date than the generally accepted dates of the invention of their patterns in the court workshops[16]. The development of the floral and cloudband design also seems to have reached a final stage some time before the first example is recorded in a Western painting (1598, cat.343).

Still, the Cairene Ottoman carpets and the so-called 'Transylvanian' carpets are examples of types included in Netherlandish paintings relatively shortly after the design is assumed to have been invented. Some of the earliest examples recorded in these Netherlandish paintings were apparently represented at breakpoints in the stylistic developments of the carpet patterns. For example, 'Lotto' carpets with cartouche-borders appear for the first time in Flemish and Dutch pictures, whereas 'Lotto' carpets with kufic borders are seldom found in Netherlandish painting; the latter border design ran apparently out of fashion at the time these carpets were starting to be regularly depicted in the Netherlands. The final stage in the stylistical development of the larger part of these carpet patterns may therefore have preceded their earliest appearance in Flemish and Dutch paintings.

In Persian and Anatolian carpets in 16th century (mostly Italian) paintings this stage had not yet been reached; the examples in late 16th and 17th century paintings are mostly stereotyped simpler examples or show only slight variations on the classical themes. It would however be too extreme to assume that the finer of such carpets were therefore all woven during the 16th century or earlier, or that, in the case of Persia, from the time Shah Abbas the Great started to stimulate the export of pile carpets early in the 17th century, only relatively simple examples were produced. The Flemish and Dutch painters depicted mainly those carpets which were easily accessible to them; undoubtedly these were the average types of carpets commonly found in commerce, which offered the largest profit to the East-India companies and which must have been present in the Netherlands in the largest numbers. More costly and elaborate examples were certainly also produced contemporaneously, and may consequently have been traded to the West as well, but most likely in far smaller numbers. It is not surprising, therefore, that these richer pieces are relatively far less often found in Western paintings; an excellent example of the phenomenon is the case of the so-called 'Polonaise' carpets in Netherlandish paintings (p.67f). For all these reasons, carpets showing a richer design should therefore not necessarily be dated as relatively early examples, simply because late 16th or 17th century Western paintings

only show the somewhat simpler variants. Another example is the carpet production in India, which started as late as the end of the 16th century. In the course of the 17th century, some very fine pieces were woven in India, the best of which were decorated with naturalistically executed representations of flowering plants (see p.80), but at the same time India seems to have produced massive quantities of relatively cheap carpets with stereotyped designs. The Western tradesman could order them woven as fine or as coarse as they liked: *soo fijn en groff als men begeert* (see p.78).

Many fine-quality Indian carpets were represented in Netherlandish paintings, some of which even show representations of animals in the field (e.g. cat.731,732); coarser carpets with typically Indian design elements have also been found (e.g. cat.713). It only seems logical to assume that in other weaving centres Western merchants could also have purchased very fine pieces with carefully drawn patterns as well as the ordinary examples that formed the bulk of their commercial efforts.

FLORAL CARPETS: INFORMATION FROM THE PICTORIAL SOURCES

Unfortunately, the attribution of carpets to certain weaving areas is not as certain as one would expect from comparing the designs of the floral carpets discussed in Chapters IV, V and VII. In Chapter V we discussed carpets that in their decoration system show ornaments suggesting Indian origins for the designs. As we have seen, this does not exclude the possibility that carpets with floral patterns of which only a small part is represented in a particular painting may have been erroneously included in Chapter IV (Persian carpets), even though the actual carpets used as models may have had distinctively Indian design elements in parts of their patterns that were, for whatever reason, not represented by the painter. In other words, the line dividing the sections of Persian and Indian carpets in the diagram is not as secure as the diagram suggests. Moreover, the line dividing the sections of the Indian carpets and the carpets relating to the 'Scheunemann' type (Chapter VII) becomes somewhat blurred when we realize that many examples of the latter group also bear Indian design elements in their decoration. (cf. e.g. cat.952). Perhaps the conclusion drawn in Chapter V, stating that 'it seems plausible that nearly a third of the carpets used as models by Dutch and Flemish painters originated from Indian workshops' should be reconsidered; perhaps the share of Indian carpets in 16th and 17th century Netherlandish painting was larger than that. Things appear even more complicated if we compare a carpet with Indian design elements in *Portrait of Copes van Hasselt* by Abraham van den Hecken (cat.682) to a similar surviving carpet[17]. In a short article written on the occasion of the 1988 Maastricht exhibition *Carpets in 17th Century Netherlandish Paintings*, Ian Bennett attributed the surviving carpet to Persia, despite the Indian motifs in its pattern, and noted that the actual rug also contains ornaments drawn in the Persian style as well[18]. The characteristics of this particular carpet thus indicate that commercially successful types were quite likely copied carefully in other, perhaps distant weaving areas, and consequently these copies were represented in paintings, such as the carpet in the painting by van den Hecken. Similar authentic examples are a 'Lotto' carpet that we have tentatively attributed to Eastern Europe[19] and a Medallion Ushak carpet sometimes said to have been woven in Poland[20]. Such carpets, if represented by painters, would undoubtedly have been attributed in this publication without comment *ad hoc*. This problem demonstrates therefore the complexity of the question of the attribution of some of the carpets in Netherlandish and other paintings. This question remains especially unanswered in the case of the 'Scheunemann' carpets (Chapter VI) and the related group (Chapter VII), as it is not even certain if the place of production was located in the Orient or in Europe itself. In the case of the related group, some may suggest an Anatolian[21], Persian[22] or Indian origin (see p.115f). However, the subject of this study is limited to the pictorial sources on the one hand and the carpet patterns on the other hand, and the pictorial sources maintain a stony silence as to the actual provenance of the rugs, as they do to the finer details of technique and the exact nature of dyestuffs. It is therefore often hazardous to attribute carpets to a certain weaving area on the basis of their pattern alone. At any rate, it is too early to interpret the *oranje/blanje/bleu* colour scheme of the inner guard border of the ei3 carpets (see p.119) as representations of the Dutch flag at the time of the Republic of the Seven United Provinces!

THE WRITTEN SOURCES

In the sections of the Conclusion directly above, and also in some of the preceding chapters, we have quoted written sources from archives of the East-India companies and Netherlandish inventory lists. These sources can add useful information to the results of the study of the pictorial sources, and vice versa. This was especially apparent in the study of Indian carpets in paintings. Still, not much attention has been given to the Western documentary source materials. The reason for this can easily be deduced from the sources quoted in this study; usually these sources include only brief descriptions of carpets which seldom allow identification of the type.

As we have seen, a carpet described in an inventory as *Turcx* may have been woven anywhere. This vagueness of the written sources

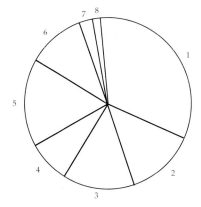

Schematic representation of the relative share of individual carpet types in Netherlandish painting, 1540-1700. 1. Carpets attributed to Persia; 2. Carpets with Indian design elements; 3. Unidentified carpets of the 'Scheunemann' type; 4. Unidentified carpets related to the 'Scheunemann' type. 5. Anatolian carpets with 'Lotto' design; 7. Other Anatolian carpets; 8. Mamluk and Cairene Ottoman carpets; 9. 'Chessboard' rugs.

is especially regrettable in the case of the carpet types that could possibly be attributed to Occidental, rather than Oriental workshops (Chapters VI and VII). It would be most desirable to find 17th century sources in Dutch municipal archives indicating locations where pile carpets were being produced, parallel to the 16th century Flemish source proving that pile carpets were woven in Antwerp: *Car la se font (...) des tapis de Turquie ou imitez tels*[23]. The chances that similar entries will be found in Dutch archives are unlikely, unfortunately. Such a source would have to come to light by accident, but it is not very likely that such a happy event will happen. The Dutch word for carpet is identical to that for tapestry: *tapijt*. A crucial documentary entry may for that reason remain unrecognized even when it falls into the hands of the researcher.

RELATION BETWEEN THE PICTORIAL SOURCES AND SURVIVING ORIENTAL CARPETS

The results of this study of carpets in Flemish and Dutch paintings have emerged after exhaustive reference to materials relating to the study of surviving carpets from the 16th and 17th century available to the author from various public and private collections. On one level, the applicability of the results of this study will be judged by the usefulness of the pictorial sources presented here relative to the art historical study of surviving authentic carpets. Eventually it may perhaps be possible to compare the results published in this study with those of systematic studies of individual groups of carpets from this period. The model presented in the dissertation of Dr.Friedrich Spuhler, including a list of all 'Polonaise' carpets known in 1968, deserves to be followed by other scholars[24]. Similar systematic studies of surviving Persian and Indian carpets, as well as carpets from other weaving areas, might result in conclusions that could be compared to those of the present study of carpets in paintings.

It can be expected that the conclusions of future studies will to a certain extent concur with those formulated in this study, but they will undoubtedly also differ in some aspects: the pictorial sources listed in the present study are all of Flemish or Dutch origin, whereas almost all surviving 16th and 17th century carpets have been preserved in countries other than Holland and Belgium. Still, the combination of a systematic study of carpets in paintings and future systematic research of surviving pieces may result in important conclusions about matters such as trade relations, datings, and provenance. As already mentioned, only a tiny fraction has been preserved of the thousands of Oriental carpets that must have been traded to the Netherlands in the 16th and 17th century; the representations of over nine hundred pile carpets recorded here in Flemish and Dutch paintings only afford us a glimpse of the enormous numbers of these costly items of luxury that must have been present at one time in the houses, palaces, corporation halls and churches of the Netherlands. Unfortunate as the loss of these carpets may be, the Flemish and Dutch painters nevertheless show us an imposing record of the carpets that were once present in the Low Countries, in all their variety and richness.

fig.129 North-West Persian carpet, Staatliche Museen, Islamisches Museum, Berlin.

CATALOGUE

In this Catalogue most of the
illustrations show details of the
paintings in order to represent
the depicted carpets more clearly.
The dimensions mentioned in the
text however refer to the size of
the complete painting.

EGYPTIAN CARPETS

1
Unknown Flemish artist

Portrait of Prince Philip in 1587
Prado, Madrid
17th century
121 x 83 cm

(di1)

The painting is presumably a
copy after an unknown 16th
century original. Prince Philip is
standing on a carpet with the
characteristic lobed medallions of
the Mamluk group in the main
border.

1a
Unknown artist, French school
The Three de Coligny Brothers
Royal Picture Gallery The
Mauritshuis, The Hague, on loan
to municipal museum Het
Prinsenhof, Delft.
c. 1555
191 x 163 cm
Literature: Ydema 1984, p.24-25

di1

1b
Unknown artist, English school
*Portrait of a Man, presumed to be
Adam Duff of Clunyberg*
Private collection, England
1590-1620
Literature: Beattie 1964, p.8; ill.3

di1

1c
Unknown artist, English school
*Portrait of a Lady, presumed to be
the wife of Adam Duff of Clunyberg*
Sale Sotheby's London, 13/12/
78, Lot 37
126 x 100 cm

di1

2
Balen, H. van and Brueghel, J.

Bacchanal
Bayerische
Staatsgemäldesammlungen, Alte
Pinakothek, Munich
1615-20
42 x 70 cm
Literature: Ydema 1989, p.302-
303

d221; d222 (di2)

2a
Baschenis, E. (circle of)
Still-life with Musical Instruments
Sale Christie's London 12-7-1985,
Lot 132
c. 1670
89.5 x 127 cm
See illustration p.24

di2/d222

2b
Bassano, L.
Portrait of a Man with a Statuette
Coll. H.M. The Queen of England
c. 1592
Literature: White, cat.29

di1?

2c
Bassano, L.

Portrait of Daniel Hopfer II
Fairfax Murray sale, Berlin,
November 1929
c. 1595
Literature: Mills 1981, nr.A6

di1

2d
Bassano, L.
Portrait of Alvisi Corradini
Museo Civico, Padua
c. 1601
Literature: Mills 1981, nr.A7

di1

2e
Bassano, L.
Portrait of a Lady
Sale Sotheby's London 13/12/78
Lot 37
c. 1610
Literature: Mills 1981, nr.A5

di1

2f
Bassano, L.

Portrait of an Unknown Man
Sale Finarte (Milan) 3/11/82, Lot
46
85 x 67 cm

1590-1610

di1

2g
Bellini, G.
*The Doge Loredan and Four
Advisers* (or 4 family members)
Sale Nemes, Munich 16/6/31
Lot 24
1507
Literature: Mills 1981, nr.A1

di1

3
Bronckhorst, G. van de

*Merry Company with a Girl Playing
the Lute*
Herzog Anton Ullrich-Museum,
Braunschweig
c. 1625
141 x 205.7 cm

di2/d222

3a
Champaigne, Ph. de

*The Mayor and the Municipal
Council of the City of Paris*
Louvre, Paris
1648

di2

4
Codde, P.

The Lute Player
Philadelphia Museum of Art,
Philadelphia
c. 1650
35.3 x 44.3 cm

di2/d221

5
Finsonius, L.
Annunciation
Present whereabouts unknown.
c. 1612
175 x 218 cm
See illustration p.20

di2/d221

6
Francken, A.
The Last Supper
Koninklijk Museum voor Schone
Kunsten, Antwerp
1570
245 x 270 cm
See illustration p.20

di1

7
Gijsbrechts, C.

Still-life with a Servant
Present location unknown
1657

di2/ig121,og121

Cf. Pagnano nr.29

8
Janssens, A.

Triptychon of the Schildersambacht
(Painter's Guild) *in Mechelen*
St.Romboutskathedraal,
Mechelen
c. 1620
293 x 248 cm

di1

9
Lundens, G.
Portrait of Joris van Oorschot
Foundation Familiefonds Boreel,
The Netherlands
1656
51 x 46 cm
Literature: Haarlem 1986, cat.34

di2/d222

10
Lundens, G.
Portrait of the Wife of Joris van Oorschot
Foundation Familiefonds Boreel,
The Netherlands
1656
51 x 46 cm
Literature: Haarlem 1986, cat.34

di2/d222

10a
Moretto, A. (attr. to)
Portraits of Young Ladies of the House of Martinengo
Palazzo Martinengo-Salvadego,
Brescia
1542 or earlier
Literature: Mills 1981, nr.A2

di1

10b
Moroni, G. (attr. to)
Portrait of a Man
Sale Drouot, Paris 18/12/20
c. 1550
Literature: Mills 1981, nr.A3

di1

11
Mijtens, D.

Portrait of Nicolo Morino
Coll. Lord Sackville, Knole, Kent
1622
215 x 137 cm
Literature: Brussels 1973, cat.42

di2

12
Mijtens, D.
Portrait of Charles, Prince of Wales
Coll. Mrs. P.A. Tritton, Parham
Park, Pulborough, West Sussex
1623
182,5 x 140 cm
See illustration p.25

di2/d222?

13
Palamedesz, A.
Portrait of an Unknown Woman
Wallraf-Richartz Museum,
Cologne
1665
112 x 89.5 cm
Literature: cat. 1986, p.70,
Abb.378

di2?/d222?/ig12,og12

It is uncertain if the rug in this
painting belongs to the Ottoman
Cairene group, as only a small
part is represented and the
pattern is not rendered in a
careful way.

13a
Palma (Giovane), J.
Venus and Cupid
Coll. H.M. The Queen of England
c. 1590
Literature: White cat.174

di1?

14
Rubens, P. or Dyck, A. van
Portrait of a Lady, Member of the Imperial Family, with her Grand-child
Sale van Diemen, Berlin 26/4/
35,Lot 81
c. 1620
215 x 130 cm

di1

15
Rubens, P. and Brueghel, J.

Christ in the House of Mary
Dublin, National Gallery of
Ireland
1610-20

di2/d222

15a
Tintoretto, J. or Tintoretto, D.
The Doge Pietro Loredan Praying for the End of Famine
Palazzo Ducale, Venice
1581-4
Literature: Mills 1981, nr.A4

di1

16
Venne, A. van der

Geckie met de Kous
Museum Narodowe, Warsaw
c. 1630
54 x 75 cm

di2/d221

17
Vonck, E.
Portrait of an Elderly Couple
Private collection, Germany
c. 1640
30 x 35 cm
Literature: Hali IX (34), p.6,
Ydema 1988, p.20
See illustration p.24

di2/d222

For the field design compare the
Tucher von Simmelsdorf Cairene
rug (Ydema 1988, ill. p.21)

LOTTO CARPETS

18
Unknown, possibly Flemish artist
Portrait of a Man
Present location unknown
1598
Literature: Mills 1981, nr.21

aiv3/a7

19
Unknown Dutch painter

Portrait of an Unknown Man
Foundation Bakker, Amsterdam
1511
49.5 x 38.5 cm

aiv3

Cf. Dimand/Mailey fig. 162

20
Unknown Flemish painter
Portrait of Jean de Muelnaere
Begijnhof, Bruges
1670
91.5 x 71.3 cm

aiv2

21
Unknown Dutch Painter
Portrait of a Man at a Table
Louvre, Paris
c.1640
See illustration p.36

aiv2/a93

For the pattern of the inner guard
border see Elias, *Portrait of a Man
aged 34.* The carpet has a dark
blue field.

22
Aldewerelt, H. van
Portrait of a Family
Sale Mak van Waay Amsterdam
12/4/21-1
1664
196 x 155 cm

a2/g14 (aiv)

23
Baen, J. de (attr. to)

Portrait of Mr. Jacob de Witt
Museum Mr. Simon van Gijn,
Dordrecht
c.1670
130 x 102 cm

aiv/a6/ig10 (aiv2)

Sketchy representation.

24
Backer, J.
Bacchus and Ariadne
Present location unknown
1643
85.1 x 153.7 cm
Literature: Sumowski II, p.214

aiv/a6/g14

25
Balen, H. van
Fire (War)
Sale Gerhardt Berlin 10/11/11-35
1610-20

aiv2/a2/g14

Small carpet. The outer guard has
no ornaments.

26
Balen, H. van
Moses Beats the Rock
Museum, Pommersfelden
1610-20
62 x 92 cm
Literature: cat. 1894, nr.17

aiv2/a2

27
Balen, H. van and Brueghel, J.
Herse and her Servants
Gemäldegalerie, Kassel
1610-20
28 x 21 cm
Literature: Schnackenburg pl.5

aiv3/a2/g14

Sketchy representation of the
field design and unusual
drawing of the cartouche pattern
in the border. The painter may
have worked from a preparatory
study without having the original
carpet in his studio.

28
Balen, H. van and Brueghel, J.
Spring
Bayerische Staats Gemälde
Sammlungen, Munich
1616
56 x 84

aiv2/a2/g14,og41

The field and the main border are
separated by a barber-pole
ornament.

29
Balen, H. van and Brueghel, J.
Winter
Bayerische Staats Gemälde
Sammlungen, Munich
1616
56 x 84 cm
Literature: H. Rudolph in:
Festschrift W. Pinder p.423, ill.6

aiv2/a2/g14

Cf. the same artist's *Spring.* The
carpet is draped over the buffet.

30
Balen, H. van

The Baptism of Christ
Sale Sotheby's London 22/2/84-
66
1610-20
140 x 201 cm

aiv3

The rug is used as a kind of
garment by a putto.

31
Balen, H. van
Collecting the Manna
Herzog Anton Ullrich Museum,
Braunschweig
1610-20
166 x 241 cm

aiv (aiv3)

32
Balen, H. van
The Feast of the Gods
The Dayton Art Institute, Dayton,
O.
1610-20
55 x 93 cm
Literature: New Orleans 1963,
cat.14

aiv

On the buffet. Both the field and
the border have a red ground.

33
Balen, H. van
The Wedding of Peleus and Thetis
Koninklijk Museum voor Schone
Kunsten, Brussels
1615-25
54.2 x 76 cm

aiv/a2/g14?

34
Berckheyde, J.
Man Preparing Dyes
Museum der Bildenden Künste,
Leipzig
1670-80
33.5 x 27.5 cm
Literature: cat. 1959, nr.988, p.56

aiv

Apparently an unusually coarse
piece. The border pattern cannot
be identified.

35
Berckheyde, J.
A Self-portrait
Uffizi, Florence
1675
36 x 30.7 cm
Literature: Amsterdam 1984,
p.224 afb.a

aiv

Cf. id. *Man Preparing Dyes.*

36
Bisschop, C.
A Young Man and a Cavalier
Metropolitan Museum of Art,
New York
1660-70

aiv/a6

37
Bloemaert, H.

Allegory of Winter
Mrs. Bruel Dumphail
(Morayshire) 1953
1631
104.1 x 83.8 cm

aiv

38
Bloemaert, H.
Winter
Present location unknown
1631
81 x 98 cm
Literature: Amsterdam (Rijks-
museum) 1918, nr.526

aiv

cf. id. *Allegory of Winter*

39
Bloemaert, H.
A Smiling Girl Pickpocketing
Sale Christie's London 2/12/77-6
1632
127 x 103 cm

aiv/a2?

The cartouches in the main
border are diamond-shaped.

40
Boel, P.
Still-life with Animals
Sale Fievez Brussels 17/5/23-6
c.1660
118 x 171 cm

a92 (aiv)

41
Brakenburg, R.

Merry Company
Present location unknown
1680-1700

aiv/a6

42
Bray, J. de
*Regents of the St.Lucasguild in
Haarlem*
Rijksmuseum, Amsterdam
1675
130 x 184 cm
Literature: van Thiel p.142

a2/ig9 (aiv)

43
Brekelendam, Q.
*A Soldier Drinking in an Inn with a
Young Woman*
Sale Christie's London 12/12/86-
16
1664
45.2 x 36.2 cm

a92 (aiv)

44
Bronchorst, J. van
Musical Party
Centraal Museum, Utrecht
1640-50
115 x 154 cm

Literature: Mills 1981, nr.56

aiv4

Sketchy representation. The
ornaments are too large
compared to the dimensions of
the field.

45
Bronchorst, J. van
Solomon Adoring Pagan Gods
Bob Jones University Art
Collection, Greenville
1642
170 x 157 cm
Literature: Mills 1981, nr.54

aiv4/a2/g14,og134

46
Bronchorst, J. van
The Prodigal Son
Herzog Anton Ullrich Museum,
Braunschweig
1644
142 x 206 cm
Literature: Mills 1981, nr.55

aiv4/a2/g14

47
Bronchorst, J. van
Merry Party with a Violin Player
Hermitage, Leningrad
1640-50
Literature: Kuznetsov nr.110

aiv4/a2/g14

48
Brueghel, J. the Elder
The Touch
Prado, Madrid
c.1618
Literature: cat.1980, p.233

aiv2/a6/og6

49
Brueghel, J. the Elder and
Balen, H. van

*The Reconciliation of Jacob and
Laban*
Sale Sotheby's London 9/4/86-5
c.1615
46 x 68.5 cm

aiv2/a2/g14

50
Brueghel, J. the Elder and
Balen, H. van

The Banquet of Acheloos
K. and V. Waterman Gallery,
Amsterdam 1984
c.1620
54.5 x 92 cm

aiv4/a2/g14

51
Brueghel, J. the Elder and
Balen, H. van

Allegory of the Five Senses
K. and V. Waterman Gallery,
Amsterdam 1987
c.1620
61.5 x 100.5

aiv4/a2/914

52
Brueghel, J.
Sight and Smell
Prado, Madrid
c.1618
175 x 263 cm
Literature: Mills 1981, nr.42

aiv2/a2/og41

53
Brueghel, J.
The Taste
Prado, Madrid
1618
64 x 108 cm
Literature: Mills 1981, nr.41

aiv2/a2/ig14

54
Brueghel, J. the Younger
A Monkey Feast
Sale Sotheby's London 9/4/86-3
162(4?)
26 x 34 cm

aiv/a2/g14 (aiv2)

Sketchy representation. The field
and the main border are
separated by a barber-pole stripe.

55
Brugghen, H. ter
King David Accompanied by Angels
Narodowe Museum, Warsaw
1628

150 x 190 cm
Literature: Bialostocki 1957,
ill.184

a6/g14 (aiv3)

Sketchy representation.

56
Brugghen, H. ter
Annunciation
Municipal Museum, Diest
1629
See illustration p.16

aiv3/a6/og6 (g14)

Careful representation. Cf.
Dimand/Mailey fig.162

57
Brugghen, H. ter
*Girl with a Lute and a Man with a
Violin*
Borghese Gallery, Rome
1629

aiv3/a6/g14

58
Burgh, H. van der
Portrait of a Family
Present location unknown
1660-65
89 x 132 cm
Literature: Valentiner, P. de
Hoogh, p.238

aiv3/a2/ig6

Sketchy representation.

59
Burgh, H. van der
Interior with a Musical Party
Sale Sotheby London 6/7/66-114
1660-65

Literature: Mills 1981, nr.66

aiv/a6

60
Burgh, H. van der
The Tickled Sleeper
Sale Christie's London 15/5/71-
110
1660-70
Literature: Mills 1981, nr.67

aiv/a2

61
Burgh, H. van der
Interior Scene
Sale Christie's London 14/5/71-
110
1660-70

aiv3/a2

62
Claeuw, J. de
Still-life with Skull and Violin
Sale Spink Berlin 28/3/74-227
1643
75.5 x 96 cm

aiv/a8

Cf. the border design of a rug in
the Rijksmuseum (Erkelens 1977,
cat.4 (ill.)). Careless
representation with additional
ornaments which may well have
been invented by the painter.

63
Codde, P.

Man Smoking at a Table
Sale F. Muller Amsterdam 25/4/
11-17
c. 1630
31 x 36 cm

aiv3/a2

64
Coosemans, A.
Still-life with Animals
Sale Fievez Brussels 17/5/23-6
c. 1670
118 x 131 cm

a93 (aiv)

65
Coques, G.
Portrait of a Family
Sale F.Muller Amsterdam, 24/9/
18-43
1645-55

aiv3

Clumsy representation. The
borders have an unusual design,
possibly invented by the painter.
The field design is too large
compared to the dimensions of
the rug.

66
Coques, G.
An Aristocratic Antwerp Family
Museum of Fine Arts, Budapest
1660-70
65.5 x 89.5 cm
Literature: Mills 1981, nr.73

aiv2/a11

The Lotto field ornaments are too
large. The fringes at all four sides
of the rug are unusual, and have
either been added in Europe or
invented by the painter. John
Mills surmised that the rug might
have been a flat-woven textile
with the Lotto design; there is
however no indication that such
textiles have ever existed.

67
Duck, J.
Merry Company
Musée d'Art, Nîmes
1640-50
Literature: Mills 1981, nr.57

aiv3/a2/g14,og43?

68
Duck, J.
Musical Company
Sale Christie's London 12/12/75-
126
1640-50
Literature: Mills 1981, nr.58

aiv2/a2/g14,og41

69
Duck, J.
*A Brothel Scene, with an Old
Woman Stealing Money from a
Sleeping Man*
Sale Christie's London 12/11/75-
126
1645-50
31.7 x 45.5 cm

aiv2/a93/ig64,og64

Blue field, with changing ground
colour.

70
Dullaert, H.
'Piskijker'
Municipal museum, Groningen
43 x 54 cm

a2 (aiv)

71
Duyster, W.
The Tric-trac Players
National Gallery, London
1620-25
41 x 67.6 cm
Literature: Mills 1981, nr.47

aiv3/a2/ig14

72
Dyck, A. van
Portrait of the Countess of Arundel
Sale Munich 12/4/37-684
1630s
Literature: Mills 1981, nr.51

aiv2/a93/ig43?

Sketchy representation.
Changing ground colour in the
possibly blue field.

73
Dyck, A. van
*Portrait of Elizabeth, Countess of
Peterborough*
Private collection, Edinburgh
1630s
Literature: Mills 1981, nr.52

aiv/a93

Cf. id. *Portrait of the Countess of
Arundel.* The inner guard border
seems to have a geometrical
pattern of stepped diamonds.

74
Dyck, A. van
Portrait of Anna van Craesbecke
Gemäldegalerie, Kassel
1634-36
Literature: Mills 1981, nr.53

a2/g14?,og43 (aiv)

The rug has a green flat-woven
'elem' strip and red fringes.

75
Dyck, A. van (attr. to)
Portrait of Charles I
Private collection, England
c. 1630
Literature: King 1987, p.25

aiv/a93/og64?

76
Eliasz (Pickenoy), N.

Portrait of a Man Aged 34
Hermitage, Leningrad
1630
122 x 89 cm

aiv/a93/ig13 (aiv2)

The Lotto design is carelessly
represented, whereas the border
design is painted with much
more care. The changing colour
of the ground is clearly visible.
The inner guard has an unusual
pattern of diamond-shaped
compartments with octagons,
separated by smaller diamonds.

77
Fabritius, B.

St. Peter in the House of Cornelius
Herzog Anton Ulrich Museum,
Braunschweig
1653
91 x 116 cm
Literature: cat. 1983, p.65

aiv4/a2/ig6

78
Floris, F.
The van Berchem Family
Wuyts-van Campen and Baron
Caroly Museum, Lierre
1561
Literature: Mills 1981, nr.18

aiv2/a11/ig64,og43

The border has a green ground,
with kufic ornaments similar to
those in the carpet illustrated by
Pagnano, nr.8.

79
Forbes, P.
Still-life
Sale Christie's London 11/3/84-
49
1663
132 x 110 cm

aiv/a6/ig64,og103

80
Francken, F.
The Justice of Seleucus
Sale Berlin 29/3/27-129
1620s?
73 x 104 cm

a93 (aiv2)

Sketchy representation. The field
shows a clumsy version of Lotto-
like ornaments; the border with a
changing ground colour (cf.
Yetkin 1981 pl.35) is more
carefully depicted.

81
Gallis, P. (attr. to)

Still-life
Present location unknown
1653 (?)
75 x 68 cm

aiv/a2/og82 (aiv3)

82
Gelder, A. de
Portrait of the Painter
Hermitage, Leningrad
c. 1690
79 x 64 cm
Literature: Haak 1984, ill.926

aiv

Sketchy representation.

83
Gheeraedts, M.
Portrait of Francis Howard
Viscount Cowdray, Cowdray
Park
1611
Literature: Mills 1981, nr.34

aiv3/a6

Clumsy representation, as if the
painter worked after a
preparatory study. The guard
border has a stylized meandering
floral stem. Cf. Hannover 1987,
nr.3

84
Gheeraedts, M.
Portrait of Ludowick Stuart, Duke of Richmond and Lennox
Duke of Bedford, Woburn Abbey
1610-20
Literature: Mills 1981, nr.25

aiv2

The field has a changing ground colour. Cf. Mills 1981, nr.23; also: Bode 1902, ill.62

85
Gheeraedts, M.
Portrait of Francis Manners, 6th Duke of Rutland
Duke of Bedford, Woburn Abbey
1610-20
Literature: Mills 1981, nr.24

aiv2

86
Gheeraedts, M.
A Woman Holding a Dove
Earl of Chichester, Summer Park
1610-20
Literature: Mills 1981, nr.26

aiv2/a2

87
Gheeraedts, M.
Portrait of Sir Anthony Mildmay
Emmanuel College, Cambridge
1610-20
Literature: Mills 1981, nr.27

aiv2

88
Gheeraedts, M. (attr. to)
Portrait of Robert Sydney, 1st Earl of Leicester
Marquess of Bath, Longleat
c. 1615
Literature: Mills 1981, nr.38

aiv2

The minimal narrow border has linked diamonds.

89
Heerschop, H.
Solomon at the Death-bed of David
town hall, Montfoord (Utrecht)
1649

aiv/a2/g14

Careless representation with several unauthentic additional ornaments. The painter may not have had the original rug in his studio while doing this painting.

90
Helst, B. van der
Portrait of Vice-Admiral Johan de Liefde
Rijksmuseum, Amsterdam
1668
139 x 122 cm
Literature: van Thiel p.269

aiv3/a6

The unusual colouring (most yellow and brown shades) and the carelessly drawn border design suggest that van der Helst worked after a preparatory study. The inner guard border is replaced by three stripes without decoration.

91
Honthorst, G. van
The Merry Fiddler
Rijksmuseum, Amsterdam
1623
108 x 89 cm
Literature: van Thiel p.285

aiv/a2/og6 (aiv2)

92
Honthorst, G. van
Artemisia
University Art Museum, Princeton, New Jersey
c. 1635
Literature: Amsterdam (God en de goden) 1981, p.117

aiv

Sketchy representation. The field is green. Cf. id. *A Soldier Lighting a Pipe.*

93
Honthorst, G. van (attr. to)
A Soldier Lighting a Pipe with a Maidservant Pouring Wine (fragment)
1630-40?
Sale Christie's London 11/12/84-57
99.7 x 83.2 cm

aiv2/a11

The colouring is unusual; the field is green with yellow arabesques and red dots. For the border design see Pagnano nr.7. Cf. id. *Artemisia.*

94
Honthorst, G. van
Elisabeth Stuart, Queen of Bohemia
Sale Sotheby London 27/11/86-36
c. 1631
214 x 146 cm

aiv3

Cf. id. *Frederik V, Count Palatine* (pendant).

95
Honthorst, G. van
Frederik V, Count Palatine
Sale Sotheby's London 27/11/86-35
1631
214 x 146 cm

aiv3

Cf. id. *Elisabeth Stuart, Queen of Bohemia* (pendant). Carelessly rendered. The Lotto design is partly drawn in other colours than the usual yellow, as can be seen, mutatis mutandis, in a Lotto rug in Berlin (Spuhler 1987, nr.7). Some additional unauthentic ornaments suggest that the painter worked after a preparatory study.

96
Honthorst, G. van
Three Daughters of Frederik Hendrik (Musical Party)
Sale Christie's New York, 18/1/83-7
1644
88 x 105 cm

aiv/a93/ig6 (aiv2)

Careless representation of the field design, which is on a blue ground with red cartouches. Cf. id. *Portrait of a Young Woman Painting a Portrait*; id. *Three Young Women with Musical Instruments and Flowers.*

97
Honthorst, G. van

Portrait of a Young Woman Painting a Portrait
Present location unknown
1648
135 x 111 cm
Literature: sale Bukowski Stockholm 16/4/58-192

aiv/a93/ig6 (aiv2)

Careless representation of the field design. The original rug seems to have had a blue field and red cartouches. The border has a changing ground colour. Cf. id. *Three Daughters of Frederik Hendrik*; id. *Three Young Women with Musical Instruments and Flowers.*

98
Honthorst, G. van
Chariclea is Recognised by her Parents
Kronborg Castle, Copenhagen
1635
Literature: Christian IV and Europe, The 19th Art Exhibition of the Council of Europe, Copenhagen 1988, p.83-84

aiv2/ig64

Blue field. The main border stripe and the outer guard are not depicted.

99
Honthorst, G. van
Three Young Women with Musical Instruments and Flowers
Hermitage, Leningrad
1649
120 x 187 cm

Literature: cat. 1958, nr.3339

aiv2/a93/ig6

The rug has a changing ground colour. Cf. id. *Three Daughters of Frederik Hendrik*; id. *Portrait of a Young Woman Painting a Portrait*.

99-2
Honthorst, G. van
A Self-portrait
Rijksmuseum Amsterdam
1655
117 x 94.5 cm
Literature: van Thiel p.286

a93/og64

99-3
Honthorst, G. van
Portrait of Sophia Coopmans, Wife of the Artist
Rijksmuseum Amsterdam
1655
117 x 94.5 cm
Literature: van Thiel p.64

a93/ig64,og64

100
Hooch, P. de
A Woman Reading, with a Child
Present location unknown
1662-66
58 x 76 cm
Literature: Sutton cat. 50

a6/og134 (aiv)

101
Hooch, P. de
Card Players Beside a Fireplace, with an Embracing Couple and a Servant
Louvre, Paris
1663-5
Literature: Sutton cat. 58

a6 (aiv)

102
Janssens, A.
Madonna and St. John
Museo de Arte, Ponce
(Puerto Rico)
c. 1600
152 x 119 cm
Literature: sale Christie's London
14/12/56-47

aiv/iig13,ig64

103
Janssens, A. (attr. to)

Venus at her Toilet
Frank Uhlig Gallery, Vienna 1957
1600-20
165 x 120 cm

aiv/a2/ig134,og46

104
Jordaens, J.
Portrait of Judge Steengracht
Sale Anderson Gallery, New York 20/4/39-32
c. 1630
111.8 x 79.9 cm

aiv2

105
Key, W.

Portrait of a Man at a Table, Aged 59
Koninklijk Museum voor Schone Kunsten, Antwerp
1543
90 x 81 cm

aiv/a132 (aiv2)

Stiff representation. The pointed geometrical forms at the sides protruding into the field are unusual. The design of the inner guard border could be identical to that of a guard border of an example in the Keir collection (Spuhler 1978, cat.15).

106
Keyser, Th. de
Portrait of Three Children and a Man
Rijksmuseum, Amsterdam
1622
135 x 94 cm (fragments)
Literature: van Thiel p.318

a2/g14 (aiv)

The field is left plain. The inner guard border has a chevron ornament.

107
Keyser, Th. de (attr. to)
The Tric-trac Players
Sale Nemes Paris 17/6/13-55
1620-30
85 x 68 cm

aiv3/a91/og422

The Lotto ornaments are too large in comparison to the dimensions of the rug. The field colour is light, possibly even white.

108
Kick, S.
Hunters in an Interior
Statens Museum, Copenhagen
1640-50
97 x 75.5 cm
Literature: cat. Dublin 1986, fig.212

aiv/a6/g14,og422 (aiv2)

109
Lievens, J. (attr. to)
Esther and Ahasverus
Sale Dorotheum, Vienna 12/9/64
1630-35
85 x 123 cm

aiv2

110
Linschoten, J.H. van (attr. to)
Portrait of a Man Aged 28
Museum Bisdom van Vliet, Haastrecht
1584

aiv3

111
Luttichuys, S.
A Still-life with a late Ming Gold and White Faceted Jar
Sale Christie's London 25/10/85-49
1640-60
94 x 78.7 cm

aiv/a6

The rug has a yellow flat-woven elem and red fringes.

112
Maes, N.
Girl Rocking a Cradle
National Gallery, London
1654-9
40.4 x 32.6 cm
Literature: Valentiner 1924, nr.26

aiv/a6

Cf. id. *Girl with Apples*

113
Maes, N.
Girl with Apples
Metropolitan Museum of Art, New York
c. 1655
54 x 45 cm
Literature: Valentiner 1924, nr.24

aiv/a6

114
Maes, N.
Portrait of a Man
Sale Christie's London 14/7/78-103
1657
123.1 x 100.3 cm

a6/ig103 (aiv)

115
Maes, N.
Portrait of Captain Verschuer
Sale O.Strauss a.o., Frankfurt 11/12/34
1674
124 x 100 cm

aiv/a6

116
Maes, N. (attr. to)

Still-life
Louvre, Paris
c. 1670

aiv/a6/g43

117
Mander, C. van or Isaacs, P.
St.John the Baptist Preaching
J. Weitzner Gallery, London 1971
1580-1600
82.5 x 162.5 cm
See illustration p.32

aiv3/a2/ig6

118
Massys, J.
Merry Company
National Museum, Stockholm
c. 1555
97 x 134 cm
Literature: Ydema 1985, p.125-28

aiv/a93/ig8

119
Meer, B. van der

Still-life with Servant
Alte Pinakothek, Munich
c. 1685
150.7 x 117.6 cm
Literature: Haak 1984, ill.1100

aiv/og422 (aiv3)

The border design cannot be identified with certainty. It seems to be based upon the a6 design. Since van der Meer painted the worn condition of the rug with painstaking care, it seems improbable that he would have been less careful in copying the details of the design. Still, the border design of the rug in the painting is not known from surviving examples.

120
Mesdach, S.
Portrait of Sir Peter Courten
Rijksmuseum, Amsterdam
1617
194 x 109 cm
Literature: Mills 1981, nr.39

aiv3/a2/gi4,og48

121
Metsu, G.
Woman with a Glass and a Tankard
Louvre, Paris
1657-60
28 x 26 cm
Literature: Robinson cat.20

a2? (aiv)

Sketchy representation.

122
Metsu, G.
The Hunter's Present
Rijksmuseum, Amsterdam
1655-60
Literature: Robinson cat.24

aiv/a2/ig9

Sketchy representation.

123
Metsu, G.
Couple at the Table
Rijksmuseum, Amsterdam
35.5 x 29 cm
1657-62
Literature: Robinson cat.72

aiv

Sketchy representation.

124
Metsu, G.
The Music Lesson
National Gallery, London
1657-60
37 x 31 cm
Literature: Robinson cat.73

aiv/a2/ig9

Sketchy representation.

125
Metsu, G.
The Letter-writer Surprised
Wallace collection, London
1655-60
46 x 39 cm
Literature: Robinson cat.74

aiv?/a2/g14

Sketchy representation.

126
Metsu, G.
A Man Writing a Letter
Musée Fabre, Montpellier
1655-60
Literature: Robinson cat.75

aiv/a2/ig9

Sketchy representation.

127
Metsu, G.
The Oyster Meal
Hermitage, Leningrad
1660-63
56 x 41 cm
Literature: Robinson cat.78

aiv?/a2?/ig9?

Sketchy representation.

128
Metsu, G.
The Hunter's Gift
Uffizi, Florence
1660-3
56 x 50 cm
Literature: Robinson cat.132

aiv/a2/g14

Sketchy representation. The field and the main border are separated by a barber's pole ornament.

129
Metsu, G.
The Intruder
National Gallery, Washington
1660-3
65 x 57 cm
Literature: Robinson cat.133

aiv/a2?/ig9

Sketchy representation.

130
Metsu, G.
The Oyster Meal
Hermitage, Leningrad

1655-60
56 x 46 cm
Literature: Robinson cat.137

a2/g14 (aiv)

Sketchy representation. The field and the main border are separated by a barber-pole stripe.

131
Metsu, G.
Girl Playing a Lute
Gemäldegalerie, Kassel
c. 1660
36 x 30 cm
Literature: Robinson cat.141

a2/og82

The rug has a red border with blue cartouches, and a yellow guard border. At the upper or lower end the rug has a yellow, narrow flatwoven elem. Apparently the rug was somewhat worn: some threads of the elem are hanging between the fringes.

132
Metsu, G.
Woman with a Glass of Wine and a Soldier
Louvre, Paris
1663
63 x 47 cm
Literature: Robinson cat.142

aiv/a2/g14

Sketchy representation. The field and the main border are separated by a barber-pole stripe.

133
Metsu, G.
Woman Playing the Lute and a Boy Playing with a Dog
Uffizi, Florence
c. 1663
31.3 x 27.5 cm
Literature: Robinson cat.202

aiv/a2/g14

Sketchy representation. The field and the main border are separated by a barber-pole stripe.

134
Mieris, F. van (attr. to)
A Painter in his Studio
Detroit Institute of Arts, Detroit
1650-60
90.8 x 76.7 cm
Literature: Naumann cat. C31

aiv2

Sketchy representation. The rug seems to have a changing ground colour: a blue field with red cartouches. Naumann suggests an attribution of this painting to Michiel van Musscher or Jacob Berckheyde (Naumann II, p.146-7, cat. C31 fig.17).

135
Moeyaert, N.
Portrait of The Catholic Priest Leonardus Marius
Museum Amstelkring, Amsterdam
1643

a2 (aiv)

A second version of this portrait was painted by Moeyaert in 1647 (Schwartz 1986, p.52).

136
Moeyaert, N.
The Choice Between Old and Young
Rijksmuseum, Amsterdam
1640-50
113.5 x 127.5 cm
Literature: van Thiel p.391

a2 (aiv)

The field is left undecorated.

137
Musscher, M. van
Peasant Offering Poultry to a Lawyer
Sale Christie's London 18/4/80-89
1668
44.5 x 39.3 cm

a6/og36 (aiv)

138
Musscher, M. van

Portrait of Margaretha van Hardenbroek
Present location unknown
1680-90
36.5 x 30 cm

aiv3/a6/ig8,og103

139
Mijtens, D. (attr. to)
Portrait of Robert Devereux, 3rd Earl of Sussex
National Portrait Gallery, London (on loan from the Duke of Portland)
1610-20
Literature: Mills 1981, nr.33

aiv2/a16

Dr. Mills suggests an English or Flemish origin of the rug, as the field is divided into triangular and octagonal compartments, a feature unknown from surviving Lotto carpets.

140
Neer, E. van der
Portrait of a Couple in an Interior
Städtisches Kunstmuseum, Dusseldorf
1700
96 x 79 cm
Literature: Dusseldorf (Joh. Wilhelm) 1958, cat.38

aiv3/a6/og134

Careful representation. The rug has a broad, flatwove elem, presumably in a yellow colour, with yellow fringes. The inner guard has a thin running stem with stylized scrolls.

141
Ochtervelt, J. (attr. to)
A Soldier and a Maid in a Window-bay
Formerly Hermitage, Leningrad
1660-80
Literature: sale van Diemen & co, Berlin 25/1/35-43

a92/og103 (aiv)

Cf. id. *Musical Party in a Window.*

142
Ochtervelt, J. (attr. to)
Musical Party in a Window
California Palace of the Legion of Honor, San Francisco
1660-80
58.7 x 48.8 cm
Literature: Kuretsky cat.D-5

a92/og103 (aiv)

The carpet has a narrow, presumably red flat-woven elem, and red fringes. Cf. id. *Musical Party in a Window.*

143
Oost, J. van
St. Augustin Washing Christ's Feet
Stedelijk van Groeningen Museum, Bruges
1645-55
271 x 168 cm
Literature: Mills 1981, nr. 60

aiv2/a2/g14,og48

The carpet has a broad flat-woven elem, presumably red, and red fringes.

144
Oost, J. van
Portrait of Everard Tristan
Sale Stockholm (Ivar Krenger)
14/9/32-68
1646
57 x 33 cm

aiv2/a11/ig64

Cf. id. *Portrait of Wilhelmina Bezaete* (pendant). compare Erdmann 1956, Abb.26.

145
Oost, J. van
Portrait of Wilhelmina Bezaete, Wife of Everard Tristan
Sale Stockholm 14/9/32-69
1646
57 x 33 cm

aiv2/a11/ig64

Cf. id. *Portrait of Everard Tristan* (pendant)

146
Palamedesz, A.
A Man Taking his Boots off
Sale Sotheby's Monaco 22/6/85-135
c. 1650
37.5 x 31 cm

aiv/a2/ig14

147
Pot, H. (attr. to)
Merry Company
Sale F.Muller Amsterdam 3/5/34-138
1615-25
56.5 x 71 cm

a2/ig64 (aiv)

Sketchy representation. The carpet is shown with fringes on all four sides (cf. Coques, *Portrait of Jacques van Eyck and his Family*?).

148
Pourbus, F. (attr. to)
Frances Howard, Duchess of Richmond and Lennox
Marquess of Bath Longleat (Wilts.)
c. 1620
218 x 124 cm

a93 (aiv2)

No changing ground in the main border. The design of the field and the guard borders is hard to identify; the field seems to have a red ground with blue clusters like the Von Bode Lotto (Bode 1902, Abb.62).

149
Ravesteyn, J.A. van
Portrait of an Unknown Officer
Royal Picture Gallery The Mauritshuis, The Hague
1621
115 x 97 cm
Literature: cat. 1985, nr.455
See illustration p.30

aiv4

The border has an unidentified design of large S-forms with stylized lotus flowers and other floral ornaments.

150
Ravesteyn, J.A. van
Portrait of an Unknown Gentleman
Sale Paris Drouot 8/12/48-38 as Th. de Keyser
1627
115 x 85 cm

aiv4.

The carpet has a very light, possibly even white field colour. Possibly the same carpet as represented in id. *Unknown Officer*; id. *Portrait of an Unknown Man*.

151
Ravesteyn, J.A. van
Portrait of an Unknown Man
Palazzo Pitti, Florence
1625-30
127 x 90 cm
Literature: cat. 1937, nr.255
(as A. de Vries)

aiv4

152
Rootius, J.A. (attr. to)
Portrait of a Family
Present location unknown
1640-50
150 x 218 cm
Literature: BM 47 (1925) November, p.XXX

a6/ig86,og51 (aiv)

The field is left without decoration.

153
Rossum, J. van
Portrait of an Unknown Woman, Thought to be Anna of Burgundy
Rijksmuseum, Amsterdam
1662
117 x 93 cm
Literature: Mills 1981, nr.63

aiv2

154
Rossum, J. van
Portrait of Geertruid Vermeulen, Wife of dr. Joan Blaeu
Amsterdams Historisch Museum, Amsterdam
1663
Literature: cat. 1975/79, nr.383
See illustration p.28

aiv2

Cf. id. *Portrait of an Unknown Woman, Thought to be Anna of Burgundy*.

155
Rubens, P.
The Four Philosophers
Palazzo Pitti, Florence
1611-2
Literature: Mills 1981, nr.35

aiv/a2

Sketchy representation. Both the field and the border have a red ground.

156
Rubens, P. and Brueghel, J.

The Feast of Achelous
Metropolitan Museum of Art, New York
1614-15
107.9 x 163.8 cm
Literature: Liedtke 1984 II, Plate XIV, fig.75

aiv4/a2

Cf. Végh & Layer nr.4

157
Schalcken, G.
A Woman Singing and a Man with a Cittern
National Gallery, London
1665-70
26.8 x 20.4 cm
Literature: Mills 1983, pl.26

aiv2/a6/ig103?

158
Schalcken, G.
Venus with the Burning Arrow of Eros
Gemäldegalerie, Kassel
1690
69 x 53 cm
Literature: Amsterdam 1989, cat.43

a92

159
Seghers, G.
Saint Eligius Before the Holy Virgin
Musée des Beaux-Arts, Valenciennes
1635-50
240 x 225 cm
Literature: cat. 1931, nr.97

aiv/a2 (aiv3)

Careful representation. The inner guard has a simple decoration of dots.

160
Sibilla, G.
Solon Before Croesus
Hessisches Landesmuseum, Darmstadt
c. 1645

aiv

161
Slingelant, P. van
Young Woman with a Child and a Servant
Wallraf Richartz Museum, Cologne
1660-70
39 x 34 cm
Literature: cat. 1964, nr.37

aiv/a6

Sketchy representation. The rug apparently had a small field, compared to the dimensions of the border. Cf. Hannover 1987, nr.3.

162
Steen, J.
A Young Woman Playing the Lute
coll. J.B.Scholten, Enschede
1660-62
55 x 43.5 cm
Literature: Braun cat.137

a6/g14 (aiv3)

Sketchy representation.

163
Steen, J.
Scene in a Brothel
Corcoran Art Gallery, Washington
1667
63 x 53 cm
Literature: Braun cat.279

aiv/a6 (aiv3)

164
Steen, J.
The Wedding of Tobias
Herzog Anton Ullrich Museum,
Braunschweig
1667
131 x 172 cm
Literature: Braun cat.281

aiv/a6/ig8 (aiv3)

Mills assumed that the rug is
decorated in the 'kilim' style; this
identification of the design is
indeed supported by several
details. The representation is
rather sketchy; it is patched up
with several loose elements of the
Lotto design. The flatwoven elem
at one end of the rug is light blue,
at the other end it has red, light
blue and yellow stripes. The
fringes are red.

165
Steen, J.
*The Banquet of Antony and
Cleopatra*
University Museum, Göttingen
1667
67.5 x 58.5 cm
Literature: Braun cat.283

aiv3/a6/ig8,og102

166
Steen, J.
*The Banquet of Antony and
Cleopatra*
Private collection,
The Netherlands
1667-8
105 x 90 cm
Literature: Braun cat.287

aiv/a6 (aiv3)

167
Steen, J.
Amnon and Thamar
Wallraf Richartz Museum,
Cologne
1668-70
67 x 83 cm
Literature: Braun cat.310

aiv/a6/ig14 (aiv3)

168
Steenwyck II, H. van and a
follower of J.Brueghel the Elder
Croesus and Solon
National Gallery, London
1620s
31.1 x 22.9 cm
Literature: Mills 1983, pl.23 and
p.38

aiv2/a2

169
Streeck, J. van
Still-life with a Servant
Alte Pinakothek, Munich
1680-87
143.4 x 120.5 cm
Literature: cat. 1983, p.510

aiv (aiv3)

Cf. id. *An Oriental Bowl with Fruit
and a Glass of Wine on a Rug on a
Terrace*; id. *Still-life with Fruits and
Porcelain*

170
Streeck, J. van
Still-life
Rijksmuseum Muiderslot,
Muiden
1650-70
142 x 119 cm

aiv (aiv3)

Cf. id. *Still-life with a Servant.*

171
Streeck, J. van or Meer, B. van der
Still-life with Silver Objects
Louvre, Paris
1650-60
83 x 102 cm
Literature: cat. 1922, nr.2437
(p.100)

aiv/a6/og64 (aiv3)

Sketchy representation. Cf. id.
Still-life with a Servant.

172
Streeck, J. van

*An Oriental Bowl with Fruit and a
Glass of Wine on a Rug on a Table*
Sale Christie's New York 15/1/
86-152
c. 1660
63.5 x 66 cm

aiv3/a2/ig14?

173
Streeck. J. van
Still-life with Fruits and Porcelain
D.Hoogendijk Gallery, Amster-
dam 1947
c. 1660
88 x 105 cm
Literature: Bergstrom, nr.234

aiv3/a6

The inner guard border seems to
be decorated with small rosettes.

174
Streeck, J. van
Still-life
Private collection
1655-70
83 x 101 cm
Literature: Haak 1984, ill. 1099

aiv3/ig72

175
Tengnagel, J.

*King David with his Harp, a Family
Portrait Group to the Right*
Sale Sotheby's London 5/7/84
1610-20
56.5 x 72.5 cm

a6/a2 (aiv)
a2 (aiv)

The rug on the table has a border
with the cloudband pattern,
whereas the field is decorated
with the cartouche border design.
This combination is without any
doubt invented by the painter.
The second rug on the painting
has the same cartouche border;
the field design is not visible.

176
Tengnagel, J.
*Circe Transforms Ulysses' Friends
into Pigs*
Sale Mak Dordrecht 30/11/81-95
1612
44.5 x 64 cm

aiv/a2

177
Tengnagel, J.
*Banquet of Seventeen Members of
the Archers' Civil Guard Company
of Captain Geurt van Beuningen*
Rijksmuseum, Amsterdam
1613
155 x 264 cm
Literature: van Thiel p.535

a6 (aiv)

178
Teniers, A.
Monkeys Feasting
Sale Sotheby's London 12/12/84-
177
1650-70
35 x 27 cm

aiv/a2/g14 (aiv2)

Sketchy representation.

179
Terborch, G.
A Couple Drinking Wine
Buckingham Palace, London
c. 1660
42 x 32 cm
Literature: Gudlaugsson ill.166

a6?/og64 (aiv)

The rug is shown from the
reverse side.

180
Terborch, G.
Interior with Dancing Couple
Coll. Mrs. R. Greville, Polesden
Lacey (National Trust)
c. 1660
76 x 68 cm
Literature: Gudlaugsson ill.187

a6/og64 (aiv3)

181
Terborch, G.
Young Woman Reading a Letter
Wallace Collection, London
c. 1662
43 x 32 cm
Literature: Mills 1981, nr.64

aiv3/a6/og64

The rug has a green flatwoven
elem and yellow or green fringes.

182
Terborch, G.
A Lady with a Letter
Athenaeum, Helsinki
c. 1665
38.3 x 34 cm
Literature: Mills 1981, nr.70

aiv/a6/g14,og6? (aiv3)

Cf. id. *Young Woman Reading a
Letter.*

183
Tielius, J.

*Portrait of Anna Catharina van
Renesse*
Coll. d'Oultremont, Stockey
(Belgium)
1678
36 x 30 cm

aiv3/a6?

184
Tielius, J.
*Portrait of Two Women Making
Music*
Gemeentemuseum, The Hague
1680-90
38.5 x 29.5 cm

aiv/ig82 (aiv2/a93)

The careful way in which the
painter depicted the individual
knots suggests a reliable
representation of the original
model; the arabesques however
are inconsistently drawn. The
field has a blue ground, and red
cartouches. The possibility that
this carpet is in fact related to the
carpets discussed in Chapter VII
can not be excluded.

185
Toorenvliet, J. (attr. to)
The Doctor's Visit
Staatliche Kunsthalle, Karlsruhe
c. 1670
Literature: Lauts p.420, nr.1806

aiv/a6/g14? (aiv3)

186
Valckert, W. van de
*Five Governors, presumably of the
Groot Kramers Guild*
Staatliche Museen zu Berlin,
Gemäldegalerie, Berlin (East)
1622
135 x 187 cm
Literature: Mills 1981, nr.46

aiv2/a6/g14,og46

187
Velde, E. van de
Musical party
State-owned Art Collections
Dept., The Hague, on loan to the
Frans Hals Museum, Haarlem
1615-20

aiv

The rug is draped over the buffet.

188
Verkolje, J. (attr. to)
*A Young Boy with a Viola da
Gamba*
Wawel, Cracow
1675-80
Literature: Bialostocki 1957, pl.X
See illustration p.32

a92 (aiv)

The inner guard border has three
plain stripes.

189
Verkolje, N. (attr. to)
Scene in a Brothel
Sale Lempertz, Cologne 28/5/63-
157
1686
71 x 79.5 cm

a2/g14 (aiv)

The field and the main border are
separated by a barber-pole stripe.

190
Vermeer, J.
*Christ in the House of Mary and
Martha*
National Gallery of Scotland,
Edinburgh
1654-6
160 x 142 cm
Literature: Blankert 1978, cat.1

aiv/a2/ig64,og8 (aiv3)

The elem is yellow; the fringes
are red or yellow. Cf. id. *Girl
Asleep at a Table.*

191
Vermeer, J.
Girl Asleep at a Table
Metropolitan Museum of Art,
New York
c. 1657
86.5 x 76 cm
Literature: Blankert 1978, cat.4

aiv3/a2/og8

According to Mills (nr.62)
uncertain style field. However,

the saw-tooth outlines of the
arabesques in the field are clearly
visible.

192
Victors, J.

The Blessing of Jacob
Narodowe Muzeum, Warsaw
after 1672?
136 x 190 cm
Literature: Bialostocki 1957, ill.
251

aiv/a2/g14,og43

The function of the rug in the
painting is remarkable: it is used
on the bed.

193
Visscher, C. (attr. to)

*Portrait of the Goldsmith François
Coenraedz. Messingh*
Duivenvoorde Castle, Voorschoten
1582

aiv2

The field design has additional,

presumably not authentic
ornaments.

194
Voorhout, J.
Still-life with a Woman at an Easel
Worcester Art Museum,
Worcester Massachusetts
1680-90
148.5 x 40.3 cm
Literature: Kuretsky cat. D-10

a6 (aiv)

195
Vos, C. de

The Painter, his Wife and Son
Present location unknown
1625-35
197 x 163 cm

aiv/a11

Cf. Pagnano 9.

196
Vos, C. de
Portrait of the Artist and his Family
Koninklijk Museum voor Schone
Kunsten, Brussels
1621
Literature: Mills 1981, nr.43

aiv2/a93/ig64,og8

The rug has a blue field and red
cartouches. The red border has
no changing ground colour (cf.
id., *Portrait of F. Veckmans*); the
elem has a red and a green stripe;
the fringes are green.

197
Vos, C. de, or Francken, F. II
Interior of Rubens's Drawingroom
National Museum, Stockholm
c. 1621
Literature: Speth-Holterhoff,
ill.26

aiv/a93

Presumably a blue field colour.
The representation is drawn in a
rather sketchy fashion. It is
remarkable to see that in many
paintings showing interiors of
picture galleries, in which the
paintings hanging on the walls or
handled by the visitors of the
galleries, are represented in so
much detail, the carpets on the
table are often painted with little
care. Cf. e.g. the illustrations in
Speth-Holterhoff; several carpets
are included in the cabinets while
only a few are clearly
recognizable.

198
Vos, C. de
Portrait of a Lawyer
Herzog Anton Ullrich Museum,
Braunschweig
1622
123 x 94 cm
Literature: Mills 1981, nr.44

aiv2/a93/ig64

Blue field, with changing ground
colour.

199
Vos, C. de

*Portrait of a Scholar with his Little
Daughter*
Bode Museum, Berlin (East)
c. 1625

aiv2

Blue field, with changing field
colour.

200
Vos, C. de

*Portrait of the Sollicitor Barthel van
den Berghe*
Koninklijk Museum voor Schone
Kunsten, Antwerp
1620-25

aiv2/a93/ig64

201
Vos, C. de

Portrait of F. Veckmans
Museum Mayer van den Bergh,
Antwerp
1620-25

aiv2/a93/ig64

202
Vos, S. de
The Magnanimity of Scipio
Wallraf Richartz Museum,
Cologne 1645-55
197 x 166 cm

aiv/a11 (aiv2)

The carpet is very large. The
representation of the design is
not careful in all details (Cf. id.
The Generosity of Scipio); the
painter may have worked after a
preparative drawing. This
assumption could also explain
the careless drawing of the kufic
ornaments. There are no guard
borders shown. The rug
apparently has fringes on all four
sides (cf. Coques, *Portrait of
Jacques van Eyck and his family?*).

203
Vos, S. de
The Generosity of Scipio
Earl of Bradfort, Weston
1640-50
71 x 99 cm

aiv2/a11

The dimensions of the rug are
enlarged; the Lotto ornaments are
consequently enlarged too. Cf.
id. *The Magnanimity of Scipio*. For
the drawing of the kufic
ornaments cf. Spuhler 1978
cat.17.

204
Vos, S. de
Merry Company
Hermitage, Leningrad
c. 1650
45 x 67.5 cm
Literature: cat.1958, nr.619

aiv2/a11?

205
Weenix, J.
*Portrait of Peter Count von Nahuys
and Catharina Soeten*
Sale Sotheby's Amsterdam 22/4/
80-96
1685-95
129 x 119 cm

aiv3/a61

MEDALLION USHAK CARPETS

206
Ceulen, C. Janssens van
*Portrait of a Man, Presumed to be
Thomas Savile, Earl of Sussex*
Duke of Buccleuch, Boughton
(Scotland)
1640-50
205 x 126 cm

av./a16/ig102,og102

The dark central medallion has a
fine curved outline. It stands on
a presumably red ground with

light coloured floral ornaments. A simpler version of the border pattern can be found in the inner guard border of a Medallion Ushak in Colonial Williamsburg (Lanier cat. 28.)

207
Ceulen, C. Janssens van
Portrait of Frances Devereux, Marchioness of Hertford
Lord Leconfield, Petworth
1633
203 x 127 cm

av.

208
Dyck, A. van
The Fourth Count of Pembroke, and his Family
Coll. Lord Pembroke, Wilton House
c. 1635
330 x 510 cm
Literature: E.Larsen, Anton van Dyck 2, Werkverzeichnis, nr.578

eii./d15/ig64,og64 (av.)

209
Heda, W.
A Still-life
Sale Palais d'Orsay, Paris 21/11/78-56
1664
94 x 68.5 cm

d15 (eii.;av.)

209-2
Heere, L. de
The Family of Henry VIII
Indeley Castle collection, Gloucestershire
1570-75
129.5 x 180.3 cm
Literature: Sotheby's Art at Auction 1989-90, p.18

av.

210
Honthorst, G. van
Portrait of Christiana, Countess of Cavendish with her Children
Coll. The Duke of Devonshire, Chatsworth
1628

av./a12/og64

211
Honthorst, G. van
Portrait of Amalia van Solms
Huis Ten Bosch, The Hague
1650
331 x 195 cm

See illustration p.42

av.

212
Hooch, P. de
A Party of Four Figures, with a Man Entering a Doorway
Museu Nacional de Arte Antiga, Lisbon
1663-65
Literature: Sutton cat. 57

eii. (av.)

213
Horst, G.W. (attr. to)
A Still-life
Brera, Miland
1640-50
Literature: cat.1942, nr.795

av./ig62

The floral ornaments in the field are clumsily drawn.

214
Janssens, H.
Portrait of a Couple in a Courtyard, with a Boy
Hallwyl, Stockholm
63 x 57.5 cm
Literature: cat. 1930, Groep, XXXII, nr.B.28

av. (eii.)

Sketchy representation. The rug may have been coarse, judging from the representation of the floral ornaments in the field, and the form of the corner medallion; cf. Vermeer, *The Music Lesson.*

214-2
Moreelse, P.
Portrait of Lucas van Voorst
Rafael Valls Gallery, London
1988
c. 1628
Literature: C.de Jonge, Paulus Moreelse, Portret- en Genreschilder te Utrecht 1571-1638, Assen/Gorcum 1938, nr. 91a, pl. 73

av.

215
Mijtens, D.

Portrait of Lady Martha Cranfield, Countess of Monmouth
Coll. Lord Sackville, Knole
c. 1622
213 x 128 cm

av.

The outlines of the presumably dark blue medallion are quite stiff. The red field has stylized floral ornaments. Cf. Lanier, pl.31.

216
Mijtens, D.
Portrait of Prince Frederik Hendrik
Sale Christie's London 25/6/65-32
c. 1635
200 x 140 cm
See illustration p.45

av.

217
Mijtens, D.
Lord Admiral Charles Howard, 1st Earl of Nottingham
National Maritime Museum, London
c. 1615
251.5 x 145 cm
Literature: cat. 1988, p.285

aix2/a11
av

218
Noordt, J. van
Woman at her Toilet
Koninklijk Museum voor Schone Kunsten, Brussels
1670
75.5 x 62.5 cm
Literature: cat. 1984, p.212

eii./g84/ig102 (av.)

Apparently a very coarse carpet.

219
Noordt, J. van
Woman at her Toilet
Formerly coll. Semenov, St.Petersburg
c. 1670
Literature: J.O.Kronig, Joan van Noordt, in: Onze Kunst XI (1911), p.156-158

eii./ig102 (av.)

Cf. id. *Woman at her Toilet*, Brussels.

220
Oost, J. van

Portrait of a Theologist and his Clerk
Groeningemuseum, Bruges
1668
116 x 222 cm
Literature: cat.1983, p.65

av.

Careful representation. The central medallion is dark blue with green outlines; the floral ornaments on the red ground are also green. The pendant motif is dark blue.

221
Schalcken, G.
The Visit to the Doctor
Wallraf-Richartz Museum, Cologne
1669
34 x 29 cm
Literature: cat. 1986, p.77, Abb.403

av.

222
Steen, J.

Soo gewonne, soo verteert'
Museum Boymans-van
Beuningen, Rotterdam
1661
Literature: Braun cat.143

eii./d15/ig64,og64 (av.)

223
Steen, J.
The Love-sick Girl
Alte Pinakothek, Munich
1661-63
61 x 52.1 cm
Literature: Braun cat.154

eii./d15/ig64,og64 (av.)

224
Steen, J.
*'Daer baet geen medecyn, want het is
minnepyn'*
Landesmuseum, Schwerin
c. 1662
62.5 x 52 cm
Literature: Braun cat.155

eii./d15/ig64,og64 (av.)

225
Streeck, J. van
Still-life with a Nautilus Cup
Sale Sotheby's London 3/4/85-
176
63 x 51 cm

eii./d15/ig64,og64 (av.)

Cf. Jan Steen, *'Soo gewonne, soo
verteert'*.

226
Terborch, G.

*A Woman Making Music with Two
Men*
National Gallery, London
c. 1670
67.6 x 57.8 cm
Literature: Mills 1983, pl.34

av./a12/ig86,og83

The border has a meandering
vine with lotus flowers and
leaves. Cf. Pagnano nr. 16.

227
Verkolje, N.
Young Couple with a Dog
Gallery Nijstad, The Hague 1984
1694
49 x 43 cm
See illustration p.45

av. (eii.)

228
Vermeer, J.
The Procuress
Staatliche Gemäldegalerie,
Dresden
1656
143 x 130 cm
Literature: Blankert cat.3
See illustration p.43

av./a16/og86

229
Vermeer, J.
*Girl Reading a Letter at an Open
Window*
Staatliche Gemäldegalerie,
Dresden
c. 1659
83 x 64.5 cm
Literature: Blankert cat.6

eii./d15 (av.)

230
Vermeer, J.
The Music Lesson
Royal collections, Buckingham
Palace, London
c. 1664
73.6 x 64.1 cm
Literature: Blankert cat.16

eii./d15/og102 (av.)

231
Vermeer, J.
The Concert
Isabella Stewart Gardner
Museum, Boston (stolen, April,
1990)
c. 1664
69 x 63 cm
Literature: Blankert cat.17

eii./d15/og102 (av.)

DOUBLE-NICHE USHAK CARPETS

232
Claesz. van Utrecht, C.
Annunciation
Gemäldegalerie, Leipzig
c. 1525
See illustration p.40

avii/a6/og48

233
Dou, G.
*Girl Playing the Virginals at a Table
Covered by a Rug*
Present location unknown
c. 1660
38 x 30.5 cm

Literature: Dijck 1987, nr.130

avii/a7/og43

Cf. id. *Woman Looking Out of a
Window.*

234
Dou, G.
Woman Looking Out of a Window
Narodowe Museum, Prague
c. 1660
38 x 29.5 cm
See illustration p.41

avii/a7/ig51,og43

Cf. id. *Girl Playing the Virginals at
a Table Covered by a Rug.* Cf. also
Pagnano nr.45.

235
Dyck, A. van
*The Three Eldest Children of
Charles I*
Galleria Sabauda, Turin
1635
151 x 154 cm
Literature: Larsen 2, nr.577

avii/a7/ig51,og43?

236
Maes, N.
Woman Reading at a Table
Koninklijk Paleis voor Schone
Kunsten, Brussels
1650-55
70.5 x 51 cm
Literature: cat. 1984, p.180

avii/a7/ig51?

The central medallion has a white
colour.

237
Mierevelt, M.J. van
Portrait of Prince Rupert
Royal Collections, England
1625
Literature: Mills 1983, fig.16

avii/a7/ig421,og421

The spandrels have a cloudband
pattern.

238
Ochtervelt, J.
Family Portrait
Fogg Art Museum, Cambridge
(Massachusetts)
1663
97 x 85 cm
Literature: Kuretsky cat.18

a7/ig421,og421 (avii)

The rug seems to have yellow elems and yellow fringes.

239
Ochtervelt, J.
The Lemon Slice
c. 1667
48.5 x 37.5 cm
Literature: Kuretsky cat.37

avii/a7/og42

240
Pluym, K. van der (attr. to)

A Philosopher
National Museum, Warsaw
c. 1660
75 x 82 cm

avii/a7

241
Ravesteyn, J.A. van

Portrait of Arent Hermansz Hem
Sale Christie's New York 18/6/
82-44
1620-25
215.9 x 133.4 cm

a61 (avii)

242
Renesse, C. van
Christ before Pilate
North Carolina Museum of Art
1660-70
118.7 x 96.5 cm
Literature: Steel p.103

a7 (avii)

The field is left empty.

243
Steen, J.
A Lady at her Toilet
H.M. the Queen of England
1663
65 x 53 cm
Literature: Braun cat.178

avii./a6?

The red field is framed with white borders; the spandrels are white too. Red fringes. Cf. id. *Moses Breaks the Crown of Pharao*h.

244
Steen, J.
'Soo voer gesongen, soo na gepepen'
Royal Picture Gallery The Mauritshuis, The Hague
1663-5
134 x 163 cm
Literature: Braun cat.201

a62 (avii)

Only a small part of the border is visible. It shows a stiff version of the cloudband design. The border is white; cf. id. *A Lady at her Toilet*; id. *Moses Breaks the Crown of Pharaoh*; id. *The Human Life*.

245
Steen, J.
'Soo voorgesonghen, soo naegepepen'
Musée Fabre, Montpellier
1663-5
87 x 71 cm
Literature: Braun cat.202

avii./a62/ig14,og8

The rug has a red field with red borders and spandrels; the latter are decorated with cloudband ornaments. An elem is missing.

246
Steen, J.
The Human Life
Royal Picture Gallery The Mauritshuis, The Hague
1665-67
68.2 x 82 cm

Literature: Braun cat.261
See illustration p.41

avii./a62

Cf. id. *'Soo voorgesonghen, soo naegepepen'*; id. *A Lady at her Toilet*; id. *Moses Breaks the Crown of Pharaoh*.

247
Steen, J.
Moses Breaks the Crown of Pharaoh
c. 1670
78 x 79 cm
Literature: Braun cat.328

avii./a62/ig14a,og72

The carpet is shown three times: once on the podium, and twice on the baldachin. The colouring is presumably identical to the other Ushak Double-niche rugs painted by Steen. Again, the cloudband border design is of the simpler version, as is usual for white-ground Anatolian carpets (cf. Pagnano nrs.13,15).

248
Voort, C. van der
Portrait of a Man
National Museum, Copenhagen
1622
149 x 94 cm

avii

249
Voort, C. van der
Portrait of a Man Aged 26
Hallwyll Museum, Stockholm
1623
126 x 94 cm

avii.?/a62/ig131

The arabesques in the spandrels have various different colours (Cf. Hali VII (1985), 4, p.7)

250
Vos, C. de

Portrait of a Family
Koninklijk Paleis voor Schone Kunsten, Antwerp

avii./a7

251
Zeeuw, C. de
Family Portrait
Landesmuseum, Munster
1564
Literature: Mills 1983 (B), ill.20

avii/a6/ig5?,og5

The authentic model may have had arabesques in the spandrels, which are clumsily painted by de Zeeuw. The floral ornaments in the field are undoubtedly invented by the painter.

TRANSYLVANIAN CARPETS

252
Unknown Dutch artist

Portrait of an Unknown Lady
Sale F.Muller, Amsterdam 23/2/
04-17
1644

axi2/a3?/ig11

Cf. Pagnano 202.

253
Backer, A.
Four Governesses of the Burgher Orphanage
Amsterdams Historisch Museum, Amsterdam
1683
Literature: Mills 1988, p.43, O. Ydema, Turkse tapijten op Nederlandse schilderijen, in: H. Theunissen e.a., p.143.

axi3

254
Boel, P
Still-life with Peaches
Sale Sotheby's London 10/7/63-145
1650-60
53 x 70 cm

axi./a3/ig11,og11

Cf. Pagnano 202

255
Codde, P.
A Lady at her Toilet
Louvre, Paris
1660

axi.1/a3/ig11,og43

Possibly the rug which Pieter Codde used as a model for this painting was of some age in 1660, as it has arabesques in the corner medallions and an archaic undulating stem in the outer guard border. It seems that the rug had two niches at the end side; cf. de Keyser, *Portrait of an Unknown Man.*

256
Eeckhout, G. van de
Jozef Explaining The Dreams of the Pharaoh (or Daniel Explaining the Dreams of Nebuchadnezzar?)
Sale Dorotheum Vienna, sept. 1970, as J. Ovens
1660-70?
101.3 x 126.6 cm

axi2/a31

The rug has a dark field and spandrels in a light colour. Cf. Pagnano 202 for the field design.

257
Graat, B.
Portrait of Some Members of the Deutz (?) Family
Collection Jkvr. P.Boreel, Beverwijk
1658

Literature: Exh. cat. Drie Eeuwen Portret in Nederland, Amsterdam 1952, nr. 41

a31/ig11,og11 (axi)

Stiff representation of the design. The border is too narrow in comparison to the field. The carpet is shown with fringes and elems on four sides, which seems an invention by the painter rather than a historical characteristic of the authentic model.

258
Gijsels, P.
Still-life near a Fountain
Rijksmuseum, Amsterdam
1670-80
38 x 47 cm
Literature: van Thiel p. 251

axi/a31/ig11,og11

259
Hooch, P. de
Family Portrait Group Making Music
The Cleveland Museum of Art, Cleveland
1663
100 x 119 cm
Literature: Sutton cat. 53
See illustration p.52

axi3/a15/ig13

A very similar surviving example is the Rothschild-Carlowitz rug, which is kept in the Planner collection, Graz, Austria (Hali X (1988), 3, p.43).

260
Kessel, J. van
Asia
Alte Pinakothek, Munich
1664-6
Literature: Berlin 1985, p.41

axi2/a31/ig11,og11

The border has no starform cartouches. The elem and the fringes are green.

261
Keyser, Th. de
Portrait of Constantijn Huygens and his Clerk
National Gallery, London
1627
92.4 x 63.9 cm
Literature: Mills 1983 (A), Pl.28

axi1/a31/ig11,og11

Cf. Pagnano 201.

262
Keyser, Th. de
Portrait of an Unknown Man
Louvre, Paris
1632
78 x 52 cm
Literature: O. Ydema, Turkse tapijten op Nederlandse schilderijen, in: H. Theunissen e.a., p.143-4, pl.13
See illustration p.47

axi1/a31/ig11,og11

Usually, 'Transylvanian' carpets have a niche at both end sides of the field. A group of relatively early 'Transylvanian' prayer rugs with only one niche also exists (e.g. Végh and Layer 1977, nr.11). In paintings it is not possible to determine whether the 'Transylvanian' rug in the painter's atelier had one or two niches, unless he had represented it in such a way that both ends of the field would be visible. The rug in this and other portraits by Thomas de Keyser may have had two niches at one end (for which reason the representations are very interesting, as surviving examples of this variant are unknown). Still, because in all his portraits de Keyser showed the rug with medallions in the visible end of the field, the possibility exists that the rug may have had niches on the other end of the field as well. Otherwise one would expect an occasional representation showing the rug from the lower end without the corner medallions.

263
Keyser, Th. de

Portrait of an Unknown Woman
Gemäldegalerie, Berlin-Dahlem

c. 1632
78 x 52 cm

axi1/a31/ig11,og11

Cf. id. *Portrait of an Unknown Man* (pendant).

264
Keyser, Th. de
Portrait of a Couple at a Table
Musée des Beaux-Arts, Rouen
1625-35
53 x 45 cm
Literature: Oldenbourg cat.130

axi1/a31/ig11,og11

Cf. id. *Portrait of Constantijn Huygens and his Clerk*

265
Man, C. de

Portrait of a Woman Giving a Letter to a Man
Musée des Beaux-Arts, Marseille
1665 c
64 x 60 cm

axi/a3/ig11,og11

Cf. Pagnano 202. The rug is shown from the reverse side.

265-2
Man, C. de
The Faint
Present location unknown
1666
See illustration p.50

axi2

266
Man, C. de

Interior of a House, with a Servant
Sale Fievez, Brussels 8/5/29-77
1666
65 x 58 cm

axi2/a32/og11

267
Man, C. de
The Chessplayers
Museum of Fine Arts, Budapest
c. 1670
97.5 x 85 cm
Literature: London 1984, pl.117

a32/ig11,og11 (axi)

Comparatively simple design of
the border. Cf. Spuhler 1978 cat.
28. The rug has a yellow elem
and red fringes.

268
Man, C. de
Portrait of a Young Scholar
Collection F. Spliethoff, Baren-
drecht
c. 1680
74 x 60.5 cm
Literature: Plietsch pl.115

axi/a3/og11

269
Netscher, C.
*Lady Feeding a Parrot and a Man
with a Monkey*
Columbus Museum of Art, Ohio
1664
34.3 x 27.9 cm

axi2/a31/ig11,og11

Cf. Pagnano 202

270
Netscher, C.
*Couple Making Music in an Arched
Window-bay*
Gemäldegalerie, Dresden
1665

43.5 x 34 cm
See illustration p.50

axi2/a17/ig11,og11

271
Netscher, C.
The Music Lesson
Royal Picture Gallery The
Mauritshuis, The Hague
1665
Literature: Amsterdam 1989,
nr.31b

axi/a17/ig11,og11

Cf. id. *Couple Making Music in an
Arched Window-bay.*

272
Netscher, C.
Woman Teaching a Child to Read
National Gallery, London
c. 1669
45.1 x 37 cm
Literature: cat. 1960, nr.844;
Amsterdam 1989, nr.33

axi/a32/ig11,og11

273
Netscher, C.
*Young Servant Handing a Silver
Plate with Apples to a Young
Woman*
Collection Duke of Rutland,
Belvoir Castle
1665
39 x 32 cm

axi/a3/ig11,og11

Cf. id. *The Music Lesson*, Alte
Pinakothek, Munich

274
Netscher, C.

Lady at her Toilet
Gemäldegalerie, Dresden

1665
43.5 x 34 cm

axi2/a31/ig11,og11

Cf. id. *The Music Lesson*, Alte
Pinakothek, Munich

275
Netscher, C.
*Two Men and Two Women in an
Interior Playing Cards*
Metropolitan Museum of Art,
New York
1660-70
47.5 x 42.5

axi2/a3/ig11

276
Netscher, C.
A Boy Blowing Bubbles
Sale Christie's New York, 10/1/
80-238a
c. 1665
22.8 x 17.8 cm

axi2/a31/ig11.og11

Cf. id. *The Music Lesson*, Dresden

277
Netscher, C.
The Music Lesson
Gemäldegalerie, Dresden
1666

axi2/a31/ig11,og11

cf. id. *The Music Lesson*, Alte
Pinakothek Munich. The
cartouches are white and yellow.
The elems are green with a red
stripe; the fringes are red. For the
decoration of the spandrels cf.
Bennett p.202, ill. upper left side
on the page.

278
Netscher, C.
Brothelscene
Sale Sotheby's London 19/4/37-
14
1660-70
37,5 x 32,5 cm

axi2/a31/ig11,og11

Cf. Pagnano 202

279
Netscher, C.
The Present
Gemäldegalerie, Kassel
1667
25 x 21 cm
Literature: Hofstede de Groot,
nr.131

axi/ig11

Cf. id. *The Music Lesson*, Alte
Pinakothek, Munich

280
Netscher, C.
The Music Lesson
Alte Pinakothek, Munich
1665
50.4 x 45.7 cm
Literature: Philadelphia 1984,
pl.76

axi/a3/ig11,og11

The rug has a red field, red main
border and red guard border. The
spandrels are brown or purple;
the cartouches in the main
border, as far as they are visible,
are green. There is no lamp
hanging in the top of the niche,
but a floral ornament (cf. Spuhler
1978, cat.27). The elem and the
fringes are green.

281
Netscher, C.

*A Woman Singing at a Table and a
Man Playing the Lute*
Musée des Beaux-Arts, Rouen
1665-75

axi2/a3/ig11,og11 (a31)

Cf. id. *The Music Lesson*, Munich

282
Netscher, C.

Portrait of Mr. Matthias van Remswinckel (1618-99), Vice Chancellor of Brandenburg
State-owned Art Collections Department, The Hague
c. 1670
69 x 54 cm

axi2/a3/ig11,og11

283
Netscher, C. (after)
A Musical Party
National Gallery, London
1665-75
55.5 x 45 cm
Literature: Mills 1983 (A), Pl.30

axi2/a31/ig11,og11

Cf. id. *The Music Lesson*, Alte Pinakothek, Munich

284
Netscher, C.
Dutch Lady (portrait of the painter's wife?)
Metropolitan Museum of Art, New York
c. 1670
30 x 26.2 cm

axi2/a3?/ig11

Cf. id. *The Music Lesson*, Alte Pinakothek, Munich

285
Netscher, C.
The Death of Cleopatra
Staatliche Kunsthalle, Karlsruhe
1673
53.5 x 44 cm

axi

286
Netscher, C.
Portrait of a Young Girl with Fruit, and a Servant
Coll. Earl of Northbrook, London
c. 1680
33.1 x 72.4 cm

g11 (axi)

287
Netscher, C.
Portrait of a Young Girl
Koetser Gallery, London 1961
1680
50.8 x 41 cm

a3?/ig11,og11 (axi)

288
Netscher, C. (attr. to)

Portrait of a Young Man
Sale J.Schroeffl, Vienna 17/10/ 21-42
50 x 42 cm

axi.2/a3

289
Ochtervelt, J. (after)
Merry Company at a Table
North Carolina Museum of Art, Raleigh
c. 1675 or later
46.5 x 46.5 cm
Literature: Kuretsky D-6

axi2/a31/ig11

290
Rubens, P. or Thomas, J.
Annunciation
Sale Lepke Berlin 10-11-1911, nr.106

axi/a3/ig11,og11

The cartouche design at the end side of the rug has only been represented in half, which seems a historical detail; the weaver may have had to shorten the rug on the loom because the warps were too short.

291
Steen, J.
The Doctor's Visit
Wellington Museum, London
c. 1663
47.5 x 41 cm
Literature: Braun cat.186

a31/ig11 (axi)

292
Tilborgh, G. van
A Collection of Paintings
Coll. Cook, Richmond
120 x 176 cm
Literature: E. de Callatay, in: Belgisch Tijdschrift voor Oudheidkunde en Kunstgeschiedenis XXIX (1960) 1-4, p.161, fig.5

a3/ig11,og11 (axi)

293
Toorenvliet, J.

Portrait of Carel Quina, Knight of the Holy Sepulchre, Amsterdam-born Explorer of Asia
Rijksmuseum, Amsterdam
1669
40 x 31 cm
Literature: van Thiel, p.543

a15 (axi3)

294
Toorenvliet, J.
'Piskijker'
Galerie Mullenmeister, Sohngen 1973 (Art Market)
1670-80
48 x 32 cm

axi/a17/ig10,og11

295
Toorenvliet, J.

The Doctor's Visit
Museum of Fine Arts, Budapest

1670-80
51 x 40 cm
Literature: cat. 1931, nr.560

axi2

Cf. Végh & Layer 1977, pl.17.

296
Valckert, W. van de
*The Company of Captain Albert
Coenraets Burgh and Lieutenant
Peter Evertsz Hulft, Amsterdam*
Amsterdams Historisch Museum,
Amsterdam
1625
169.5 x 270
Literature: van Thiel p.554

a31/ig11 (axi)

Only a very small part of the field
is visible, which makes it very
difficult to identify the field
design. It seems to have been
decorated with, among others, a
floral ornament, and stylized
leaves on stiff stems. This would
suggest that the rug did not have
a quarter medallion in that corner
of the field, as quarter medallions
usually do not have similar
ornaments. Perhaps Valckert here
presents the only single-niche
Transylvanian prayer rug of this
group recorded so far in painting.
However, since the decoration of
the small visible part can not be
linked with certainty to the
ornaments in the lower end
corners of similar single-niche
prayer rugs (e.g. Végh and Layer
1977, nr.11; Dimand/Mailey
1973, fig.176), the identification of
the field pattern is still uncertain.

297
Verkolje, J.

Nursery Scene
Louvre, Paris
1675
58 x 51 cm
Literature: Kuretsky fig. 85

axi2/a31/ig11,og11

298
Verkolje, J.
*Young Woman Talking to a Dog,
and a Servant*
State-owned art Collections
Department, The Hague
1679
52 x 47.5 cm

axi

299
Vos, C. de
Portrait of Abraham Grapheus
Koninklijk Paleis voor Schone
Kunsten, Antwerp
1620

a3/g11a (axi)

300
Witte, E. de
*Portrait of a Family, Presumed to be
Nicolaas Listing, His Wife Geertruyt
Spiegel and Their Godchild*
Alte Pinakothek, Munich
1678
68.5 x 86.5 cm
Literature: cat. 1983, p.571

axi2/a31/ig13,og102

Smyrna Carpets

301
Boonen, A.
*Portrait of Cornelis, Nicolaes and
Catharina Jacoba Geelvinck*
sale Christie's London 4/5/79-29
1690-1700

50.7 x 38.1 cm

axii/a4/ig83

302
Bronchorst, J. van
Allegorical Portrait of a Family
Sale Lempertz Köln 26/11/31-
652
1656
186 x 230 cm

axii/a4

303
Bronchorst, J. van

Vanitas
Sale Christie's London 2/7/76-16
1650-60
76.2 x 100.4 cm

axii/g12/ig5

Cf. Willem Duyster, *Tric-trac
Players*, Hermitage. For the
rosette border cf. Hannover 1987,
nr.59. The field has a dark
ground.

304
Coques, G.
*A Collector of Drawings and his
Family*
Gemäldegalerie, Kassel
1645-60
47.2 x 63.8 cm
Literature: Schnackenburg nr.73

a12/g12 (axii)

305
Duyster, W.
Tric-trac Players
Rijksmuseum, Amsterdam
30.5 x 40 cm
c. 1630
Literature: van Thiel p.207 (ill.)

axii/g12/

Cf. id. *Tric-trac Players*, Hermitage. The carpet has a dark blue
field.

306
Duyster, W. (attr. to)

Tric-trac Players
Hermitage, Leningrad
1625-35

axii/a4

The border with rosettes, as well
as the triple inner guard border
without decoration, is unusual
(cf. Bronchorst, *Vanitas*).

307
Hoet, G.

Portrait of a Man
Alte Pinakothek, Munich
c. 1690

axii/a16/ig6

308
Hooch, P. de
*A Woman at her Toilet, with an
Officer*
Wellington Museum, London
c. 1665
52 x 62 cm
Literature: Sutton cat.70
See illustration p.54

axii/a13/ig83,og83

Only a small part of the field is
visible. The design of the main
border stripe is remarkable. It is
known from the much later 19th

century Ladik prayer rugs (cf. J. Bailey, Ladik Prayer Rugs, in: Hali VII (1985) 4, p.18v, pl. 1 en 5).

309
Hooch, P. de
Portrait of the Jacob-Hoppesack Family
Private collection, England
1670
97 x 114.5 cm
Literature: Sutton cat.92

axii/a4/ig83,og83?

310
Lairesse, G. de
Portrait of a Man, Presumed to be Philipp von Zesen
Gemäldegalerie, Kassel
1682
141 x 115 cm

axii/ig12

311
Musscher, M. van
Portrait of a Geographer
Sale Lepke Berlin 3/12/29-30
c. 1660
44 x 35 cm

axii

The carpet has a dark coloured field.

312
Musscher, M. van
A Gentleman with Mandolin and a Lady in an Interior
Sale Petit Amsterdam 19/6/13-50
c. 1670
67.5 x 63.5 cm
Literature: Gaehtgens cat.9b

axii/a4

The carpet has a dark coloured field.

312-2
Musscher, M. van
Portrait of Thomas Hees
Rijksmuseum , Amsterdam
1687
See illustration p.75

axii/g12

313
Musscher, M. van

Woman Giving a Coin to a Servant
Sale Lepke Berlin 20/2/12-330
1669
74.5 x 65 cm

axii/a4

Rather small rug. It has a dark coloured field.

314
Musscher, M. van

The Doctor's Visit
Present location unknown
c. 1675
50 x 39 cm

axii/a4

Large carpet. Cf. id. *Musical Party in a Courtyard*. The carpet has a dark blue field.

315
Musscher, M. van

Portrait of a Family in an Interior
Duke of Buccleuch, Boughton, Scotland
c. 1670
71 x 59 cm

axii/a4/ig86,og86

The place of the carpet, on the floor, is highly unusual for 17th century Dutch genre paintings. Cf. id. *Portrait of Thomas Hees*; Coques, *Portrait of a Couple in an Interior*. The carpet has a dark coloured field.

316
Musscher, M. van
Portrait of Sara Antheunis
Sale Frederik Muller Amsterdam, 9/12/1902-44
1671
100.5 x 88.5 cm

axii?/a4?

The carpet has a dark coloured field.

317
Musscher, M. van

Musical Party in a Courtyard
State-owned Art Collections Dept., The Hague
1674 or 1676
64.5 x 72 cm
Literature: cat. Gemeente-museum Arnhem 1965, p.106

axii/a4

The carpet has a dark blue field.

318
Musscher, M. van

An Alchemist in his Studio
Sale Cologne 5/6/1893-79
1670-80
41 x 36 cm

axii/a16/ig51

The carpet has a dark coloured field.

319
Musscher, M. van
Portrait of a Family in an Amster-dam Courtyard
Royal Picture Gallery The Mauritshuis, The Hague
1681
90 x 106 cm
Literature: cat.1985, nr.123

axii/a16

Cf. id. *An Alchemist in his Studio.* The carpet has a dark blue field.

320
Musscher, M. van

Portrait of Balichje Hulft and her Son Valerius
Private collection,
The Netherlands
1682
83 x 72 cm

axii

321
Musscher, M. van

Portrait of Godfried Hinter
Formerly coll. Chanenko, Kiev
1688
58 x 49 cm

axii/a16/ig46?

Cf. id. *An Alchemist in his Studio.* The carpet has a dark coloured field.

322
Musscher, M. van

Portrait of a Geographer
Private collection, Brussels
1680-90

axii

The carpet presumably has a yellow or green field.

323
Musscher, M. van

Girl Feeding Grapes to a Parrot
Present location unknown
1680
60 x 46 cm

axii/a4/og121

The carpet has a dark coloured field.

324
Musscher, M. van

Lady Playing the Lute
Montreal Museum of Fine Arts,
Montreal
c. 1680

axii

325
Musscher, M. van (circle)

Portrait of an Unknown Man
Private collection, Germany 1944
1670-80

axii

326
Naiveu, M.
Portrait of an Unknown Man
Museum of Fine Arts, Budapest
c. 1700
62.5 x 52.5 cm

axii

Cf. id. *Portrait of an Unknown Woman* (pendant).

327
Naiveu, M.
Portrait of an Unknown Woman
Museum of Fine Arts, Budapest
c. 1700
62.5 x 52.5 cm

axii

Cf. id. *Portrait of an Unknown Man*
(pendant).

328
Netscher, C. or Netscher, Con.
Portrait of a Woman and a Child
Gallery R. Lamm, Paris 1960
51 x 42.5 cm
Literature: sale P.Brandt,
Amsterdam 12/10/54-122

axii/a4/ig43b,og43b

329
Schalcken, G.
A Lady Feeding a Parrot at a Niche
Sale Christie's London 22/10/82-
115
42 x 33 cm

axii

330
Slingelant, P. van
Woman with a Lute
California Palace of the Legion of
Honor, San Francisco
1677
23 x 18.7 cm

axii/a4/ig86,og51

331
Slingelant, P. van

Portrait of Sara van Peenen
Centraal Museum, Utrecht
1687
42.3 x 32.1 cm

axii/a4/ig43,og83

The red cartouches are placed on
a red ground. The field is blue;
the elem is red as are the fringes.

332
Sorgh, H.

*Portrait of a Man, Writing at a
Table*
National Museum, Warsaw
1663
81 x 75 cm

axii

The border design is unusual for
Smyrna carpets.

Chessboard Carpets

332a
Unknown artist, possibly Italian
school

Still-life
Collection Prof.dr. Grottanelli,
Rome 1951

axiv/a5

333
Claesz, P.
Still-life with Turkey Pie
Rijksmuseum, Amsterdam
1627

75 x 132 cm

axiv/a5

Only a small part of the field
design is visible. The border has

334
Gheeraedts, M.
Portrait of Queen Elizabeth
Private collection, England
1580s
Literature: Mills 1981, nr. C2

axiv

335
Kick, S.

the usual cartouche design on a
dark purple ground.

*Five Young Men at a Table, One of
them Playing the Flute*
Staatliche Kunsthalle, Stuttgart
1645-50
54 x 41 cm

axiv/a5/ig6

There can be little doubt about
the identification of the rug in
this painting. Still, it is
remarkable that Simon Kick
changed the ground colour of the
border; as several details like the
pattern of the guard borders are
identical with those of other
representations of 'Chessboard'
carpets in his work, all
representations seem to have
been drawn by Kick after the
same model.

336
Kick, S.
Portrait of a Woman at a Table
Ashmolean Museum of Art,
Oxford
1645-50
61 x 50 cm
Literature: Mills 1981, nr. C6

axiv/a5

337
Kick, S.
*Painter Portraying a Man with a
Wineglass*
National Gallery of Ireland,
Dublin
1645-50
91.4 x 71.1 cm

axiv/a5

338
Kick, S.
Woman at her Toilet, and a Maid
Museum für Bildenden Künsten,
Leipzig
1648
55 x 41 cm

axiv/a5

339
Kruys, C.
Still-life
Sale Christie's London 21/7/72-
100
1640-50
90 x 78.5 cm

axiv/a5

340
Metsu, G.
Music Party
Metropolitan Museum of Art,
New York
1659
61.5 x 54.3 cm
Literature: Philadelphia 1984,
cat.72, pl.66

axiv/a5

341
Mijtens, D.

*Portrait of Susan Villiers, Countess
of Denbigh*
Sale Christie's London 1/7/38-96
1625-30
202 x 117 cm

a5 (axiv)

342
Neer, E. van der
The Faint
Private collection

1680
52 x 43 cm
Literature: Amsterdam 1989,
nr.27

a5

The border pattern seems to
point at a relation between this
carpet and the 'Chessboard' rugs,
although the field pattern is
different. Since the relation
cannot be established with more
certainty, this example is not
included in the diagram on p.56.

342a
Roos, Th.

The Death of Damocles
Gallery Konrad O. Bernheimer,
Munich/London 1989
1672
56 x 66 cm

a5

Roos left the field undecorated,
which appears to be a caprice of
the painter rather than an
objective registration of the
authentic rug which he may have
had in his studio; the cumulation
of objects represented in detail by
Roos appears to have dictated a
less ornamented background in
the scene.

PERSIAN CARPETS

343
Unknown Flemish artist

*Portrait of Jean Charles de la Faille,
Lord of Rymenam, aged 30*
Koninklijk Museum voor Schone
Kunsten, Brussels
1598
107.2 x 77.2 cm
Literature: cat. 1984, p.408

bi./b1/ig62?

A somewhat stiff representation,
possibly made after a
preparatory study.

344
Unknown Dutch artist
Portrait of an Unknown Lady
Sale Sotheby's, New York, 30/5/
79-78
c. 1630
71 x 54.5 cm

bi./b2/ig92,og4

345
Aelst, W. van

Still-life with Flowers
Eugene Slatter Gallery, London
1954
c. 1660
91.4 x 65.1 cm

bi./b1/ig64,og44

346
Aelst, W. van (attr. to)
Still-life with Flowers
Present location unknown
c. 1660
76.2 x 63.5 cm
Literature: Apollo nov. 1968,
p.LV (ill.)

ig62 (bi.)

347
Anraadt, Pieter van
*Six Regents and the Housemaster of
the Oude Zijds Institute for the
Outdoor Relief of the Poor*
Amsterdams Historisch Museum,

Amsterdam
1675
237 x 425 cm
Literature: van Thiel p. 84;
Ydema 1986, p.17, fig.2

bi./b1/ig11c,og47

Impressive representation of the
floral and cloudband pattern. The
large rug had rows of four
spiralling scrolls instead of two,
as most of these carpets in Dutch
paintings have. Similar, but
somewhat richer in design is a
carpet illustrated by Pagnano,
nr.120. The latter rug has a more
complicated system of secondary
scrolling vines and also animal
figures.

348
Backhuyzen, L.

A Self-portrait
Rijksmuseum, Amsterdam
1699
190 x 150 cm
Literature: van Thiel p.96

biv/ig46

The field is filled with large birds
and floral ornaments.

349
Berckheyde, J.

Portrait of a Painter
Present location unknown
c. 1660
44 x 36 cm

bi./b1/ig46

350
Boel, J.
Still-life with a Dead Swan
Koninklijk Paleis voor Schone
Kunsten, Antwerp
c. 1660
237 x 229 cm
Literature: Greindl 1983, nr.3

bi./b1?/og86?

351
Boel, J.
Still-life with Dead Animals
Private collection, Brussels 1983
c. 1660
169 x 236 cm
Literature: Greindl 1983, nr.4

bi./b1?/og86

352
Boel, P.
A Still-life with Pets and Trophies of War
Gemäldegalerie, Kassel
c. 1648
172 x 249 cm
Literature: Schnackenburg, pl.39

bi./b1/ig45

At the upper and/or lower sides

the carpet ends in a narrow elem
of irregular flat weave, and long
fringes formed by plaited warps.
Cf. Pagnano 105 for the border
design.

353
Bol, F.
Portrait of Johanna Mercier
van de Poll-Wolters-Quina
Foundation, Zeist
134 x 98 cm
c. 1645
Literature: Blankert cat.154,
pl.165

bi./b5 (bii.)

354
Bol, F.
The String of Pearls
Philips collection, Eindhoven
1649
143.5 x 178 cm
Literature: Blankert cat.168,
pl.179

bi./b5/ig45 (bii.)

355
Bol, F.
*Four Governors of the Lepers'
Asylum*
Amsterdams Historisch Museum,
Amsterdam
1649
224 x 310 cm
Literature: van Thiel, p. 123
See illustration p.68

bii./b5/ig45,og44

356
Bol, F.
Portrait of a Boy
Castle Howard collection
1652
160.0 x 147.5 cm
Literature: Blankert cat.138,
pl.149

b5/ig45,og44 (bii.)

The field is left plain. Cf. id.
Portrait of the Artist and his Wife.

357
Bol, F.
Five Officers of the Gouda Militia
Municipal Museum, Gouda
1653
213 x 252 cm
Literature: Blankert cat.178,
pl.190

bi./b5/ig45?,og44 (bii.)

358
Bol, F
*Portrait of the Artist and his Wife
Lisbeth Dell*
Louvre, Paris
1654
205 x 180 cm
Literature: Blankert cat.174-1,
pl.186

b5/ig45,og44 (bii.)

The field is left plain.

359
Bol, F.

*The Headmen of the Amsterdam
Wine Merchants Guild*
Alte Pinakothek, Munich
c. 1655
193.5 x 305 cm
Literature: Blankert cat.180,
pl.192

bi./b5/ig45,og44 (bii.)

360
Bol, F.
*Six Regents and the Beadle of the
Nieuwe Zijds Institute for the
Outdoor Relief of the Poor*

Rijksmuseum, Amsterdam
1657
143 x 192 cm
Literature: van Thiel p. 124 (ill.)

bi./b5/ig45 (bii.)

361
Bol, F.
Gentleman Sitting at a Table
Hermitage, Leningrad
1657
129.5 x 100 cm
Literature: Blankert cat.105-1,
pl.106a

bi./og44 (bii.)

362
Bol, F.

*Four Governors of the Lepers'
Asylum*
Amsterdams Historisch Museum,
Amsterdam
1668
224 x 310 cm
Literature: Blankert cat.177,
pl.189

bi./b1/ig47,og46

363
Bol, F.
Portrait of a Gentleman
Brodie Castle, Scotland
1669
109 x 89 cm
Literature: Blankert cat.116,
pl.125

bi./b5/ig45,og44 (bii.)

364
Boonen, A.
Six Regents of the Spinhuis (house of correction) and the Nieuwe Werkhuis (new workhouse) in Amsterdam
Amsterdams Historisch Museum, Amsterdam
1699
191.5 x 297 cm
Literature: van Thiel, p.128

bi.?

365
Bor, P.
Portrait of the van Vanevelt Family
St. Pieters and Blokland Gasthuis, Amersfoort
1628
102 x 303 cm
Literature: Haarlem 1986, cat.74
See illustration p.66

b5/ig46 (bi.)

366
Bray, J. de
Odysseus Discovered among the Daughters of Lykomedes
Narodowe Museum, Warsaw
1664

bi./b6

Sketchy representation. As far as can be seen on the representation, the border has oblong and circular lobed cartouches, filling the entire width of the border.

367
Brueghel, J.

Hearing
formerly Prado, Madrid
1610-20
65 x 107 cm

b1/ig89,og46 (bi.)

The field is left plain.

368
Brueghel, J. and Rubens, P.
Sight

Prado, Madrid
1610-20
70 x 112
Literature: sale Paris 26/4/07-5

bi./b1

369
Bronchorst, J. van
Merry Company
Present location unknown
1640-50
88 x 136 cm
Literature: cat. Chanenko Kieff 1899, nr.261, album 102

bi./b1?/ig46

370
Bronchorst, J. van
Cleopatra
Schloss Gruenewald, Berlin
1640-50
160 x 135 cm
Literature: Gen. Kat. I, nr. 5469

b1 (bi.)

371
Ceulen, C. Janssens van
William II as a Child
Coll. H.M. the Queen, Windsor Castle
1658
162.5 x 116.5 cm

biv/b71/ig46

The field has S-stems with large palmettes, lotus flowers etc, as are found in the b1 border design (cf. Rijksmuseum fragment R.B.K. 1956-49).

372
Christian, J.
Portrait of the Painter
Sale Christie's, London 21/11/52-56
1677
39.3 x 31.6 cm

bi./b74/ig11d,og71

The field pattern is drawn in a similar way in a carpet in the

collection of E.Cittone (Pagnano nr.107), although the latter carpet has a somewhat richer design. The decoration of the main border is less elegantly drawn.

3/3
Codde, P.
A Party with a Dancer
Present location unknown
1603-6
54 x 86.5 cm
Literature: Cat. Mauritshuis 1983, ill.5

bi./b1

Sketchy representation. The inner guard has a geometrical design of small waves interchanged with rosettes (cf. Pagnano nr.108).

374
Coques, G.

Group Portrait in a Courtyard
Sale Sotheby's, London 6/7/66-79
1665-75
55 x 68 cm

bvi./b1/ig45,og47?

The field has a rich variant of the floral and cloudband design, like the carpet represented on a painting by van Anraadt, *Six Regents and the Housemaster of the Oude Zijds Institute for the Outdoor Relief of the Poor*. The representation by Coques is less elegantly painted, as is most obvious in the rendering of the main border design. The carpet has a triple inner guard border.

375
Coques,G.
A Family Group
Sale Sotheby's, London 3/12/1924-63
1665-75
84.5 x 110 cm

bi./b1

376
Court, M. de la

Lambert Twant and his Four Sons
The Netherlandish PTT Museum, The Hague
1695
115 x 138 cm

bi./b1/ig62

The design is represented in a more lively drawing than that of the surviving floral and cloudband carpets. This could indicate that the painter did not have the original model in his studio when he painted this representation. Note the pinwheel rosette in the field and the large serrated leaves sprouting from the cloudband in the field. For similar characteristics cf. Ellis 1988, nr.62 and fig.62a.

377
Crayer, C. de
Christ Manifesting Himself to St.Julian
Koninklijk Paleis voor Schone Kunsten, Brussels
1623
287 x 200 cm
Literature: cat. 1984, p.80

b1/ig11a,og46. (bi.)

The field is left plain.

378
Crayer, C. de

The Representatives of the Clergy
and Nobility Rendering Account to
Christ
Alte Pinakothek, Munich
1630-35
303 x 148 cm
Literature: cat. 1898, nr.747

bi.?/b1/ig62,og89

379
Crayer, C. de
The Coronation of St.Rosalie
Municipal Museum, Ghent
1641
290 x 220 cm

bi./b1/og46

380
Crayer, Caspar de
The Purification of Mary
Sale Weber e.a., Brussels 21/12/
25-35
1644
205 x 163 cm

bi./b1/ig11a,og46

The border has a stiff floral
design. Cf. id. The Representatives
of the Clergy and Nobility Rendering Account to Christ; id. Christ
Manifesting Himself to St.Julian; id.
Annunciation.

381
Crayer, C. de
Annunciation
Gemäldegalerie, Vienna
c. 1630
333 x 238 cm
Literature: Vlieghe 1972, I, nr.
A93 and II, fig.94

bi./b1/ig11a,og46

382
Cuyp, A.

Burgomaster and City Council of
Dordrecht
formerly Sir Frederick Cook,
Richmond
c. 1640

biv/b6 (ci.?)

The painter may have worked
from a preparatory study, and
obscured the gray spots in his
memory by the sketchy
representation. The field has
large, directional plants (cf.Sarre/
Trenkwald 1979, pl.30). It is
framed by a triple guard border,
showing among others the g11
and g71 design.

383
Diepenbeek, A. van
Epitaph of Francis Movins
Alte Pinakothek, Munich
1625-30
203 x 148 cm
Literature: Steadman, fig.26

bi./b1/ig62,og89

384
Dou, G.

A Violin Player in a Window-bay
sale Christie's, London 11/6/71-
94
c. 1655
26.7 x 34.3 cm

bi./b73

384a
Dou, G.
'Piskijker'
Kunsthistorisches Museum,
Vienna
1653

bi./b73

385
Dyck, A. van
Portrait of Marchesa Balbi
National Gallery, Washington
1621
183 x 122 cm
Literature: Larsen, nr.194

bi./b1

386
Dyck, A. van
Portrait of Paolina Adorno,
Marchesa di Brignole-Sale and her
Son
National Gallery of Art,
Washington
1621-25
189.2 x 139.7 cm
Literature: Larsen, nr.225

bi./b1/ig46?

Sketchy representation.

387
Dyck, A. van
Portrait of a Man, Assumed to be
Lucas van Uffel
Metropolitan Museum of Art,
New York
c. 1622
124 x 100.6 cm
Literature: Liedtke, col.pl.VI

bi./b6 (ci.)

388
Dyck, A. van
P.P. Rubens with his son Albert
Hermitage, Leningrad
c. 1623
134 x 112 cm
Literature: cat. 1958, nr.7728

bi./b1/ig6

389
Dyck, A. van
Portrait of an Unknown Genoese
Lady
Staatliche Museen Preussischer
Kulturbesitz, Berlin-Dahlem
1623-24
200 x 116 cm
Literature: Larsen, nr.216

bi./b1

390
Dyck, A. van
Portrait of the Lomelli Family
National Gallery of Scotland,
Edinburgh
1623-25
265 x 250 cm
Literature: Larsen, nr.257

b1/og46? (bi.)

Sketchy representation.

391
Dyck, A. van
Portrait of Marchesa Lomelli with
Two of her Children at Prayer
Museu de Arte, Sao Paulo
1623-25
Literature: Larsen, nr.258

b1 (bi.)

Sketchy representation.

392
Dyck, A. van
Portrait of Paolina Adorno,
Marchesa di Brignole-Sale
Frick Collection, New York
1621-25
230.8 x 156.5 cm
Literature: Larsen, nr.226

bi./b1

Sketchy representation.

393
Dyck, A. van
Portrait of Giovanni Vincenzo
Imperiale
Koninklijk Museum voor Schone
Kunsten, Brussels
1626
210 x 147 cm
Literature: Larsen, nr.282

b1/og46? (bi.)

394
Eliasz (Pickenoy), N.

Portrait of Andries Rijckaert
Private collection,
The Netherlands
1628
121 x 89 cm

bi./b1/ig63

395
Eliasz (Pickenoy), N.
Portrait of an Unknown Man
Frost & Reed Gallery, London
1958
1630-40
Literature: *Connoisseur*, June 1958,
p.CIV

bi./b1/ig63

cf. id. *Portrait of Andries Rijckaert*

396
Eliasz (Pickenoy), N.

The Company of Capt. Dirck
Theuling en Lt. Pieter Adriaensz
Raep
Amsterdams Historisch Museum,
Amsterdam
1639
202 x 340.5 cm
Literature: van Thiel, p. 217

bi./b1/ig62,0g89

The floral ornaments of the
border are stiffly drawn.

397
Eliasz (Pickenoy), N.

Portrait of a Gentleman, Aged 67
Newhouse Galleries, New York
1989
c. 1640
109.2 x 82.5 cm

bi./ig62

398
Eliasz (Pickenoy), N. (attr. to)

Portrait of a Man Aged 41
Kunsthalle, Bremen
1632

bi./b1/ig11b

399
Everdingen, C. van
Count William III Grants a Charter
to the Polderboard of Rijnland
Hoogheemraadschap, Leyden
1654
218 x 212 cm
See illustration p.63

bi./b1/ig46

400
Everdingen, C. van

Portrait of Wollebrandt Geleynsz. de
Jongh
Municipal Museum, Alkmaar
1674
212 x 205 cm

bi./b7/ig10?

For the border pattern cf. Spuhler
1968, nrs.18-20. The carpet has
fringes on all sides. Wollebrandt
Geleynsz de Jongh was a chief
merchant of the Dutch East India
Company in Persia.

401
Fris, J.
Still-life with Helmet and Skull
Sale Sotheby's, London 30/11/
83-97
1666
108 x 84.5 cm

(bi.)

The guard borders have
alternating ovals and S-motifs.

402
Gabron, G.
Still-life with Roasted Poultry
Private collection, Naples
1646
80 x 100 cm
Literature: sale Rinuccini, Rome
29/4/05-24

bi./b1/ig46

403
Gijsbrechts, C.

Vanitas Still-life
Statens Museum for Kunst,
Copenhagen
1670
132 x 183 cm

bvi/b7/iig10,ig11d,og3?

404
Gijsbrechts, C.
Still-life with a Lobster and Fruits
Statens Museum for Kunst,
Copenhagen
1672
See illustration p.68

b74 (bi.)

405
Haensbergen, J. van
Portrait of a Member of the Bredehoff Family
Centraal Museum, Utrecht
1695
55 x 46 cm
Cat. 1952, p.51-52 (without ill.)

bi.

Some of the details differ from
the design in surviving examples.

406
Haye, R. de la (attr. to)
Two Women in an Arched Window
Sale Bukowski, Stockholm 11/
11/64-200 (as C. Netscher)
c. 1680
46.5 x 37.5 cm

bi./og44

407
Haye, R. de la
Woman Feeding her Parrot
Present location unknown
1670-90
32 x 26.5 cm
Literature: Oud Holland 1950,
p.242

b1/og44 (bi.)

408
Haye, R. de la
Three Children with a Cat and a Dog on a Balcony
Sale Christie's, London 17/12/
81-19
1660
48.5 x 39.5 cm

b1/ig46?,og44 (bi.)

The broad border has a rich floral
design.

409
Hecken, A. van den
Still-life with Fruits, a Lobster and Musical Instruments
Sale Sotheby's, London 6/7/83-
20
164.
121 x 174 cm

bi./b1/ig62 (og89 or g46)

The carpet has a red field, a dark
blue main border and a white
outer guard border. The latter
has at the lower or upper end
side the g46, and at the left or
right side the g89 design.

410
Heerschop, H.

A Writer
Hallwyl, Stockholm
1660-70
55 x 48 cm

b1/ig46 (bi.)

For the design of the inner guard
border cf. Pagnano nr.150.

411
Helst, B. van der

Portrait of Anthonie Reepmaker and his Wife and Children
Louvre, Paris
1669
192 x 149 cm
Literature: cat. 1979, p.69

b1?/ig89,og89? (bi.)

The border has palmettes,
flanked by large birds.

412
Helst, B. van der
Portrait of a Gentleman
Sale Mak van Waay, Amsterdam
4/10/1949-31
c. 1650
198 x 123 cm
See illustration p.71

bv./b7/g132

The drawing of the spiralling
scrolls, the floral ornaments and
the small chi-motifs indicate a
North-West Persian origin. The
border design is also
characteristic of North-West
Persian carpets (cf. Erdmann
1955, Abb.59; also: Pagnano
nr.64). The presence of a g132
ornament in the inner guard
cannot be explained.

413
Helst, B. van der
Officers of the Harquebusiers' Civic Guard
Amsterdams Historisch Museum,
Amsterdam
1655
171 x 283 cm
Literature: Schwartz 1986, p.35

bi./b1/ig11a/og47

414
Hooch, P. de
A Party of Four Figures at a Table
Metropolitan Museum of Art,
New York
1663-5
Dimensions not indicated
Literature: Sutton cat.56

bi./b1/ig63

The fringes are presumably
formed by the plaiting of the
ends of the warps.

415
Hooch, P. de
The Council Chamber of the Burgomasters in the Town Hall in Amsterdam
Thyssen-Bornemisza collection,
Lugano
1664-6
112.5 x 99 cm
Literature: Sutton cat.66

bi./b1?

416
Hooch, P. de
A Musical Party in a Hall
Museum der Bildenden Künste,
Leipzig
1664-6
81 x 68.3 cm
Literature: Sutton cat.68

bi./b1/ig11b?

417
Hooch, P. de
*A Man Playing a Lute and a Woman
Singing*
Present location unknown
c. 1670
73.5 x 62.2 cm
Literature: Sutton cat.95

bi./b74

418
Hooch, P. de
Woman and Child with a Parrot
Present location unknown
1673
Literature: Sutton cat.105

bi./b74/og47?

419
Hooch, P. de
*A Merry Company with a
Trumpeter*
Staatliche Museen Preussischer
Kulturbesitz, Berlin-Dahlem
1673-5
85 x 92 cm
Literature: Sutton cat.107

bi./b74

420
Hooch, P. de
A Musical Party with Four Figures
Academy of Arts, Honolulu
1674
98 x 115 cm
Literature: Sutton cat.108

bi./b74

421
Hooch, P. de
A Music Party with Five Figures
Statens Museum for Kunst,
Copenhagen
c. 1674
92 x 105.5 cm
Literature: Sutton cat.109

bi./b74

422
Hooch, P. de
A Party of Six Figures
Philadelphia Museum of Art,

Philadelphia
c. 1675
82 x 100 cm
Literature: Sutton cat.114

bi.?/b1?

423
Hooch, P. de
A Party of Four Figures at a Table
Corcoran Gallery of Art,
Washington
1675-7
86.3 x 69.8 cm
Literature: Sutton cat.121

bi./b1/ig62,og46?

424
Hooch, P. de
A Couple with a Parrot
Wallraf Richartz Museum,
Cologne
1675-7
73 x 62 cm
Literature: Sutton cat.122

bi./b74

Cf. Pagnano 107 for the field
design.

425
Hooch, P. de
A Doctor and a Sick Woman
Present location unknown
1675-80
65 x 56 cm
Literature: Sutton cat.132

bi./b74

426
Hooch, P. de
*A Man with a Book and Two
Women*
Staatliche Museen,
Gemäldegalerie, Berlin (East)
1676
63.5 x 75 cm
Literature: Sutton cat.133

bi./b74

427
Hooch, P. de
A Musical Party in a Courtyard
National Gallery, London
1677
83.5 x 68.5 cm
Literature: Sutton cat.134

bi./b74

428
Hooch, P. de
*A Woman with a Lute and a Man
with a Violin*

Present location unknown
1678 or later
66 x 59 cm
Literature: Sutton cat.138

bi./b2/og46?

429
Hooch, P. de
*A Couple Playing Music at a Table,
with a Serving Woman*
Hermitage, Leningrad
c. 1680
65 x 53 cm
Literature: Sutton cat.146

bi./b74

430
Hooch, P. de
*A Man Offering a Letter to a Lady
Feeding a Parrot*
Present location unknown
1681 or later
Literature: Sutton cat.149

bi./b74

Schematic representation.

431
Hooch, P. de
*A Woman Kneeling by a Fire, with
Figures at a Table*
Present location unknown
1681 or later
67.3 x 83.8 cm
Literature: Sutton cat.153

bi./b74

432
Hooch, P. de
*A Woman Kneeling by a Fire, with a
Musical Company*
C. Mumenthaler collection
1681 or later
68 x 82.5 cm
Literature: Sutton cat.154

bi./b74

433
Jongh, L. de
Tric-trac Players
Sale Sotheby's, New York 9/10/
1980-23
c. 1660
63 x 47 cm

bi./b7/ig74

The carpet has a rich floral design
of scrolling vines with large
palmettes and wavy cloudbands.
The light-coloured main border
has an unusual design of S-stems
with cartouche-shaped, stylized

palmette forms, and elegant
small cloudbands.

434
Kalf, W.
*Still-life with Chinese Porcelain,
Glass objects and a Piece of Bread on
a Silver Plate*
Kurpfälzisches Museum,
Heidelberg
1653-56
66.5 x 52.2 cm
Literature: Grisebach, cat.73

bi./ig11b

435
Kalf, W.
*Still-life with a Piece of Bread and
Glass Objects on a Silver Plate*
formerly Dr. J. van Gelder,
Arnhem
1653-55
64 x 56 cm
Literature: Grisebach, cat.74

bi./b1/ig11b

436
Kalf, W.
*Still-life with Glass Objects and
Fruits*
Musée Crozatier, Le Puy-en-
Velay
1653-55
70 x 60 cm
Literature: Grisebach, cat.75

bi./b1/ig11,og46?

437
Kalf, W.
*Still-life with Glass Objects and
Fruits*
National Museum, Prague
1653-55
64 x 71.5 cm
Literature: Grisebach, cat.76

bi./ig11b,og46

438
Kalf, W.
*Still-life with the Drinking-Horn of
the St. Sebastian Guild*
National Gallery, London
c. 1653
86.4 x 102.2
Literature: Grisebach, cat.77

bi.?/b1/ig11b,og46

439
Kalf, W.
*Still-life with the Drinking-Horn of
the St. Sebastian Guild*
National Gallery, London
c. 1655

128 x 106 cm
Literature: Grisebach, cat.78

bi.?/ig11b,og46?

440
Kalf, W.
Still-life with Goblet and Fruits
Hermitage, Leningrad
c. 1655
105 x 88 cm
Literature: Grisebach, cat.79

b1/og46 (bi.)

441
Kalf, W.
Still-life with a Glass and Fruits
Museum Boymans-van
Beuningen, Rotterdam
1655
62 x 56 cm
Literature: Grisebach, cat.82

b1/og46 (bi.)

442
Kalf, W.
Still-life with a Glass and Fruits
Staatliche Museen Preussischer
Kulturbesitz, Berlin
1655-60
65 x 56 cm
Literature: Grisebach, cat.83

bi.?/ig11b,og46

443
Kalf, W.
*Still-life with Glass Objects and
Fruits*
Museum of Fine Arts,
Springfield, Mass.
1655-60
98 x 73 cm
Literature: Grisebach, cat.84

bi.

Cf. Pagnano 204

444
Kalf, W.
*Still-life with Glass Objects and
Fruits*
Collection of the University of
Lund, Lund
1655-60
57.5 x 49 cm
Literature: Grisebach, cat.86

bi1/ig62,og46

445
Kalf, W.
*Still-life with a Goblet, Glass Objects
and Fruits*
Art Gallery, Glasgow

c. 1660
84 x 70 cm
Literature: Grisebach, cat.88

bi.?/ig6,og46

446
Kalf, W.
*Still-life with Glass Objects and
Fruits on a Silver Plate*
City Art Gallery, Manchester
1656-58
53 x 46 cm
Literature: Grisebach, cat.90

bi.?/b1?

447
Kalf, W.
*Still-life with a Cup-holder, Glass
Objects and a Chinese Vase*
Musée de Picardie, Amiens
c. 1660
101 x 83 cm
Literature: Grisebach, cat.92

b1/ig62,og46

448
Kalf, W.
*Still-life with Glass Objects and
Fruits*
Metropolitan Museum of Art,
New York
1659
58 x 51 cm
Literature: Grisebach, cat.94

ig62 (bi./b1)

449
Kalf, W.
*Still-life with Glass Objects and a
Pomegranate*
Present location unknown
c. 1660
64 x 53 cm
Literature: Grisebach, cat.95

og46 (b1)

450
Kalf, W.
*Still-life with Glass Objects and a
Pomegranate*
Kunsthalle, Bremen
1659
65.5 x 52.5 cm
Literature: Grisebach, cat.96

b1/ig62,og46 (bi.)

451
Kalf, W.
*Still-life with Glass Objects, a
Pomegranate and a Half-peeled
Lemon*
Royal Picture Gallery The

Mauritshuis, The Hague
c. 1659
50 x 42.5 cm
Literature: Grisebach, cat.97

ig62 (bi.)

452
Kalf, W.
*Still-life with a Glass and Fruits on a
Silver Plate*
Collection John C. Johnson,
Philadelphia
c. 1659
50 x 42.5 cm
Literature: Grisebach, cat.98

bi.

453
Kalf, W.
*Still-life with Glass Objects and
Fruits on a Chinese Dish*
Formerly Neues Palais, Potsdam
c. 1659
66 x 55
Literature: Grisebach, cat.99

bi.?

454
Kalf, W.
Still-life with a Goblet and Fruits
Institute of Arts, Detroit
c. 1660
58 x 49 cm
Literature: Grisebach, cat.100

bi.

455
Kalf, W.
*Still-life with Glass Objects and
Fruits*
National Gallery, Washington
c. 1660
64.5 x 54 cm
Literature: Grisebach, cat.102

bi.?/og46?

456
Kalf, W.
*Still-life with a Silver Goblet, Glass
Objects and Fruits*
Present location unknown
c. 1660
76 x 64 cm
Literature: Grisebach, cat.103

bi./ig62,og46

457
Kalf, W.
*Still-life with a Silver Goblet, Glass
Objects and Fruits*
Ashmolean Art Museum, Oxford
c. 1662

66 x 55 cm
Literature: Grisebach, cat.104

bi.?/og46?

458
Kalf, W.
*Still-life with a Silver Goblet, a
Glass and Fruits*
Kunsthalle, Hanover
c. 1661
65.5 x 54 cm
Literature: Grisebach, cat.105

bi.?/og46

459
Kalf, W.
*Still-life with a Silver Goblet and a
Chinese Sugar-bowl*
Collection G. Henle, Duisburg
1963
1661
66 x 50.5 cm
Literature: Grisebach, cat.106

b1/ig62,og46? (bi.)

460
Kalf, W.
*Still-life with a Chinese Sugar-bowl
and a Half-peeled Lemon*
Formerly Gemäldegalerie,
Dresden
1661
48 x 41 cm
Literature: Grisebach, cat.107

og46 (bi.)

461
Kalf, W.
*Still-life with Glass Objects, a
Chinese Sugar-bowl and Fruits*
C. Janet Gallery, New York 1984
1660-65
77.5 x 63.5 cm
Literature: Grisebach, cat.108

b1?/og46? (bi.)

462
Kalf, W.
*Still-life with a Nautilus Cup, a
Glass and Fruits on a Chinese Dish*
Thyssen-Bornemisza collection,
Lugano
1661
64 x 55 cm
Literature: Grisebach, cat.109

bi./b1/og46

463
Kalf, W.
*Still-life with a Nautilus Cup, a
Glass and Fruits on a Chinese Dish*
Musée des Beaux Arts,

Strasbourg
c. 1661
68 x 57 cm
Literature: Grisebach, cat.110

bi.

464
Kalf, W.
Still-life with a Nautilus Cup, Glass Objects and Fruits
Emile Wolf, New York
c. 1661
69 x 58 cm
Literature: Grisebach, cat.111

b1?/og46? (bi.)

465
Kalf, W.
Still-life with Nautilus Cup, Glass Objects and Fruits
Formerly Kaiser Friedrich Museum, Berlin
1664
64 x 53 cm
Literature: Grisebach, cat.112

bi./og46

466
Kalf, W.
Still-life with Nautilus Cup, Glass Objects and Fruits
Pushkin Museum, Moscow
1659-62
76 x 62 cm
Literature: Grisebach, cat.113

bi./og46?

467
Kalf, W.
Still-life with Glass Objects, a Chinese Sugar-bowl and Fruits
Art market, Knoedler 1962
1659-62
58 x 51 cm
Literature: Grisebach, cat.114

bi.?/og46

468
Kalf, W.
Still-life with Glass Objects, a Chinese Sugar-bowl and Fruits
Staatliche Museen Preussischer Kulturbesitz, Berlin-Dahlem
1662
58 x 51 cm
Literature: Grisebach, cat.115

bi.?/og46

469
Kalf, W.
Still-life with Glass Objects, a Chinese Sugar-bowl and a Half-peeled Lemon
Statens Museum for Kunst, Copenhagen
1662
66.5 x 55 cm
Literature: Grisebach, cat.116

bi./b1/ig62,og46

470
Kalf, W.
Still-life with a Nautilus Cup, a Glass Goblet and a Chinese Sugar-bowl on a Silver Plate
Thyssen-Bornemisza 1960
166(1?)
80 x 65 cm
Literature: Grisebach, cat.117

bi./b1/og46

471
Kalf, W.
Still-life with a Nautilus Cup and Glass Objects on a Silver Plate
Collection E.G. Buehrle, Zurich
c. 1662
66.5 x 56 cm
Literature: Grisebach, cat.118

bi.

472
Kalf, W.
Still-life with Silver Objects, a Nautilus Cup and Fruits on a Chinese Plate
Collection J.G. Johnson, Philadelphia
1662
121 x 105 cm
Literature: Grisebach, cat.119

bi./ig62,og46

473
Kalf, W.
Still-life with Chinese Artefacts and Fruits
Baroness Gabriele Bentinck, Paris (on loan to Kunstmuseum, Bern)
1660-65
111 x 84 cm
Literature: Grisebach, cat.120

bi./b1/og46

474
Kalf, W.
Still-life with Glass Objects, a Chinese Dish and Fruits on a Silver Plate
Custodia Foundation, Institut Néerlandais, Paris
c. 1662
53 x 42.5 cm
Literature: Grisebach, cat.121

b1?

475
Kalf, W.
Still-life with Silver Objects and Fruits in a Chinese Bowl
Staatliches Museum, Schwerin
1663
78.5 x 66.7 cm
Literature: Grisebach, cat.122

bi.?/og46?

476
Kalf, W.
Still-life with Silver Objects and Fruits on a Chinese dish
Art Gallery, Glasgow
c. 1663
69 x 57 cm
Literature: Grisebach, cat.123

bi.?

477
Kalf, W.
Still-life with Glass Objects, a Chinese Sugar-bowl and Fruits on a Silver Plate
State-owned Art Collections Dept., The Hague
c. 1670
55 x 47 cm
Literature: Grisebach, cat.124

bi.

478
Kalf, W.
Still-life with Cup-holder and Fruits on a Chinese Dish
Staatliches Museum, Schwerin
1663
61 x 47.9 cm
Literature: Grisebach, cat.125

bi.?

479
Kalf, W.
Still-life with a Cup-holder, Glass Objects and a Chinese Dish with Fruits on a Silver Plate
Cleveland Museum of Art, Cleveland, Ohio
c. 1670
60.4 x 50.2 cm
Literature: Grisebach, cat.126

bi./b1/og46

480
Kalf, W.
Still-life with a Glass and Fruits on a Silver Plate
Musée des Beaux-Arts, Strasbourg
c. 1665

49 x 41 cm
Literature: Grisebach, cat.127

bi.?

481
Kalf, W.
Still-life with a Glass and Fruits on a Silver Plate
National Gallery of Victoria, Melbourne
c. 1665
53 x 44 cm
Literature: Grisebach, cat.128

bi.

482
Kalf, W.
Still-life with Glass Objects and a Chinese Dish with Fruits on a Silver Plate
Portland Art Museum, Portland, Oregon
c. 1670
51 x 41 cm
Literature: Grisebach, cat.130

bi.?

483
Kalf, W.
Still-life with Glass Objects and Fruits
Collection dr. H.A. Wetzlar, Amsterdam
c. 1670
36.5 x 26 cm
Literature: Grisebach, cat.132

b1/og46 (bi.)

484
Kalf, W.
Still-life with Glass Objects and Fruits on a Chinese Dish
Collection Dr. H. Girardet, Kettwig/Ruhr
c. 1670
55 x 45.5 cm
Literature: Grisebach, cat.133

bi.?

485
Kalf, W.
Still-life with Glass Objects and Fruits on a Chinese Dish
Museum voor Stad en Lande, Groningen
c. 1670
45 x 36 cm
Literature: Grisebach, cat.134

bi.?

486
Kalf, W.
*Still-life with a Cup-holder, a Glass,
a Chinese Vase and Fruits on a
Silver Plate*
J. Herron Art Museum, Indiana-
polis
1669
78 x 66 cm
Literature: Grisebach, cat.135

bi./b1/og46

487
Kalf, W.
*Still-life with a Nautilus Cup, a
Glass and a Half-peeled Melon on a
Silver Plate*
Museum der Bildenden Künste,
Leipzig
1669
52.5 x 43 cm
Literature: Grisebach, cat.136

bi.

488
Kalf, W.
*Still-life with a Chinese Vase, Fruits
and a Watch*
Louvre, Paris
1670-80
58 x 71 cm
Literature: Grisebach, cat.137

bi./ig62,og46

489
Kalf, W.
*Still-life with Silver Artefacts and a
Chinese Dish with Fruits*
Statens Museum for Kunst,
Copenhagen
1678
67 x 55 cm
Literature: Grisebach, cat.138

bi./ig62,og46

490
Kalf, W.
*Still-life with a Silver Goblet, a
Nautilus Cup, Glass Objects and
Fruits on a Chinese Dish*
Sale Fischer, Lucerne 24/11/70-
236
1678-80
57.5 x 52 cm
Literature: Grisebach, cat.139

bi.

491
Kalf, W.
*Still-life with a Nautilus Cup and a
Chinese Sugar-bowl*
Present location unknown
c. 1680

66 x 50 cm
Literature: Grisebach, cat.140

b1? (bi.)

492
Kalf, W.
Still-life with Silver Objects
Staatliche Kunstsammlungen,
Weimar
1680
82.5 x 71.8
Literature: Grisebach, cat.141

bi.?/og46?

493
Kemper, G.
Portrait of a Man Playing the Cello
Kunstgalerie, Dusseldorf
1646
54.4 x 42.7 cm
Literature: Bernt IV, nr. 148

bi./b1

Cf. id.: *Portrait of a Young Man
Aged 20, Holding a Violin*

494
Kemper, G.
*Portrait of a Young Man Aged 20,
Holding a Violin*
National Gallery of Ireland,
Dublin
1645
49 x 41 cm
Literature: cat. 1986, nr.806

bi./b1/ig89,og89?

495
Kemper, G.
A Man Greeting a Woman
Municipal Museum De Lakenhal,
Leiden
1659
Literature: cat. 1983, nr.233, p.182

bi./b2/ig13

496
Keyser, Th. de
Portrait of a Gentleman
Present location unknown
1630-35
66 x 47.5 cm
Literature: Oldenbourg cat.141

bi./b1/ig71?

497
Keyser, Th. de

Portrait of David Bailly
Present location unknown
c. 1630
73.7 x 53.7 cm

bi./b1/ig71

498
Keyser, Th. de
Portrait of a Scholar
Royal Picture Gallery The
Mauritshuis, The Hague
1631
82.5 x 61 cm

bi./b1/ig45,og44

499
Keyser, Th. de
Portrait of a Young Silversmith
Coll. Marquess of Bath
1630
66 x 54 cm
See illustration p.10

bi./b1/ig71,og8

Presumably a representation of
the same original carpet as in
Keyser's two portraits in
Copenhagen, and the portrait in
the Mauritshuis. Cf. Pagnano
nr.107 for the design of the outer
guard border.

500
Keyser, Th.de

Portrait of a Gentleman Aged 45
Present location unknown
1631
50 x 41.5 cm

bi./b1/ig71

Pendant of id. *Portrait of a Lady.*
Cf. Pagnano nr.104.

501
Keyser, Th. de
Portrait of a Lady
Statens Museum for Kunst,
Copenhagen
c. 1631
50 x 41.5 cm
Literature: BM CXIII (1971), p.825

bi./b1/ig71

Pendant of id. *Portrait of a
Gentleman Aged 45*; presumably
the same richly designed carpet.
The inner guard border has two
subguards with the barber pole
ornament (Cf. Pagnano 126, inner
guard border). At the upper or
the lower end the carpet has an
elem with a chevron motif.

502
Keyser, Th. de
Portrait of a Family
Wallraf-Richartz Museum,
Cologne
1640
102.5 x 85 cm
Literature: cat. 1986, p.41,
Abb.344

bi./b1

503
Keyser, Th. de (attr. to)
A Couple in an Interior
National Gallery of Ireland,
Dublin
c. 1630
32 x 36 cm

bi./b1/og89

504
Kuyl, G. van de
The Magnanimity of Scipio
Sale Koller Zurich 30/10/73-2789
1640-50
148 x 212 cm
Lit. Oud Holland 91 (1977), 3,
p.166-194, afb.3

bi./b1/ig47?

505
Kuyl, G. van de
Musical Party
Coll. Sir George Leon, Bart.,
London
c. 1650
124.5 x 180.5 cm
Lit. Oud Holland 91 (1977), 3,
p.166-194, afb.10

bi./b1/ig62

506
Lachtropius, N. or Ruysch, R.

Still-life with Flowers
Sale Sotheby's, London 9/3/83-
94
1680-90
73.5 x 61 cm

bi./ig8,og11b?

The S-motives of the green inner
guard border are red and yellow;
the fringes are white or yellow.

507
Loo, J. van
Musical Company
Thyssen-Bornemisza Collection,
Lugano
c. 1650
73 x 65.5 cm
Literature: Philadelphia 1983,
pl.87

bi./b52/ig46,og44

The design is carefully
represented. Remarkable is the
palmette in the corner of the
border, which points inwards
instead of outwards. The rug has
no fringes.

508
Luttichuys, S.
Still-life
Sale Lange, Berlin, 7/4/38-16
c. 1650
57.5 x 45 cm

bi./b2

509
Luttichuys, Is. or Helst, B. van
der
Portrait of a Man
Sale Sotheby's Monte Carlo, 16/
6/89-475
c. 1660
147 x 120 cm

bi./b1/ig62

510
Maes, N.
*Six Governors of the Amsterdam
Surgeons' Guild*
Amsterdams Historisch Museum,
Amsterdam
1680-81
130.5 x 195.5 cm
Literature: van Thiel p.358 (ill.)

bi.?/b1

511
Meer, B. van der
Still-life with a Parrot
Kunsthistorisches Museum,
Vienna

1689
142 x 110 cm
Literature: cat. 1884, nr.997

bi.?/bi/ig46,og45?

512
Metsu, G.
The Doctor's Visit
Hermitage, Leningrad
c. 1663
61 x 48 cm
Literature: Robinson cat.138

bi./b1/ig62

cf. id. *A Young Woman Composing
Music*

513
Metsu, G.
Woman Playing the Viola da Gamba
M.H. de Young Memorial
Museum, San Francisco
1663
Literature: Robinson cat.143

bi./b1/ig6

514
Metsu, G.
Man Writing a Letter
Sir Alfred Beit, Blessington
1663-5
52.5 x 40.2 cm
Literature: Robinson cat.145

bi./b1/ig62,og46?

Cf. id. *Woman Playing the Viola da
Gamba*

515
Metsu, G.

A Visit to the Nursery
Metropolitan Museum of Art,
New York
1660-67
Literature: Ydema 1988, p.532

b8/ig47? (bv)

516
Metsu, G.
Woman in a Blue Satin Robe
Art Market, London 1974
1667
57 x 43.2 cm
Literature: Robinson cat.153

bi./b2/ig92,og46?

Cf. Pagnano nr.107.

517
Metsu, G.
A Young Woman Composing Music
Royal Picture Gallery The
Mauritshuis, The Hague
c. 1667
38 x 34 cm
Literature: Robinson cat.158
See illustration p.125

bi./b1/ig62,og45?

The carpet has the usual
colouring: a red field, a blue
border and an orange outer
guard border. The glossy shine of
the fringes might indicate that
these were made of silk.

518
Metsu. G.
Woman Writing a Letter and a Dog
Private collection, Wassenaar
1659

49.4 x 33.7 cm
Literature: Robinson cat.208

bi./b1/ig62,og45?

519
Mierevelt, M.J. van

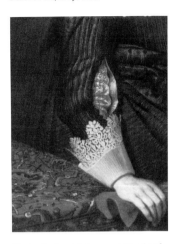

Portrait of an Unknown Man Aged 29
Art Market, Abels Cologne 1955
1632
111 x 83.5 cm

bi./ig45

Cf. Pagnano 107.

520
Mierevelt, M.J. van (circle)
Portrait of an Unknown Gentleman
Sale Sotheby's, Monaco 9/12/84-554
1655
110.5 x 81 cm

bi./ig63

Rather crude representation. The diamonds in the inner guard border are each composed of four stylized leaves.

521
Mierevelt, M.J. van
Portrait of a Woman Aged 52
Museum, Lyon
1631
110 x 82 cm
Literature: sale Lady Evelyn Lister, London 12/7/22-67

bi.

Cf. Spuhler 1978, nr.48.

522
Mieris, F. van
A Sleeping Courtesan
Uffizi museum, Florence
1669?

27.5 x 22.5 cm
Literature: Naumann pl.75

bi.?/b1/ig46,og46

523
Mieris, F. van
The Doctor's Visit
Kunsthistorisches Museum, Vienna
1657
33 x 27 cm

bi.

524
Mieris, F. van
Girl Stringing Pearls
Musée Fabre, Montpellier
1659
22 x 17 cm
Literature: Naumann pl.25

bi./b7?/ig92

Cf. Pagnano 107. also id. *The Puppy.*

525
Mieris, F. van
The Puppy
Hermitage, Leningrad
c. 1660
Literature: Naumann cat.32

bi./b7/ig92

Cf. id. *Girl Stringing Pearls*; Eiland 1979, fig.123.

526
Mieris, F. van

The Cloth Shop
Kunsthistorisches Museum, Vienna
1660
34 x 27 cm
Literature: Naumann cat.31

bi./b1/ig13,og46

The inner guard seems to have a row of rosettes on a thin vine, alternated by red and blue leaflets. The fringes are red.

527
Mieris, F. van
The Oyster Meal
Royal Picture Gallery The Mauritshuis, The Hague
1661
27 x 21 cm
Literature: Naumann pl.36

b1/ig13,og46 (bi.)

528
Mieris, F. van
Teasing the Pet
Royal Picture Gallery The Mauritshuis, The Hague
1660
27.5 x 20 cm
Literature: Philadelphia 1984, pl.58

bi./b1/ig13,og46

Cf. id. *The Cloth Shop*

529
Mieris, F. van
A Lady Examining Herself in a Mirror
Gemäldegalerie, Berlin-Dahlem
c. 1662
30 x 23 cm
Literature: Naumann pl.46

bi.?/b1/ig13,og46?

Cf. id. *Teasing the Pet*

530
Mieris, F. van
A Woman at her Toilet
Duke of Sutherland
c. 1663
27.5 x 22.5 cm
Literature: Naumann pl.51

bi./b7/ig92,og46

531
Mieris, F. van
A Woman Singing
Present location unknown
c. 1671
Literature: Naumann pl.86

bi.?/b1/ig46,og46

Cf. id. *The Puppy*

532
Mieris, F. van (attr. to)

Portrait of an Unknown Man
Present location unknown
1660-70
Literature: Hofstede de Groot nr.265

bi./b2/og46

533
Mieris, F. van (attr. to)
Young Woman at her Toilet
Gemäldegalerie, Dresden
1667
27 x 22 cm
Literature: Naumann pl.69

bi.?/b1/ig46?,og46

534
Mieris, F. van and Mieris, W. van
Portrait of a Woman Holding a Mirror
Present location unknown
c. 1670
44 x 33 cm
Literature: Naumann cat. B27

bvi?

Apparently a coarse carpet. The spiralling scrolls do not end in lanceolate leaves, but in flowerbuds (Cf. Pagnano nr.149). The painting was probably made in collaboration with Willem van Mieris.

535
Mieris, W. van
Preciosa
Museum für Bildenden Künste, Leipzig
c. 1700
52 x 46 cm
Literature: Hofstede de Groot nr.31 (as F. van Mieris)

bi./b8/ig46,og46

Cf. J. van der Sluys, *Allegorical Scene*. The border has a comparable row of cartouches, here however without cloud-bands; instead it has short stems ending in flowerbuds above and below the starform cartouches. Cf. also Willem van Mieris, *Sophonisba Decides to Accept the Poisoned Cup*, Amsterdam 1989, nr.21a, and the 1741 representation of presumably the same carpet by Frans van Mieris the Younger in his *Three Generations of Painters from the van Mieris Family*, l.c., 21d

536
Mieris, W. van
Woman Reading a Music Book
Earl of Northbrook, London
c. 1671
21.5 x 18.5 cm

bi./b1/ig46,og46

537
Mieris, W. van
Domestic Scene
Narodowe Museum, Prague
1680-90
51.5 x 42.5 cm

bi./b2/ig46,og46

538
Mieris, W. van
Preciosa
Palazzo Bianco, Genoa
1687
33 x 42 cm

bi./b2/ig46,og46

539
Mieris, W. van
A Drinker and a Trumpet Player
Art Market, E. Speelman, London
1958
1689
24.7 x 19.7 cm
Literature: Hofstede de Groot nr.296

bi./b1/og46

540
Mieris, W. van

Antony and Cleopatra
Wallace Collection, London
1691
47 x 37 cm

bi./b2?/ig46,og46

541
Mieris, W. van
The Doctor's Visit
Hermitage, Leningrad
1695
23.5 x 20 cm
Literature: Kuznetsov nr.117

bi.

542
Mieris, W. van
Elegant Couple
City Art Gallery, Manchester
1695
24.7 x 20.6 cm
Literature: E.Elen-Clifford, in: Leids Kunsthistorisch Jaarboek IV (1985), p.152-3, fig.6

bi.

543
Mieris, W. van
Three Children Blowing Bubbles
Louvre, Paris
1690-1700
31 x 26 cm
Literature: cat. 1922, nr.2473

bi./b1

544
Mieris, W. van
Esther before Ahasverus
Brera, Milan
c. 1700
47 x 63 cm
Literature: HdG 16

bi./b2/ig46,og46

Cf. id. *Preciosa*. In the centre of the field appears a kind of medallion formed by elegant leaves.

545
Mieris, W. van
An Old and a Young Woman
Sale Bukowski, Stockholm 4/4/ 62-194
c. 1700
40 x 30 cm

bi.

546
Moreelse, P.
Portrait of an Unknown Man
Sale Christie's, London 8/7/77-17
c. 1625
196.8 x 125.7 cm

bi./b7/ig46?,og46

The carpet has a lobed medallion in the centre of the field.

547
Musscher, M. van

Portrait of Three Children
Museum Boymans-van Beuningen, Rotterdam
1690
48.3 x 40.5 cm

bi.?/b2?/ig92,og46

The carpet is shown from the reverse side.

548
Musscher, M. van (attr. to)

Portrait of a Lady with a Guitar
Present location unknown
35.5 x 28 cm
c. 1690

bi.

549
Musscher, M. van

Portrait of a Man with a Watch
Art Market, G. Le Roy, Brussels
1940
1660-80
42 x 32 cm

bi./b73/ig92

Cf. Pieter van Slingelant, *Portrait of J. van Crombrugge*

550
Musscher, M. van
Portrait of a Man
Sale Christie's, London 14/3/75-83
1690
46.9 x 38.1 cm

bi.

Portrait of Nicolaas Calkoen
State-owned Art Collections
Dept, The Hague.
1696
56 x 50 cm

bi./ig86

The field has a floral pattern of stiff vines. Cf. id. *Portrait of Agatha van Loon* (pendant); J. Verkolje, *Woman Washing her Feet and a Servant*; also id. *Portrait of a Lady and her Child*

552
Musscher, M. van
Portrait of Agatha van Loon, Wife of Nicolaas Calkoen
State-owned Art Collections
Department, The Hague
1696
56 x 50 cm

bi.

553
Musscher, M. van

Portrait of Admiral J.F. Lefort
Musée d'Art et d'Histoire,
Geneva
1698
71 x 60 cm

bi./b1/ig46

554
Musscher, M. van or Naiveu, M.
Tric-trac players
Sale d'Oultremont, Amsterdam
27/6/1889-6
1680-90

bi.?/b8/ig46,og46?

555
Mijtens, D. (attr. to)
Portrait of George Villiers, 1st Duke of Buckingham
National Maritime Museum,
London
1615-25
221 x 132 cm
Literature: cat. 1988, p.286

biv

556
Naiveu, M.
In the Nursery
Metropolitan Museum of Art,
New York
1675
64.2 x 80 cm
Literature: cat. 1954, inv. 71.160

bi./b1

557
Neer, E. van der
The Lute Player
Statens Museum, Copenhagen
1670-80
60 x 52 cm

g46?/ig8,og8 (bi.)

Cf. Gonzales Coques, *Portrait of a Young Family in an Interior.*

558
Neer, E. van der
A Lady Drawing
Wallace Collection, London
1675-80
Literature: cat. 1925, pl.40

bvi

Cf. id. *The Sick Lady*

559
Neer, E. van der
Courting Couple in an Interior
Staatsgemäldesammlungen,
Aschaffenburg
16.6 (1666)
67.1 x 58.7 cm
Literature: cat. 1964, p.119

bi./b1?/ig46

560
Neer, E. van der

Woman with a Lute and a Servant
Sale Christie's, London 14/5/71-
120
1680
40.6 x 33 cm

biv

The thickness of the pile indicates
that it was made of wool. The
carpet apparently has a rich floral
design, with details possibly
rendered in gold or silver
threads.

561
Netscher, C.
'Piskijker'
Formerly Gemäldegalerie,
Dresden
1664
27 x 22 cm
Literature: Hofstede de Groot
1912, nr.74

bi./b1/ig46?,og46?

Cf. Pagnano 148

562
Netscher, C.
Woman with a Parrot
Alte Pinakothek, Munich
1666
Literature: Hofstede de Groot
1912, nr.137

bi./b1/ig45,og44

Cf. id. *Portrait of Mme de
Montespan*

563
Netscher, C.
Portrait of Mme de Montespan
Gemäldegalerie, Dresden
1670
50.5 x 38.5 cm

bi./b1/ig45,og44

Large carpet (cf. Dimand/Mailey
fig.95). The design of the inner
guard border is symmetrical,
compared to the vertical axis of
the carpet.

564
Netscher, C.

Portrait of Lady Harley
Szepmuveszeti Muzeum,
Budapest
c. 1670
54.7 x 46 cm

bi./b1

565
Netscher, C.

Vertumnus and Pomona
Sale Sotheby's, London 11/12/
85-160
c. 1670
49.5 x 39 cm

biv

Possibly a 'Polonaise' carpet; an
alternative interpretation of the
design was suggested by Mr.
Michael Franses (in discussion):
the carpet may have had a red
field with a white central
medallion and black corner
medallions.

566
Netscher, C.
*A Woman Combing the Hair of a
Child in an Interior*
Rijksmuseum, Amsterdam
1669
44.5 x 38 cm
Literature: van Thiel p.413;
Amsterdam 1989, nr.34

bi./b1/ig45

Regarding the floral ornaments,
the original carpet must have
been quite large.

567
Netscher, C.
Portrait of Abraham van Lennep
Custodia Foundation, Paris
1672
55 x 45 cm
Literature: Amsterdam 1989,

nr.35

bi./b1/ig45,og44

Cf. id. *Portrait of Mme de
Montespan.*

568
Netscher, C.
Sara, Offering Hagar to Abraham
Sale Christie's, London, 13/7/45-
76
1673
58 x 49 cm

bi./b1/ig45,og44?

Cf. id. *Portrait of Mme de
Montespan*

569
Netscher, C.
A Lady and a Child
Sale Sotheby's, Frankfurt 5/10/
81-181
1678
54 x 45.5 cm

b1/og44 (bi.)

Large carpet.

570
Netscher, C.
*Portrait of Joh. Friedrich van
Ansbach and his Wife*
Formerly Bildergalerie Sanssouci,
Potsdam
1681
Dimensions not indicated

b1. (bi.)

571
Netscher, C.
Portrait of an Unknown Woman
Museum, Stuttgart
1682
Literature: cat. 1908, nr.1350

bi./b1/ig46?

A very large carpet.

572
Netscher, C.
*Portrait of Abigail Stephens, 2nd
Wife of Sir E. Harley*
Art Museum, Budapest
1682
54.5 x 46 cm
Literature: cat. 1937, nr.244

bi./b1/ig72,og46?

573
Netscher, C. (attr. to)
A Young Woman with a Servant
Coll. Mrs. Aase Young Reusch,
Oslo 1962
c. 1670
48 x 39 cm

b1/og44

574
Ochtervelt, J.
Portrait of the Elsevier Family
Wadsworth Atheneum, Hartford
166(7?)
75 x 58 cm
Literature: Kuretsky cat.19

bi.?

575
Ochtervelt, J.
The Lovesick Girl
State-owned Art Collections Dpt,
The Hague
1667-70
48 x 42 cm
Literature: Kuretsky cat.32

bi.

The large palmette in the vertical
axis of the carpet is flanked by
large lanceolate leaves; one of
which is visible.

576
Ochtervelt, J. (attr. to)
The Tric-trac Players
Museum für Bildenden Künste,
Leipzig
1671
84 x 93 cm
Literature: Kuretsky cat.64

bi./d11/ig84,og85

Cf. Pagnano 148. The
combination of a floral and
cloudband design with this
border design is remarkable.

577
Ochtervelt, J.
The Music Lesson
City Museum and Art Gallery,
Birmingham
c. 1671
95 x 76 cm
Literature: Kuretsky cat.65

bi./b2/ig92,og46

578
Ochtervelt, J.
*Family Portrait: a Man, a Woman
with an Apple and a Child*
Norton Simon Foundation, Los
Angeles

c. 1671
91 x 79.5 cm
Literature: Kuretsky cat.66

bi./b2/ig92,og46

579
Ochtervelt, J.
Lady at the Virginals and Lutenist
Present location unknown
1671-73
Literature: Kuretsky cat.68

bi./b2?

580
Ochtervelt, J.
The Oyster Meal
Present location unknown
1671-3
87 x 72.5 cm
Literature: Kuretsky cat.71

bi./b2?/ig92

581
Ochtervelt, J.
The Betrothal
Private collection, Germany
1670-75
95 x 78 cm
Literature: Kuretsky cat.72

bi./b2/ig92,og46

582
Ochtervelt, J.
The Nursery
Private collection, Capetown
1671-73
92.6 x 74.2 cm
Literature: Kuretsky cat.73

bi./b2/ig92?

The border seems to be a bit
narrow.

583
Ochtervelt, J.
Lady and Maid Feeding a Parrot
Present location unknown
1671-73
77.5 x 94 cm
Literature: Kuretsky cat.74
See illustration p.65

bi./b2/ig92

584
Ochtervelt, J.
Lady with Servant and Dog
The New York Historical Society,
New York
1671-73
93.8 x 76 cm
Literature: Kuretsky cat.75

bi./b2/ig92?

585
Ochtervelt, J.
The Letter Reader
Private collection, Cologne
1671-1673
91 x 78 cm
Literature: Kuretsky cat.77

bi./b2/og46

586
Ochtervelt, J.
Lady with Servant and Dog
Carnegie Institute
1671-3
70 x 57 cm
Literature: Kuretsky cat.78

bi./b2/ig92,og46

587
Ochtervelt, J.
The Visit
Private collection, England
c. 1675
71 x 58 cm
Literature: Kuretsky cat.85

bi.

588
Ochtervelt, J.
The Duet
Private collection, London
1676-80
85 x 70 cm
Literature: Kuretsky cat.93

bi./b2/ig92,og46

589
Ochtervelt, J.
The Faint
Ca' d'Oro, Venice
1677
72 x 84 cm
Literature: Kuretsky cat.98

bi./b2/ig92,og46

590
Ochtervelt, J.
The Doctor's Visit
Bayerische
Staatsgemäldesammlungen,
Munich
1680-2
84.5 x 69 cm
Kuretsky cat.105

bi.?/b2?/ig92

591
Oost, J. van

Madonna and Saints
Church of Our Lady, Ghent
1648

bv/b7

The main border design has some
similarities with a fragment
shown at the Munich exhibition
of 1985 (cat.9b). The secondary
border at the side of the field, has
a meandering floral stem with
small cloudbands; the inner
subguard is only vaguely
represented. The field is
dominated by a large medallion
(cf. Pope 1120): it has in the
centre a star, from which sprout
short tendrils ending in lotus
flowers (cf. ook id. A man
contemplating over a skull). This
medallion is placed in the middle
of a larger, concentrical
medallion with a lobed outline. A
floral twig fills the remaining
space (cf. Bode 1902, Abb.10;
Munich 1985, cat.8). The field has
a floral design of stems and
flowers, quite similar to the bi.
design (cf. Erdmann 1966,
Abb.74).

592
Oost, J. van

A Man Contemplating over a Skull
Groeninge Museum, Bruges
1647
101 x 149 cm

bv/b7

Cf. id. *Madonna and Saints.*
Without any doubt a
representation of the same
original model. The inner
subguard has bars and small
dots, linked by a straight line.

593
Palamedesz, A., or Codde, P.
*An Officer and a Lady Making
Music*
Coll. G. Hulme, London 1974
1630-40
49.5 x 33 cm

bi./b1?/ig11a

594
Plaes, D. van der (attr. to)

Portrait of a Family
Present location unknown
c. 1690

bi./b74/ig46?

595
Ravesteyn, J.A. van
Portrait of a Man
Sale Wawra, Vienna 2/5/17-191
1630-50
114 x 123 cm

bi./b1/ig63

596
Ravesteyn, J.A. van (attr. to)
Portrait of an Unknown Gentleman
Sale Weissmuller, Munich 12/
15/54-925
1630-55
139 x 105 cm

bi./b1/ig46?,og46

Cf. id. *Portrait of a Lady* (pendant)

597
Ravesteyn, J.A. van (attr. to)
Portrait of a Lady
Sale Weissmuller, Munich 12/
15/54-926
1630-55
139 x 105 cm

bi./b1/ig46?/og46

Cf. id. *Portrait of an Unknown
Gentleman* (pendant)

598
Ring, P. de
Still-life
Kunsthalle, Kiel
c. 1650
100 x 85 cm
Literature: cat. 1958, p.128

bi./b1/ig46?,og46

The field pattern is not correctly
rendered in all details.

599
Roestraten, P.G. van

A Vanitas Still-life
Sale Christie's, London 5/7/85-
89
1670-80
119.4 x 115.6 cm

bi./b2

The field has too few floral
ornaments, compared with
surviving floral and cloudband
carpets, and these are sometimes
incorrectly drawn (cf. the
cloudband). The border pattern is
not symmetrical, which suggests
that the carpet is shown from the
left or right side. The field pattern
however is shown as if the carpet
is shown from the upper or lower
end side.

600
Rootius, J.A.
Portrait of a Woman Aged 32
Sale Christie's, London 28/11/30
1653
117 x 87 cm

bi.

601
Rossum, J. van
Portrait of Prof. Henricus Bornius
Private collection,
The Netherlands
1668?
40 x 30 cm
Literature: Amsterdam 1984,
cat.60

bvi.

Only a small part if the field is
visible. This part cannot be
identified with certainty. The pile
of the floral ornaments seems to
be higher than the ground, which
has apparently two different
colours. The ground may be
brocaded, as in the 'Polonaise'
carpets, but the indication is not
enough for a positive
identification.

602
Rubens, P.
The Holy Family
Palazzo Pitti, Florence
1610-15
114 x 88 cm
Literature: cat.1937, nr.139

b1/ig62,og46 (bi.)

603
Rubens, P.
*Portrait of Alatheia Talbot, Countess
of Arundel*

Alte Pinakothek, Munich
c. 1620
261 x 265 cm
Literature: Cat. 1983, nr.352

bi./b1/ig62,og46

604
Rubens, P.
*St.Mary with Jesus and St.John,
Venerated by Remorseful Sinners
and Saints*
Gemäldegalerie, Kassel
c. 1620
258 x 204 cm
Literature: B. Schnackenburg,
pl.19

bi./b1/ig62,og46?

605
Rubens, P.
Portrait of N. de Respaigne
Gemäldegalerie, Kassel
c. 1620
205.5 x 119.5 cm
Literature: B. Schnackenburg,
pl.20

bi./b1/og46

606
Rubens, P.
Birth of Louis XIII at Fontainebleau
Louvre, Paris
1623-25
394 x 295 cm
Literature: cat.1979, p.116

bv./b8

607
Rubens, P.
A Roman Triumph
National Gallery, London
c. 1628
86.8 x 163.9 cm
Literature: Mills 1983, pl.31

bi./b1/ig62

608
Rubens, P.
Helene Fourment in a Chair
Alte Pinakothek, Munich
1630
160 x 134 cm
Literature: G. Mulazzani, Peter
Paul Rubens II, Werkverzeichnis
1981, nr.457

bi./b1/ig6

609
Slingelant, P. van
*Portrait of Joh. Meerman, Burgoma-
ster of Leyden, and his Family*
Louvre, Paris

1668
52 x 44 cm
Literature: cat.1979, p.128;
Amsterdam 1989, nr.46a

bi./b1/ig62,og89

610
Slingelant, P. van
Portrait of a Man with a Watch
Rijksmuseum, Amsterdam
1680-90
25.5 x 20 cm
Literature: van Thiel p.515

bi./b2/ig46,og46

611
Slingelant, P. van
Young Woman at a Window
Gemäldegalerie, Dresden
1672
35.5 x 28 cm
Literature: Amsterdam 1989,
nr.48

bi./b1?/ig46?

612
Slingelant, P. van
Couple Teaching a Dog
Statens Museum, Copenhagen
1663
43 x 31 cm
Literature: cat. 1951, nr.665;
Amsterdam 1989, nr.46

bi./b2

613
Slingelant, P. van

Portrait of J. van Crombrugge
Museum Boymans-van
Beuningen, Rotterdam
1677
35.5 x 27.5 cm

bi./b73/ig92

Cf. Michiel van Musscher,
Portrait of a Man with a Watch.

614
Slingelant, P. van or Tol, D. van
*Portrait of a Man and a Woman in
an Interior*
Sale Sotheby's, London 15/12/
48-114
c. 1670
See illustration p.66

bi./b73/ig92

615
Sluys, J. van der
*The Orphanage at the Hooglandse
Kerkgracht in Leyden*
1684
See illustration p.70

b8/ig4 (bv.)

616
Snijders, F.
*Still-life with Precious Objects,
Fruits and Flowers*
Sale Christie's, London 23/4/82-
70
c. 1640
78.8 x 116.2 cm

b1./ig46? (bi.)

617
Spelt, A. van der
Still-life
Municipal Museum, Gouda
1661

b1?/og46 (bi.)

The carpet has red fringes

618
Steen, J.
A Lady at her Toilet
Present location unknown
c. 1657
23 x 17 cm
Literature: Braun cat.101

og46? (bi.)

For the border design cf. Spuhler
1968, b18?

619
Tempel, A. van de
*Portrait of the Governors of the
'Walenweeshuis' (orphanage) in
Amsterdam*
Amsterdams Historisch Museum,
Amsterdam
1662
123 x 152 cm

bi./b1/ig62

The border pattern shows small
dots; a feature unknown from
surviving examples.

620
Tempel, A. van de (attr. to)

Portrait of Susannah de Wilhelm (?)
Rev J.Forbes, Ampleforth Abbey,
York 1956
1659
96 x 80 cm

bi.

621
Tempel, A. van de
*The Governors of the H. Spirit
Orphanage in Leyden*
1668
146 x 196 cm

bi.

Cf. Pagnano nr.149.

622
Terborch, G.
Portrait of an Unknown Man
Present location unknown
c. 1675
47.5 x 39 cm
Literature: Gudlauggson ill.269
See illustration p.71

bv./b6/ig83,og83

Cf. Erdmann 1966, Abb.98,99;
also (border pattern) Munich
1985, cat.8

623
Terborch, G.
Portrait of an Unkown Man
Present location unknown
1677-8
46 x 40 cm
Literature: Gudlauggson 277

bi./b2/ig92,og46?

624
Valckert, W. van de
Portrait of a Man Aged 58
Sale A. Schoenlank, Koln 28/4/
1896-192
1620-25
119 x 95 cm

bi./b1

Cf. Pagnano nr.148

625
Vermeer, J.
The Glass of Wine
Gemäldegalerie, Berlin-Dahlem
1660-1
65 x 77 cm
Literature: Blankert cat.8

b1/iig131,ig46,og11e

626
Vermeer, J.
Lady Writing a Letter, with her Maid
Sir Alfred Beit, Blessington, Ireland (stolen)
c. 1671
71 x 59 cm
Literature: Blankert cat.27

bi./b1

627
Verschuring, H.
The Magistrates of the City of Gorinchem
City hall, Gorinchem
1660-65

bi./b74

Cf. Pagnano nr.134.

628
Voort, C. van der
Portrait of a Lady
Sale Sotheby's, Amsterdam 9/6/77-3
c. 1620
105 x 72 cm.

bi./b1

The floral inner guard border has apart from a meandering vine presumably also small cloud-bands.

629
Vos, C. de

172 CATALOGUE

Portrait of a Man Aged 30
Sale A. de Berghe, Brussels 26/7/30-115
1620
108 x 78 cm

bi.

630
Vos, C. de

Portrait of a Man
Dr. Miklos Rosza, Hollywood
1627
109.5 x 80

bi.

Careless representation. The carpet in this painting seems to be copied after the representation in id. *Portrait of a Man Aged 30*, 1620.

631
Vos, S. de
The Five Senses
Sale Christie's, London 9/4/37-23
1620-40
151 x 208.2 cm

bi./b1/og44

632
Vos, C. de
The Tric-trac Players
Present location unknown
1635-45
140 x 180 cm
Literature: Revue du Louvre XIV (1964), p.170-171, ill.23

b76/ig46,og11a (bi.)

The field has palmettes and lotus flowers, which are pointed inwards and outwards, with, in the heart of the ornaments, human faces. Birds are placed between the palmettes and lotus flowers. For reference one could mention the 16th century silk carpets, usually ascribed to Kashan workshops (cf. Pagnano nr.92).

633
Voskuyl, H.
Portrait of Philip Denys
Rijksmuseum, Amsterdam
1640
123.5 x 90 cm
Literature: van Thiel p.590

b1/ig62 (bi.)

Cf. id. *Portrait of Gertruy Resel* (pendant)

634
Voskuyl, H.
Portrait of Gertruy Resel
Rijksmuseum, Amsterdam
c. 1640
123.5 x 90 cm
Literature: van Thiel p.590

b1/ig62 (bi.)

Cf. id. *Portrait of Philip Denijs* (pendant)

635
Wilt, Th. van der
Elegant Couple
Sale van Diemen, Berlin 25/1/35-41
c. 1675-85
86 x 70 cm

bi.

636
Witting, D.
The Tric-trac Players
Sale Christie's, London 22/6/36-96
1630
47 x 61 cm

bi./b1

INDIAN CARPETS

637
Unknown Dutch painter
Portrait of an Unknown Lady
Sale Sotheby's, New York 12/1/79-136
c. 1650
74 x 54.5 cm

b6 (ci.)

Cf. Sorgh, *Portrait of a Young Man*; also his *Portrait of a Young Man Standing at a Table*.

638
Unknown Dutch painter
A Scholar in his Studio
Sotheby's London 16/5/84-21 (as Th.Wijk)
c. 1670
66 x 55 cm
Literature: Ydema 1986, p.2186-7
See illustration p.80

ci.

639
Unknown Flemish Painter
Cognoscenti in a Room Hung with Pictures
National Gallery, London
c. 1620
95.9 x 123.5 cm
Literature: cat. 1986, p.196

ci.

640
Anraadt, P. van
Portrait of an Unknown Man
Sale H.Houck, Amsterdam 7/5/1895-1
1664

bi./ig46 (ci.)

641
Anraadt, P. van
Portrait of an Unknown Lady
Sale H.Houck, Amsterdam 7/5/1895-2
1664

bi./ig46 (ci.)

cf. his pendant to the above work, *Portrait of an Unknown Man*

642
Backer, J.A. (attr. to)

Portrait of an Unknown Man
Koninklijk Museum voor Schone
Kunsten, Brussels
1625-1640
114 x 91.5 cm
Literature: cat. 1984, p.376

b78/ig63 (ci.?)

Only a small part of the field is
visible, showing little floral
ornaments. The main border has
S-stems ending in double leaves
(cf. for variant designs Spuhler
1968, p.28: 7a; also: Erdmann
1955, Abb. 87; cf. Jordaens,
St.Martin Curing a Possessed Man)

643
Backhuyzen, L.

Portrait of Anna de Hooghe
Rijksmuseum, Amsterdam
1690-1700

Literature: van Thiel p.96

ci./b73

The field has thin floral stems
ending in the characteristic
curved blossoms, or in rosettes
from which sprout two or more
tendrils, some bearing similar
curved blossoms. Birds and
animals in combat are placed
between these floral ornaments.

644
Baen, J. de

Portrait of Steven Wolters
Stichting v.d.Poll-Wolters-Quina,
Zeist
1687
123 x 92 cm

ci./c2/ig8,og8

The border has an unidentified
design of trefoils on C-stems and
flowers. The S-motifs in the
guardborders are alternately
rendered in two colours.

645
Baen, J. de
*Portrait of Hieronymus van
Beverningh*
Rijksmuseum, Amsterdam
1670
156 x 121.5 cm
Literature: van Thiel p.94
See illustration p.82

ci.?

646
Baen, J. de
Portrait of François van Bredehof
Sale F.Muller 14/12/48-3
1670-76
122 x 96 cm

ci./ig8

647
Baen, J. de
*Portrait of a Man, Member of the
Paedts Family*
Private collection,
The Netherlands
c. 1685
140 x 113 cm

ci.?

648
Baen, J. de

Portrait of an Unknown Man
Gallery Katz, Dieren 1938
1670-85

ci./og11c

For the design of the outer guard
border cf. an Indian carpet in
Glasgow, ill. p.83

649
Baen, J. de
Portrait of Marc du Tour
Private collection
1670-72

ci.?

650
Baen, J. de

The Syndics of the Lakenhal (Cloth
Hall) *in Leyden*
Municipal Museum 'De Laken-
hal', Leyden
1675
See illustration p.96

ci./c2/iiig46?,iig46,ig8

The S-motifs of the subguard are
rendered in two shades of the
same colour without separating
outline. Cf. Hecken, *A Still-life
with a Rumer and Fruits*. Cf. an
Indian carpet in Glasgow, ill. p.83
for the design of the field; cf.
Pagnano nr.146 for the border
design. Both border and field
have a red ground.

651
Baen, J. de

Portrait of a Man
Gallery Katz, Dieren, 1938
1679

ci./ig131

652
Baen, J. de
Portrait of Willem van den Kerckhoven
Sale Mak van Waay, Amsterdam 24/6/41-4
1680
128 x 104 cm

ci./iig131?

The red carpet has white spiralling scrolls with black outlines. A secondary system of scrolling floral stems is vaguely indicated: it is rendered in a slightly lighter shade of red than the ground.

653
Baen, J. de
Governors of the East India Company of the Chamber in Hoorn
Westfries Museum, Hoorn
1682
238 x 292.5 cm
Literature: Haak ill.1001

ci./ig131

The drawing of the scrolling stems and the floral ornaments is clearly identical to those in the rug in id., *Portrait of Hieronymus van Beverningh.*

654
Baen, J. de

Portrait of Frederik van Hoeckelum
Private collection,
The Netherlands
1683
120.5 x 96 cm

ci.

The carpet seems to be of the same type as the other carpets depicted by de Baen.

655
Baen, J. de (attr. to)
Portrait of an Unknown Lady
Sale M.H. Brugman, Ixelles 23/3/26-143
c. 1670
125 x 95 cm

ci.

The carpet could be identical to the rug in id. *Portrait of Hieronymus van Beverningh.*

656
Baen, J. de (attr. to)
Portrait of Hendrikus Fagel
State-owned art collections department, The Hague
c. 1675
63 x 54 cm

ci.?

Cf. B. van der Helst, *Portrait of Two Men*

657
Baen, J. de (attr. to)
Portrait of an Unknown Man
Sale Christie's New York 7/12/77-129 (as C. de Moor)
c. 1680

ci./ig131

658
Baen, J. de (attr. to)
Portrait of an Unknown Man
Sale F.Muller Amsterdam 25/6/24-10
1675-85
109 x 92 cm

ci./ig131

659
Boel, P.

Still-life with a Globe
Gemäldegalerie der Akademie, Vienna
c. 1660
Literature: Berlin 1985 p.44, ill.33

c2/ig46,og11b (ci)

The green border has lotus flowers and rosettes, and the curved blossoms which may be indicating an Indian origin of the rug. Remarkable is the design of the main border, which has an axis parallel to the direction of the border. The floral ornaments on one side of this axis are more or less the mirror-image of those on the other side.

660
Boonen, A.
A Man Smoking
Sale Sotheby's, London 21/3/56-8
c. 1695

ci.?/c2?/ig132

The g132 ornament seems to point to an Indian origin of this carpet.

661
Bray, J. de

Regents of the Leper's Asylum in Haarlem
Frans Hals Museum, Haarlem
1667
142 x 197.5 cm

c2/ig46,og86 (ci.)

The carpet has a highly unusual design in both the field and the border; the presence of an elaborate g46 ornament in combination with the g86 ornament (the latter was recorded rather frequently on Indian carpets in paintings) could indicate an Indian origin. Surviving carpets with this field and border design are unknown.

662
Bray, J. de
Governors of the Poor Children's Home
Frans Hals Museum, Haarlem
1663
See illustration p.92

bi./b6/iig8,ig46,og11b (ci)

The field design has fine stems and flowers of medium size. The glossy shine of the fringes suggests that these were made of silk.

663
Bray, J. de
The Haarlem Painter Abraham Casteleyn and his Wife Margarieta van Bancken
Rijksmuseum, Amsterdam
1663
84 x 108 cm
Literature: van Thiel p.141

b6/iig8?,ig46?,og11? (ci.)

Cf. id. *Governors of the Poor Children's home*

664
Codde, P.
Portrait of a Family
Rijksmuseum, Amsterdam
1642
55 x 74 cm
Literature: van Thiel, p.171

ci./c1/iig8,ig421

The red field has a repeating design of stiff floral stems, at regular intervals pointing upwards and downwards to support a lotus flower. A secondary system of straight and curved floral stems is rendered in a slightly lighter shade of red without separating outlines. This field design is unknown from surviving carpets. The border has S-stems. The possibly Indian provenance of this carpet is indicated by the presence of an accentuated subguard separating the field and the inner guard border, and by the elaborate version of the g46 decoration of the inner guard border which is found on many carpets in paintings which may have been manufactured in India.

665
Codde, P.

Portrait of a Family in a Courtyard
Art market, Berlin c. 1925
c. 1640
98 x 127 cm

ci./c2/iig71,ig132

Sketchy representation. The carpet is long and narrow. The border has amongst others palmettes, composed of small lotus flowers in a flaming arabesque. Similar palmettes can be found in the borders of the Braganza carpets (Pagnano nr.99); cf. also A. de Vries, *Regents of the Poor Children's House.*

666
Coques, G.
A Couple Making Music in an Interior
Koninklijk Museum voor Schone Kunsten, Brussels
1650-60
39 x 57 cm
Literature: cat. 1984, p.67

b6/ig132,og11? (ci.)

The location of the carpet is highly unusual: on the floor under the table. The border has a white ground (cf. Pot, *Portrait of Willem de Vrij*; Sorgh, *Portrait of a Boy Standing Near a Table*).

667
Cossiers, J.

Portrait of the Artist
Art dealer Bachstitz, The Hague
1959
c. 1625

ci./c23

The main borderstripe shows the characteristic curved blossoms. Cf. Eiland pl.45.

668
Cossiers, J. (attr. to)
David's Advice to Solomon
Sale Drouot Paris, 26/6/89-52
1630-40?
166.5 x 231 cm

ci.?/c23?/ig46

The carpet is placed on the floor, under the bed. For the border-design with lanceolate leaves, composed of smaller leaflets cf. Pagnano nr.231.

669
Doomer, L.

Moses as a Child, Crushing Pharao's Crown
Present location unknown
c. 1670
61 x 34 cm

c11/ig132,og122 (ci.)

Cf. Constantijn Netscher, *Portrait of a Boy Standing at a Stone Table with Precious Objects.*

670
Eliasz (Pickenoy), N.

Portrait of a Man
Coll. Viscount Halifax
1628
111.2 x 83.7 cm

ci/c2/iig131?

Cf. Jordaens, *St.Martin Curing a Possessed Man*

671
Gelder, N. van (attr. to)

Still-life with Nautilus Cup and Fruits
Present location unknown
1655-60

ci/c11/og8

For the field design cf. Pagnano nr.144.

672
Graat, B.
Interior Scene with Courting Couple
Sale Sotheby's, London 19/2/86-
135a
1670-80
53 x 43 cm

ci./c26?(ci.3)

Cf. Spuhler 1987, nr.124;
Musscher, *A Scholar and his Son*;
Ochtervelt, *Letter-writer and a
Maid*.

673
Graat, B.
Family Portrait on a Terrace
Royal Collections, England
c. 1670
Literature: White cat.55

ci.?/c28

674
Haye, R. de la
Lady Playing the Cello
Sale Dorotheum, Vienna 18/9/
79-62
c. 1680
32 x 24 cm

ci./c27/ig132?

Cf. Hali V (1982) 1, p.55 (ill.)

675
Hecken, A. van den
A Still-life with a Rumer and Fruits
Sale Sotheby's, London 16/7/
1980-23
1653
58.4 x 53.3 cm

c27/iiig6,iig46,ig8 (ci./c27)

The S-motifs in the inner
subguard are drawn in the same
colour, but a lighter shade than
the ground.

676
Hecken, A. van den
An Old Man Sitting at a Table
Sale J. de Winter, Giroux Brussel,
12/3/28-46
1647 of 1657
53 x 44 cm

ci./c23?/iig131?,ig46?,og11c

Cf. id. *The Repentant Judas*.

677
Hecken, A. van den

*Portrait of an Old Man in an
Interior*
Formerly coll. E.Burg-Berger,
Berlin 1936
1653-58
54.5 x 44.5 cm

ci./c23/iig6,ig46?og11c

Cf. id. *Portrait of a Philosopher in
his Studio*.

678
Hecken, A. van den

The Repentant Judas
Formerly Hermitage, Leningrad
1654

ci./b1/iig6,ig42,og11c

The field has scrolling stems with
large lanceolate leaves and
curved blossoms. Several floral
ornaments are rendered in the
same colour but a lighter tone
than the ground, without
separating outlines. Cf. *Portrait of
a Philosopher in his Studio*.

679
Hecken, A. van den

*Portrait of a Philosopher in his
Studio*
Present location unknown
1655
60 x 80 cm

ci./c23/iig6,ig46,og11c

Some of the ornaments in the
field are drawn in the same
colour, but a lighter shade, as the
ground colour.

680
Hecken, A. van den

Portrait of Cornelis Meyer
Rijksmuseum, Amsterdam
1653
81 x 64 cm
Literature: van Thiel p.262

ci./b1/ig89,og89

A secondary system of floral
ornaments with curved blossom
motifs indicates an Indian origin
of the pattern. The borders are
strongly emphasized. The white
inner guard and the red outer
guard have subguards with
geometrical decorations.

681
Hecken, A. van den
Portrait of a Scholar in his Studio
Sale Christie's London 6/2/76-75
1650-55
121.8 x 106.7 cm

ci.2/c2/iig8,ig46,og11c

Cf.J. de Meyer, *The Daughters of
Sir Matthew Decker*

682
Hecken, A. van den

Portrait of Mr. Copes van Hasselt
Present location unknown
1655?

ci.3/b6/
iiig131,iig46,ig8,og6,oog46

683
Helst, B. van der
Portrait of Two Men
Sale Sotheby's New York, 3/6/
88-58
1660-80
160 x 128 cm

ci.

Cf. Pagnano 151. A large curved
'wistaria' blossom, rendered in a
lighter shade than the ground
colour, without separating
outlines, indicates an Indian
origin of the pattern.

684
Horst, G.W.

The Lute Player and an Old Man
French & Company, New York
1957
c. 1640
121 x 95 cm

cii./ig132

Cf. id. *Musical Party*. The field is

empty, apart from large
ornaments resembling palmettes
in the corners, and a smaller,
possibly floral ornament in the
centre of the field. A small lotus
flower can be seen between the
corner ornaments.

686
Jongh, L. de
Portrait of a Family in an Interior
Amsterdams Historisch Museum,
Amsterdam (collection van der
Hoop)
1673
See illustration p.77

ci./b6/iiig131,ig132,og46

687
Jordaens, J.
*Portrait of the Antwerp Merchant
Johan Wierts*
Wallraf-Richartz Museum,
Cologne
c. 1631-36
134.5 x 108.5 cm
Literature: cat. 1986, p.39,
Abb.338

c2 (ci.)

Cf. id. *St.Martin Curing a
Possessed Man.*

688
Jordaens, J.
St.Martin Curing a Possessed Man
Koninklijk Museum voor Schone
Kunsten, Brussels
1630
432 x 269 cm
Literature: cat. 1984, p.156
See illustration p.90

ci.?/c2/og11

689
Kemper, G.

Portrait of a Family
Edel Gallery, Cologne 1989
1661
86.5 x 113 cm

ci./c27/iig131?ig132

690
Keyser, Th. de

Portrait of a Family
Sale Christie's London 5/12/69-
74
1634
82.5 x 59 cm

bi.?/c23?/ig46,og11b

Some elements of the decoration
of the border indicate that the
design is a variant of the b1
pattern: the lotus flower is
smaller than usual and shows a
somewhat different drawing, and
one of the palmettes is only
partly visible as half of the
ornament is cut off by the outer
guard border. The stiff S-stems
do not end in a scroll, but end
prematurely in a simple, almost
geometrical ornament.
Furthermore, the border has no
corner solution. The floral
ornaments in the field have an
unusual drawing with sharp
angles; the connecting stems are
not represented in the painting.
The glossy fringes may have been
made of silk.

691
Man, C. de
Still-life with a Servant and Parrot
Historisches Museum, Frankfurt
1667 or later
151 x 129 cm
See illustration p.93

ci./b6/iig8,ig132,og86

Musical Party
Koetser Gallery, New York 1953
c. 1640
85 x 75 cm

cii./c26?/ig132,og11c

Cf. id. *The Lute Player and an Old
Man.*

685
Horst, G.W.

692
Man, C. de
Discussion in a Laboratory
National Museum, Warschaw
1680-85
90 x 112 cm
Literature: Bialostocki 1957,
Abb.259

bi./c24

693
Meyer, J. de
*The Daughters of Sir Matthew
Decker*
Fitzwilliam Museum, Cambridge
1718
76 x 65 cm
See illustration p.84

ci.2/b6/iig6,ig132,ogg12

694
Mieris, W. van
*Young Woman with a Boy Blowing
Bubbles in an Arched Window*
Rijksmuseum, Amsterdam
c. 1700
36 x 28 cm
Literature: van Thiel p.387

ci./c25/ig46,og11c

The border design has no corner
solution.

695
Molenaer, J.M.
The van Loon-Ruychaven Family
Stichting Museum van Loon,
Amsterdam
1629-30
64.5 x 79 cm
Literature: Haarlem 1986, cat.47

ci.3?/c26/iig8,ig132,og122

Cf. id. *Portrait of a Family.*

696
Molenaer, J.M.
Portrait of a Family, or: *The Four
Generations*
Rijksmuseum, Amsterdam
1631

ci.3?/c26/iig8,ig132,og122

Quite unusual is the representation of chairs with an upholstering
of knotted carpet fragments. The
pattern of the upholstering seems
to be related to the design of the
carpet in *A Young Woman with a
Boy Blowing Bubbles in an Arched
Window,* attributed to Willem van
Mieris. The cushion at the lower
left side of the painting also has a
knotted pile.

697
Musscher, M. van

The Doctor's Visit
Present location unknown
1668
45 x 40 cm

ci.?/iig8

The accentuated subguard
framing the field may be an
indication that this unusual
carpet was woven in India.

698
Musscher, M. van
An Astronomer or Cartographer
Amsterdams Historisch Museum,
Amsterdam
1671
See illustration p.88

c27/ig46,og46 (ci.)

The inner guard border has a g65
guard border at the side of the
main border, while the outer
guard border has a variant of the
g71 design.

699
Musscher, M. van
Woman at a Table with a Servant
Present location unknown
1670-80
Literature: Gudlaugsson II,
T.XVIII

b6/iig8?,ig132?,og44? (ci.)

700
Musscher, M. van
*Portrait of a Man and a Woman
with a Dog*
Sale F.Muller Amsterdam 15/6/
37-55
1685
77 x 64 cm

ci./b7

The border has a variant of the b1
design, with stiff floral stems
ending in curved blossoms.
Similar blossoms can be found in
the field design.

701
Musscher, M. van
Portrait of a Family
Musée des Beaux Arts,
Chateauroux
1680-90

ci.?/c27?/iig131,ig46,og46?

702
Musscher, M. van
A Scholar and his Son
Present location unknown
1680-90
See illustration p.84

ci.3/c2

Cf. Graat, *Interior Scene with
Courting Couple*; Ochtervelt,
Letter-writer and a Maid.

703
Musscher, M. van
Portrait of Johannes Hudde,

*Burgomaster of Amsterdam and
Mathematician*
Rijksmuseum, Amsterdam
1686
57 x 49 cm
Literature: van Thiel p.404
See illustration p.78

ci./c2

704
Musscher, M. van

Boy with a Dog
Art gallery Leeman, Zutphen
1970
1690
41 x 32 cm

ci./c2/og86

Cf. id. *Portrait of an Unknown
Gentleman.* The carpet has a
border with whimsical
cartouches. Cf. an Indian carpet,
formerly in the Pannwitz
collection, ill. p.85 (border
design); also an Indian carpet in
the Metropolitan Museum of Art,
Pagnano nr.144 (field design).

705
Musscher, M. van
Portrait of a Man Writing at a Table
Private collection, Amsterdam
43 x 37 cm
1693

ci./c2

Cf. id. *Boy with a Dog*

706
Musscher, M. van
Portrait of an Unknown Gentleman
Sale Sotheby Mak van Waay 18/
10/85
1698
46.5 x 39 cm
See illustration p.89

ci./c2

Cf. id. *Boy with a Dog.*

707
Musscher, M. van (attr. to)

'Piskijker'
Present location unknown
1660-70
57 x 45 cm

ci.2?/iig8,ig46,og11c

The carpet in this painting may
well belong to the same group as
the one in Abraham van der
Hecken's *Portrait of a Scholar in
his Studio*.

708
Musscher, M. van (attr. to)

Portrait of a Man in a Silk Gown
Present location unknown
c. 1690
67 x 56 cm

ci./c2/iig62,ig46,og62

709
Musscher, M. van (attr. to)

Portrait of a Man in a Silk Gown
Musée des Beaux-Arts,
Strasbourg
c. 1690

ci./iig64,ig46

710
Musscher, M. van (follower)
*Portrait of a Family, in the
Background the Amsterdam City
Hall*
Private collection, Germany
c. 1700
See illustration p.94

ci./d16/ig102,og102 (eiii)

711
Naiveu, M.
The Card Players
Sale Christie's London 19/6/42-
30
1679
79.9 x 100.9 cm

ci.?/c28

The inner guardborder consists
of three stripes without
geometrical or floral ornaments.
The border has a meandering
stem with small rosettes and
flowerbuds on tendrils.

712
Naiveu, M.
Public Surgery
Sale Christie's London 26/6/48-
18 (as J. Victors)
1704
53 x 41 cm

ci.?/c28

Cf. id. *Woman with a Parrot in a
Window*

713
Naiveu, M.
Woman with a Parrot in a Window
State-owned Art Collections
Dept., The Hague
1715
40.5 x 32.5 cm
See illustration p.90

ci.?/c28

The carpet has in the field a
clearly depicted 'wistaria'
blossom, indicating an Indian
provenance of the pattern. Cf. id.
The Card Players; id. *Public
Surgery*.

714
Netscher, C.
*Portrait of an Architect Sitting on a
Terrace*
Sale Goeteborg 7/11/76-269
1663
63 x 73 cm

ci./c11/iig8,ig42

The field is decorated with S-
stems, ending in split leaf forms
(Cf. Spuhler 1978, nr.63).

715
Netscher, C.
Portrait of an Unknown Gentleman
Wawel Castle Museum, Crakow
c. 1675
Literature: Bialostocki 1957,
nr.287

ci.?

Cf. the carpets listed in this part
depicted by de Baen.

716
Netscher, C.
*Portrait of a Young Woman and a
Man Playing the Lute*
Coll. Herrington, Indianapolis
1670-80
53 x 45 cm
Literature: Illinois (Krannert Art
Museum) 1964, cat.22

ci./c25?/ig86,og46

The typical curved floral
ornament in the border could
indicate an Indian origin of the
rug. The field has a pattern of
stems bearing small flowers.

717
Netscher, C.

*Portrait of a Woman, Believed to be
the Painter's Wife, Playing the
Guitar*
Wallace Collection, London
35.4 x 31.3 cm

ci./c25/ig46,og11c

Cf. Willem van Mieris, *Young
Woman with a Boy Blowing Bubbles
in an Arched Window*. Remarkable
is the same lack of a corner
solution in both represented
carpets.

718
Netscher, C.

*Mme de Montespan with her Son,
the Duke of Maine, Playing Musical
Instruments*
Gemäldegalerie, Dresden
1671
48 x 37 cm

bi./ig131 (ci.)

The carpet has a rich floral
design, presumably even
including small areas brocaded
with silver or gilded threads. One
of the palmettes, cut by the
border, seems to have a
cartouche-form as is not unusual
for 'Polonaise' carpets (Pope
1939, pl.1248).

719
Netscher, C.
Portrait of an Unknown Lady
Foundation Slot Zuylen, Zuilen
1674
49 x 39.5 cm

ci./c25/ig46,og11a

720
Netscher, C.
A Woman at Prayer
Schönborn Gallery, Vienna
1665-80

ci.?/c26?/iig8?,ig46,og46

Cf. Ochtervelt (attr. to), *Letter-
writer and a Maid* for the border
design. The possible Indian
provenance is suggested by the
elaborate version of the g46
design, and the presence of an
accentuated subguard framing
the field.

721
Netscher, C.
A Man in a Silk Gown
Kunsthalle, Bremen
1681
54 x 44.8 cm

ci.?/b1?/iig131?,ig46?,og46?

722
Netscher, Con.
*Portrait of Maria Constantia and
Paulina Gillette Le Leu de Wilhelm*
Private collection
1689
50 x 40 cm
Literature: Lunsingh Scheurleer
1986, p.285

ci./c11/iig?,ig132?,og11c

The cartouches in the border
have lobed outlines.

723
Netscher, C.
A Member of the Citters Family?
Rijksmuseum, Amsterdam
c. 1680
49 x 39 cm
Literature: van Thiel p.412

b6/iig131,ig46 (ci.)

724
Netscher, C. (attr. to)

Portrait of an Unknown Man
Coll. A. Rosner, Tel Aviv 1961
1675-84
64 x 52 cm

ci./c27

The field has stiff floral stems.

725
Netscher, C. (follower)
Vertumnus and Pomona
The Dundee Museums, Dundee
1681
53.5 x 45 cm

ci.?/ig132?

726
Netscher, Con.
*Portrait of a Boy Standing at a Stone
Table with Precious Objects*
Marquess of Bath, Longleat
1680-1700
31 x 26 cm

c11/iig131,ig132,og11c (ci.)

Cf. Doomer, *Moses as a Child,
Crushing Pharao's Crown.*

727
Netscher, Con.

Portrait of an Unknown Lady
Present location unknown
1680-90
47.5 x 36 cm

ci./c27/iig8?,ig122,og86

The field has a pattern of stiff
floral stems and large palmettes,
and tendril-bearing curved
blossoms.

728
Netscher, Con.

Portrait of Three Children
Sale Sotheby's, London 6/12/67-
50
1697
53.5 x 45 cm

ci./c11/iig131?,ig132,og11c

A similar Indian carpet (Martin
fig.231) has an identical inner
guard border; the field has a
small-scale design of rosettes,
palmettes and stems making an
ogival lattice. As far as can be
seen on the painting, the carpet
there seems to have the same
field design.

729
Ochtervelt, J.

Dancing Dog
Stockholm, National Museum
1670-75
92 x 75 cm
Literature: Kuretsky cat.70

ci./c28

The field has an unidentified floral design. For the border design cf. Naiveu, *Woman with a Parrot in a Window.*

730
Ochtervelt, J. (attr. to)
Letter-writer and a Maid
Present location unknown
c. 1670
95 x 79.5 cm
Literature: Kuretsky D-21
See illustration p.90

ci.3/c26/iig8,ig46?,og46?

731
Pot, H. (attr. to)
Portrait of W. de Vrij Frederiksz Aged 34
Private collection,
The Netherlands
1634
122 x 89 cm
See illustration p.86

bii./b6/iig62,ig63 (ci.)

The field has floral ornaments and hunting animals. Cf. id. *Portrait of Aeltje Donkers, Wife of W. de Vrij* (pendant)

732
Pot, H. (attr. to)
Portrait of Aeltje Cornelisdr Danckerts, Wife of W. de Vrij
Private collection,
The Netherlands
1634
122 x 89 cm
See illustration p.86

bii./b6/iig62,ig63 (ci.)

Cf. id. *Portrait of W. de Vrij* (pendant).

733
Ravesteyn, J.A. van

Portrait of an Unknown Lady
Sale Christie's London 12/12/75-176

1631
111.8 x 76.2 cm

ci./iig8,ig46

The field has a floral design of waving stems with the typical Indian curved blossoms. Note the elaborate version of the g46 guard pattern.

734
Reesbroeck, J. van

Portrait of Balth. Moretus III
Museum Plantin, Antwerp
c. 1670

ci.

735
Slingelant, P. van (attr. to)

Boy with a Cage in an Arched Window
Sale Fisher Luzern 13/6/50-2449
(as C. Netscher)
c. 1660
47 x 35 cm

ci./c23/og11c

For the border design cf. Pagnano 231. The field has the usual

design, related to the bi pattern, enriched with curved 'wistaria' blossoms.

736
Sorgh, H.

Portrait of a Young Man Sitting at a Table
Kunstmuseum, Johannesburg
1656
51.5 x 41 cm

ci./b6/iig6,ig46?

The field has a large-scale, whimsical floral design. The cartouches in the field have been placed on a white ground. Cf. Pot (attr. to), *Portrait of W. de Vrij*; Coques, *A Couple Making Music in an Interior.*

737
Sorgh, H.

Portrait of a Young Man Standing at a Table
Present location unknown
1657

ci./b6/iig6,ig46?

Apparently the painter used the same model here as he did for the carpet in *Portrait of a Young Man Sitting at a Table*.

738
Spilberg II, J.
Feast of the Amsterdam Civic Guard in Honour of the Appointment of Burgomaster Jan van de Poll as Colonel
Amsterdams Historisch Museum, Amsterdam
1650
297.5 x 589 cm
Literature: van Thiel p.518

c27 (ci.)

739
Terborch, G.
The Visit
c. 1660
92 x 104 cm
Literature: Gudlauggson 149

ci./c25/og11c

Cf. Willem van Mieris, *A Woman with a Boy Blowing Bubbles in an Arched Window.*

740
Vaillant, B.

The Treaty of Nijmegen
Present location unknown

ci.

741
Vos, C. de
Portrait of Mathilde Lintermans, Wife of Jan Bierens and Two Children
County Museum of Art, Los Angeles
c. 1620
230 x 128 cm
Literature: Schaefer p.99

ci./b1/ig46,og11b

The field of the carpet has a stiff pattern including curved blossoms. The pattern of the subguard framing the field is unclear. The carpet has white, glossy fringes, possibly made of silk.

742
Vries, A. de
Regents of the Poor Children's House in Amsterdam
Amsterdams Historisch Museum

ci.?/c2/iig131,ig12,og11b

For the field design cf Backer, *Portrait of an Unknown Man*. The field has many ornaments in orange on a red ground; the border also has many ornaments in orange, on a green ground. The fringes are green. Cf. also Codde, *Portrait of a Family in a Courtyard* (border pattern).

743
Werff, A. van der
Portrait of Two Children with a Cat and a Guinea-pig
Royal collections, England
1681
33.9 x 27.3 cm
Literature: Gaehtgens cat.16

ci?/c23/iig6?,ig132,og46

Cf. Eiland 1979, fig. 120; the carpet in the painting however does not show the typical curved blossom motifs.

744
Wolfsen, A.
Portrait of a Child in a Window
Present location unknown
c. 1680

ci./c25/og11

Cf. W. van Mieris (attr. to), *A Woman with a Boy Blowing Bubbles in an Arched Window.*

THE 'NAMENLOSE GATTUNG'

745
Brakenburg, R.
The Husband Surprised
Sale Christie's New York 5/11/82-119
1670 or later
53 x 69.2 cm

d11/og102 (ei.)

In the catalogue of the auction this painting is described as a copy by Brakenburgh of a painting by Jan Steen; it bears the signature of Jan Steen. The carpet in the painting is not unusual for paintings by Jan Steen, but is the only example of a carpet with the d11 border recorded in a painting attributed to Brakenburg.

746
Brakenburg, R.
A Musical Party
New York Historical Society, New York
1690-95
39.5 x 49.5 cm

ei./d14/ig86,og85

The carpet has no elem. The central medallion has small reciprocal ornaments, as can be seen in the Scheunemann carpets depicted by de Hooch; these ornaments are in the latter paintings placed on the lobed ornaments which enclose the corner medallions.

747
Brakenburg, R.
Scene in an Inn
Sale Schwerdt New York, 25/4/28-37
1690-95
33 x 39.3 cm

d14 (ei.)

748
Brakenburg, R.

Scene in an Interior
Present location unknown
1690-1700
40 x 33 cm

ei./d14/og85

749
Brakenburg, R.

A Picture Gallery
Dominion Gallery, Montreal 1945
1690-95
57.8 x 71.7 cm

ei./d14/ig86,og85

Both the design of the main border stripe and the design of the outer guard border are symmetrical.

750
Brakenburg, R.
The Feast of St.Nicolas
Present location unknown
1690-1700
77.5 x 87.5 cm
Literature: Exhibition Katz Gallery, Dieren 1957, cat.3

og85 (ei.)

751
Brakenburg, R.
The Card Players
Sale Schidlof, Vienna 5/3/21-8
1690-1700
40.5 x 49 cm

ei./d14/ig86,og85

752
Brakenburg, R.

Portrait of a Young Girl
Sale Phillips, London 28/4/87
1690-95
57 x 65 cm

ei./ig84,og85

The central medallion is used like a nimbus around the head of the girl. The rug does not seem to have the d14 border; the original model may therefore have been another carpet than the one depicted by Brakenburg in other paintings; the inner guard border differs as well.

753
Brakenburg, R.
Merry Home-coming
Gallery Hoogstede, The Hague
1983
1690-95
39 x 33 cm
Literature: sale Mark, Dordrecht 4/6/16-9

ei./d14/ig86,og85

754
Brakenburg, R.
Interior of a Dutch Inn
Musée des Beaux-Arts, Bordeaux
1692
Literature: sale F. Muller, Amsterdam 22/11/10-15

ei./d14/ig86,og85

755
Brakenburg, R.

A Party in an Interior
Present location unknown
c. 1692
40.5 x 48.5 cm

ei./d14/ig86,og85

756
Brakenburg, R.
The Doctor's Visit
Present location unknown
1694
51 x 40 cm

ei./d14/ig86,og85

757
Brakenburg, R.
The Faint
Sale Dorotheum, Vienna 17/3/64
1701
35 x 29 cm

ei./d14/ig86,og85

758
Dusart, C. (attr. to)
A Man and a Woman Making Music
Art Gallery, Glasgow
1685-90
20 x 15 cm
See illustration p.106

ei./ig86

759
Dusart, C.

An Alchemist
Present location unknown
1687
32.3 x 28.1 cm

ei./ig86

The rug has a hole at the same spot as in id. *A Man and a Woman Making Music*. Perhaps Dusart used a worn carpet as a model.

760
Haye, R. de la
The Doctor's Visit
Sale Dorotheum, Vienna 17/3/64
1701
35 x 29 cm

ei./d14/ig86,og85

761
Helst, B. van der
Portrait of Maria Henrietta Stuart
Rijksmuseum, Amsterdam
1652
199.5 x 170 cm
Literature: van Thiel p.268

ei./d14/ig86,og85

The barbers-pole stripe consists of alternating red and black dots.

762
Helst, B. van der
Woman Making Music
Metropolitan Museum of Art, New York
1662
136 x 109.5 cm

ei.

Only a small part of the field is visible.

763
Helst, B. van der
Portrait of Daniel Bernard, Governor of the V.O.C.
Museum Boymans-van Beuningen, Rotterdam
1669
124 x 113 cm
Literature: cat. 1972, p.212, ill. p.80

ei./ig86

The field is red, and has white spandrels with blue stars.

764
Helst, B. van der
Portrait of a Man
Hermitage, Leningrad
1670
168 x 138
Literature: de Gelder 1921, cat.233, ill. XXXIX

ei./ig86,og85

765
Heyden, J. van der
Still-life in a Niche
Royal Picture Gallery The Mauritshuis, The Hague
1664
27 x 20.7 cm
Literature: Wagner cat.211

ei./d16/ig86,og102

The carpet has a selvedge consisting of two or three strands of yarn, apparently wrapped with wool, and a narrow elem.

766
Heyden, J. van der
Still-life with a Red Curtain
Ferdinandeum, Innsbruck
1665
26.5 x 19.5 cm
Literature: Wagner cat.212
See illustration p.104

ei./d16/ig86,og85

767
Heyden, J. van der
Still-life with an Ebony Cabinet
Kunsthalle, Hamburg
c. 1665
27 x 20.5 cm
Literature: Wagner cat.213

d16/og102 (ei.)

768
Heyden, J. van der
Still-life with a Tapestry Curtain
Kunsthalle, Hamburg
c. 1665
51 x 44.4 cm
Literature: Wagner cat.214

ei./d16/ig86,og102

769
Hooch, P. de
Woman Reading a Letter by a Window
Museum of Fine Arts, Budapest
1664
55 x 55 cm
Literature: Sutton cat.63

d17/ig88? (ei.2)

770
Hooch, P. de
A Woman Weighing Gold Coins against Silver Coins
Staatliche Museen Preussischer Kulturbesitz, Berlin
c. 1664 or later
61 x 53 cm

ei./d17/ig88,og88

771
Hooch, P. de
A Man with a Glass of Wine and a Woman Lacing her Bodice
Collection Lord Barnard, Raby Castle, Darlington
1665
53.5 x 64 cm
Literature: Sutton cat.69

ei.2/d17/ig88,og88

772
Hooch, P. de
Mother and Child by a Cradle
Rijksmuseum, Amsterdam
1665-68
36.5 x 42 cm
Literature: Sutton cat.71

ei.2/d17/ig88,og88

773
Hooch, P. de
A Musical Party on a Terrace
Present location unknown
c. 1667
67 x 79 cm
Literature: Sutton cat.76

ei.2/d17/ig88,og88

774
Hooch, P. de
Two Women and a Man Making Music

Picture Gallery, Royal Collection, Hampton Court
1667
52 x 62 cm
Literature: Sutton cat.77

ei./d17/ig88,og88 (ei.2)

775
Hooch, P. de
A Woman with a Mandolin and a Couple at a Table Singing
Taft Museum, Cincinnati
1667-70
70 x 58 cm
Literature: Sutton cat.78
See illustration p.98

ei.2/d17/ig88,og88

776
Hooch, P. de
A Woman with a Basin and a Flagon, and a Man Dressing
Metropolitan Museum of Art, New York
1667-70
61.5 x 52 cm
Literature: Sutton cat.79

ei.2/d17/ig88

777
Hooch, P. de
A Woman Reading a Letter, and a Man at a Window
National Museum, Stockholm
1668-70
57 x 49 cm
Literature: Sutton cat.85

ei.2/d17/ig88,og88

778
Hooch, P. de
A Man and Two Women Conversing
City Art Museum, Manchester
1668-70
70 x 61.8 cm
Literature: Sutton cat.86

d17/ig88,og88 (ei.2)

779
Hooch, P. de
Two Women Teaching a Child to Walk
Museum der Bildenden Künste, Leipzig
1668-72
67.5 x 59 cm
Literature: Sutton cat.87

ei.2/d17/1g88,og88

780
Hooch, P. de
A Woman Handing a Coin to a

Serving Woman with a Child
Los Angeles County Museum of Art, Los Angeles
1668-72
73 x 66 cm
Literature: Sutton cat.88

ei./d17/ig88,og88 (ei.2)

781
Hooch, P. de
Women with a Child Feeding a Parrot
Private collection, England
1668-72
79.5 x 66 cm
Literature: Sutton cat.90

d17/ig88,og88 (ei.2)

782
Hooch, P. de
Three Women and a Man with a Monkey on a Terrace
Private collection, England
1669
70 x 85.5 cm
Literature: Sutton cat.91

ei.2/d17/ig88

783
Hooch, P. de
A Man and a Serving Woman Behind a Screen, with Card Players
Present location unknown
1675-80
88 x 81 cm
Literature: Sutton cat 119

ei.2/d17/ig88

784
Hooch, P. de
A Man with a Serving Woman at a Table
Present location unknown
c. 1680
51 x 47 cm
Literature: Sutton cat.147

ei.2/d17/ig88

785
Hooch, P. de (attr. to)
A Musical Company with Four Figures
Present location unknown
1660-65
82 x 103 cm
Literature: Sutton cat.b4

ei.2/d17/ig88

786
Hooch, P. de (attr. to)
A Woman before a Mirror, with Two Women by a Hearth

Present location unknown
1665-70
35.5 x 48.2 cm
Literature: Sutton cat.b1

ei./d17/ig88,og88?

787
Hoogstraten, S. van
An Interior with a Lady
1660-70
Gallery Douwes, Amsterdam
1976
Literature: Delft Antiekbeurs 1976, Exhibition catalogue, p.9 (ill.)

ei.

Not a very clear representation.

788
Hoogstraten, S. van
Couple Playing Cards
Sale Christie's London 5/6/80-122
1660-70
65 x 72 cm

ei./d11/iig64,ig86,og85

The design of the main border stripe and the pattern of the outer guard border are symmetrical. The presence of an inner subguard is remarkable (cf. Sant-Acker, *Still-life*, id, *Still-life with Nautilus Cup*).

789
Hoogstraten, S. van (attr. to)
Couple Making Music
Present location unknown
1665 or later
55 x 61 cm
Literature: HdG, de Hooch nr.172

ei.2/d17/ig88,0g88

790
Hoogstraten, S. van (follower)
Lady Sitting Next to a Cradle with a Sleeping Child
Niedersächsisches Landes-museum, Hanover
1660-70
45.7 x 38.1 cm

ei.

791
Jongh, L. de
Portrait of a Family at a Table
Museum of Western European and Oriental Art, Riga
1670
71 x 60 cm
Literature: Kuznetsov cat.98

ei./d11/ig84,og102

792
Metsu, G.
Lady at her Toilet
Frick Collection, New York
c. 1660
48.7 x 41 cm

ei./d17?/ig102,og85

793
Mieris, J. van
Man Offering an Apple to a Man Holding a Parrot
Sale Lepke, Berlin 31/3/25-46
1680
29.5 x 23.5 cm

ei.

The representation suggests that the original rug had a very coarse weaving structure.

794
Mieris, F. van
The Music Lesson
Gemäldegalerie, Dresden
1672
41 x 31 cm
Literature: Naumann cat.89

ei./d11/ig84,og102?

795
Mieris, F. van
The Death of Lucretia
Private collection, Sweden
1679
38 x 27 cm
Literature: Naumann cat.116

ei./d11/ig84,og102?

Very careful representation. The rug seems to have a selvedge made of two separate warps or pairs of warps, overcast apparently with red wool yarns. The wefts are probably white, as can be seen at both the reverse side of the carpet and the upper side; the pile may have been worn down a little.

796
Mieris, W. van
A Young Woman Writing Down an Old Woman's Last Will
Sale Mak van Waay, Amsterdam 7/6/55-76
1720
54.5 x 44 cm

ei./ig84,og102?

797
Neer, E. van der
The Lute Player

Gemäldegalerie, Karlsruhe
1677
38.5 x 32 cm
Literature: cat. 1929,nr.279

d11/ig86,og8 (ei.)

798
Neer, E. van der
Elegant Couple in an Interior
Present location unknown
1678
82.5 x 68.4 cm
Literature: Royal Academy London 1958, Robinson Collection, cat.37 (ill.)

ei./d11/ig88?,og85

799
Netscher, C.
Portrait of an Unknown Man Seated at a Table
Sale Sotheby's London 5/7/84-391
1680 or later
44.5 x 40 cm

ei./d11/og85

800
Niwael, J.

Annunciation
Private collection, Amsterdam
1661
79.5 x 127 cm

ei./d14/og88?

801
Ochtervelt, J.
The Embracing Cavalier
Asheton Bennett Collection, Manchester
1660-63
44.6 x 35.6 cm
Literature: Kuretsky cat.14

ei.?/d11/ig84,og85?

802
Ochtervelt, J.
The Sleeping Soldier
Asheton Bennett Collection, Manchester
1660-63
46 x 37.7 cm
Literature: Kuretsky cat.15

ei./d11?/ig84,og85

803
Ochtervelt, J.
The Oyster Meal
Private Collection
1664-5
54 x 44.5 cm
Literature: Kuretsky cat.23

ei./d11/ig84

804
Ochtervelt, J.
The Oyster Meal
Museum Boymans-van Beuningen, Rotterdam
1667
43 x 33.5 cm

ei./d11/ig84

The irregularity in the inner guard border can also be found in another representation by Ochtervelt, *The Gallant Man*. This indicates the care taken by the painter in reproducing details in following the pattern of his model.

805
Ochtervelt, J.
The Concert
Private collection
c. 1667
41.2 x 39.3 cm
Literature: Kuretsky cat.38

ei./d11/ig84,og85 (2x)

806
Ochtervelt, J.
The Music Lesson
Reiss Museum, Mannheim
c. 1667
66 x 56 cm
Literature: Kuretsky cat.40

ei./d11/ig84

The corner medallions are not depicted. The borders are missing at the end of the rug.

807
Ochtervelt, J.
The Tric-trac Players
Collection E.G.Buehrle, Zurich
1667-9
58.5 x 46.5 cm
Literature: Kuretsky cat.42

ei./d11/ig84,og85

808
Ochtervelt, J.
Musician with Tric-trac Players
Wallraf-Richartz Museum, Cologne
c. 1668
63.5 x 50 cm
Literature: Kuretsky cat.44

d11/ig84 (ei.)

809
Ochtervelt, J. (attr. to)
Lady Violinist
Statens Museum, Copenhagen
1668
52.5 x 43.5 cm
Literature: Kuretsky cat.46

ei./d11/ig84,og85

The corner solution is different here from e.g. id. *Musician with Tric-trac Players*, or id. *Portrait of a Man in a Window*. No fringes present.

810
Ochtervelt, J.
Portrait of a Man in a Window
Städelsches Institut, Frankfurt
1668
29 x 23 cm
Literature: Kuretsky cat.48

d11 (ei.)

811
Ochtervelt, J.
Galanterie
Gemäldegalerie, Dresden
1669
81.5 x 60.5 cm
Literature: Kuretsky cat.53

ei./d11/ig84,og85

Cf. id. *The Oyster Meal* for the irregularity in the S-forms in the inner guard border. A similar irregularity can be seen in Adriaen van der Werff's *Portrait of an Unknown Gentleman*.

812
Ochtervelt, J.
The Dancing Dog
Private collection, England
1669
Literature: Kuretsky cat.56

ei./ig84

cf. id. *Dancing Dog*

813
Ochtervelt, J.
Dancing Dog
Wadsworth Athenaeum,
Hartford
c. 1669
72.5 x 58.5 cm
Literature: Kuretsky cat.57

ei./ig84

814
Ochtervelt, J.
The Serenade
Present location unknown
1669-70
52 x 41 cm
Literature: Kuretsky cat.59

ei.

815
Ochtervelt, J.

A Young Lady Trimming her Fingernails
National Gallery, London
1671-3
74.6 x 59 cm
Literature: Kuretsky cat.76

ei./d11/ig84,og85

816
Ochtervelt, J.
Lady and a Maid
Henry E. Huntington AG, San Marino, California
1670-75
44 x 33.6 cm
Kuretsky cat.80

ei./d11/ig84,og85

817
Ochtervelt, J.
Portrait of a Couple Making Music
Städtische Kunstsammlungen, Augsburg
1671-75
87 x 75 cm
Literature: Kuretsky cat.81

ei./d11/ig84,og85?

The corner solution is identical to the one found in id. *Lady Violinist*, but differs from the one in id. *Portrait of a Man in a Window*. If the representations are reliable, either Ochtervelt must have used two different carpets of this type as models or the corner solutions at the one

end of the carpet were different from those at the other end side.

818
Ochtervelt, J.
The Tease
Private collection, Switzerland
c. 1675
81 x 65 cm
Literature: Kuretsky cat.86

ei.?

819
Ochtervelt, J.
Lady at the Virginals
Present location unknown
1676-80
49 x 39 cm
Literature: Kuretsky cat.96

ei.

819a
Ochtervelt, J. (attr. to)
Lady in an Interior
Galerie Liechtenstein, Vienna
52 x 46 cm
Literature: Kuretsky cat.D-19

ei./d11

S.Kuretsky believes that this painting is a fake. The analysis of the design of the carpet could bring up an extra argument for rejecting the attribution of the painting to Ochtervelt; the drawing of the corner medallions is unusual, as well as the

representation of the d11 main border design and the decoration of the outer guard border (presumably g85). Moreover, the place of the carpet in the scene, namely on the floor, is rather unusual for carpets in 17th century Dutch genre paintings.

820
Sant-Acker, F. van de
Still-life
Collection A.Gatacre-de Stuers, Vorden
1668
66 x 60 cm

iig102,ig85,og85,oog102? (ei.)

Remarkable is the presence of a double inner guard border, which can also be seen on the representation of a similar rug by Sant-Acker, *Still-life with Nautilus Cup*. The carpet has a selvedge made of two or three warps or pairs of warps, overcast apparently with wool, and a narrow elem.

821
Sant-Acker, F. van de
Still-life with a Nautilus Cup
Amsterdam, Rijksmuseum
c. 1668
66 x 56.5 cm
Literature: van Thiel p.498

d12?/iig102,ig85,og85,oog102 (ei.)

Cf. id. *Still-life*

822
Slingelant, P. van

Portrait of an Unknown Family
Present location unknown
1674
64 x 53 cm

ei./d16

Cf. Jan van der Heyden, *Still-life with a Red Curtain*.

823
Steen, J.
Bookkeeper and Death
Narodni Galerie, Prague
1662-3
61 x 54 cm
Literature: Braun cat.157

d11?/ig84,og102 (ei.)

The rug presumably has a
selvedge made of two warps or
pairs of warps.

824
Steen, J.
The Faint
Sir Alfred Beit, Russborough
(Ireland)
1664-8
49 x 37 cm
Literature: Braun cat.232

ei./d11/ig84,og102

825
Steen, J.
*Hier baet geen medesyn, het is der
minne pyn*
State-owned Art Collections
Dept., The Hague
1665-66
57 x 43.5 cm
Literature: Braun cat.254

ei./d17/ig86

826
Steen, J.
The Lover
Present location unknown
1666-68
67 x58 cm
Literature: Braun cat.272

ei./d11/ig84,og102

827
Steen, J.
The Feast of St.Nicolas
Museum Boymans-van
Beuningen, Rotterdam
1667-78
58.5 x 49 cm
Literature: Braun cat.288

d11/og102 (ei.)

828
Steen, J.
Esther and Ahasuerus
Hermitage, Leningrad
1667-69
106 x 83.5 cm
Literature: Braun cat.291

ei./d11/ig84,og102 (table)
ei./d11/ig84,og84 (dais)

829
Steen, J.
*Soo d'ouden songen, pypen de
jongen*
Rijksmuseum, Amsterdam
1668
110.5 x 141 cm
Literature: Braun cat.295

ei./d11/ig84,og102

830
Steen, J.
The Infuriated Ahasuerus
Barber Institute of Fine Arts,
Birmingham
c. 1668
129 x 167 cm
Literature: Braun cat.299

ei./d11/ig84,og102

831
Steen, J.
The Feast of Epiphany
Staatliche Kunstsammlungen,
Kassel
1668
82 x 107.5 cm
Literature: Braun cat.296

ei./d11/ig84,og102

832
Steen, J.

Delilah has Samson's Hair Cut
Private collection,
The Netherlands
1668
67.5 x 82 cm
Literature: Braun cat.297

ei./d11/ig84,og102

833
Steen, J.
The Philistines Mocking Samson
Wallraf-Richartz Museum,
Cologne
1668
134 x 199 cm
Literature: Braun cat.298

ei./d11/ig84,og102

834
Steen, J.
The Sick Antiochus and Stratonike
Sale Sotheby's London 16/4/80-
72
c. 1668
48 x 60 cm
Literature: Braun cat.302

ei./d11/ig84,og102

835
Steen, J.
Farmers Consulting a Lawyer
Present location unknown
c. 1668
61 x 54 cm
Literature: Braun cat.305

d11/ig84,og102

836
Steen, J.

Antony and Cleopatra
Binnenhof, The Hague
1668-69
113 x 192 cm
Literature: Braun cat.306

ei./d11/ig84,og102

837
Steen, J.
The Wedding of Tobias and Sara
Present location unknown
1668-70
79 x 102 cm
Literature: Braun cat.309

ei./d11/ig84,og102

838
Steen, J.
*Bathsheba Receiving the Letter of
David*
Present location unknown
1668-70
38 x 31.5 cm
Literature: Braun cat.311

ei./d11/ig84,og102

839
Steen, J.
Ascagnes and Lucelle
Marquess of Bath, Longleat
1668-70
Literature: Braun cat.312

ei./d11/ig84,og102

840
Steen, J.
The Drawing Lesson
Fitzwilliam Museum, Cambridge
1668-70
41.6 x 31.1 cm
Literature: Braun cat.313

ei./d11/ig84,og84

841
Steen, J.
Doctor Examining a Young Girl
Philadelphia Museum of Art,
Philadelphia
1668-70
46.3 x 36.8 cm
Literature: Braun cat.315

ei./d11/ig84,og102

842
Steen, J.
A Doctor Writing a Prescription
Present location unknown
1668-70
48.5 x 37 cm
Literature: Braun cat.316

ei./d11/ig84,og102

The carpet seems damaged at the
end.

843
Steen, J.
The Doctor's Visit
Present location unknown
1668-70
70 x 52.5 cm
Literature: Braun cat.317

ei./d11/ig84,og102

844
Steen, J.
The Doctor's Visit
Royal Picture Gallery The
Mauritshuis, The Hague
1668-70
60.5 x 48.5 cm
Literature: Braun cat.318

ei./d11/ig84,og102

845
Steen, J.
The Seduction
Museum Bredius, The Hague
1668-72
49 x 39.5 cm
Literature: Braun cat.322
See illustration p.122

d11/og102 (ei.)

846
Steen, J.
*The Rhetoricians and the
Mischievous Song*
Allen Memorial Art Museum,
Oberlin
1668-72
44.8 x 37.2 cm
Literature: Braun cat.325

ei./d11/ig84,og102

847
Steen, J.

The Spanish Bride
Present location unknown
1668-70
110.5 x 82 cm
Literature: Braun cat.326

ei./d11/ig84?,og102?

848
Steen, J.
Hier baet geen medecijn
Present location unknown
1669-72
46 x 39.2 cm
Literature: Braun cat.331

ei./d11?/ig84,og102

849
Steen, J.
A Scene in a Brothel
Museum of Fine Arts, Budapest
1670-72
61.6 x 46 cm
Literature: Braun cat.336

ei./d11/ig84?

850
Steen, J.
The Magnanimity of Scipio
Euro Art Centre, Roermond
1671-74
92 x 151 cm
Literature: Braun cat.348

ei./d11?/ig84,og102

851
Steen, J.
Worshipping the Golden Calf
North Carolina Museum of Art,
Raleigh
1672-73
178 x 155 cm
Literature: Braun cat.351

ei./d11/ig84,og102

852
Steen, J.
The Wedding of Tobias and Sara
De Young Memorial Museum,
San Francisco
c. 1673
103 x 125 cm
Literature: Braun cat.355

ei./ig84?

853
Steen, J.

*The Philistines Mocking the
Captured Samson*
Koninklijk Paleis voor Schone
Kunsten, Antwerp
1675-76
65 x 82 cm
Literature: Braun cat.365

ei./d11/ig84

854
Steen, J.
The Wedding at Cana
Norton Simon Collection,
Los Angeles
1676
78 x 108 cm
Literature: Braun cat.369

ei./d11/ig84,og102 (2x)

855
Tempel, A. van de
Portrait of a Man
Sale Schüller Vienna 10/5/32-436
1655-70
80 x 67 cm

ei./d11/ig86,og85

856
Terborch, G.
A Lady Washing her Hands
Gemäldegalerie, Dresden
c. 1655
53 x 43 cm
Literature: Gudlaugsson ill.113

ei./d12/ig86,og85

The d17 border has S-stems like
the b1 border design. However,
the former pattern bears an
emphasis on the stems, whereas
in the b1 design the flowers are
the predominant ornaments. Cf.
Voorhout, *Footwashing*

857
Terborch, G.

A Lady Writing a Letter
Royal Picture Gallery The
Mauritshuis, The Hague
c. 1655
39 x 29.5 cm
Literature: Gudlaugsson ill.114

ei./d13/ig86,og11b

The d13 border design indicates
that the original rug that served
as a model for this painting was
not identical to the one which
Terborch used when he painted
A Lady Washing her Hands.

858
Terborch, G.
*Two Girls Making Music, and a
Servant*
Louvre, Paris
c. 1657
47 x 43 cm
Literature: Gudlaugsson ill.126
See illustration p.101

ei./d13/ig86,og11b

859
Terborch, G.
A Lady Playing the Lute and a Boy
Koninklijk Paleis voor Schone
Kunsten, Antwerp
c. 1657
31 x 27 cm
Literature: Gudlaugsson ill.128
See illustration p.101

d13/ig86,og11b (ei.)

860
Terborch, G.
The Greeting
National Gallery, Washington
about 1658
80 x 65.5 cm
Literature: Gudlaugsson ill.139

ei./d13/og11b

861
Terborch, G.
*Lady Playing the Lute, and an
Officer*
Metropolitan Museum of Art,
New York
about 1658
37 x 32.5 cm
Literature: Gudlaugsson ill.111

ei./d13/ig86,og11b

862
Terborch, G.

Lady at her Toilet
Detroit Institute of Arts, Detroit
c. 1660
71 x 58 cm
Literature: Gudlaugsson ill.165

ei./d13/ig86,og11b

863
Terborch, G.

A Girl Playing the Lute
Present location unknown
1655-60
33 x 19 cm

d13/og11b

864
Verheyen, A. (attr. to)
Lady Playing the Lute in an Arched Window
Sale Christie's London 5/7/35-22
30.4 x 22.8 cm

ei./d11/ig84,og85

865
Vois, A. de
Portrait of Joseph Hoeufft
Formerly collection mr. J.A.Grothe van Schellack, Rotterdam
1679
30 x 40.5 cm

ei.

The field shows a coat of arms, supported by mythological animal figures. Although European coats of arms can be found in several Eastern carpets (see page 67), the presence of a coat of arms could be presented as an extra argument for the attribution of this type of carpets to Dutch workshops. However, the painter could also have added the coat of arms to the design, as a reference to the identity of the sitter.

866
Voorhout, J.

A Writer and a Young Woman in an Interior
Present location unknown
1660-70
Dimensions not indicated

ei./d13/og85

867
Voorhout, J.
The Footwashing
Present location unknown
1675-80
132 x 112 cm
Literature: Kuretsky fig.92

ei./d12/ig86,og85

Cf. Terborch, *A Lady Washing her Hands*

868
Voorhout, J.
Three Women, a Child and a Servant in a Garden
Christie's London 15/7/77-40
1675-85
43.2 x 63.5 cm

ei./d13/ig84

The carpet seems to have had a small coat of arms in the main border, representing an animal figure. Cf. A.de Vois, *Portrait of Joseph Hoeufft*

869
Voorhout, J.
The Oyster Meal
National Museum, Stockholm
1680
83 x 66 cm
Literature: cat.1958, nr.687

ei.

870
Voorhout, J.
Portrait of a Lady, Seated Full Length by a Table, Draped with a 'Turkish' Carpet
Sale Christie's London 20/2/86-145
1680
172.7 x 134.6 cm
Literature: Hali VIII (1986), 2, p.88

ei./d17?/ig86

cf. id. *Portrait of a Gentleman, Seated Full Length by a Table Draped with a 'Turkish' Carpet* (pendant).

871
Voorhout, J.
Portrait of a Gentleman, Seated Full Length by a Table Draped with a 'Turkish' Carpet
Christie's London 20/2/86-144
1680
172.7 x 134.6

ei./d17?/ig86

cf. id. *Portrait of a Lady, Seated Full Length, by a Table, Draped with a 'Turkish' Carpet*

872
Voorhout, J.
A Young Man Writing a Letter
Sale Fievez Brussels 14/12/27-77
(as de Man)
1660-70
36 x 35 cm

ei./d13/ig102,og85?

873
Voorhout, J.
Joseph of Arimathea Pleading with Pontius Pilate for the Body of the Dead Christ
Sale Christie's London 26/7/68-118
1670-85

ei./d13/ig84

874
Voorhout, J.
The Hunter
Amsterdams Historisch Museum, Amsterdam
1680-85

ei./d13/ig84

875
Werff, A. van der
Portrait of a Gentleman Wearing a Grey Cloak, in a Landscape
Christie's London 17/7/86-7
1680-90
48.2 x 39.3 cm
See illustration p.107

ei./d11/og85

The carpet has a dark green main border, and orange fringes. Remarkable is a small irregularity in the design of the guard border (cf. Ochtervelt, *The Gallant Man*). The representation is done carefully enough to see that the yarns of the pile all point upwards.

876
Werff, A. van der
Portrait of an Unknown Family
Present location unknown
1680-90
Literature: Haarlem 1986, ill.60

ei./d11/og85

877
Werff, A. van der
Portrait of a Girl with Apples
Formerly A. Haije, Heemstede
1697
Dimensions not indicated

d11/og85 (ei.)

878
Werff, A. van der
Ecce Homo
Alte Pinakothek, Munich
1698
131 x 110 cm
Literature: Amsterdam 1981 (God
en de Goden) p.247

ei./d11/ig84?,og85

879
Werff, A. van der
*Portrait of Three Children, Plaiting
Crowns of Flowers*
Gemäldegalerie, Kassel
1710
31 x 23 cm

ei./d11/og85

880
Wulfraet, M.
Portrait of a Couple
Rijksmuseum, Amsterdam
1694
63 x 53 cm

ei./d11/ig86,og85

881
Wulfraet, M.
Portrait of a Man with a Pipe
(Self-portrait?)
Sale Mak Dordrecht 10/12/74-
277
1722
39 x 33 cm

ei./d11/og85

CARPETS RELATED TO THE 'NAMENLOSE GATTUNG'

882
Unknown Dutch artist
Portrait of Justus de Huybert
Rijksmuseum, Amsterdam
c. 1665
53 x 44 cm
Literature: van Thiel p.682

ei3 (eiii)

883
Backer, A.

*Portrait of Anthony de Bordes and
his Son Antoni*
Private collection, Bussum
1674 or 1679
140 x 157 cm

eiii/d12/ig102,og102

884
Boonen, A.
Governors of the Burgerweeshuis
(orphanage home) *in Amsterdam*
Amsterdams Historisch Museum,
Amsterdam
1699
See illustration p.114

eiii/d14/ig86,og86

885
Brakenburg, R.
Merry Company
Sale Christie's London 24/7/
1936-7
1690
31.8 x 40 cm

d18/ig65 (ei1, eiii)

886
Brakenburg, R.
Two Prostitutes
National Museum, Warsaw
c. 1690
40 x 33 cm
Literature: Cat. 1955, nr.67

ei1/d18/ig65 (eiii)

887
Brakenburg, R.
Merry Company
Sale F. Muller Amsterdam 22/
11/10-15a
1692
40.5 x 48.5 cm
See illustration p.108

ei1/d18/ig65 (eiii)

888
Brakenburg, R.

Couple Making Music
Present location unknown
1692

ei1/d18/ig65

Cf. id. *Merry Company*; id. *Lovers
in an Interior, with Children and in
the Background, a Merry Company*

889
Brakenburg, R.
*Portrait of a Family in an Archaic
Setting*
Private collection, Germany
1690-1700
68 x 93 cm

ei1/d18/ig65 (eiii)

890
Brakenburg, R.
Interior Scene
Sale Mak Dordrecht 26/3/12-2
1690-96
47 x 41 cm

ei1/d18,ig65? (eiii)

891
Brakenburg, R.
*Party in an Interior, with Nuns and
Priests*
Musée des Beaux Arts, Bernay
1690-96

ei1/d18/ig82c? (eiii)

892
Brakenburg, R.

*Lovers in an Interior, with Children
and in the Background a Merry
Company*
Present location unknown
1690-1700
49.5 x 40 cm

ei1/d18/ig65 (eiii)

Cf. id. *Merry Company* 1692; id.
Couple making Music. Apparently
Brakenburg used the same carpet
as a model; the carpets in both
representations have the large
medallion in the field, which
shows an overlap over the inner
guard border.

893
Brakenburg, R.

The Love-sick Girl
Present location unknown
1690-1700

ei1/d18/ig65 (eiii)

894
Bray, Jan de
*The de Bray Family as Antony and
Cleopatra*
Currier Gallery of Art, Man-
chester, New Hampshire
1669
248 x 190 cm
See illustration p.113

ei2 (eiii)

895
Brekelendam, Q.
A Family in an Interior
Collection Bentinck-Thyssen,
Ascona
c. 1660
46 x 63 cm

eiii/d18 (ei2)

896
Burgh, H. van der
The Terrace
Art Institute, Chicago
c. 1660
Literature: Haarlem 1986, ill.59b

ei2 (eiii)

897
Burgh, H. van der
The Glass of Wine
National Gallery, London
1660-70
116 x 91 cm

(ei2, eiii)

Presumably the same carpet as in id. *The Terrace*

898
Coques, G.
Portrait of a Young Family in an Interior
Sale Mak Amsterdam 19/5/1919-12
c. 1670
51 x 63 cm

eiii?/g46?/ig8,og8

The corner solution of the border, recalling the d11 design, seems to point toward an occidental origin for the carpet. The border design may be identical to that of the carpet in Constantijn Netscher's *Portrait of Three Children in a Window-bay.* Cf. also E. van der Neer, *Lute Player.*

899
Doomer, L.
Anna Presenting her Son Samuel to Heliah
Musée des Beaux Arts, Orleans
1668

ei2/d18/ig74,og9 (eiii)

The border shows a crude variant of the d18 pattern. The outer guard is missing at one of the shorter sides of the carpet.

900
Doomer, L.
A Man and a Woman by a Globe
University of Vermont,
Burlington, VT
1660
71.2 x 53 cm

ei2? (eiii)

Cf. also *Anna Presenting her son Samuel to Heliah.* Only a small part of what is possibly the same carpet is depicted.

901
Duyster, W.

Soldiers in an Inn
Sale F.Muller Amsterdam 17/10/05 (as Terborch)
c. 1625
43 x 44 cm

d19 (ei2)

902
Duyster, W.

Portrait of a Man and Woman at a Table
National Gallery of Ireland,
Dublin
c. 1625
64.2 x 51.5 cm
Literature: cat. 1986, nr.556

ei2/d19/ig74 (eiii)

903
Duyster, W.
A Young Lady Reading a Letter, and a Gentleman
Sale Christie's London 12/12/80-20
c. 1625
57.1 x 49 cm
See illustration p.110

ei2/d19/ig74 (eiii)

904
Duyster, W.
Woman with a Letter at the Virginals
Sale Christie's London 28/6/74-117
c. 1625
34.9 x 44.1 cm

ei2/d19/ig74 (eiii)

905
Duyster, W.
Plundering Soldiers
Gemäldegalerie, Dresden
c. 1625
33.5 x 42.5 cm
Literature: Dresden 1962, cat.9 (as J.Duck)

ei2/d19 (eiii)

906
Fabritius, B.
Portrait of W. van der Helm and his Family
Rijksmuseum, Amsterdam
1655
148 x 127.5 cm
Literature: van Thiel p.224 (ill.)
See illustration p.116

ei2/b75?/ig65? (eiii)

907
Haensbergen, J. van
Portrait of Le Rocher de la Resnaye
Sale Fievez Brussels 21/2/28-29
1691
51 x 42 cm

ei3 (eiii)

The inner guard border has parallel stripes without decoration.

908
Haye, R. de la

Three Children Decorating a Stone Putto with Flowers
Sale Christie's London 9/2/79-130
c. 1690
47.7 x 37.5 cm

ei3/d03 (eiii)

909
Haye, R. de la
A Woman Playing the Virginals
Sale Ehrich Gallery, New York 12/11/24-33 (as P. de Hooch)
1670-80
35.5 x 27.9 cm

eiii

910
Haye, R. de la (attr. to)

A Woman Sitting at a Table with a Music Book, and a Viola da Gamba
Sale Arents, Parke Bernet New York 15/12/29-371
1670-80
38 x 30 cm

eiii

911
Haye, R. de la (attr. to)

A Couple Making Music
Private collection, England
1670-80
39 x 32 cm

eiii

912
Hecken, A. van den

Philosopher at a Table
Present location unknown
64 x 50
c. 1655

(eiii)

The carpet is decorated with a version of the 15th century Anatolian stars-and-bars design.

913
Helst, B. van der
The Four Governors of the Archers' Civil Guard (the St.Sebastian Guard)
Rijksmuseum, Amsterdam
1653
183 x 268 cm
Literature: van Thiel p.268

(eiii)

The exceptionally coarse carpet has a high pile with a simple geometric pattern of concentric squares. It has at the upper and lower edges thick braids of plaited warps. The pattern vaguely reminds of Southern Persian 'Gabbeth' carpets. cf. Hali 53, October 1990, pp. 7, 62, 63.

914
Hondecoeter, M. d'
The Menagerie
c. 1685
135 x 116.5
Literature: van Thiel p.282

eiii

915
Man, C. de
Man Weighing Gold
Sale Fievez Brussels 16/12/29-58
1665-75
65 x 80 cm
See illustration p.117

eiii/iig6,ig133,og102

916
Metsu, G.
Couple Making Music
Collection Viscount Bearsted
1660-65
39.5 x 29 cm

d01 (ei2?)

Presumably a coarse carpet. It seems to have had a fluffy texture, although a comparison with other carpets depicted by Metsu indicates that this might be explained by the style of the painter rather than by the technique of the carpet he painted.

917
Musscher, M.van
A Scholar in his Studio
Fürsterliche Hohenzollernsche Sammlungen, Sigmaringen
1669?
45 x 38 cm

d18 (ei1;eiii)

918
Musscher, M. van
Portrait of a Lady and her Child
Sale Christie's London 10/5/35-118
1691
54.5 x 62.2 cm

ei1/ig86? (eiii)

919
Naiveu, M.
A Family Portrait with a Landscape Beyond
Sale Sotheby Mak van Waay, Amsterdam 2/6/1986-87
1675-80
139 x 129 cm

eiii

Cf. id. *A Scholar in his Studio*

920
Naiveu, M.

A Scholar in his Studio
Sale Christie's London 26/6/64-53
1677
63 x 45 cm

eiii

Cf. his *A Family Portrait with a Landscape Beyond*

921
Neer, E. van der
The Visit
Koninklijk Paleis voor Schone Kunsten, Antwerp
1664?
65 x 55.5 cm
literature: cat. 1948, nr.732

eiii?/g46?

The field, as far as is visible in the painting, shows a floral pattern of curved vines with lotus flowers and rosettes. The border is relatively narrow. Compare for the border Verkolje's *The Message*.

922
Neer, E. van der
A Lady Playing the Lute in an Interior
Koetser Gallery, Zurich 1973
about 1680
44.5 x 35.5 cm

See illustration p.121

ei2/b75/ig6 (eiii)

923
Neer, E. van der
Woman Playing the Lute
Sale Sotheby's London 21/6/50-92 (as F. van Mieris)
c. 1677
27.5 x 23 cm

eiii

Cf. id. *A Lady Playing the Lute in an Interior*

924
Neer, E. van der
A Lady Playing the Lute
Gemäldegalerie, Karlsruhe
1677
38.5 x 32 cm

eiii?/iig8,ig86

For the pattern of the main border compare the same artist's *Woman Playing the Lute*; also Cornelis de Man, *Man Weighing Gold*.

925
Netscher, C.
The Bicker van Zwieten (?) Children
Museum für Bildenden Künste, Leipzig
1676
49 x 40 cm

ei3/d03 (eiii)

The form of the palmettes in the main border recalls some ornaments in the d11 pattern.

926
Netscher, C.
Portrait of a Man in a Silk Robe Sitting at a Table
Wawel Castle Museum, Krakow
1675 c
Literature: Bialostocki ill.286
See illustration p.118

ei3/d03? (eiii)

The inner guard border has parallel stripes without decoration.

927
Netscher, C.

A Self-portrait
Hermitage, Leningrad
1675-80
42 x 41 cm

ei3/d03 (eiii)

928
Netscher, C. or Haensbergen, J.
van
*Portrait of an Unknown Man in a
Silk Robe*
Sale Mak Amsterdam 14/10/18-
75
1670-80
55 x 44 cm

ei3/d03 (eiii)

929
Netscher, C.

*Portrait of a Lady, Seated, in a Blue
and White Dress, Leaning on a Table
Draped with a Carpet.*
Sale Christie's New York 13/3/
80-51 (as Nicolaes Maes)
1670-80
56.5 x 45 cm

ei3/d03 (eiii)

930
Netscher, C.

Portrait of Pieter Six
Städtisches Kunstmuseum,
Frankfurt
1677
47.8 x 39.8 cm
Literature: cat.1924, nr.885

ei3/d03 (eiii)

931
Netscher, C.
Portrait of Sir William Temple
Sale Christie's London 25/2/66-4
1671

ei3 (eiii)

Cf. Netscher, Con., *Portrait of
Three Children in a Window-bay.*

932
Netscher, C. (attr. to)

*Portrait of a Lady, Sitting at a Table
Playing the Lute*
Present location unknown
43.5 x 36 cm

eiii

933
Netscher, C. (attr. to) or Verkolje J.
*Portrait of a Mother and her Child,
Being Served by a Negro Boy.*
Sale Berlin 29/10/1888-58
1670-85
64 x 51 cm

eiii/d1/ig46,og11a

This painting may have been
painted by Verkolje. Cf. Jan
Verkolje, *Portrait of a Naval
Officer.*

934
Netscher, Con.
*Portrait of Three Children in a
Window-bay*
Sale Peretz Cologne 12/10/74
c. 1710
53.5 x 44 cm

ei3/d03 (eiii)

Cf. Adriaen van der Werff, *Two
Children Playing with a Mouse-trap.*

935
Ochtervelt, J. (attr. to)
*Lutenist and a Woman Drinking
Wine*
Staatliche Kunstsammlungen,
Dessau
1670-80
37 x 32 cm
Literature: Kuretsky D-17

ei1/d18

The inner guard border has
square compartments with
diagonal lines.

936
Ochtervelt, J. (circle)

Artist with a Female Student
Rheinisches Landesmuseum,
Bonn
1665-80
72.5 x 59 cm
Literature: Kuretsky D-9

ei2/b75/ig6 (eiii)

The field has a repeating floral
design of palmettes and rosettes,
interchanged with a stylized
ornament composed of four
leaflets radiating from a central
diamond. Cf. B. Fabritius, *Portrait
of W. van der Helm and his Family.*

937
Ochtervelt, J. (circle)
A Man and a Woman at a Table
Private collection, London
1670-80
59.4 x 46.5 cm
Literature: Kuretsky cat.D-26

ei2/b75 (eiii)

Coarse carpet with an apparently
fluffy texture. Cf. Ochtervelt, J.
(attr. to), *Artist with a Female
Student.*

938
Rossum, J. van
Portrait of a Young Lady
Sale Lempertz Cologne 11/12/
29-56
1678
128 x 104 cm

eiii/d15/ig63

Careful representation. The field
has concentric diamonds. The
carpet has a very coarse weaving
structure.

939
Rossum, J. van
Portrait of Jan Willemsz Verbrugge and his Wife
Rotterdams Historisch Museum, Rotterdam
1670
191 x 190 cm
See illustration p.116

eiii/d11/ig86,og86

940
Steen, J.
'Hier baet geen medesyn, het is der minne pyn'
State-owned Art Collections Department, The Hague
1665-66
62 x 47 cm
Literature: Braun cat.254

ei1/d18/ig86

941
Terborch, G.
Portrait of Pieter de Graeff
Private collection, Germany
1674?
36 x 31 cm
Literature: Gudlaugsson ill.263

ei3/d12?/ig85,og85 (eiii)

The colours of this carpet are related to those of the group first described by Brigitte Scheunemann. The field is red, with light green and orange ornaments, the main border is dark blue and has a white inner guard and an orange outer guard border. One of the palmettes is replaced by a cartouche filled with a rosette.

942
Verkolje, J.

Young Lady at her Toilet
Sale Sotheby's Monaco 13/6/82-19

1680-85
52.5 x 43.5 cm

ei2/ig46 (eiii)

The carpet has a very narrow border, with a decoration which is primarily known from guard borders. The original model may have had a more complex bordering, but Verkolje apparently chose to depict only the inner guard border. Cf. Thomas van der Wilt, *Couple Playing Tric-trac.*

943
Verkolje, J.
Portrait of a Naval Officer
Thos Agnew & Sons Gallery, London 1974
c. 1680
See illustration p.111

eiii/d1/ig46,og11

943-2
Verkolje, J.

Portrait of Petronella Bogaert
Frans Hals Museum, Haarlem
1679
55.5 x 47 cm

eiii/d1/ig46,og11a

Cf. id. *Portrait of a Naval Officer*

944
Verkolje, J.
Portrait of Three Children in a Garden
Leger Galleries 1961
1676
55 x 66.25 cm
See illustration p.120

ei3/d03/ig84?,og84? (eiii)

The red field is framed by a dark blue border, with a white inner and a red outer guard stripe. The

fringes are white. The rug may have had a selvedge made of two or three warps or pairs of warps, overcast apparently with wool. Cf. Adriaen van der Werff, *Two Children Playing with a Mouse-trap.*

945
Verkolje, J.

The Approach
Gemäldegalerie, Dresden
1670-80
70 x 66 cm
Literature: Haak 1984, ill.993

eiii/iig6,ig133,og102

946
Verkolje, J.
Merry Company
Sale Mak van Waay, Amsterdam 23/5/67-483 (as N.Verkolje)
1670-80
65 x 76 cm

eiii/iig6,ig133,og102

947
Verkolje, J.
The Message
Royal Picture Gallery The Mauritshuis, The Hague
1674
59 x 53.5 cm
See illustration p.116

eiii/iig6,ig133,og102

Cf. his *Merry Company*; also his *The Approach*; also Cornelis de Man, *Man Weighing Gold.* The field is red with many orange accents. The colour scheme of the main border stripe is more or less identical to that of the d11 borders.

948
Vermeer, J.
Woman with a Water Jug
Metropolitan Museum of Art, New York
c. 1662
45.7 x 42 cm
Literature: Blankert cat.12

eiii/d11/ig102,og85

949
Verschuring, H.

Young Woman Playing the Cittern
Würtembergische Staatsgalerie, Stuttgart
1670-80
34 x 26 cm
Literature: cat. 1931, nr.426

eiii/b75/ig65?

Cf. Verkolje, *Young Woman Playing the Lute in an Interior*

950
Vois, A. de

Portrait of an Unknown Man
Louvre, Paris
1680
39 x 31 cm

eiii/d14/ig86,og86,oog102

The presence of the fringes suggests that the beholder is looking at one of the ends of the carpet, but the pattern of the field indicates the view is from the side. Possibly the carpet had added fringes on all four sides. This carpet is difficult to classify. The field pattern with the h1 motif points at an Indian origin, but the border seems more related to the d14 design. Several undecorated bands accompanying the subguards could justify the classification of the carpet as belonging to the eiii group.

951
Weenix, J.
Portrait of Abraham van Bronckhorst
Rijksmuseum, Amsterdam
1688
87 x 73.5 cm
Literature: van Thiel p.595

ei2/d14

The inner guard border is not decorated with either floral or abstract ornaments.

952
Weenix, J.

Portrait of Lodewina Schey
Sale Sotheby's London 20/4/88
1680-90

ei2/d14

The large carpet in this portrait illustrates one of the major problems of a study of carpets in paintings. The field pattern is strongly related to Indian patterns, as identified in works such as Michiel van Musscher's *Portrait of an Unknown Gentleman*, whereas in the case of the carpet painted by Jan Weenix, the pattern is more or less identical but the carpet in question is classified as belonging to a very different group. If only a small part of the carpet in question had been visible, namely the part displaying two down-ward pointing palmettes and the h1

motif, and if no indications of the empty inner guard border and the d14 main border had been visible, it would have been classified as an Indian carpet just like the one represented by Musscher. In other words, it is quite possible that some of the carpets of which only a small part is visible in the paintings, are in this study classified as Indian, while the original models may in fact have belonged to the same group as the one painted by Weenix.

953
Weenix, J.

A Portrait of Three Children with Birds and a Dog
Museum of Fine Art, Budapest
1680-90
64 x 60 cm

ei2/d14 (eiii)

Apparently the same carpet as in the same artist's *Portrait of Abraham van Bronckhorst*; his *Portrait of Lodewina Schey*; and his *Portrait of a Lady and her Child in a Landscape*. Noteworthy is the decoration of the outer guard border, which shows in part the g85 ornament, associated with the carpets of the 'namenlose Gattung', and in part a geometrical motif consisting of X-motifs interchanged with some kind of abstract leaflets, perhaps in combination with an undulating stem.

954
Weenix, J.
Portrait of a Lady and her Child in a Landscape
Art Market, Boehler, Munich
1976 (as Constantijn Netscher)
c. 1680-90
87 x 72.2 cm

ei2/d14

955
Werff, A. van der
Couple Playing Music
Gallery Richard Green
1674-78
48 x 35.5 cm
Literature: Gaehtgens cat.

d11/ig86

Cf. van Rossum, *Portrait of Jan Willemsz Verbrugge and his Wife*.

956
Werff, A. van der
Two Men Playing Chess
Staatliche Museen, Schwerin
1679
49 x 37 cm
Literature: Gaehtgens cat.12
See illustration p.115

eiii/d11/ig86,og86

Cf. van Rossum, *Portrait of Jan Willemsz Verbrugge and his Wife*.

957
Adriaen van der Werff,

Portrait of a Lady
Sale Dorotheum Vienna, 3/11/71-137
1682
78 x 64 cm
Literature: Gaehtgens cat.136

ei3

958
Werff, A. van der

Portrait of an Elegant Lady Holding Flowers
Present location unknown
1682
79.7 x 64.5 cm
Literature: Gaehtgens cat.135

eiii/d11/ig86,og86

Cf. van Rossum, *Portrait of Jan Willemsz Verbrugge and his Wife*.

959
Werff, A. van der
Two Children Playing with a Mouse-trap
Gallery J. van Haeften, London
1984
1692
34.4 x 26.2 cm

ei3/d03/ig86,og86 (eiii)

The carpet has a red field and a dark blue or black main border. The guard borders seem to have a green ground, and the fringes are red. Cf. Con. Netscher, *Portrait of Three Children in a Window-bay*.

960
Wilt, Th. van der

Couple Playing Backgammon
Staatliche Museen zu Berlin, Berlin
c. 1680
71 x 57 cm

ei2/d1/ig46,og11 (eiii)

LIST OF CODES

FIELD PATTERNS OF ANATOLIAN CARPETS AND CHECKERBOARD CARPETS

ai.   Reserved
aii.   Reserved
aiii.   Reserved
aiv   'Lotto' design
aiv2   'Lotto' design, 'Anatolian style'
aiv3   'Lotto' design, 'Kilim style'
aiv4   'Lotto' design, 'Ornamented style'
av.   Medallion Ushak design
avi.   Reserved
avii.   Double-niche Ushak design
aviii   Reserved
aix   Reserved
ax.   Reserved
axi.   'Transylvanian' rug designs
axi.1   'Transylvanian' rug designs including arabesques in the spandrels
axi.2   'Transylvanian' rug designs including floral ornaments in the spandrels
axi.3   'Transylvanian' rug design: Anatolian variants of the Cairene Ottoman prayer rugs; see fig. p.52
axii.   'Smyrna' design
axiii   Reserved
axiv   'Checkerboard' or 'Chess-board' design

FIELD PATTERNS OF PERSIAN AND INDO-PERSIAN CARPETS

bi.   Floral and cloudband designs. See e.g. fig. p.58
bii.   Floral designs including representations of animals
biii   Floral design composed of stiff stems connecting opposed palmettes or lotusflowers
biv   Other floral carpet designs except North-West Persian designs
bv   North-West Persian designs

FIELD PATTERNS OF INDIAN CARPETS

ci.   Floral designs in the Persian tradition, showing Indian design elements
cii.   Indian designs

FIELD PATTERNS OF CARPETS ATTRIBUTED TO EGYPT

di1   Mamluk designs
di2   Ottoman Cairene designs

FIELD PATTERNS OF THE 'NAMENLOSE GATTUNG' AND RELATED CARPETS

ei.   The 'Scheunemann' design
ei1   Crude unidentified floral designs; see Chapter VII. Only a reconstruction of the medallion that is frequently included in this design could be drawn.

ei2   Crude unidentified floral designs; see Chapter VII.
ei3   Crude floral designs

eii.   Variant Medallion Ushak design
eiii   Other unidentified designs

MAIN BORDER PATTERNS OF ANATOLIAN CARPETS AND 'CHECKERBOARD' CARPETS

a2   Cartouche design of the 'Lotto' carpets

a3   Cartouche design of the 'Transylvanian' carpets

a4   Cartouche design of the 'Smyrna' carpets

a5   Cartouche design of the 'Checkerboard' carpets

a6   Cloudband designs, e.g. of 'Lotto' carpets and Double-niche Ushak carpets

a7   Floral border design of the Double-niche Ushak carpets

a8   Reserved
a91   Stylized floral 'S' stems
a92   Rosette design of the 'Lotto' carpets

a93   Border design of the blue-ground 'Lotto' carpets

a94   The so-called 'Eli-belinde' ornament

a10   Reserved
a11   Kufic ornaments

a12   Reserved
a13   Reserved
a14   Reserved
a15   Anatolian variant of the d222 pattern
a16   Other border patterns
a17   Meandering leaf design of the 'Transylvanian' carpets

PERSIAN BORDER PATTERNS

b1   'S' stems

b2   Repetitive design of coiling stems

b3   Reserved
b4   Reserved
b5   Stems with large interlacing leaves

b6   Lobed and Shield-form cartouches

b71   Reserved
b72   Reserved
b73   'S' stems

b74   'S' stems

b75   Reserved
b76   Floral stems in combination of representations of animals
b8   Lobed and star-form cartouches

INDIAN BORDER PATTERNS

c1   Cartouche designs
c11   Star-form cartouche design

c2   Other Indian designs
c23   'S' stems enhanced with small red rosettes

c24   Meandering stem with small flower calyxes

c25   Floral stems with curved leaves, without corner solutions

c26 Twin 'S' stems

c27 'Flaming' leaves

OTHER MAIN BORDER PATTERNS

d01 Reserved

d02 Reserved

d03 Meandering stem

d11 Irregular floral stem; see fig. 101, p. 100

d12 'S' stems of the 'namenlose Gattung'

d13 Cartouche design of the 'namenlose Gattung'

d14 'S' leave and rosette design

d15 Cartouche design

d16 Lobed and Shield-form cartouches, cf. b6

d17 'S' stems of the 'namenlose Gattung'

d18 'S' stems with coarse flowers

d2 Egyptian designs

d21 Mamluk designs

d221 Ottoman Cairene design with tulips and pomegranates

---

d222 Ottoman Cairene design with double lanceolate leaves

GUARD BORDER PATTERNS

g1 Reserved

g2 Reserved

g3 Reserved

g4 Meandering stems

g41 Reserved

g42 Reserved

g43 Stylized meandering stem

g44 Meandering stem with floral sprays

g45 Double meandering stem

g46 Single meandering stem

g47 Double meandering stem, one of which bears a special emphasis

g48 Stylized meandering ornament

g5 Stylized stem

g6 Geometrical zig-zag ornaments

g61 Reserved

g62 Zig-zag line forming triangular compartments filled with small dots

g63 Diamond-form ornaments interchanged with smaller diamonds

---

g64 Double zig-zag ornament

g65 Zig-zag ornament with stylized leaves

g71 Oblong cartouches, interchanged with dots

g72 Single diamond-form ornaments

g73 Reserved

g74 'X' motifs interchanged with hexagons

g8 'S' motifs

g81 Reserved

g82 Reserved

g83 Stylized 'S' forms with octagons

g84 Thin 'S' ornaments

g85 Broad 'S' ornaments

g86 'S' stems with hearts and stylized leaves

g87 Reserved

g88 Stylized meandering stem with crosses and leaves

g89 Floral 'S' stems

g9 'Barber's pole' ornament

g91 Reserved

g92 'Chevron' ornament

---

g10 Elaborately drawn 'Z' motifs

g102 Simple 'Z' motif

g103 Other 'Z' motif

g11 Reciprocal ornaments

g11a Elaborately drawn reciprocal ornament

g11b Stylized reciprocal ornament

g11c Variant elaborately drawn reciprocal ornament

g11d Reciprocal heart-shaped ornament

g11e Reciprocal ornament, e.g. of the 'Transylvanian' carpets

g12 Rosettes

g122 Rosettes interchanged with colonettes

g13 Other designs

g131 'X' motifs interchanged with dots

g132 Shield-form ornaments with small volutes

g133 Stylized heart-forms and 'Z' motifs

g134 Stylized 'Z' motif

g14 No inner guard present

Notes

Notes Introduction

1. Mills 1983 (A), p. 4
2. L.c., pl. 3, 14, 15
3. These three rugs all belong to the Amsterdam Sephardic Community. The best known is the 16th century Small Silk Kashan; see Erdmann 1966, fig.183. The second rug, a 'Polonaise', is listed by F.Spuhler in his 1968 doctoral thesis, nr.5. The third, described as a 17th century woollen rug, is unpublished and at the time of writing has not been available for inspection
4. See Mills 1978 (A)
5. Mills, l.c., p.239
6. Lessing 1877
6a. Yetkin 1981, ill. p. 38
7. Panofsky, figs. 240, 248, 252
8. L.c., fig.247
9. Mills 1983 (A), p.14
10. Mills l.c., pl.7
11. Mills l.c., p.18
12. Mills l.c., pl.5-7
13. Mills l.c., nr.1
14. See Kuznetsov fig.138
15. Cf. Milan 1982, p.32
16. London 1983, p.84
17. Mills 1983 (B), p.19
18. In 18th century paintings, carpets are still represented regularly. One can even assume that there is a continuous tradition in the Low Countries of covering tables with pile weavings such as Oriental carpets up to the present day. From the pictorial sources, it appears that, in the eighteenth century, the carpets imported were mainly simple and coarse Anatolian products which were probably not acquired by the consumer as pièce de résistance in his interior any more, but rather as common furnishings (e.g. Cornelis Troost, *Couple Making Music in an Interior*, van Thiel p.543). This also accounts for the introduction in the 18th century of large wall-to-wall floor carpets with the Medallion-Ushak design, which were not only imported from Anatolia (one such example is kept in the Lakenhal in Leyden) but manufactured in The Netherlands also, well into the 20th century (a good example is the carpeting in castle Duyvenvoorde in Voorschoten. It appears that in the 17th century, carpets were luxury items which were used with much care, whereas in the 18th century these pile weavings were considered less costly and often used on the floors. This would explain the loss of almost all 16th and 17th century carpets in the Netherlands, which were used up on the floors in the 18th and 19th centuries
19. Scheunemann 1954, p.51-65; Mills 1981 (B)
20. Ter Kuile 1985
21. Beattie 1972, p.39-40
22. Streynsham Master 1679-1680, p.171
23. See Bennett 1988
24. N.Y. Willemin, Monuments Français inédits pour servir à l'histoire des arts depuis le VIe siècle jusqu'au commencement du XVIIe, Paris 1839, pl.209
25. Cf. Enay 1977, p.7 and Spuhler 1978 (B), p.11
26. Lessing 1877, p.5
27. Lessing l.c., p.7
28. Karabacek 1881, p.119-137
29. Bode 1892
30. E.g. F.R.Martin 1908, pp.74, 124
31. Pope 1939, p.2269
32. The Western pictorial sources are mentioned twice: o.c. p.2258, note 1; p.2364, note 1
33. Humboldt Universität, Berlin, unpublished
34. E.g. Scheunemann o.c., p.94-95
35. Scheunemann 1959
36. See for example Erdmann 1955, E.Kühnel in his revised 1955 edition of von Bode's Vorderasiatische Knüpfteppiche; Ellis 1965; Dimand 1973; Bennett 1977
37. Mills 1977, 1978 (A+B), id. 1981 (A)
38. Mills 1981 (B)
39. Mills 1983 (A)
40. Mills 1983 (B)
41. Duverger 1987, p.159
42. Cf. Beattie 1964, p.11
43. Ydema 1988 (B)
44. Mills 1988
45. Ellis 1984, p.3
46. RGP 34, p.163-4; see p.51
47. Similarly de Groot, whose attention was focused on the history of the diplomatic relations between the Ottoman Empire and the Dutch Republic 1610-1630.

Notes Egyptian carpets

1. Beattie 1964, p. 4-14
2. Mills 1981 (A), p.53
3. Hali IV, 1981, p. 38, fig.2
4. Ydema 1984
5. Cf. Denny 1979, p.8-9
6. Denny op. cit., p.6
7. Pinner and Franses 1981, p.39
8. Thevenot 1665, 2, X, p.272
9. See London 1983, text part with cat.nr.50
10. Kühnel-Bellinger 1957, pl. XXVI
11. London 1983, nr.50
12. Cf. Denny loc.cit.; Pinner and Franses 1981

Notes Anatolian and Chessboard Carpets

1. Mills 1981 (B), p. 281, nr.1
2. Mills, l.c., nr.12
3. Bode 1902, p.99, 100
4. Scheunemann 1954, p.51-65
5. L.c., p.57
6. L.c., p.65
7. Ellis 1975
8. Reimer 1984
9. Ellis 1986, p.174
10. L.c.
11. Mills 1981, nr.7
11a. Shortly before publication of this book the author came across a painting by Caravaggio, *The Lute Player* (c. 1596/97).This painting was discovered in 1990 as a genuine Caravaggio, and represents a carpet of the 'Lotto' type. As the 'Lotto' carpet which the artist used as a model seems to have included small scrolling ornaments, which are a characteristic of the so-called 'ornamented style', it appears that this Italian painting could well be the earliest one to include an ornamented style 'Lotto' carpet. Cf. Keith Christiansen, A Caravaggio Rediscovered, the Lute Player. The Metropolitan Museum of Art, New York, 1990.
12. Mills 1981, p.287-88
13. L.c., nr.34
14. Curatola 1983, pl.1
15. Mills 1981, p.288
16. See Washington 1974, nr.31, Munich 1978, nr.4, Spuhler 1978 (B), nr.18, Lanier nr.19, London 1983, nr.32
17. Eskenazi 1981, Tav.8, Dimand/Mailey fig.160, London 1983, nr.35, Amsterdam 1977, nr.5; ill.9b
18. Pagnano nr.12
19. Scheunemann 1954, p.57
20. Mills 1981, p.289
21. L.c., p.288
22. McMullan 1965, p.224; Yetkin 1981, p.57
23. London 1983, nr.33
24. Mills 1981, p.288
25. E.g. Mills l.c., nr.4
26. L.c., p.288
27. Munich 1978, Old Eastern Carpets, Masterpieces in German Private Collections, by F. Spuhler a.o., p.46
28. London 1983, cat.nr.40
29. Mills 1983 (B), p.16
30. Franses and Pinner 1984, p.374. nr.30
31. L.C., p.373
32. Raby, J., (B)

33. L.c. p.177f
34. Pinner 1986, p.293
35. Inalcik 1986, p.59
36. Quoted in: Inalcik 1986, p.55
37. Raby 1986 (B), p.185
38. E.g. Lanier 1975, nr.31
39. E.g. Lanier 1975, nr.2
40. Guiccardini 1560, p.155
41. Spuhler 1987, nr.14
42. E.g. the Thyssen-Bornemisza Medallion Ushak carpet, Beattie 1972, pl.XIV
43. Lanier 1975, nrs.29-32
44. Cf. a fragmentary preserved example in Berlin, Spuhler 1987, nr.13
45. Spuhler 1987 (A), p.35
46. Beattie 1972, nr.XIV; Spuhler 1987, nr.12
47. Lanier 1975, nr.31
48. Erdmann 1955, pl.VIII
49. Dimand/Mailey fig.167
50. E.g. Yetkin 1981, p.76,77
51. See p.103f
52. Anthony van Dyck, cat.208
53. Batari 1980, p.82f; Budapest 1986, no page numbers indicated
54. See p.40; Munich 1978, nrs.11,12; London 1983, nr.47
55. See p.40; Munich 1978, nrs.9,10
56. Végh and Layer 1977, text with plate 11; also London 1983, p.77,78
57. Compare Washington 1974, nrs. I, III, VI, VII, XI and many others
58. London 1983, p.78
59. Végh and Layer 1977, nr.16
60. Végh and Layer 1977, nr.17
61. E.g. Bode 1902, p.77
62. E.g. Mills 1978, pl.28, London 1983, p.78, Ydema 1988 (B), p.22 (ill.)
63. Cf. Bennett 1977, p.205; Spuhler 1987 (A), nr.27
64. See also Robert Feke's Isaac Royall and Family, 1741, Fogg Art Museum, Cambridge, illustrated in Bennett 1977, p.206
65. Budapest 1986, fig. IV
66. Végh & Layer 1977, nrs. 16, 17
67. Denny 1979, p.8-9
68. Mills 1988, p.43

69. RGP 9, p.296
70. L.c., p.612
71. L.c., p.612-5
72. RGP 34, p.163
73. Bruyn 1985, p.120
74. Inv. 467-1883; Hali IV (1981), 1, p.46, ill.12
75. Munich 1978, cat.20
76. Dimand/Mailey fig.168
77. See also Pagnano nr.53
78. C.G.Ellis, in correspondence
79. See Bailey 1985, figs.2,7
80. See p.25
81. See p.19-20
82. Mills 1981 (A), p.54-55
83. Mills 1981 (A), p.55
84. Ellis 1984
85. Spuhler 1986, p.264-265
86. Spuhler 1986, p.261
87. Spuhler 1986, p.266

NOTES PERSIAN CARPETS

1. Subgroups can be distinguished, on the basis of systematic variations of the pattern, or, in surviving specimens, weaving characteristics and materials. Due to the limitations of this study subgroups could not be catalogued as such or discussed separately.
2. See also p.78 (top)
3. Kämpffer p.156. Engelbert Kämpffer visited the Persian court in 1684-85
4. Cf. Broecke p.85
5. E.g. Dimand/Mailey, figs.71,76
6. Irwin 1955, p.18f.
7. Beattie 1972, pl.VII
8. Pagnano nr.149, fig.4b
9. E.g. Dimand/Mailey p.68, ill.95
10. Spuhler 1968, p.281, reconstruction nr.9
11. L.c., p.283-4
12. Williamstown, cat.31, ill.11
13. Eskenazi, Tav.28
14. Hali VI (1983), 1, p.10
15. Ellis 1965, q.v.
16. Spuhler 1968, p.279, nr.4;
17. Bode/Kühnel 1955, Abb.87
18. Ellis 1988, fig.62a
19. Cf. Spuhler 1985, nr.8; Dimand/Mailey ill.63
20. Cf. Pagnano nr.64, Erdmann

1955, Abb.59
21. London 1983, cat.65
22. Herbert 1638, p.156
23. Tavernier 1692, Kap.15, S.520-21
24. Ketelaar p.143
25. Spuhler 1968, p.160
26. Spuhler loc. cit., p.16; Dimand/Mailey cat.17; fig.84
27. Spuhler l.c.
28. RGP 72, p.144
29. RGP 72, p.452
30. RGP 104, p.483
31. Tavernier 1692, p.23,24
32. RGP 112, p.421
33. L.c., p.549
34. RGP 150, p.222
35. RPG 112, p.650
36. Ibid. p.700
37. Ibid. p.765; see also: RGP 125, p. 177, 306
38. RGP 134, p.158
39. Spuhler 1987 (B), p.34
40. Ibid., p.34,35
41. Texeira, p.243
42. RGP 72, p.452
43. Tavernier 1692, p. 319
44. Mandelslo 1658, Ch.19, p. 68
45. Pelsaert p.148
46. L.c. p.264
47. Krusinski, cited in Spuhler 1968, p.142
48. Cf. Beattie 1976, cat. 50, 51
49. Pope 1939, pl.1248
50. Dimand/Mailey fig.86
51. L.c. p.83-4, ill.83
52. Ibid, fig.94
53. Pagnano nr.131
54. Spuhler 1968, pp.94, 284, nr.22a
55. Beattie 1976
56. Texeira, p.243
57. Kämpffer, p.202: the most splendid carpets he saw were those from Kerman including in their designs representations of animals.
58. Cf. Beattie 1976, pl.2
59. L.c., p.26f

NOTES INDIAN CARPETS

1. Dapper 1672, p.72
2. Texeira, p.83
3. Abul Fazl, p.55
4. E.g. Walker 1982, p.253
5. Records of Fort St.George: Diary and Consultation Book,

1679-80. Madras 1912, p.100
6. Beattie 1972, p.40
7. Cf. Franses 1981, p.48
8. Irwin, p.18
9. Irwin, p.19
10. Ibid.
11. Unpublished. cf. RGP 72, p.130
11a. Broecke, p.320
12. Pelsaert, p.254
13. RGP 125, p.501-2
14. Irwin, l.c.
15. Ydema 1988, p.20
16. Van Thiel, p.466, ill.
17. Skelton, p.151f
18. Ydema 1986, p.184
19. Eiland, p.136
20. Cf. Brisch pl.24; Spuhler 1987 (A), nr.125
21. Sarre, 1931
22. Bode/Kühnel 1955, p.106
23. Ellis, 1972
24. Eiland, p.157-60
25. Walker, p.256-57
26. Eiland, ill.116
27. O.c. ill.117
28. O.c. p.146
29. Dimand/Mailey fig.134; Pagnano nr.146
30. Spuhler 1987, nr.124
31. Hali II (1979), 3, advertisement p.44
32. Spuhler 1978 (B), nr.54
33. Ellis 1972, p.280
34. Spuhler 1978 (B), nr.54
35. Ellis 1972, p.280
36. Ellis 1988, p.157
37. Inv. 1966.1182, for illustration see Ellis 1972, fig.18
38. The technical characteristics seem to point to another place of origin, see Ellis 1972, p.280
39. See for example Eiland, ill.131
40. E.g. Pagnano nr.108
41. Eiland, fig.116
42. See above, note 38.
43. See p.195, cat.952

NOTES 'NAMENLOSE GATTUNG'

1. Scheunemann 1954, pp.111-24
2. Scheunemann 1959, p.80. Scheunemann was not too sure about her reconstruction

due to the fact that she found the representations of the d11 border pattern rather poor.

3. L.c. p.89
4. Eg. Pagnano nr.144
5. Scheunemann 1954, Abb.10
6. Cf. Naumann I, colour plate between pages 112-13
7. Scheunemann 1954, p.111
8. Scheunemann 1959, p.89: 'a coarse and loose weaving structure'.
9. L.c., p.82
10. Scheunemann 1954, p.123. She assumed that this group could not have been made in Persia.
11. L.c., p.121
12. L.c.
13. Scheunemann 1954, p.124
14. Scheunemann 1959, p.82-3
15. L.c. p.84
16. L.c. p.80
17. Dimand/Mailey ill.116,117; Scheunemann 1959, p.85
18. L.c.
19. L.c. Abb.10
20. Erdmann 1955, ill.50
21. Cf. Pagnano nrs.131,132
22. Scheunemann 1959, p.89. She assumed that this group presents a late phase in the development of the arche-typal pattern, which in her opinion explains the inclu-sion of the design elements borrowed from some other thesaurus of patterns.
23. Ellis 1984
24. Scheunemann 1959, p.89. These carpets were probably quickly worn off as a result of their coarse and loose weav-ing structure.
24a.Cf. Sluyter 1990, p.17. Rosemarijn Hoekstra is cur-rently preparing a disserta-tion on this subject.
24b.In correspondence and in dis-cussion. Mrs. Ellis plans to publish the results of this study soon.
25. Scheunemann 1954, p.121. She assumed that the type must have been developed some time before the first ex-amples reached Europe.

NOTES RELATED TO THE 'NAMENLOSE GATTUNG'

1. Eiland fig.120
2. Compare to a similar cartouche in a surviving rug, Bode 1902, Abb.10
3. See fig.100, p.98
4. Curatola fig.11
5. E.g. Erdmann 1955, Abb.87
6. Spuhler 1987 (A), nr.124
7. Housego 1987, fig.2
8. Washington 1980, nr.89

NOTES CONCLUSION

1. WA 3074-5a/b
1a. Philadelphia 1984, pl.110
2. Thornton 1981, fig.95
3. Duverger 1985, p.70
4. RGP 147, p.182
5. E.g. Duverger 1984, p.11, 18, 78, 187 etc.
6. Ibid, p.197
7. Ibid. p.414
8. Ellis 1984, p.2
9. RGP 34, p.163-4
10. Ibid. p.163
11. Duverger 1985, p.195
11a.Ydema 1989, p.147 and ill.111
12. RGP 147, p.209
13. Duverger 1985, p.70
14. Ibid.
15. Duverger 1984, p.408
16. Cf. Raby 1986 (B), p.185
17. Bennett 1988 (B), fig. p.728
18. Bennett 1988 (B)
19. Hali VI (1984), 4, p.5
20. Spuhler 1987 (A), cat.14
21. Cf. Balpinar/Hirsch 1988, pl.57
22. Cf. Aschenbrenner nr. 27
23. Guiccardini 1560, p.155
24. Spuhler 1968.

LITERATURE

Abul Fazl, *Ain-i Akbari*, translated by H.Blochmann, Calcutta 1873

Amsterdam, Rijksmuseum, *Tot lering en Vermaak, Bekentenissen van Hollandse genrevoorstellingen uit de 17de eeuw*, Exh.cat. Amsterdam 1976

Amsterdam, Rijksmuseum, *Oosterse tapijten uit de schenking Van Aardenne*, by A.M.L.E. Mulder-Erkelens, Exh.cat. Amsterdam 1977

Amsterdam, Rijksmuseum, *God en de Goden, Verhalen uit de bijbelse en klassieke oudheid door Rembrandt en zijn tijdgenoten*, by A.Blankert a.o., Exh.cat. Amsterdam 1981

Amsterdam, Rijksmuseum, *Prijst de Lijst, de Hollandse schilderijenlijst in de zeventiende eeuw*, by P. van Thiel and C. de Bruyn Kops, Exh.cat. Amsterdam 1984

Amsterdam, Tropenmuseum, *Indigo*, by L. Oei a.o., Exh.cat. Amsterdam 1985

Amsterdam, Rijksmuseum, *De Hollandse Fijnschilders, van Gerard Dou tot Adriaen van der Werff*, by Peter Hecht. Exh.cat. Amsterdam-Maarssen/The Hague 1989

Antwerp, Koninklijk Museum voor Schone Kunsten-Antwerpen, *Beschrijvende Catalogus I-Oude Meesters*, by A. Delen, Antwerp 1948

Arndt, K. *Altniederlaendische Malerei in der Gemäldegalerie Berlin*, Berlin 1968

Aschaffenburg, Galerie Aschaffenburg, *Katalog der Bayerischen Staatsgemäldesammlungen*, by A. Brochhagen a.o., Munich 1964

Aschenbrenner, E., *Orientteppiche*, Band 2: *Persische Teppiche*, Munich 1981

Bailly, J., Ladik Prayer Rugs, in: *Hali* VII, 1985, p.19f

Balpinar, B., Establishing the Cultural Context of a group of Anatolian Cicim Prayer Rugs, in: *Hali* IV (1982), 3, p.262-67

Balpinar, B. and Hirsch, U., *Carpets of the Vakiflar Museum Istanbul*, Wesel 1988

Batari, F., Turkish Rugs in Hungary, in: *Hali* III (1980), 2, p.82-90

Beattie, M., Britain and the Oriental Carpet, in:

Leeds Arts Calendar LV (1964), p.1, 4-15

Beattie, M., *The Thyssen-Bornemisza Collection of Oriental Rugs*, Ticino 1972

Beattie, M., *Carpets of Central Persia. With special reference to rugs of Kirman.* Westerham 1976.

Bennett, I. (ed.), *Rugs and Carpets of the World*, New York 1977

Bennett, I., Isfahan 'Strapwork' Carpets, in: *Hali* X, (1988 (A)), p.35-43

Bennett, I., Teppiche auf holländischen Gemälden des 17. Jahrhunderts, in: *Weltkunst* LVIII (1988 (B)), 5, p.728-731

Bergamo, *Catalogo Provvisorio della Galleria di Palazzo Bianco*, Bergamo 1950

Bergstrom, I., *Dutch Still-life Painting in the Seventeenth Century*, London 1956

Berlin, *Jagdschloss Grünewald*, by M. Kühn (intr.), Berlin 1960

Berlin, *Museum für Islamische Kunst*, by K. Brisch a.o., Berlin 1979

Berlin, *Europa und die Kaiser von China 1240-1816*, Exh.cat. Frankfurt am Main 1985

Bernt, W., *Die niederländischen Maler und Zeichner des 17. Jahrhunderts*, Munich 1979/80

Bialostocki, J. and Walicki, M., *Europäische Malerei in polnischen Sammlungen*, Warsaw 1957

Blankert, A., *Amsterdams Historisch Museum, Schilderijen daterend van voor 1800*, voorlopige catalogus, Amsterdam 1975/1979

Blankert, A., *Ferdinand Bol, Rembrandt's Pupil*, Doornspyk 1982

Blankert, A., *Vermeer of Delft*, Oxford 1987

Bode, W. von, Altorientalische Tierteppiche, in: *Orientalische Teppiche*, by A. von Scala (ed.), Vienna/London/Paris 1892

Bode, W. von, *Vorderasiatische Knüpfteppiche aus älterer Zeit*, Leipzig 1902

Bode, W. von and Kühnel, E. *Vorderasiatische Knüpfteppiche aus alter Zeit*, Braunschweig 1955

Braun, K., *Alle tot nu toe bekende schilderijen van Jan Steen*, Rotterdam 1980

Braunschweig, *Herzog Anton Ulrich Museum Braunschweig, Die holländischen Gemälde, kritisches Verzeichnis mit 485 Abbildungen*, bearbeitet von Rüdiger Klesmann, Braunschweig 1983

Bremen, *Handbuch der Kunsthalle Bremen*, by G. Busch and H. Keller, Bremen 1954

Bremen, *Katalog der Kunsthalle*, by S. Waltmann, Bremen 1939

Brisch, K. a.0., *Museum für Islamische Kunst Berlin*, Katalog 1972², Berlin 1979

Broecke, P. van den, Pieter van den Broecke in Azie, uitgegeven door W.Coolhaas in: *Werken* , Linschoten-Vereniging, LXIV, The Hague, 1963

Brown, Ch., *Carel Fabritius, Complete edition with a catalogue raisonne*, Oxford 1981

Brussels, *Koninklijke Musea voor Schone Kunsten van België, Departement Oude Kunst, Inventariscatalogus van de Oude Schilderkunst*, Brussels 1984

Bruijn, J. and Eyck van Eslinga, E. van, Aan 'wijffje lief', Brieven van zeekapitein Eland Du Bois aan zijn vrouw (1669-1674), in: *Nederlandse Historische Bronnen* V (1985), p.111-146

Budapest, *Szepmuveszeti Muzeum, A Regi Keptar Katalogusa*, by P.Andor, Budapest 1937

Budapest, The Museum of Applied Arts, *Five Hundred Years in the Art of Ottoman-Turkish Carpetmaking*, by F.Batari, Exh.cat. Budapest 1986

Cologne, *Katalog der niederländischen Gemälde von 1550 bis 1800 im Wallraf-Richartz-Museum und im öffentlichen Besitz der Stadt Köln*, by H. Vey, and A. Kesting, Cologne 1967

Cologne, *Wallraf-Richartz-Museum Köln, Vollständiges Verzeichnis der Gemäldesammlung*, Cologne/Milan 1986

Copenhagen, *Royal Museum of Fine Arts, Catalogue of old foreign paintings*, Copenhagen 1951

Copenhagen, *Katalog over Äldre Malerier, Statens Museum for Kunst*, Copenhagen 1946

Curatola, G. and Spallanzani, M., *Lo Specchio del Bargello, Tappeti-Carpets*, Florence 1983

Dapper, O., *Asia, of Naukeurige Beschryving van het Rijk des Grooten Mogols, en een groot gedeelte van Indien. Beneffens een volkome Beschryving van geheel Persie, Georgie, Mengrelle en andere Gebuurgewesten. Beschreven door dr. Olfert Dapper*, Amsterdam 1672

Delft, Prinsenhof, *Oosterse tapijten*, by P. Aaldering and P.Otten, Exh.cat. Delft 1948

Delft, Prinsenhof, *De Hugenoten in Nederland*, Exh.cat. Delft 1963

Denny, W., The Origin of the Designs of Ottoman Court Carpets, in: *Hali* II (1979), 1, p.6-11

Dimand, M.S. and Mailey, J., *Oriental Rugs in the Metropolitan Museum of Art*, New York 1973

Dresden, *Katalog der königlichen Gemäldegalerie zu Dresden*, by K. Woermann, Dresden 1908

Dresden, *Die staatliche Gemäldegalerie zu Dresden, Katalog der alten Meister*, Dresden 1930

Dresden, Gemäldegalerie 1962, *Holländische und flämische Meister des 17. Jahrhunderts*, Exh.cat. Dresden 1962

Dijck, L. van and Koopmans, T., *The Harpsichord in Dutch Art before 1800*, Amsterdam/ Zutphen 1987

Dublin, *Dutch Seventeenth and Eighteenth Century Paintings in the National Gallery of Ireland, A complete catalogue*, by H. Potterton, Dublin 1986

Duverger, E., *Antwerpse Kunstinventarissen uit de zeventiende eeuw*, Vol. 1: 1600-1617, Brussels 1984

Duverger, E., *Antwerpse Kunstinventarissen uit de zeventiende eeuw*, Vol. 2: 1618-1626, Brussels 1985

Duverger, E., *Over Oosterse en Westerse vloer- en tafeltapijten van vroeger in Vlaanderen, in: Brugge en de Tapijtkunst*, Exh. cat. Bruges, 1987, p.149-161

Eiland, M., *Chinese and Exotic Rugs*, London 1979

Ellis, C.G., Some Compartment Designs for Carpets, and Herat, in: *Textile Museum Journal* I (1965), 4, p.42-56

Ellis, C.G., The Portuguese Carpets of Gujarat, in: *Islamic Art in the Metropolitan Museum of Art*, by R.Ettinghausen (ed.), p.267-290, New York 1972

Ellis, C.G., The 'Lotto' Pattern as a Fashion in Carpets, in: *Festschrift für P.W. Meister*, p.19-31, Hamburg 1975

Ellis, C.G., Confusion from the Dutch!, in: *Oriental Rug Review*, June 1984, p.2-3

Ellis, C.G., On 'Holbein' and 'Lotto' Rugs, in: *Oriental Carpet and Textile Studies* II (1986), p.163-176

Ellis, C.G., *Oriental Carpets in the Philadelphia Museum of Art*, London 1988

Enay, M.-E., and Azadi, S., Einhundert Jahre Orientteppich Literatur 1877-1977, Hanover 1977

Erdmann, K., *Der orientalische Knüpfteppich. Versuch einer Darstellung seiner Geschichte*, Tübingen 1955

Erdmann, K., *Siebenhundert Jahre Orientteppich*, Herford 1966

Erdmann, K., *The History of the Early Turkish Carpet*, London 1977

Eskenazi, Gallery, cf. Milan

Florence, *La Galleria Pitti*, by A. Jahn-Rusconi, Rome 1937

Franses, M., catalogue part in: *Milan* 1981, q.v.

Franses, M. and Pinner, R., Turkish Carpets in the Victoria & Albert Museum part 1: The 'Classical' Carpets of the 15th to 17th Century, in: *Hali* VI (1984), 4, p.357-381

Fredericksen, B., *Catalogue of the Paintings in the J. Paul Getty Museum*, Los Angeles 1972

Friedlaender, M., *Antonis Mor and his Contemporaries*, Leyden/Brussels 1975

Gaehtgens, B., *Adriaen van der Werff 1659-1722*, Munich 1987

Gelder, J. de, *Bartolomeus van der Helst*, Rotterdam 1921

Genova, *Cattalogo Provvisorio della Galleria di Palazzo Bianco*, Genoa 1950

Greindl, E., *Les Peintres Flamands de Nature Morte au XVIIe Siecle*, Sterrebeek 1983

Grisebach, L., *Willem Kalf*, Berlin 1974

Groot, A.H. de, *The Ottoman Empire and the Dutch Republic, A History of the Earliest Diplomatic Relations*, diss. Leiden/Istanbul 1978

Gudlaugsson, S., *Gerard Ter Borch*, The Hague 1959

Guiccardini, R.H. Tawney & E. Power, *Tudor Economic Documents*, p. 155: 'Guiccardini's Description of the Trade of Antwerp, 1560'

Haak, B., *Hollandse Schilders in de Gouden Eeuw*, Amsterdam 1984

Haarlem, Frans Hals Museum, *Portretten van echt en trouw, Huwelijk en gezin in de Nederlandse kunst van de zeventiende eeuw*, by E. de Jongh, Exh.cat. Zwolle/Haarlem 1986

Herbert, Th., *Some years of travels into Africa & Asia the great. Especially describing the Famous Empires of Persia and Industant. As also divers other kingdoms in the Orientall Indies, and I-les adjacent*, London 1638

Hofstede de Groot, *Beschreibendes und kritisches Verzeichnis der Werke der hervorragendsten Holländischen Maler des XVII. Jahrhunderts I: Jan Steen, Gabriel Metsu, Gerard Dou, Pieter de Hooch, Carel Fabritius, Johannes Vermeer*, Esslingen a.N./Paris 1907

Hofstede de Groot, *Beschreibendes und kritisches Verzeichnis der Werke der hervorragendsten Holländischen Maler des XVII. Jahrhunderts IV: Gerard Ter Borch, Caspar Netscher, Godfried Schalcken, Pieter van Slingeland, Eglon van der Neer*, Esslingen a.N./Paris 1912

Housego, J., 18th Century Persian Carpets: Continuity and Change, in: *Oriental Carpet and Textile Studies* III, 1987, I, p.40-51

Inalcik, H., The Yürüks: their Origins, Expansion and Economic Role, in: *Oriental Carpet and Textile Studies* II (1986), p.39-66

Irwin, J., Indian Textile Trade in the Seventeenth Century, in: *Journal of Indian Textile History* I (1955), p.5-33

Kämpffer, E., *Am Hofe des persischen Grosskönigs (1684-85). Das erste Buch der Amoenitates exoticae. Eingeleitet und in deutscher Bearbeitung herausgegeben von Walther Hinz*, Leipzig 1940

Karabacek, J., *Die persische Nadelmalerei Susandschird*, Leipzig 1881

Kassel, *Die Gemäldegalerie der staatlichen Kunstsammlungen Kassel*, by E. Herzog, Hanau 1969

Ketelaar, J., *Journaal van Ketelaar's hofreis naar den Groot Mogol te Lahore. 1711-1713, uitgegeven door J.Ph. Vogel*, The Hague 1937

Kiel, Kunsthalle, *Katalog der Gemäldegalerie*, Kiel 1958

King, D., The Carpet Collection of King Charles I, in: *Oriental Carpet and Textile Studies* III (1987), 1, p.22-27

Kuile, O. ter, Twee 'Van Huysum' Bloemstillevens door Frederik van Royen (ca 1645-1723), Hofschilder te Berlijn, in: *Tableau* VIII (1985), 3, p.29-31

Kühnel, E. and Bellinger, L., *Cairene Rugs and Others Technically Related*, Washington 1957

Kuretsky, S., *The Paintings of Jacob Ochtervelt (1634-1682)*, Oxford 1979

Kuznetsov, Y. and Linnik, I., *Dutch Painting in Soviet Museums*, Amsterdam/Leningrad 1982

Landreau, A. and Yohe, R., *Flowers of the Yayla, Yorok weaving of the Toros mountains*, Washington 1983

Lanier, M., *English and Oriental Carpets at Williamsburg*, Williamsburg 1975

Larsen, E., *Anton van Dyck, Werkverzeichnis*, Frankfurt/Berlin/Vienna 1980

Lessing, J., *Alte orientalische Teppichmuster nach Bildern und Originalen des XV.-XVI. Jahrhunderts*, Berlin 1877

Lauts, J. *Staatliche Kunsthalle Karlsruhe, Katalog Alte Meister bis 1800*, Karlsruhe, 1972

Leipzig, *Museum der bildenden Künste Leipzig*, by G. Winkler, Leipzig 1979

Leiden, *Catalogus van de schilderijen en tekeningen. Leiden, Stedelijk Museum De Lakenhal*, Leiden 1983

Liebaers, H. *Vlaamse Kunst van de Oorsprong tot Heden*, Antwerp 1985

Liedtke, W.A., *Flemish Paintings in the Metropolitan Museum of Art*, New York 1984

London, *National Gallery, Illustrated General Catalogue*, London 1986

London, *Concise Catalogue of Oil Paintings in the National Maritime Museum*, Suffolk, 1988

London, *Wallace Collection Catalogues, Pictures and Drawings (illustrations)*, London 1925

London, Royal Academy of Arts, *Dutch Pictures 1450-1750*, Exh.cat. London 1952

London, Royal Academy of Arts, *The Robinson Collection: Paintings from the collection of the late Sir J.B. Robinson, lent by the Princess Labia*, Exh.cat. London 1958

London, Hayward Gallery 1983, *The Eastern Carpet in the Western World, Selected and arranged by Donald King and David Sylvester*, Exh.cat. London 1983

London 1984, see Philadelphia 1984

Lunsing Scheurleer, Th.H. a.o., *Het Rapenburg, Geschiedenis van een Leidse gracht 1: Groenhazenburch*, Leiden 1986

Madrid, Prado, *El Siglo de Rembrandt*, Exh.cat. Madrid 1985

Manchester, *Art Gallery, Catalogue of Paintings and Drawings from the Asheton-Bennett Collection*, Manchester 1965

Martin, F.R., *A History of Oriental Carpets before 1800*, Vienna 1908

McMullan, J.V., *Islamic Carpets*, New York 1965

Milan, Gallery Eskenazi, *Il Tappeto Orientale dal XV al XVIII Secolo*, Exh. cat. Milan 1981

Mills, J., *Carpets in Pictures*, London 1977

Mills, J., Early Animal Carpets in Western Paintings - A Review, in: *Hali* I (1978 (A)), 3, p.234-43

Mills, J., Small Pattern Holbein Carpets in Western Paintings, in: *Hali* I (1978 (B)), 4, p.326-34

Mills, J., East Mediterranean Carpets in Western Paintings, in: *Hali* IV (1981(A)),1,p.53-55

Mills, J., 'Lotto' Carpets in Western Paintings, in: *Hali* III (1981 (B)), 4, p.278-89

Mills, J., *Carpets in Paintings*, London 1983 (A)

Mills, J., The Coming of the Carpet to the West, in: *The Eastern Carpet in the Western World, Selected and arranged by Donald King and David Sylvester*, Exh.cat. London 1983 (B), p.11-23

Mills, J., Near Eastern Carpets in Italian Paintings, in: *Oriental Carpet and Textile Studies* II (1986), p.109-122

Mills, J., Carpets in 17th Century Dutch Paintings, in: *Hali* X (1988), 3, p.42-44

Munich, *Katalog der Gemälde-Sammlung der königlichen Älteren Pinakothek*, Munich 1898

Munich, *Alte Pinakothek Muenchen, kurzes Verzeichnis der Bilder, amtliche Ausgabe 1957*, Munich 1957

Munich 1978, see Spuhler, F.

Munich, *Alte Pinakothek, München, mit einen Gesamtverzeichnis aller ausgestellten Gemälde*, Munich 1980

Munich, *Alte Pinakothek München. Erlauterungen zu den ausgestellten Gemälden*, Munich 1983

Leipzig, *Meisterwerke im Museum der bildenden Künste zu Leipzig übergeben von der Sowjetunion*, Leipzig 1959

Naumann, O., *Frans van Mieris (1635-1681) the Elder*, Doornspijk 1981

New York, *European Paintings in the Metropolitan Museum of Art, by artists born in or before 1865, a summary catalogue*, by K. Baetjer, New York 1980

New York, *The Frick Collection, an illustrated catalogue, Vol. I, Paintings, American, British, Dutch, Flemish and German*, New York 1968

New Orleans, *Fetes de la Palette*, Exh.cat. New Orleans 1963

Oldenbourg, R., *Thomas de Keysers Tätigkeit als Maler, ein Beitrag zur Geschichte des holländischen Porträts*, Leipzig 1911

Olearius, A., *Vermehrte newe Beschreibung der Muscowitischen und Persischen Reyse so durch gelegenheit einer Holsteinischen Gesandschafft and den Russischen Zaar und König in Persien geschehen*, Schleswig 1656

Pagnano, G., *L'Arte del Tappeto Orientale ed Europeo dalle origini al XVIII secolo*, Busto Arsizio 1983

Paris, Louvre, *Catalogue des Pentures exposées dans les Galeries III: Ecoles Flamande, Hollandaise, Allemande et Anglaise*, by L. Demonts, Paris 1922

Paris, Louvre, *Catalogue sommaire illustrée des peintures du Musée du Louvre I: Ecoles flamande et hollandaise*, by Brejon de Lavergnée, A. a.o., Paris 1979

Paris, *De Rembrandt a Vermeer, Les peintres hollandais au Mauritshuis de La Haye*, by B.Broos a.o., Exh.cat. Paris 1984

Pelsaert, F., *De geschriften van Francisco Pelsaert over Mughal Indie, 1627, Kroniek en Remonstrantie, uitgegeven door D.Kolff en H. van Santen*, The Hague 1979

Philadelphia, Philadelphia Museum of Art, *Masters of Seventeenth Century Dutch Genre Painting*, by P. Sutton a.o., Exh.cat. Philadelphia/Berlin/London 1984

Pinner, R. and Franses, M., East Mediterranean Carpets in the Victoria & Albert Museum, The East Mediterranean Carpet Collection, in: *Hali* IV, 1981, p.37-52

Pinner, R., References to Carpet Production and Trade, in: *Oriental Carpet and Textile Studies* II (1986), p.291-296

Plietzsch, E., *Holländische und flämische Maler des XVII Jahrhunderts*, Leipzig 1960

Pommersfelden, *Verzeignis der Gemälde in gräflich Schönborn-Wilsentheidschen Besitz*, by Th. von Frimmel, Pommersfelden 1894

Pont, D., *Barent Fabritius 1624-1673*, Utrecht 1958

Pope, A.U., *A Survey of Persian Art*, London 1939

Potsdam, *Die Gemälde in der Bildergalerie Sanssouci*, Potsdam 1964

Raby, J. (A), Court and Export: Part 1: Market Demands in Ottoman Carpets 1450-1550, in: *Oriental Carpet and Textile Studies* II (1986), p.29-38

Raby, J. (B), Court and Export: Part 2. The Ushak Carpets, in: *Oriental Carpet and Textile Studies* II (1986), p.177-188

Reimer, T.O., Observations on Some Minor Features of Lotto Rugs, in: *Hali* VI, 1984, 2, p.144f

RGP 9/10, *Bronnen tot de Geschiedenis van den Levantschen Handel, I: 1590-1660*, by K. Heering, Rijksgeschiedkundige Publicatiën, The Hague 1910

RGP 34, *Bronnen tot de Geschiedenis van den Levantschen Handel, II: 1661-1726*, by K. Heering, Rijksgeschiedkundige Publicatiën, The Hague 1917

RGP 72, *Bronnen tot de Geschiedenis der Oostindische Compagnie in Perzië, I: 1611-1638*, by H. Dunlop, Rijksgeschiedkundige Publicatiën, The Hague 1930

RGP 74, *Pieter van Dam's beschryvinge van de Oostindische Compagnie*, 2nd vol, I, by F. Stapel, Rijksgeschiedkundige Publicatiën, The Hague 1931

RGP 104, *Generale Missiven van Gouverneurs-Generaal en Raden aan Heren XVII der Verenigde Oostindische Compagnie, I: 1610-1638*, by W.Ph. Coolhaas, Rijksgeschiedkundige Publicatiën, The Hague 1960

RGP 112, *Generale Missiven van Gouverneurs-Generaal en Raden aan Heren XVII der Verenigde Oostindische Compagnie, II: 1639-1655*, by W.Ph. Coolhaas, Rijksgeschiedkundige Publicatiën, The Hague 1964

RPG 125, *Generale Missiven van Gouverneurs-Generaal en Raden aan Heren XVII der Verenigde Oostindische Compagnie, III: 1655-1674*, by W.Ph. Coolhaas, The Hague 1968

RPG 134, *Generale Missiven van Gouverneurs-Generaal en Raden aan Heren XVII der Verenigde Oostindische Compagnie, IV: 1657-1685*, The Hague 1971

RGP 147, *Inventarissen van de inboedels in de verblijven van de Oranjes en daarmede gelijk te stellen stukken 1567-1795 I: Inventarissen Nasau-Oranje 1567-1712*, by S.W.A. Drossaers and Th.H. Lunsingh Scheurleer, Rijksgeschiedkundige Publicatiën, The Hague 1974

RGP 148, *Inventarissen van de inboedels in de verblijven van de Oranjes en daarmede gelijk te stellen stukken 1567-1795 I: Inventarissen Nasau-Dietz 1587-1763*, by S.W.A. Drossaers and Th.H. Lunsingh Scheurleer, Rijksgeschiedkundige Publicatiën, The Hague 1974

RGP 150, *Generale Missiven van Gouverneurs-Generaal en Raden aan Heren XVII der Verenigde Oostindische Compagnie, V: 1686-1697*, by W.Ph. Coolhaas, Rijksgeschiedkundige Publicatiën, The Hague 1975

Robinson, F., *Gabriel Metsu (1629-1667), A Study of His Place in Dutch Genre Painting of he Golden Age*, New York 1974

Rotterdam, Museum Boymans-van Beuningen Rotterdam, *Old Paintings 1400-1900*, Rotterdam 1972

Sarre, F., A 'Portuguese' carpet from Knole, in: *The Burlington Magazine* III (1931), pp.214-219

Sarre, F. and Trenkwald, H., *Alt-orientalische Teppiche*, (2 vols.), Vienna/Leipzig 1926

Sarre, F. and Trenkwald, H., *Old Oriental Carpets*, New York 1979

Schaefer, S. and Fusco, P., *European Painting and Sculpture in the Los Angeles Museum of Art*, Los Angeles 1987

Scheunemann, B., *Anatolische Teppiche auf abendländischen Gemälden*, diss. Berlin 1954 (typed manuscript)

Scheunemann, B., Eine unbekannte Teppichgattung, in: *Kunst des Orients* III (1959), p.78-89

Schwarz, G., *The Dutch World of Painting*, Vancouver 1986

Sheffield 1976, Mappin Art Gallery, *Carpets of Central Persia*, by M. Beattie, Exh.cat. Sheffield/Birmingham 1976

Skelton, R., A Decorative Motif in Mughal Art, in: *Aspects of Indian Art, papers presented in a symposium at the Los Angeles County Museum of Art*, Leyden 1972

Sluyter, E.J., Hoe realistisch is de Noord-Nederlandse schilderkunst van de 17de eeuw? De problemen van een vraagstelling, in: *Leidschrift* VI (1990), 3, p.5-39

Spuhler, F., *Seidene Repräsentationsteppiche der mittleren bis späteren Safawidenzeit, die sog. Polenteppiche*, diss. Berlin 1968

Spuhler, F., *Berlin, Wien, München. Ihre Bedeutung in der Entwicklung der Orientteppichforschung*, in: *Alte Orientteppiche, Meisterstücke aus deutschen Privatsammlungen*, Munich 1978 (A), p.11-18

Spuhler, F., *Islamic Carpets and Textiles in the Keir Collection*, London 1978 (B)

Spuhler, F., *Classical Fragments and Carpets*, in: *Old Eastern Carpets, Masterpieces in German Private Collections*, Exhib. cat. Munich (Staatliche Museums zur Völkerkunde) 1985, p.11-26

Spuhler, F., 'Chessboard' Rugs, in: *Oriental Carpet and Textile Studies* II (1986), p.261-269

Spuhler, F., *Die Orientteppiche im Museum für Islamische Kunst Berlin*, Munich 1987 (A)

Spuhler, F. a.o., *Denmark's Coronation Carpets*, Copenhagen 1987 (B)

Spelt-Holterhoff, S., *Les Peintres Flamands de Cabinets d'Amateurs au XVIIième Siecle*, Brussels 1957

Steadman, D.W., *Abraham van Diepenbeek, Seventeenth-Century Flemish Painter*, Michigan 1982

Steel, D.H., *Baroque painting from the Bob Jones University Collection, North Carolina Museum of Art*, Raleigh 1984

Streynsham, Master, in: *Records of Fort St. George: Diary and Consultation Book, 1679-80*, Madras 1912, p.100

Stuttgart, *Verzeichnis der Gemäldesammlung im Königlichen Museum der Bildenden Künste zu Stuttgart, bearbeitet von Prof. K. Lange*, Stuttgart 1907

Sutton, P., *Pieter de Hooch*, Oxford 1980

Tavernier, J.B., *Les six voyages qu'il a fait en Turquie, en Perse et aux Indes, pendant l' espace de 40 ans*, Paris 1692

Texeira, P., *The travels of Pedro Texeira; with his 'Kings of Hormuz', and Extracts from his 'Kings of Persia'*. Translated and Annotated by William F. Sinclair, with further notes and an introduction by Donald Ferguson, London 1902

The Hague, *The Royal Cabinet of Paintings, illustrated general catalogue*, by H.R. Hoetink (introduction), The Hague 1977

The Hague, *The Royal Picture Gallery Mauritshuis*, by H.R. Hoetink (ed), Amsterdam/New York 1985

Theunissen, H. a.o., *Topkapi & Turkomanie, Turks-Nederlandse Ontmoetingen sinds 1600*, Amsterdam 1989

Thevenot, J. de, *Relation d'un Voyage fait au Levant par Monsieur de Thevenot*, Paris 1665

Thiel, P. van, *All the paintings of the Rijksmuseum in Amsterdam*, Amsterdam/Maarssen 1976

Thornton, P., *Seventeenth-Century Interior Decorating in England, France and Holland*, 3rd ed. New Haven/London 1981

Tübingen, Technisches Rathaus, *Holländische Kabinettmalerei -unbekannte und wenig bekannte niederländische Gemälde und Handzeichnungen*, Exh. cat. Tübingen 1967

Ungaretti, G. and Bianconi, P., *L'opera completa di Vermeer*, Milan 1967

Utrecht, *Catalogus der Schilderijen, Centraal Museum*, Utrecht 1952

Utrecht, Centraal Museum, *Caravaggio en de Nederlanden*, Exh.cat. Utrecht/Antwerp1952

Valenciennes, *Catalogue illustre et annote des oeuvres exposées au Palais des Beaux Arts de la Ville de Valenciennes*, Valenciennes 1931

Valentijn, F., *Keurlyke Beschryving van Choromandel, Pegu, Arrakan, Bengale, Mocha, Van 't Nederlandsch Comptoir in Persien, en eenige fraaje Zaaken van Persepolis overblijfselen* V, Dordrecht/Amsterdam 1726

Valentiner, W., *P. de Hooch, des Meisters Gemälde in 180 Abb.*, no place or date indicated

Valentiner, W., *Nicolaes Maes*, Stuttgart 1924

Végh, G. and Layer, K. (ed: M. and C. Dall'Oglio), *Turkish Rugs in Transylvania*, Fishguard 1977

Vienna, *Kunsthistorische Sammlungen des Allerhöchsten Kaiserhauses: Die Gemälde*, by E. Engerth, Vienna 1884

Vienna, *Die Kunsthistorische Sammlungen des Allerhöchsten Kaiserhauses: Die Gemäldegalerie, Alte Meister*, Vienna/Leipzig 1907

Vlieghe, H., *Caspar de Crayer, sa vie et ses oeuvres*, Brussels 1972

Wagner, H., *Jan van der Heyden*, Amsterdam/Haarlem 1971

Walker, D., Classical Indian Rugs, in: *Hali* IV (1982), 3, p.252-257

Washington, Textile Museum, *Prayer Rugs*, by R.Ettinghausen and others, Exh.cat. Washington 1974

Washington , Textile Museum, *Turkmen, Tribal Carpets and Traditions*, by L. Mackie and J. Thompson (ed.), Exh.cat. Washington 1980

White, *The Dutch Pictures in the Collection of her Majesty the Queen*, Cambridge 1982

Wilckens, L. von, Oriental Carpets in the German Speaking Countries and the Netherlands, in: *Oriental Carpet and Textile Studies* II (1986), p.139-150

Willemin, N.Y., *Monuments Français inedits pour servir a l'histoire des arts depuis le VIe siecle jusqu'au commencement du XVIIe*, Paris 1839

Williamstown (Massachusetts), *The Grand Mogul, Imperial Painting in India, 1600-1660*, by M.C. Beach, Exh.cat. Williamstown 1978

Ydema, O., Zestiende-eeuwse Mammelukkentapijten in Nederland, in: *Antiek* XIX (1984), 1, p.18-26

Ydema, O., Een Zeldzaam Oosters Tapijt in het Rijksmuseum, in: *Antiek* 20 (1985), 3, p.124-130

Ydema, O., Zeldzame herinneringen aan de hoftapijten van de Groot-Moghul in Lahore, in: *Bulletin van het Rijksmuseum* XXXIV, 1986, I, p.183-188

Ydema, O. Ein indischer Teppich, eine ungewöhnliche Darstellung auf einem Gemälde des 17. Jahrhunderts, in: *Weltkunst* LVI (1986), 16, p.2186-2187

Ydema, O., Teleurstellende alcatifen, een aspect van de handel met Moghul-India, in: *Aziatische Kunst, Mededelingenblad van de Vereniging van Vrienden van Aziatische Kunst* XVI (1986), 5, p.16-21

Ydema, O., 'Polentapijten', in: *Antiek* XXII, (1988 (A)), 10, p.529-532

Ydema, O., Carpets in 17th Century Dutch and Flemish Painting in: *Exhibition catalogue The European Fine Art Fair*, Maastricht 1988 (B), p.15-28

Ydema, O. De Osmaanse Tapijten van Bacchus, in: *Antiek* XXIV (1989), p.298-303

Ydema, O., Turkse tapijten op Nederlandse schilderijen, in: *Topkapi & Turkomanië, Turks-Nederlandse Ontmoetigen sinds 1600*, Amsterdam 1989, p.140-147

Yetkin, S., *Historical Turkish Carpets*, Istanbul 1981

INDEX OF PAINTERS

Italic page numbers indicate to illustrations or their captions.

PICTURE CREDITS

ACKNOWLEDGEMENTS

I would like to thank the many scholars who have assisted me in every way they could. In particular I am deeply grateful to Dr. Walter B. Denny, Professor of Art History at the University of Massachusetts, who gave me advice during the process of collecting the material, commended the early versions of the manuscript and later edited the text for publication. I am likewise deeply indebted to Dr. C. Willemijn Fock, Professor of Art History at Leiden University, who supervised this dissertation from its onset in 1985 and paved the way to the acceptance in 1990.

I am also grateful to Dr. John Mills, who invited me to his house, showed me his personal files and allowed me to make notes on depictions of carpets in Netherlandish paintings which he had found. Several examples would certainly have escaped my attention without his much valued help. Michael Franses kindly went through my files, gave his opinion on many portrayals and allowed me access to his impressive photographic files. I am indebted to him and to the other dealers who have disinterestedly lent me transparencies for illustrations in this book.

Monique van Wijngaarden spent many hours translating the larger part of the original manuscript into English and made the first critical observations on my text. Patricia Walker also translated parts of the original manuscript. Early on Dr. Hetty Dellemijn MD assisted me in collecting material in the Rijksbureau voor Kunsthistorische Documentatie (RKD) in The Hague, and searched through the archives of the Dutch East India Company in the Centraal Rijksarchief in The Hague for written sources. Dr. and Mrs. Christian Gutjahr have been particularly supportive, the former assisting me for many weeks in the RKD, and the latter devoting herself to baby-sitting in order to enable me to work on this study. Mr. G. Kotting and his staff at the RKD, Old Master Paintings Department, advised me on such matters as the dating of paintings and attributions, patiently tolerated the search that led to my turning upside down hundreds of maps in their photographic archives and supplied me with a large quantity of photographs of paintings whose present whereabouts are unknown. Dr. Pieter van Thiel and his staff of the Old Master Paintings Department at the Rijksmuseum in Amsterdam, with equal patience allowed me to make use of the photographic archives of his department, for which I am also very grateful. Pauline Scheurleer, keeper of Asian art at the Rijksmuseum, helped by lending me articles and books on Moghul Indian carpets. Kees Burgers, formerly keeper of textiles at the Rijksmuseum, deserves a special word of thanks since it was he, who years ago first suggested to me the subject of this dissertation. I would also like to thank those who have helped me to overcome difficulties with my computer: Titia and Jan Harmsen, Reinier Speelman, Rino Verhoeven and Frank Manshande.

Last but not least, I would like to thank my wife Mary-Ann for her support during the time I have been working on the present study. For once the cliché is justified, since, literally, without her help this book would not have seen the light of day.